U0524835

山东省海洋"精品旅游"社会服务创新团队项目（编号：057）、国家社会科学基金一般项目"基于条件价值评估法的群岛旅游资源非使用价值评估嵌入效应问题研究"（编号：17BGL247）、中国博士后科学基金项目"舟山群岛旅游资源非使用价值评估两个范围问题研究"（编号：2019M662308）

群岛旅游资源
非使用价值估值研究

肖建红 ◎ 著

中国社会科学出版社

图书在版编目（CIP）数据

群岛旅游资源非使用价值估值研究/肖建红著 .—北京：中国社会科学出版社，2022.1
ISBN 978－7－5203－9569－4

Ⅰ.①群… Ⅱ.①肖… Ⅲ.①群岛—旅游资源—研究—海南 Ⅳ.①F592.766

中国版本图书馆CIP数据核字（2022）第012598号

出 版 人	赵剑英
责任编辑	刘晓红
责任校对	周晓东
责任印制	戴 宽

出　版	中国社会科学出版社
社　址	北京鼓楼西大街甲158号
邮　编	100720
网　址	http://www.csspw.cn
发行部	010－84083685
门市部	010－84029450
经　销	新华书店及其他书店

印　刷	北京君升印刷有限公司
装　订	廊坊市广阳区广增装订厂
版　次	2022年1月第1版
印　次	2022年1月第1次印刷

开　本	710×1000　1/16
印　张	18.25
插　页	2
字　数	309千字
定　价	99.00元

凡购买中国社会科学出版社图书，如有质量问题请与本社营销中心联系调换
电话：010－84083683
版权所有　侵权必究

前 言

群岛是一种吸引游客的特色资源,许多世界著名的旅游度假胜地在群岛地区,如马尔代夫群岛、塞舌尔群岛、巴哈马群岛、巴利阿里群岛、夏威夷群岛等。我国是一个海洋大国,据最新统计,我国共有海岛11000余个,其中,长山群岛、庙岛群岛、舟山群岛、川山群岛、万山群岛、三亚附近岛群等多个旅游业已形成一定规模的群岛或岛群。群岛旅游资源易受到台风等极端天气和旅游业发展的影响,需要不断地对其进行保护或恢复。对群岛旅游资源进行非市场价值评估,是对其进行保护或恢复成本—收益分析的前提和基础。因此,如何科学有效地对群岛旅游资源进行非市场价值评估,是目前学术界亟待解决的重要问题。群岛旅游资源非市场价值包括使用价值和非使用价值,本书运用条件价值评估法,选取黄渤海区—庙岛群岛、东海区—舟山群岛、南海区—三亚及其附近岛屿等典型群岛旅游目的地作为案例地,评估了海滩、海洋地质遗迹、海洋文化、珊瑚礁四种代表性群岛海洋旅游资源的非使用价值。

本书以课题研究过程中的多篇文章为基础,对研究内容和研究方法进行了统一归纳和整理。全书分为四篇,十二章。第一篇是研究基础,包括国内外研究现状、理论基础和数据来源三章内容;第二篇是群岛旅游资源非使用价值估值比较研究,包括群岛旅游资源非使用价值估值比较Ⅰ、群岛旅游资源非使用价值估值比较Ⅱ和群岛旅游资源非使用价值估值比较Ⅲ三章内容;第三篇是群岛旅游资源非使用价值评估嵌入效应问题研究,包括嵌入效应问题研究总体框架和研究思路、嵌入效应问题研究庙岛群岛案例、嵌入效应问题研究舟山群岛案例和嵌入效应问题研究三亚及其附近岛屿案例四章内容;第四篇是研究结论,包括群岛旅游资源非使用价值估值比较和群岛旅游资源非使用价值评估嵌入效应问题两章内容。

  本书的研究内容和出版得到了国家社会科学基金项目（17BGL247）、山东省海洋"精品旅游"社会服务创新团队项目（057）和中国博士后科学基金项目（2019M662308）的资助；项目调研过程中得到了九丈崖景区、月牙湾景区、望夫礁景区、普陀山风景区管委会、朱家尖国际沙雕艺术广场景区、桃花岛茅草屋码头、岱山县鹿栏晴沙景区、嵊泗县基湖景区和南长涂景区、亚龙湾景区、大东海景区、西岛景区、蜈支洲岛景区及长岛、舟山和三亚多个政府相关部门和海岛村委会的支持，在此表示衷心感谢！同时，感谢陈宇菲、丁晓婷、高雪、刘宏斌、李锋、王文波、张晓慧、李小嵩、王飞、程文虹、吴艺晖等博士研究生、硕士研究生为问卷调查或课题研究付出的努力；感谢导师胡金焱教授对研究过程的指导和帮助；感谢中国社会科学出版社的责任编辑刘晓红女士及其团队卓有成效的工作。

  群岛旅游资源非使用价值估值是一项非常具有挑战意义的工作，本书的研究内容只是一项初步研究成果。由于笔者水平有限，书中不足之处，请各位专家、学者批评指正。

肖建红
2021 年 6 月于青岛

目 录

第一篇 研究基础

第一章 国内外研究现状 ……………………………………… 3
第一节 CVM 的有效性和可靠性研究 …………………… 3
第二节 基于 CVM 的海洋旅游资源非市场经济价值评估
研究 …………………………………………………… 14
第三节 CVM 的嵌入效应问题研究 ……………………… 22

第二章 理论基础 ……………………………………………… 31
第一节 非使用价值估值比较研究理论基础 ……………… 31
第二节 嵌入效应问题研究理论基础 ……………………… 37

第三章 数据来源 ……………………………………………… 65
第一节 群岛案例地 ………………………………………… 65
第二节 调查问卷设计 ……………………………………… 68
第三节 调查实施 …………………………………………… 73

第二篇 群岛旅游资源非使用价值估值比较研究

第四章 群岛旅游资源非使用价值估值比较 I ………………… 79
第一节 估值比较 I 计量经济模型 ………………………… 79

第二节　估值比较Ⅰ描述性统计分析 …………………………… 83
　　第三节　估值比较Ⅰ结果分析 ………………………………… 99
　　第四节　估值比较Ⅰ结论 ……………………………………… 108

第五章　群岛旅游资源非使用价值估值比较Ⅱ ……………………… 110
　　第一节　估值比较Ⅱ WTP 计算公式 ………………………… 110
　　第二节　估值比较Ⅱ描述性统计分析 ………………………… 111
　　第三节　估值比较Ⅱ结果分析 ………………………………… 121
　　第四节　估值比较Ⅱ结论及进一步分析 ……………………… 127

第六章　群岛旅游资源非使用价值估值比较Ⅲ ……………………… 131
　　第一节　估值比较Ⅲ模型与分类 ……………………………… 131
　　第二节　估值比较Ⅲ描述性统计分析 ………………………… 133
　　第三节　估值比较Ⅲ WTP 差异性分析 ……………………… 138
　　第四节　估值比较Ⅲ WTP 调整 ……………………………… 144
　　第五节　估值比较Ⅲ广义定序 logit 模型分析 ……………… 147
　　第六节　估值比较Ⅲ讨论与结论 ……………………………… 149

第三篇　群岛旅游资源非使用价值评估嵌入效应问题研究

第七章　嵌入效应问题研究总体框架和研究思路 ………………… 157
　　第一节　总体框架 ……………………………………………… 157
　　第二节　研究思路 ……………………………………………… 159

第八章　嵌入效应问题研究庙岛群岛案例 ………………………… 161
　　第一节　庙岛群岛嵌入效应验证方案设计 …………………… 161
　　第二节　庙岛群岛嵌入效应验证方案实施 …………………… 163
　　第三节　庙岛群岛结果分析 …………………………………… 166
　　第四节　庙岛群岛结论 ………………………………………… 170

第九章　嵌入效应问题研究舟山群岛案例 … 171
第一节　舟山群岛研究框架 … 171
第二节　舟山群岛嵌入效应验证方案设计 … 171
第三节　舟山群岛嵌入效应验证方案实施 … 176
第四节　舟山群岛结果分析 … 181
第五节　舟山群岛结论 … 193

第十章　嵌入效应问题研究三亚及其附近岛屿案例 … 196
第一节　三亚及其附近岛屿嵌入效应验证方案设计 … 196
第二节　三亚及其附近岛屿嵌入效应验证方案实施 … 199
第三节　三亚及其附近岛屿结果分析 … 201
第四节　三亚及其附近岛屿结论 … 213

第四篇　研究结论

第十一章　群岛旅游资源非使用价值估值比较 … 217

第十二章　群岛旅游资源非使用价值评估嵌入效应问题 … 219

附录 … 221

参考文献 … 259

第一篇 研究基础

第一章
国内外研究现状

第一节 CVM 的有效性和可靠性研究

一 研究重点

条件价值评估法（Contingent Valuation Method，CVM）是最重要的非市场经济价值（Non-market Economic Valuation）评估方法，被广泛应用于环境经济、健康经济、文化经济、旅游经济、交通安全、生物多样性保护、生态系统服务等多个领域，研究范围几乎涵盖了世界上每一个国家。[①] CVM 通过调查，建立一个公共物品数量或质量变化的假想市场，引导受访者在这些假想市场中做出选择；CVM 最常用的调查询问受访者的格式是陈述他们对公共物品供给水平增加或避免供给水平减少的支付意愿（Willingness to Pay，WTP）。[②] 希克斯方法测算福利 4 类方法中的另外 2 类：询问受访者陈述他们忍受公共物品供给特定损失的补偿意愿（Willingness to Accept，WTA），或者放弃一些预期得到公共物

[①] Ian J. Bateman, et al., "Economic Valuation of Policies for Managing Acidity in Remote Mountain Lakes: Examining Validity through Scope Sensitivity Testing", *Aquatic Sciences*, Vol. 67, No. 3, September 2005; Melville Saayman, et al., "Willingness to Pay: Who are the Cheap Talkers?", *Annals of Tourism Research*, Vol. 56, January 2016; Patrick Lloyd-Smith, et al., "Moving Beyond the Contingent Valuation Versus Choice Experiment Debate: Presentation Effects in Stated Preference", *Land Economics*, Vol. 96, No. 1, February 2020.

[②] Ian J. Bateman, et al., "Economic Valuation of Policies for Managing Acidity in Remote Mountain Lakes: Examining Validity through Scope Sensitivity Testing", *Aquatic Sciences*, Vol. 67, No. 3, September 2005.

品供给的 WTA。① CVM 思想源于 Ciriacy – Wantrup②，Davis 第一个应用了该方法③；20 世纪 70—80 年代，CVM 的具体案例应用是研究的重点④；20 世纪 90 年代至今，CVM 的有效性和可靠性问题成为研究的焦点⑤。目前，CVM 的有效性和可靠性相关研究的重点是如何处理以下几个主要问题：①假想偏差（Hypothetical Bias），受访者在假想市场与真实市场的反

---

① Ian J. Bateman, et al., "Estimating Four Hicksian Welfare Measures for a Public Good: A Contingent Valuation Investigation", *Land Economics*, Vol. 76, No. 3, August 2000; Ian J. Bateman, et al., "Economic Valuation of Policies for Managing Acidity in Remote Mountain Lakes: Examining Validity through Scope Sensitivity Testing", *Aquatic Sciences*, Vol. 67, No. 3, September 2005.

② S. V. Ciriacy – Wantrup, "Capital Returns from Soil – conservation Practices", *Journal of Farm Economics*, Vol. 29, No. 4, November 1947.

③ Robert Kenneth Davis, *The Value of Outdoor Recreation: An Economic Study of the Maine Woods*, Cambridge, England: Harvard University, 1963.

④ Sevda Birdir, et al., "Willingness to Pay as an Economic Instrument for Coastal Tourism Management: Cases from Mersin, Turkey", *Tourism Management*, Vol. 36, No. 3, June 2013.

⑤ Mary Jo Kealy, et al., "Reliability and Predictive Validity of Contingent Values: Does the Nature of the Good Matter?", *Journal of Environmental Economics and Management*, Vol. 19, No. 3, November 1990; Kenneth Arrow, et al., "Report of the NOAA Panel on Contingent Valuation", *Federal Register*, Vol. 58, No. 10, January 1993; Richard T. Carson, et al., "Contingent Valuation: Controversies and Evidence", *Environmental and Resource Economics*, Vol. 19, No. 2, June 2001; L. Venkatachalam, "The Contingent Valuation Method: A Review", *Environmental Impact Assessment Review*, Vol. 24, No. 1, January 2004; Daniel R. Petrolia and Tae – Goun Kim, "Preventing Land Loss in Coastal Louisiana: Estimates of WTP and WTA", *Journal of Environmental Management*, Vol. 92, No. 3, March 2011; Louinord Voltaire, et al., "Dealing with Preference Uncertainty in Contingent Willingness to Pay for a Nature Protection Program: A New Approach", *Ecological Economics*, Vol. 88, April 2013; Tuba Tunçel and James K. Hammitt, "A New Meta – analysis on the WTP/WTA Disparity", *Journal of Environmental Economics and Management*, Vol. 68, No. 1, July 2014; John Armbrecht, "Use Value of Cultural Experiences: A Comparison of Contingent Valuation and Travel Cost", *Tourism Management*, Vol. 42, June 2014; Dambala Gelo and Steven F. Koch, "Contingent Valuation of Community Forestry Programs in Ethiopia: Controlling for Preference Anomalies in Double – bounded CVM", *Ecological Economics*, Vol. 114, June 2015; Melville Saayman, et al., "Willingness to Pay: Who are the Cheap Talkers?", *Annals of Tourism Research*, Vol. 56, January 2016; Hilary Ndambiri, et al., "Scope Effects of Respondent Uncertainty in Contingent Valuation: Evidence from Motorized Emission Reductions in the City of Nairobi, Kenya", *Journal of Environmental Planning and Management*, Vol. 60, No. 1, January 2017; Nicolas Borzykowski, et al., "Scope Effects in Contingent Valuation: Does the Assumed Statistical Distribution of WTP Matter?", *Ecological Economics*, Vol. 144, February 2018; J. R. Molina, et al., "The Role of Flagship Species in the Economic Valuation of Wildfire Impacts: An Application to two Mediterranean Protected Areas", *Science of the Total Environment*, Vol. 675, July 2019.

应不一致而产生的偏差①;②信息偏差(Information Bias),受访者对待估物品特征、自身预算约束、替代品、其他人的 WTP 值等信息掌握不充分而产生的偏差②;③策略性偏差(Strategic Bias),受访者故意违背自己的真实支付意愿而产生的偏差③;④设计偏差(Design Bias),初始值、支付方式、引导技术、估值问题顺序等确定不当而产生的偏差④;⑤抗议性反应偏差(Protest Responses Bias),受访者倾向于反对假想市场而引起的偏差⑤;

---

① John Loomis, et al., "Improving Validity Experiments of Contingent Valuation Methods: Results of Efforts to Reduce the Disparity of Hypothetical and Actual Willingness to Pay", *Land Economics*, Vol. 72, No. 4, November 1996; Magnus Johannesson, et al., "An Experimental Comparison of Dichotomous Choice Contingent Valuation Questions and Real Purchase Decisions", *Applied Economics*, Vol. 30, No. 5, February 1998; James J. Murphy, et al., "A Meta-analysis of Hypothetical Bias in Stated Preference Valuation", *Environmental and Resource Economics*, Vol. 30, No. 3, March 2005; Robert J. Johnston, "Is Hypothetical Bias Universal? Validating Contingent Responses Using a Binding Public Referendum", *Journal of Environmental Economics and Management*, Vol. 52, No. 1, July 2006; Choong-Ki Lee and James W. Mjelde, "Valuation of Ecotourism Resources Using a Contingent Valuation Method: The Case of the Korean DMZ", *Ecological Economics*, Vol. 63, No. 2-3, August 2007.

② John C. Bergstrom, et al., "The Impact of Information on Environmental Commodity Valuation Decisions", *American Journal of Agricultural Economics*, Vol. 72, No. 3, August 1990; Icek Ajzen, et al., "Information Bias in Contingent Valuation: Effects of Personal Relevance, Quality of Information, and Motivational Orientation", *Journal of Environmental Economics and Management*, Vol. 30, No. 1, January 1996.

③ Robert Cameron Mitchell and Richard T. Carson, *Using Surveys to Value Public Goods: The Contingent Valuation Method*, Washington: Resources for the Future, 1989, pp. 107-126.

④ Patricia A. Champ, et al., "Using Donation Mechanisms to Value Nonuse Benefits from Public Goods", *Journal of Environmental Economics and Management*, Vol. 33, No. 2, June 1997; Mavra Stithou and Riccardo Scarpa, "Collective Versus Voluntary Payment in Contingent Valuation for the Conservation of Marine Biodiversity: An Exploratory Study from Zakynthos, Greece", *Ocean & Coastal Management*, Vol. 56, February 2012.

⑤ Jürgen Meyerhoff and Ulf Liebe, "Protest Beliefs in Contingent Valuation: Explaining Their Motivation", *Ecological Economics*, Vol. 57, No. 4, June 2006; Dominika A. Dziegielewska and Robert Mendelsohn, "Does 'No' Mean 'No'? A Protest Methodology", *Environmental and Resource Economics*, Vol. 38, No. 1, September 2007; Roy Brouwer and Julia Martín-Ortega, "Modeling Self-censoring of Polluter Pays Protest Votes in Stated Preference Research to Support Resource Damage Estimations in Environmental Liability", *Resource and Energy Economics*, Vol. 34, No. 1, January 2012; Jürgen Meyerhoff, et al., "A Meta-study Investigating the Sources of Protest Behaviour in Stated Preference Surveys", *Environmental and Resource Economics*, Vol. 58, No. 1, May 2014; Alex Y. Lo and C. Y. Jim, "Protest Response and Willingness to Pay for Culturally Significant Urban Trees: Implications for Contingent Valuation Method", *Ecological Economics*, Vol. 114, June 2015.

⑥WTA/WTP 不对称①；⑦嵌入效应。②

二 研究对象和研究问题

目前，从 CVM 的有效性和可靠性研究对象选择来看（表 1.1 和表 1.2），国外主要涉及海岛③、海湾④/海岸⑤、河流⑥、森林⑦、峡谷⑧、

---

① Daniel R. Petrolia and Tae‑Goun Kim, "Preventing Land Loss in Coastal Louisiana: Estimates of WTP and WTA", *Journal of Environmental Management*, Vol. 92, No. 3, March 2011; Tuba Tunçel and James K. Hammitt, "A New Meta‑analysis on the WTP/WTA Disparity", *Journal of Environmental Economics and Management*, Vol. 68, No. 1, July 2014.

② Ian J. Bateman, et al., "Does Part‑whole Bias Exist? An Experimental Investigation", *The Economic Journal*, Vol. 107, March 1997; Kunt Veisten, et al., "Scope Insensitivity in Contingent Valuation of Complex Environmental Amenities", *Journal of Environmental Management*, Vol. 73, No. 4, December 2004.

③ Carlisle A. Pemberton, et al., "Cultural Bias in Contingent Valuation of Copper Mining in the Commonwealth of Dominica", *Ecological Economics*, Vol. 70, No. 1, November 2010; John Loomis and Luis E. Santiago, "Testing Differences in Estimation of River Recreation Benefits for International and Domestic Tourists as a Function of Single‑versus Multiple‑destination Day Trips", *Journal of Hospitality Marketing & Management*, Vol. 20, No. 2, 2011; Ju‑Yeon Kim, et al., "Comparing Willingness‑to‑pay between Residents and Non‑residents when Correcting Hypothetical Bias: Case of Endangered Spotted Seal in South Korea", *Ecological Economics*, Vol. 78, June 2012; Mavra Stithou and Riccardo Scarpa, "Collective Versus Voluntary Payment in Contingent Valuation for the Conservation of Marine Biodiversity: An Exploratory Study from Zakynthos, Greece", *Ocean & Coastal Management*, Vol. 56, February 2012.

④ Louinord Voltaire, et al., "Dealing with Preference Uncertainty in Contingent Willingness to Pay for a Nature Protection Program: A New Approach", *Ecological Economics*, Vol. 88, April 2013.

⑤ Daniel R. Petrolia and Tae‑Goun Kim, "Preventing Land Loss in Coastal Louisiana: Estimates of WTP and WTA", *Journal of Environmental Management*, Vol. 92, No. 3, March 2011.

⑥ Ronald Sutherland and Richard G. Walsh, "Effect of Distance on the Preservation Value of Water Quality", *Land Economics*, Vol. 61, No. 3, August 1985; John B. Loomis, "How Large is the Extent of the Market for Public Goods: Evidence from a Nationwide Contingent Valuation Survey", *Applied Economics*, Vol. 28, No. 7, February 1996; Ian J. Bateman, et al., "The Aggregation of Environmental Benefit Values: Welfare Measures, Distance Decay and Total WTP", *Ecological Economics*, Vol. 60, No. 2, December 2006.

⑦ John B. Loomis and Armando González‑Cabán, "The Importance of the Market Area Determination for Estimating Aggregate Benefits of Public Goods: Testing Differences in Resident and Nonresident Willingness to Pay", *Agricultural and Resource Economics Review*, Vol. 25, No. 2, October 1996; Jürgen Meyerhoff and Ulf Liebe, "Protest Beliefs in Contingent Valuation: Explaining Their Motivation", *Ecological Economics*, Vol. 57, No. 4, June 2006; Dambala Gelo and Steven F. Koch, "Contingent Valuation of Community Forestry Programs in Ethiopia: Controlling for Preference Anomalies in Double‑bounded CVM", *Ecological Economics*, Vol. 114, June 2015.

⑧ Patricia A. Champ, et al., "Using Donation Mechanisms to Value Nonuse Benefits from Public Goods", *Journal of Environmental Economics and Management*, Vol. 33, No. 2, June 1997.

音乐厅/艺术馆①、节事②、自然保护区③、空气污染④、消除有毒物质泄漏灾害⑤、供水项目⑥等研究对象，国内主要涉及流域⑦、河流⑧、游憩资源⑨、森林⑩、群岛⑪、海湾经济区⑫、固体废弃物管理⑬、空气

---

① John Armbrecht, "Use Value of Cultural Experiences: A Comparison of Contingent Valuation and Travel Cost", *Tourism Management*, Vol. 42, June 2014.

② Melville Saayman, et al., "Willingness to Pay: Who are the Cheap Talkers?", *Annals of Tourism Research*, Vol. 56, January 2016.

③ Matleena Kniivilä, "Users and Non-users of Conservation Areas: Are there Differences in WTP, Motives and the Validity of Responses in CVM Surveys?", *Ecological Economics*, Vol. 59, No. 4, October 2006.

④ Dominika A. Dziegielewska and Robert Mendelsohn, "Does 'No' Mean 'No'? A Protest Methodology", *Environmental and Resource Economics*, Vol. 38, No. 1, September 2007.

⑤ Roy Brouwer and Julia Martín-Ortega, "Modeling Self-censoring of Polluter Pays Protest Votes in Stated Preference Research to Support Resource Damage Estimations in Environmental Liability", *Resource and Energy Economics*, Vol. 34, No. 1, January 2012.

⑥ Robert J. Johnston, "Is Hypothetical Bias Universal? Validating Contingent Responses Using a Binding Public Referendum", *Journal of Environmental Economics and Management*, Vol. 52, No. 1, July 2006.

⑦ 徐中民等：《额济纳旗生态系统服务恢复价值评估方法的比较与应用》，《生态学报》2003年第9期；张志强等：《黑河流域张掖市生态系统服务恢复价值评估研究——连续型和离散型条件价值评估方法的比较应用》，《自然资源学报》2004年第2期；蔡志坚等：《条件价值评估的有效性与可靠性改善——理论、方法与应用》，《生态学报》2011年第10期；徐大伟等：《流域生态补偿意愿的WTP与WTA差异性研究：基于辽河中游地区居民的CVM调查》，《自然资源学报》2013年第3期。

⑧ 赵军等：《环境与生态系统服务价值的WTA/WTP不对称》，《环境科学学报》2007年第5期；张翼飞等：《大城市非本地户籍人口对城市河流治理支付意愿的特征研究——基于上海和南京样本的CVM调查》，《复旦学报》（自然科学版）2014年第1期；敖长林等：《空间尺度下公众对环境保护的支付意愿度量方法及实证研究》，《资源科学》2015年第11期。

⑨ 许丽忠等：《条件价值法评估旅游资源非使用价值的可靠性检验》，《生态学报》2007年第10期；张茵等：《用条件估值法评估九寨沟的游憩价值——CVM方法的校正与比较》，《经济地理》2010年第7期；董雪旺等：《条件价值法中的偏差分析及信度和效度检验——以九寨沟游憩价值评估为例》，《地理学报》2011年第2期。

⑩ 张明军等：《不确定性影响下的平均支付意愿参数估计》，《生态学报》2007年第9期。

⑪ 肖建红等：《基于CVM的旅游相关资源价值评估总体范围扩展方法研究》，《自然资源学报》2013年第9期；肖建红等：《不同资源类型不同非使用价值——四种典型海洋旅游资源非使用价值支付意愿研究》，《旅游科学》2019年第4期；肖建红等：《群岛旅游地海洋旅游资源非使用价值支付意愿偏好研究——以山东庙岛群岛、浙江舟山群岛和海南三亚及其岛屿为例》，《中国人口·资源与环境》2019年第8期。

⑫ 刘亚萍等：《环境价值评估中的WTP值和WTA值测算与非对称性——以广西北部湾经济区滨海生态环境保护为例》，《生态学报》2015年第9期。

⑬ 金建君等：《条件价值法在澳门固体废弃物管理经济价值评估中的比较研究》，《地球科学进展》2006年第6期。

污染①等研究对象。从国内外研究对象选择的范围来看,国外比国内范围广,涉及了诸如艺术②、节事③、灾害④等国内目前 CVM 的有效性和可靠性研究很少关注的领域;从国内外研究对象选择的侧重点来看,国外选择海岛、河流、森林等作为研究对象的成果较多,国内选择流域、河流、游憩资源等作为研究对象的成果较多。

从 CVM 的有效性和可靠性关注的问题来看(表 1.1 和表 1.2),国外主要关注的问题涉及假想偏差⑤、抗议性偏差⑥、信息偏差⑦、设计偏差⑧、

---

① 曾贤刚等:《基于 CVM 的城市大气细颗粒物健康风险的经济评估——以北京市为例》,《中国环境科学》2015 年第 7 期。

② John Armbrecht, "Use Value of Cultural Experiences: A Comparison of Contingent Valuation and Travel Cost", *Tourism Management*, Vol. 42, June 2014.

③ Melville Saayman, et al., "Willingness to Pay: Who are the Cheap Talkers?", *Annals of Tourism Research*, Vol. 56, January 2016.

④ Roy Brouwer and Julia Martín – Ortega, "Modeling Self – censoring of Polluter Pays Protest Votes in Stated Preference Research to Support Resource Damage Estimations in Environmental Liability", *Resource and Energy Economics*, Vol. 34, No. 1, January 2012.

⑤ Robert J. Johnston, "Is Hypothetical Bias Universal? Validating Contingent Responses Using a Binding Public Referendum", *Journal of Environmental Economics and Management*, Vol. 52, No. 1, July 2006; Ju – Yeon Kim, et al., "Comparing Willingness – to – pay between Residents and Non – residents when Correcting Hypothetical Bias: Case of Endangered Spotted Seal in South Korea", *Ecological Economics*, Vol. 78, June 2012; Melville Saayman, et al., "Willingness to Pay: Who are the Cheap Talkers?", *Annals of Tourism Research*, Vol. 56, January 2016.

⑥ Jürgen Meyerhoff and Ulf Liebe, "Protest Beliefs in Contingent Valuation: Explaining Their Motivation", *Ecological Economics*, Vol. 57, No. 4, June 2006; Dominika A. Dziegielewska and Robert Mendelsohn, "Does 'No' Mean 'No'? A Protest Methodology", *Environmental and Resource Economics*, Vol. 38, No. 1, September 2007; Roy Brouwer and Julia Martín – Ortega, "Modeling Self – censoring of Polluter Pays Protest Votes in Stated Preference Research to Support Resource Damage Estimations in Environmental Liability", *Resource and Energy Economics*, Vol. 34, No. 1, January 2012.

⑦ Matleena Kniivilä, "Users and Non – users of Conservation Areas: Are there Differences in WTP, Motives and the Validity of Responses in CVM Surveys?", *Ecological Economics*, Vol. 59, No. 4, October 2006.

⑧ Patricia A. Champ, et al., "Using Donation Mechanisms to Value Nonuse Benefits from Public Goods", *Journal of Environmental Economics and Management*, Vol. 33, No. 2, June 1997; Mavra Stithou and Riccardo Scarpa, "Collective Versus Voluntary Payment in Contingent Valuation for the Conservation of Marine Biodiversity: An Exploratory Study from Zakynthos, Greece", *Ocean & Coastal Management*, Vol. 56, February 2012.

WTA/WTP 不对称[1]、总体范围[2]、文化偏差[3]、距离衰减[4]、偏好不确定[5]、偏好异常[6]、样本差异[7]、方法对比[8]等方面，国内主要关注的问题涉及设计偏差[9]、WTA/WTP 不对称[10]、距离衰减[11]、总体范围[12]、支

---

[1] Daniel R. Petrolia and Tae-Goun Kim, "Preventing Land Loss in Coastal Louisiana: Estimates of WTP and WTA", *Journal of Environmental Management*, Vol. 92, No. 3, March 2011.

[2] John B. Loomis and Armando González-Cabán, "The Importance of the Market Area Determination for Estimating Aggregate Benefits of Public Goods: Testing Differences in Resident and Nonresident Willingness to Pay", *Agricultural and Resource Economics Review*, Vol. 25, No. 2, October 1996; John B. Loomis, "How Large is the Extent of the Market for Public Goods: Evidence from a Nationwide Contingent Valuation Survey", *Applied Economics*, Vol. 28, No. 7, February 1996.

[3] Carlisle A. Pemberton, et al., "Cultural Bias in Contingent Valuation of Copper Mining in the Commonwealth of Dominica", *Ecological Economics*, Vol. 70, No. 1, November 2010.

[4] Ronald Sutherland and Richard G. Walsh, "Effect of Distance on the Preservation Value of Water Quality", *Land Economics*, Vol. 61, No. 3, August 1985; Ian J. Bateman, et al., "The Aggregation of Environmental Benefit Values: Welfare Measures, Distance Decay and Total WTP", *Ecological Economics*, Vol. 60, No. 2, December 2006.

[5] Louinord Voltaire, et al., "Dealing with Preference Uncertainty in Contingent Willingness to Pay for a Nature Protection Program: A New Approach", *Ecological Economics*, Vol. 88, April 2013.

[6] Dambala Gelo and Steven F. Koch, "Contingent Valuation of Community Forestry Programs in Ethiopia: Controlling for Preference Anomalies in Double-bounded CVM", *Ecological Economics*, Vol. 114, June 2015.

[7] John Loomis and Luis E. Santiago, "Testing Differences in Estimation of River Recreation Benefits for International and Domestic Tourists as a Function of Single-versus Multiple-destination Day Trips", *Journal of Hospitality Marketing & Management*, Vol. 20, No. 2, 2011.

[8] John Armbrecht, "Use Value of Cultural Experiences: A Comparison of Contingent Valuation and Travel Cost", *Tourism Management*, Vol. 42, June 2014.

[9] 刘亚萍等：《环境价值评估中的 WTP 值和 WTA 值测算与非对称性——以广西北部湾经济区滨海生态环境保护为例》，《生态学报》2015 年第 9 期；徐中民等：《额济纳旗生态系统服务恢复价值评估方法的比较与应用》，《生态学报》2003 年第 9 期；张志强等：《黑河流域张掖市生态系统服务恢复价值评估研究——连续型和离散型条件价值评估方法的比较应用》，《自然资源学报》2004 年第 2 期；张茵等：《用条件估值法评估九寨沟的游憩价值——CVM 方法的校正与比较》，《经济地理》2010 年第 7 期；肖建红等：《条件价值评估法自愿支付工具与强制支付工具比较研究——以沂蒙湖国家水利风景区游憩价值评估为例》，《中国人口·资源与环境》2018 年第 3 期。

[10] 赵军等：《环境与生态系统服务价值的 WTA/WTP 不对称》，《环境科学学报》2007 年第 5 期；徐大伟等：《流域生态补偿意愿的 WTP 与 WTA 差异性研究：基于辽河中游地区居民的 CVM 调查》，《自然资源学报》2013 年第 3 期。

[11] 敖长林等：《空间尺度下公众对环境保护的支付意愿度量方法及实证研究》，《资源科学》2015 年第 11 期。

[12] 肖建红等：《基于 CVM 的旅游相关资源价值评估总体范围扩展方法研究》，《自然资源学报》2013 年第 9 期。

付意愿不确定性①、样本差异②、方法对比③、风险认知④等方面。从国内外关注问题的范围来看，国外比国内范围广，国外专门研究假想偏差、抗议性偏差、信息偏差、设计偏差、WTA/WTP 不对称等主要问题的成果较多；国内专门研究设计偏差（如引导技术）的研究成果较多，近期对 WTA/WTP 不对称问题比较关注；但是，国内专门研究假想偏差、抗议性偏差、信息偏差等主要问题的成果较少。

　　目前，从国外 CVM 的有效性和可靠性研究成果来看（见表1.1），涉及海岛或群岛方面的，主要关注文化偏差、假想偏差和总体范围、样本差异、设计偏差等问题。如 Pemberton 等通过调查多米尼克国城市居民、农村居民、加勒比人和游客4组样本，研究了文化偏差对铜矿开采引起多米尼克环境资源损失估值的影响⑤；Kim 等通过调查韩国非当地（首尔市、仁川市、京畿道省）居民和当地（白翎岛）居民样本，研究了白翎岛斑海豹保护估值中的假想偏差和总体范围确定问题⑥；Loomis 和 Santiago 通过调查不同类型（国内/国外和单一/多目的地）的游客样本，研究了样本差异对波多黎各自由邦热带雨林河流游憩项目估值的影响⑦；Stithou 和 Scarpa 通过调查外国游客，研究了希腊爱奥尼亚群岛扎金索斯岛国家海洋公园海龟（控制海滩游客数量）和地中海僧海豹（在岛的西北创建僧海豹保护区）保护项目，自愿支付（捐赠）和强制支付（上岛费或额外机场税）方式的差异⑧。从国内 CVM 的有效性和可靠性研究成果来看（见表1.2），涉及海岛或群岛方面的研究成果较少。

---

① 张明军等：《不确定性影响下的平均支付意愿参数估计》，《生态学报》2007年第9期。
② 张翼飞等：《大城市非本地户籍人口对城市河流治理支付意愿的特征研究——基于上海和南京样本的 CVM 调查》，《复旦学报》（自然科学版）2014年第1期。
③ 金建君等：《条件价值法在澳门固体废弃物管理经济价值评估中的比较研究》，《地球科学进展》2006年第6期。
④ 曾贤刚等：《基于 CVM 的城市大气细颗粒物健康风险的经济评估——以北京市为例》，《中国环境科学》2015年第7期。
⑤ Carlisle A. Pemberton, et al., "Cultural Bias in Contingent Valuation of Copper Mining in the Commonwealth of Dominica", Ecological Economics, Vol. 70, No. 1, November 2010.
⑥ Ju-Yeon Kim, et al., "Comparing Willingness-to-pay between Residents and Non-residents when Correcting Hypothetical Bias: Case of Endangered Spotted Seal in South Korea", Ecological Economics, Vol. 78, June 2012.
⑦ John Loomis and Luis E. Santiago, "Testing Differences in Estimation of River Recreation Benefits for International and Domestic Tourists as a Function of Single-versus Multiple-destination Day Trips", Journal of Hospitality Marketing & Management, Vol. 20, No. 2, 2011.
⑧ Mavra Stithou and Riccardo Scarpa, "Collective Versus Voluntary Payment in Contingent Valuation for the Conservation of Marine Biodiversity: An Exploratory Study from Zakynthos, Greece", Ocean & Coastal Management, Vol. 56, February 2012.

表1.1　选取的国外关于 CVM 有效性和可靠性研究的典型案例①

作者（年份）	估值内容	关注的问题	选择对象
Pemberton et al.（2010）	多米尼克国开采铜矿环境影响	文化偏差	海岛
Kim et al.（2012）	韩国白翎岛斑海豹保护	假想偏差	
Loomis & Santiago（2011）	波多黎各自治邦雨林游憩项目	样本差异	
Stithou & Scarpa（2012）	希腊扎金索斯岛海龟和僧海豹保护	设计偏差	

---

① Carlisle A. Pemberton, et al., "Cultural Bias in Contingent Valuation of Copper Mining in the Commonwealth of Dominica", *Ecological Economics*, Vol. 70, No. 1, November 2010; Ju - Yeon Kim, et al., "Comparing Willingness - to - pay between Residents and Non - residents when Correcting Hypothetical Bias: Case of Endangered Spotted Seal in South Korea", *Ecological Economics*, Vol. 78, June 2012; John Loomis and Luis E. Santiago, "Testing Differences in Estimation of River Recreation Benefits for International and Domestic Tourists as a Function of Single - versus Multiple - destination Day Trips", *Journal of Hospitality Marketing & Management*, Vol. 20, No. 2, 2011; Mavra Stithou and Riccardo Scarpa, "Collective Versus Voluntary Payment in Contingent Valuation for the Conservation of Marine Biodiversity: An Exploratory Study from Zakynthos, Greece", *Ocean & Coastal Management*, Vol. 56, February 2012; Louinord Voltaire, et al., "Dealing with Preference Uncertainty in Contingent Willingness to Pay for a Nature Protection Program: A New Approach", *Ecological Economics*, Vol. 88, April 2013; Daniel R. Petrolia and Tae - Goun Kim, "Preventing Land Loss in Coastal Louisiana: Estimates of WTP and WTA", *Journal of Environmental Management*, Vol. 92, No. 3, March 2011; John B. Loomis, "How Large is the Extent of the Market for Public Goods: Evidence from a Nationwide Contingent Valuation Survey", *Applied Economics*, Vol. 28, No. 7, February 1996; Ronald Sutherland and Richard G. Walsh, "Effect of Distance on the Preservation Value of Water Quality", *Land Economics*, Vol. 61, No. 3, August 1985; Ian J. Bateman, et al., "The Aggregation of Environmental Benefit Values: Welfare Measures, Distance Decay and Total WTP", *Ecological Economics*, Vol. 60, No. 2, December 2006; John B. Loomis and Armando González - Cabán, "The Importance of the Market Area Determination for Estimating Aggregate Benefits of Public Goods: Testing Differences in Resident and Nonresident Willingness to Pay", *Agricultural and Resource Economics Review*, Vol. 25, No. 2, October 1996; Jürgen Meyerhoff and Ulf Liebe, "Protest Beliefs in Contingent Valuation: Explaining Their Motivation", *Ecological Economics*, Vol. 57, No. 4, June 2006; Dambala Gelo and Steven F. Koch, "Contingent Valuation of Community Forestry Programs in Ethiopia: Controlling for Preference Anomalies in Double - bounded CVM", *Ecological Economics*, Vol. 114, June 2015; Patricia A. Champ, et al., "Using Donation Mechanisms to Value Nonuse Benefits from Public Goods", *Journal of Environmental Economics and Management*, Vol. 33, No. 2, June 1997; John Armbrecht, "Use Value of Cultural Experiences: A Comparison of Contingent Valuation and Travel Cost", *Tourism Management*, Vol. 42, June 2014; Melville Saayman, et al., "Willingness to Pay: Who are the Cheap Talkers?", *Annals of Tourism Research*, Vol. 56, January 2016; Matleena Kniivilä, "Users and Non - users of Conservation Areas: Are there Differences in WTP, Motives and the Validity of Responses in CVM Surveys?", *Ecological Economics*, Vol. 59, No. 4, October 2006; Dominika A. Dziegielewska and Robert Mendelsohn, "Does 'No' Mean 'No'? A Protest Methodology", *Environmental and Resource Economics*, Vol. 38, No. 1, September 2007; Roy Brouwer and Julia Martín - Ortega, "Modeling Self - censoring of Polluter Pays Protest Votes in Stated Preference Research to Support Resource Damage Estimations in Environmental Liability", *Resource and Energy Economics*, Vol. 34, No. 1, January 2012.

续表

作者（年份）	估值内容	关注的问题	选择对象
Voltaire et al.（2013）	法国莫尔比昂海湾自然资源保护	偏好不确定	海湾/海岸
Petrolia & Kim（2011）	美国路易斯安那沿海土地流失防护	WTA/WTP	
Loomis（1996）	美国艾奥瓦河河流恢复（拆坝）	总体范围	河流
Sutherland & Walsh（1985）	美国弗拉特黑德河水质影响（采煤）	距离衰减	
Bateman et al.（2006）	英国伯明翰城市河流水质提高	距离衰减	
Loomis & González–Cabán（1996）	美国加利福尼亚和俄勒冈原始森林消防管理	总体范围	森林
Meyerhoff & Liebe（2006）	德国森林生物多样性保护	抗议性偏差	
Gelo & Koch（2015）	埃塞俄比亚社区林业项目	偏好异常	
Champ et al.（1997）	美国亚利桑那大峡谷公路拆除项目	设计偏差	峡谷
Armbrecht（2014）	瑞典瓦拉音乐厅和北欧水彩博物馆文化体验	方法对比	音乐厅/艺术馆
Saayman et al.（2016）	南非疯狂葡萄酒节绿色活动（植树）	假想偏差	节事
Kniivilä（2006）	芬兰伊洛曼齐市自然保护区保护	信息偏差	自然保护区
Dziegielewska & Mendelsohn（2007）	波兰空气污染8个方面损害	抗议性偏差	空气污染
Brouwer & Martín–Ortega（2012）	西班牙南部塞维利亚多尼亚纳公园保护（消除毒物泄漏灾害）	抗议性偏差	消除灾害
Johnston（2006）	美国北锡楚埃特供水项目	假想偏差	供水项目

表1.2　选取的国内关于CVM有效性和可靠性研究的典型案例①

作者（年份）	估值内容	关注的问题	选择对象
蔡志坚等（2011）	长江流域南京段生态系统恢复	有效性和可靠性	流域
徐大伟等（2013）	辽河中游地区资源、生态环境保护	WTA/WTP	
徐中民等（2003）	黑河流域额济纳旗生态系统恢复	设计偏差	
张志强等（2004）	黑河流域张掖市生态系统恢复	设计偏差	

---

① 蔡志坚等：《条件价值评估的有效性与可靠性改善——理论、方法与应用》，《生态学报》2011年第10期；徐大伟等：《流域生态补偿意愿的WTP与WTA差异性研究：基于辽河中游地区居民的CVM调查》，《自然资源学报》2013年第3期；徐中民等：《额济纳旗生态系统服务恢复价值评估方法的比较与应用》，《生态学报》2003年第9期；张志强等：《黑河流域张掖市生态系统服务恢复价值评估研究——连续型和离散型条件价值评估方法的（转下页）

续表

作者（年份）	估值内容	关注的问题	选择对象
张翼飞等（2014）	上海和南京城市河流环境治理	样本差异	河流
敖长林等（2015）	松花江环境治理	距离衰减	河流
赵军等（2007）	上海城市河流环境维护	WTA/WTP	河流
肖建红等（2018）	山东沂河资源保护	支付方式	河流
董雪旺等（2011）	四川九寨沟自然旅游资源	信度和效度检验	游憩资源
许丽忠等（2007）	福建武夷山自然、文化旅游资源	可靠性检验	游憩资源
张茵和蔡运龙（2010）	四川九寨沟自然旅游资源	设计偏差	游憩资源
张明军等（2007）	甘肃小陇山林区生态保护（宝天高速）	不确定性	森林
肖建红等（2013，2019）	群岛旅游资源	支付意愿偏好	群岛
刘亚萍等（2015）	广西北部湾经济区滨海生态环境保护	WTA/WTP	经济区
金建君和王志石（2006）	澳门固体废弃物管理	方法对比	废弃物
曾贤刚等（2015）	北京市大气细颗粒物健康风险	风险认知	空气污染

（接上页）比较应用》，《自然资源学报》2004年第2期；张翼飞等：《大城市非本地户籍人口对城市河流治理支付意愿的特征研究——基于上海和南京样本的CVM调查》，《复旦学报》（自然科学版）2014年第1期；敖长林等：《空间尺度下公众对环境保护的支付意愿度量方法及实证研究》，《资源科学》2015年第11期；赵军等：《环境与生态系统服务价值的WTA/WTP不对称》，《环境科学学报》2007年第5期；肖建红等：《条件价值评估法自愿支付工具与强制支付工具比较研究——以沂蒙湖国家水利风景区游憩价值评估为例》，《中国人口·资源与环境》2018年第3期；董雪旺等：《条件价值法中的偏差分析及信度和效度检验——以九寨沟游憩价值评估为例》，《地理学报》2011年第2期；许丽忠等：《条件价值法评估旅游资源非使用价值的可靠性检验》，《生态学报》2007年第10期；张茵等：《用条件估值法评估九寨沟的游憩价值——CVM方法的校正与比较》，《经济地理》2010年第7期；张明军等：《不确定性影响下的平均支付意愿参数估计》，《生态学报》2007年第9期；肖建红等：《基于CVM的旅游相关资源价值评估总体范围扩展方法研究》，《自然资源学报》2013年第9期；肖建红等：《群岛旅游地海洋旅游资源非使用价值支付意愿偏好研究——以山东庙岛群岛、浙江舟山群岛和海南三亚及其岛屿为例》，《中国人口·资源与环境》2019年第8期；刘亚萍等：《环境价值评估中的WTP值和WTA值测算与非对称性——以广西北部湾经济区滨海生态环境保护为例》，《生态学报》2015年第9期；金建君等：《条件价值法在澳门固体废弃物管理经济价值评估中的比较研究》，《地球科学进展》2006年第6期；曾贤刚等：《基于CVM的城市大气细颗粒物健康风险的经济评估——以北京市为例》，《中国环境科学》2015年第7期。

第二节 基于 CVM 的海洋旅游资源非市场经济价值评估研究

一 研究背景

目前，非市场经济价值（Non-market Economic Valuation）评估研究主要集中在陆地系统，而对海洋系统的关注则相对不足。[①] 国内有限的研究集中在海滩、湿地和生物多样性的研究方面，而对海洋地质遗迹、珊瑚礁等典型海洋旅游资源的关注则较为欠缺。[②] 海洋和海岸系统覆盖了地球表面的 70%，提供了广泛的直接使用价值、间接使用价值和非使用价值。[③] 中国作为一个海洋大国，大陆和岛屿岸线达 32000 千米，面积大于 500 平方米的海岛超过 7300 个（数据来自《2016 年中国海洋统计年鉴》）。2013 年 7 月，习近平总书记在中共中央政治局第八次集体学习时强调"要进一步关心海洋、认识海洋、经略海洋，推动我国海洋强国建设不断取得新成就"（中华人民共和国中央人民政府网站，2013）；2018 年 6 月，习总书记考察青岛时再次强调"建设海洋强国，必须进一步关心海洋、认识海洋、经略海洋，加快海洋科技创新步伐"（中华人民共和国中央人民政府网站，2018）。事实上，"关心海

[①] Adriana Ressurreição, et al., "Economic Valuation of Species Loss in the Open Sea", *Ecological Economics*, Vol. 70, No. 4, February 2011; R. Kerry Turner, et al., "Valuing Nature: Lessons Learned and Future Research Directions", *Ecological Economics*, Vol. 46, No. 3, October 2003; P. C. Boxall, et al., "Analysis of the Economic Benefits Associated with the Recovery of Threatened Marine Mammal Species in the Canadian St. Lawrence Estuary", *Marine Policy*, Vol. 36, No. 1, January 2012.

[②] 肖建红等：《不同资源类型不同非使用价值——四种典型海洋旅游资源非使用价值支付意愿研究》，《旅游科学》2019 年第 4 期；肖建红等：《群岛旅游地海洋旅游资源非使用价值支付意愿偏好研究——以山东庙岛群岛、浙江舟山群岛和海南三亚及其岛屿为例》，《中国人口·资源与环境》2019 年第 8 期。

[③] N. J. Beaumont, et al., "Identification, Definition and Quantification of Goods and Services Provided by Marine Biodiversity: Implications for the Ecosystem Approach", *Marine Pollution Bulletin*, Vol. 54, No. 3, March 2007; Annabelle Cruz-Trinidad, et al., "How Much are the Bolinao-Anda Coral Reefs Worth?", *Ocean & Coastal Management*, Vol. 54, No. 9, September 2011; Natasha Charmaine A. Tamayo, et al., "National Estimates of Values of Philippine Reefs' Ecosystem Services", *Ecological Economics*, Vol. 146, April 2018.

洋、认识海洋、经略海洋"核心思想就是要"保护和可持续利用海洋和海洋资源以促进可持续发展"(中华人民共和国外交部网站，2016)。

据文化和旅游部统计，2017 年，我国国内游客量达到 50 亿人次（中华人民共和国文化和旅游部网站，2018）；截至 2020 年，国内旅游市场规模预计将达到 67 亿人次（中华人民共和国中央人民政府网站，2016）。作为一种对游客颇具吸引力的特色资源，许多海岛或海岸地区已发展成为世界著名的旅游度假胜地。如中国庙岛群岛、舟山群岛、万山群岛、三亚及其附近岛屿等海岛或海岸地区已成为海洋旅游业集聚发展的重点区域。2007—2017 年，中国海洋旅游业发展迅猛，海洋旅游业增加值由 3242 亿元增加到 14636 亿元，增长了 3.50 倍（同期全国海洋生产总值增长了 2.10 倍）；相应地，海洋旅游业增加值占海洋生产总值比例由 13% 增至 19%，提高了 6 个百分点（中华人民共和国自然资源部网站，2008，2018）。海洋旅游业已发展成为我国海洋经济的重要支柱产业，科学有效地保护和可持续利用海洋旅游资源以促进海洋旅游业可持续发展，对我国国民经济和社会发展至关重要。

二 研究现状

海洋旅游资源非市场经济价值包含使用价值（Use/Active – use Values）和非使用价值（Non – use/Passive – use Values）[①]，其中，前者是指人们与海洋旅游资源或栖息地的互动和海洋旅游资源的实际使用，主要与消费者剩余和现实娱乐使用有关，后者则涉及人们偏好，与非使用满足收益有关[②]，具体包括存在价值（Existence Value）、遗赠价值

[①] P. C. Boxall, et al., "Analysis of the Economic Benefits Associated with the Recovery of Threatened Marine Mammal Species in the Canadian St. Lawrence Estuary", *Marine Policy*, Vol. 36, No. 1, January 2012; Rodelio F. Subade and Herminia A. Francisco, "Do Non – users Value Coral Reefs? Economic Valuation of Conserving Tubbataha Reefs, Philippines", *Ecological Economics*, Vol. 102, June 2014; Annabelle Cruz – Trinidad, et al., "How Much are the Bolinao – Anda Coral Reefs Worth?", *Ocean & Coastal Management*, Vol. 54, No. 9, September 2011.

[②] Rodelio F. Subade, "Mechanisms to Capture Economic Values of Marine Biodiversity: The Case of Tubbataha Reefs UNESCO World Heritage Site, Philippines", *Marine Policy*, Vol. 31, No. 2, March 2007; Natasha Charmaine A. Tamayo, et al., "National Estimates of Values of Philippine Reefs' Ecosystem Services", *Ecological Economics*, Vol. 146, April 2018.

(Bequest Value) 和选择价值（Option Value）。① 非使用价值是海洋旅游资源非市场经济价值的重要组成部分，是否包含非使用价值对海洋旅游资源保护或恢复工程的成本—收益分析具有重要影响。② 海洋旅游资源易受到台风等极端天气和旅游开发的影响，需要不断地对其（如台风侵蚀的海滩、潜水影响的珊瑚礁等）进行保护或恢复，对海洋旅游资源进行非市场经济价值评估，将有助于提升决策者判定在海洋旅游资源保护和管理方面支出和投资的有效水平③，进而为实现海洋旅游业可持续发展提供重要保障。目前，CVM 已被广泛应用于海洋生物、珊瑚礁、海滩等海洋资源的非市场经济价值评估中④（见表 1.3），研究案例地主要聚焦于日本、墨西哥、中国、瑞典、英国、美国、塞舌尔群岛、亚速尔群岛等。目前，基于 CVM 的海洋旅游资源非市场经济价值评估相关研究，主要体现出以下五方面特征：①从成果分布来看，国外

---

① Annika Batel, et al., "Valuing Visitor Willingness to Pay for Marine Conservation: The Case of the Proposed Cres – Lošinj Marine Protected Area, Croatia", *Ocean & Coastal Management*, Vol. 95, July 2014; S. Marzetti, et al., "Visitors' Awareness of ICZM and WTP for Beach Preservation in Four European Mediterranean Regions", *Marine Policy*, Vol. 63, January 2016; Luke Fitzpatrick, et al., "Threshold Effects in Meta – analyses with Application to Benefit Transfer for Coral Reef Valuation", *Ecological Economics*, Vol. 133, March 2017.

② Rodelio F. Subade and Herminia A. Francisco, "Do Non – users Value Coral Reefs? Economic Valuation of Conserving Tubbataha Reefs, Philippines", *Ecological Economics*, Vol. 102, June 2014; Michelle Cazabon – Mannette, et al., "Estimates of the Non – market Value of Sea Turtles in Tobago Using Stated Preference Techniques", *Journal of Environmental Management*, Vol. 192, May 2017.

③ R. Brouwer R., et al., "Public Willingness to Pay for Alternative Management Regimes of Remote Marine Protected Areas in the North Sea", *Marine Policy*, Vol. 68, June 2016.

④ William Wei – Chun Tseng, et al., "Estimating the Willingness to Pay to Protect Coral Reefs from Potential Damage Caused by Climate Change: The Evidence from Taiwan", *Marine Pollution Bulletin*, Vol. 101, No. 2, December 2015; Seul – Ye Lim, et al., "Public Willingness to Pay for Transforming Jogyesa Buddhist Temple in Seoul, Korea into a Cultural Tourism Resource", *Sustainability*, Vol. 8, No. 9, September 2016; Rodelio F. Subade and Herminia A. Francisco, "Do Non – users Value Coral Reefs? Economic Valuation of Conserving Tubbataha Reefs, Philippines", *Ecological Economics*, Vol. 102, June 2014; Rathnayake Mudiyanselage Wasantha Rathnayake, "'Turtle Watching': A Strategy for Endangered Marine Turtle Conservation through Community Participation in Sri Lanka", *Ocean & Coastal Management*, Vol. 119, January 2016; Juan C. Trujillo, et al., "Coral Reefs Under Threat in a Caribbean Marine Protected Area: Assessing Divers' Willingness to Pay Toward Conservation", *Marine Policy*, Vol. 68, June 2016; Abderraouf Dribek and Louinord Voltaire, "Contingent Valuation Analysis of Willingness to Pay for Beach Erosion Control through the Stabiplage Technique: A Study in Djerba (Tunisia)", *Marine Policy*, Vol. 86, December 2017.

研究相对成熟并主要以由海岛、群岛或海岸带组成的海洋公园、海洋保护区或小岛屿国家为研究对象,评估相关区域内海洋旅游资源的非市场经济价值[1],而国内相关成果较少并主要集中在对群岛旅游景区、滨海城市的海洋公园或海水浴场等单个案例或单一资源研究中[2];②从资源类型来看,当前研究主要聚焦在珊瑚礁、海滩或海洋生物三类海洋旅游资源的分析上[3],且多数文献只关注一类海洋旅游资源,而对两类及以上海洋旅游资源非市场经济价值的评估和对比分析则少有文献涉及;③从调查对象选择来看,当前研究的调查对象主要以游客或居民等单一调研对象为主[4],缺乏以游客和居民为共同调研对象的系统性研究成果;④从评估内容来看,当前研究主要以评估使用价值(门票收入、潜水收益、游憩价值、使用费、保护基金等)和非市场经济价值(使用价值和非使用价值)为主[5],而鲜有文献对海洋旅游资源非使用价值

---

[1] Rodelio F. Subade and Herminia A. Francisco, "Do Non–users Value Coral Reefs? Economic Valuation of Conserving Tubbataha Reefs, Philippines", *Ecological Economics*, Vol. 102, June 2014; Sevda Birdir, et al., "Willingness to Pay as an Economic Instrument for Coastal Tourism Management: Cases from Mersin, Turkey", *Tourism Management*, Vol. 36, No. 3, June 2013; P. Mwebaze, et al., "Economic Valuation of the Influence of Invasive Alien Species on the Economy of the Seychelles Islands", *Ecological Economics*, Vol. 69, No. 12, October 2010.

[2] 肖建红等:《基于CVM的旅游相关资源价值评估总体范围扩展方法研究》,《自然资源学报》2013年第9期;李作志等:《滨海旅游活动的经济价值评价——以大连为例》,《中国人口·资源与环境》2010年第10期;刘佳等:《浒苔绿潮影响下滨海旅游环境价值损失及影响因素——以青岛市海水浴场为例》,《资源科学》2018年第2期。

[3] Edgar Robles–Zavala and Alejandra Guadalupe Chang Reynoso, "The Recreational Value of Coral Reefs in the Mexican Pacific", *Ocean & Coastal Management*, Vol. 157, May 2018; Bruna Alves, et al., "Coastal Erosion Perception and Willingness to Pay for Beach Management (Cadiz, Spain)", *Journal of Coastal Conservation*, Vol. 19, No. 3, June 2015; Michelle Cazabon–Mannette, et al., "Estimates of the Non–market Value of Sea Turtles in Tobago Using Stated Preference Techniques", *Journal of Environmental Management*, Vol. 192, May 2017.

[4] John C. Whitehead and Suzanne S. Finney, "Willingness to Pay for Submerged Maritime Cultural Resources", *Journal of Cultural Economics*, Vol. 27, No. 3–4, November 2003; Juan C. Trujillo, et al., "Coral Reefs Under Threat in a Caribbean Marine Protected Area: Assessing Divers' Willingness to Pay Toward Conservation", *Marine Policy*, Vol. 68, June 2016; Marina Farr, et al., "The Non–consumptive (tourism) 'Value' of Marine Species in the Northern Section of the Great Barrier Reef", *Marine Policy*, Vol. 43, January 2014; 肖建红等:《基于CVM的旅游相关资源价值评估总体范围扩展方法研究》,《自然资源学报》2013年第9期。

[5] Kevin P. Ransom and Stephen C. Mangi, "Valuing Recreational Benefits of Coral Reefs: The Case of Mombasa Marine National Park and Reserve, Kenya", *Environmental Management*, Vol. 45, No. 1, January 2010; Juliana Castaño–Isaza, et al., "Valuing Beaches to Develop Payment for Ecosystem Services Schemes in Colombia's Seaflower Marine Protected Area", *Ecosystem Services*, Vol. 11, February 2015; 李作志等:《滨海旅游活动的经济价值评价——以大连为例》,《中国人口·资源与环境》2010年第10期。

进行专门性、系统性的探索评估；⑤从调查样本量来看，现有研究样本量多在 1000 份以内尤其以 500 份以内居多，而基于大样本数据如 2000 份以上的评估研究则尤为欠缺[①]；事实上，大样本数据分析在揭示公众偏好方面更具可靠性和精准性，而样本规模过小则不利于基于样本统计意义的典型规律的揭示。可见，当前基于 CVM 海洋旅游资源非市场经济价值研究成果存在案例地及资源类型单一，样本规模相对较小且代表性不足以及非使用价值专题研究欠缺等问题，亟待基于多案例、多资源和具有大样本数据支撑的海洋旅游资源非使用价值专门性研究的推进。

表 1.3　海洋旅游资源非市场经济价值（使用价值和非使用价值）评估主要研究成果[②]

作者（年份）	研究区域	关注核心资源	调查对象	引导方式	估值内容	样本量
Arin et al.（2002）	菲律宾阿尼洛、麦克坦岛和阿罗拉海洋保护区	珊瑚礁	潜水游客	支付卡式	门票收入	129

---

① Marina Farr, et al., "The Non-consumptive (tourism) 'Value' of Marine Species in the Northern Section of the Great Barrier Reef", *Marine Policy*, Vol. 43, January 2014.

② Tijen Arin and Randall A. Kramer, "Divers' Willingness to Pay to Visit Marine Sanctuaries: An Exploratory Study", *Ocean & Coastal Management*, Vol. 45, No. 2-3, February 2002; Siti Aznor Ahmad and Nick Hanley, "Willingness to Pay for Reducing Crowding Effect Damages in Marine Parks in Malaysia", *The Singapore Economic Review*, Vol. 54, No. 1, April 2009; James Francis Casey, et al., "Are Tourists Willing to Pay Additional Fees to Protect Corals in Mexico?", *Journal of Sustainable Tourism*, Vol. 18, No. 4, May 2010; John Asafu-Adjaye and Sorada Tapsuwan, "A Contingent Valuation Study of Scuba Diving Benefits: Case Study in Mu Ko Similan Marine National Park, Thailand", *Tourism Management*, Vol. 29, No. 6, December 2008; Juan C. Trujillo, et al., "Coral Reefs Under Threat in a Caribbean Marine Protected Area: Assessing Divers' Willingness to Pay Toward Conservation", *Marine Policy*, Vol. 68, June 2016; Kevin P. Ransom and Stephen C. Mangi, "Valuing Recreational Benefits of Coral Reefs: The Case of Mombasa Marine National Park and Reserve, Kenya", *Environmental Management*, Vol. 45, No. 1, January 2010; Edgar Robles-Zavala and Alejandra Guadalupe Chang Reynoso, "The Recreational Value of Coral Reefs in the Mexican Pacific", *Ocean & Coastal Management*, Vol. 157, May 2018; Steven M. Thur, "User Fees as Sustainable Financing Mechanisms for Marine Protected Areas: An Application to the Bonaire National Marine Park", *Marine Policy*, Vol. 34, No. 1, January 2010; Rodelio F. Subade and Herminia A. Francisco, "Do Non-users Value Coral Reefs? Economic Valuation of Conserving Tubbataha Reefs, Philippines", *Ecological Economics*, Vol. 102, June 2014; Ivana Logar and Jeroen C. J. M. van den Bergh, "Respondent Uncertainty in Contingent Valuation of Preventing Beach Erosion: An Analysis with a Polychotomous Choice Question", *Journal of Environmental Management*, Vol. 113, December 2012; A. Kontogianni, et al., "Eliciting Beach Users' Willingness to Pay for Protecting European Beaches from Beachrock Processes", *Ocean & Coastal Management*, Vol. 98, September 2014; Bruna Alves, et al., "Coastal Erosion Perception and Willingness to Pay for Beach （转下页）

续表

作者（年份）	研究区域	关注核心资源	调查对象	引导方式	估值内容	样本量
Ahmad et al.（2009）	马来西亚芭雅岛、热浪岛和刁曼岛国家海洋公园	珊瑚礁	游客	二分式	门票收入	338
Casey et al.（2010）	墨西哥里维埃拉玛雅地区	珊瑚礁	（讲英语）游客	二分式	门票收入	398

（接上页）Management（Cadiz, Spain）", *Journal of Coastal Conservation*, Vol. 19, No. 3, June 2015; E. Koutrakis, et al., "ICZM and Coastal Defence Perception by Beach Users: Lessons from the Mediterranean Coastal Area", *Ocean & Coastal Management*, Vol. 54, No. 11, November 2011; Juliana Castaño-Isaza, et al., "Valuing Beaches to Develop Payment for Ecosystem Services Schemes in Colombia's Seaflower Marine Protected Area", *Ecosystem Services*, Vol. 11, February 2015; Abderraouf Dribek and Louinord Voltaire, "Contingent Valuation Analysis of Willingness to Pay for Beach Erosion Control through the Stabiplage Technique: A Study in Djerba (Tunisia)", *Marine Policy*, Vol. 86, December 2017; Sevda Birdir, et al., "Willingness to Pay as an Economic Instrument for Coastal Tourism Management: Cases from Mersin, Turkey", *Tourism Management*, Vol. 36, No. 3, June 2013; T. Enriquez-Acevedo, et al., "Willingness to Pay for Beach Ecosystem Services: The Case Study of Three Colombian Beaches", *Ocean & Coastal Management*, Vol. 161, July 2018; Nikoleta Jones, "Visitors' Perceptions on the Management of an Important Nesting Site for Loggerhead Sea Turtle (Caretta Caretta L.): The Case of Rethymno Coastal Area in Greece", *Ocean & Coastal Management*, Vol. 54, No. 8, August 2011; Rathnayake Mudiyanselage Wasantha Rathnayake, " 'Turtle Watching': A Strategy for Endangered Marine Turtle Conservation through Community Participation in Sri Lanka", *Ocean & Coastal Management*, Vol. 119, January 2016; Michelle Cazabon-Mannette, et al., "Estimates of the Non-market Value of Sea Turtles in Tobago Using Stated Preference Techniques", *Journal of Environmental Management*, Vol. 192, May 2017; P. Mwebaze, et al., "Economic Valuation of the Influence of Invasive Alien Species on the Economy of the Seychelles Islands", *Ecological Economics*, Vol. 69, No. 12, October 2010; Marina Farr, et al., "The Non-consumptive (tourism) 'Value' of Marine Species in the Northern Section of the Great Barrier Reef", *Marine Policy*, Vol. 43, January 2014; Mavra Stithou and Riccardo Scarpa, "Collective Versus Voluntary Payment in Contingent Valuation for the Conservation of Marine Biodiversity: An Exploratory Study from Zakynthos, Greece", *Ocean & Coastal Management*, Vol. 56, February 2012; Paulo Torres, et al., "Dead or Alive: The Growing Importance of Shark Diving in the Mid-Atlantic Region", *Journal of Nature Conservation*, Vol. 36, April 2017; Adriana Ressurreição, et al., "Different Cultures, Different Values: The Role of Cultural Variation in Public's WTP for Marine Species Conservation", *Biological Conservation*, Vol. 145, No. 1, January 2012; John C. Whitehead and Suzanne S. Finney, "Willingness to Pay for Submerged Maritime Cultural Resources", *Journal of Cultural Economics*, Vol. 27, No. 3-4, November 2003; Annika Batel, et al., "Valuing Visitor Willingness to Pay for Marine Conservation: The Case of the Proposed Cres-Lošinj Marine Protected Area, Croatia", *Ocean & Coastal Management*, Vol. 95, July 2014; Anatoli Togridou, et al., "Determinants of Visitors' Willingness to Pay for the National Marine Park of Zakynthos, Greece", *Ecological Economics*, Vol. 60, No. 1, November 2006; 李作志等：《滨海旅游活动的经济价值评价——以大连为例》，《中国人口·资源与环境》2010年第10期；肖建红等：《基于CVM的旅游相关资源价值评估总体范围扩展方法研究》，《自然资源学报》2013年第9期；刘佳等：《浒苔绿潮影响下滨海旅游环境价值损失及影响因素——以青岛市海水浴场为例》，《资源科学》2018年第2期。

续表

作者（年份）	研究区域	关注核心资源	调查对象	引导方式	估值内容	样本量
Asafu-Adjaye et al.（2008）	泰国斯米兰群岛国家海洋公园	珊瑚礁	潜水游客	二分式	潜水收益	424
Trujillo et al.（2016）	哥伦比亚加勒比海罗萨里奥和圣贝尔纳多国家自然公园	珊瑚礁	潜水游客	二分式	潜水收益	474
Ransom et al.（2010）	肯尼亚蒙巴萨国家海洋公园	珊瑚礁	（观看过珊瑚礁）游客	开放式	游憩价值	285
Robles-Zavala et al.（2018）	墨西哥卡波普尔莫、玛丽特斯和瓦图尔科三大珊瑚礁区	珊瑚礁	游客	二分式	游憩价值	943
Thur（2010）	荷属安的列斯群岛博内尔岛国家海洋公园	珊瑚礁	（美国）潜水游客	支付卡式	使用费	299
Subade et al.（2014）	菲律宾图巴塔哈群礁国家海洋公园	珊瑚礁	（距公园较远）奎松市居民	二分式	非使用价值	800
Logar et al.（2012）	克罗地亚茨里克韦尼察	（2个）海滩	游客	二分式	门票收入	745
Kontogianni et al.（2014）	希腊莱斯沃斯岛	（2个）海滩	（欧洲）游客	开放式	保护基金	106
Alves et al.（2015）	西班牙加的斯海岸	（3个）海滩	使用者	开放式	使用价值	765
Koutrakis et al.（2011）	欧洲（希腊、意大利和法国）地中海海岸	（5个）海滩	游客	开放式	使用价值和非使用价值	1462
Castaño-Isaza et al.（2015）	哥伦比亚圣安德列斯岛、普罗维登西亚岛和圣卡塔利娜岛海葵海洋保护区	海滩	游客	二分式和开放式	使用价值和非使用价值	1793
Dribek et al.（2017）	突尼斯杰尔巴岛	海滩	居民和游客	（区间）支付卡式	使用价值和非使用价值	474

续表

作者（年份）	研究区域	关注核心资源	调查对象	引导方式	估值内容	样本量
Birdir et al. (2013)	土耳其梅尔辛南海岸	（3个）海滩	游客	支付卡式	非市场价值	432
Enriquez-Acevedo et al. (2018)	哥伦比亚加勒比海地区	（3个）海滩	游客	（区间）支付卡式	海滩生态系统服务价值	425
Jones et al. (2011)	希腊雷西姆诺海岸地区	海洋生物（海龟）	游客	开放式	住宿税/门票收入	156
Rathnayake (2016)	斯里兰卡瑞卡瓦海龟保护区	海洋生物（海龟）	游客	二分式	门票收入	900
Cazabon-Mannette et al. (2017)	特立尼达和多巴哥的多巴哥岛	海洋生物（海龟）	（国际）游客	支付卡式	非使用价值	221
Mwebaze et al. (2010)	塞舌尔群岛	海洋生物（绿海龟和塞舌尔鹊鸲）	游客	支付卡式	非市场价值	300
Farr et al. (2014)	澳大利亚大堡礁北段	海洋生物（鲸鱼和海豚、鲨鱼和鳐鱼、大鱼、海龟等）	游客	支付卡式	（非消费旅游）使用价值	2180
Stithou et al. (2012)	希腊爱奥尼亚群岛扎金索斯岛国家海洋公园	海洋生物（龟鳖和地中海僧海豹）	（国际）游客	开放式	非市场价值	100
Torres et al. (2017)	葡萄牙亚速尔群岛	海洋生物（鲨鱼）	（观看鲨鱼）潜水游客	（区间）支付卡式	（观看鲨鱼）潜水收益	144
Ressurreição et al. (2012)	葡萄牙亚速尔群岛、波兰格但斯克湾和英国锡利群岛	海洋生物（海洋哺乳动物、海鸟、鱼类、海洋无脊椎动物和藻类）	居民和游客	支付卡式	使用价值和非使用价值	1502
Whitehead & Finney (2003)	美国北卡罗来纳州	海洋文化（历史沉船）	（本州）居民	二分式	非市场价值	913

续表

作者（年份）	研究区域	关注核心资源	调查对象	引导方式	估值内容	样本量
Batel et al.（2014）	克罗地亚茨雷斯群岛洛希尼岛海洋保护区	海洋旅游资源	游客	二分式	使用价值和非使用价值	150
Togridou et al.（2006）	希腊爱奥尼亚群岛扎金索斯岛国家海洋公园	海洋旅游资源	游客	开放式	使用价值和非使用价值	495
李作志等（2010）	中国大连市老虎滩海洋公园、傅家庄浴场、星海广场和星海公园	海滩及近海海域	游客	二分式	游憩价值	1276
肖建红等（2013）	中国舟山群岛普陀金三角旅游区	海洋旅游资源	游客	支付卡式	存在价值	498
刘佳和刘宁（2018）	中国青岛市第一、第二、第六海水浴场和石老人海水浴场	滨海旅游环境	游客和网络用户	支付卡式	保护价值	550

第三节　CVM的嵌入效应问题研究

一　嵌入效应问题相关概念

嵌入效应问题，被不同学者称为范围效应（Scope Effect）[1]、嵌入效应（Embedding Effect）[2]、顺序效应（Sequence Effect）[3]、次可加效应（Sub-additivity Effect）[4]、象征偏差（Symbolic Bias）[5]、部分——整

---

[1] W. Michael Hanemann, "Valuing the Environment through Contingent Valuation", *The Journal of Economic Perspectives*, Vol. 8, No. 4, February 1994.

[2] Daniel Kahneman and Jack L. Knetsch, "Valuing Public Goods: The Purchase of Moral Satisfaction", *Journal of Environmental Economics and Management*, Vol. 22, No. 1, January 1992.

[3] Diane P. Dupont, "CVM Embedding Effects When There are Active, Potentially Active and Passive Users of Environmental Goods", *Environmental and Resource Economics*, Vol. 25, No. 3, July 2003.

[4] Thomas C. Brown and John W. Duffield, "Testing Part-whole Valuation Effects in Contingent Valuation of Instream Flow Protection", *Water Resources Research*, Vol. 31, No. 9, September 1995.

[5] Richard T. Carson and Robert Cameron Mitchell, "Sequencing and Nesting in Contingent Valuation Surveys", *Journal of Environmental Economics and Management*, Vol. 28, No. 2, March 1995.

体偏差(Part-whole Bias)[1]、分解偏差(Disaggregation Bias)[2]、规则嵌入(Regular Embedding)和完全嵌入(Perfect Embedding)[3],它是指相同公共物品作为更具包容性公共物品一部分被估值的 WTP 比其单独被估值的 WTP 低[4],或相同公共物品不同调查得到广泛变动的 WTP[5],或公共物品与更具包容性公共物品被估值 WTP 差异不大[6],或 WTP 变化的程度与待估公共物品范围变化的程度不一致[7],或待估公共物品的WTP取决于估值问题顺序[8],或待估公共物品整体变化的 WTP 比个体变化独立估值再加总的 WTP 低[9],或受访者对待估公共物品一般象征意义而不是具体供给水平的 WTP[10]。尽管上述这些概念含义略有差异,但是,它们都是指 CVM 对待估公共物品进行估值时,出现了嵌入效应问题。公共物品估值范围(Scope)嵌入通常分为数量(Quantitative)范围嵌入、分类/定性(Categorical/Qualitative)范围嵌

---

[1] Kevin J. Boyle, et al., "An Investigation of Part – whole Biases in Contingent – valuation Studies", *Journal of Environmental Economics and Management*, Vol. 27, No. 1, July 1994.

[2] Robert Cameron Mitchell and Richard T. Carson, *Using Surveys to Value Public Goods: The Contingent Valuation Method*, Washington: Resources for the Future, 1989, pp. 107 – 126.

[3] Henrik Svedsäter, "Contingent Valuation of Global Environmental Resources: Test of Perfect and Regular Embedding", *Journal of Economic Psychology*, Vol. 21, No. 6, December 2000.

[4] Daniel Kahneman and Jack L. Knetsch, "Valuing Public Goods: The Purchase of Moral Satisfaction", *Journal of Environmental Economics and Management*, Vol. 22, No. 1, January 1992.

[5] Peter A. Diamond and Jerry A. Hausman, "Contingent Valuation: Is Some Number Better than no Number?", *The Journal of Economic Perspectives*, Vol. 8, No. 4, Fall 1994.

[6] Glenn W. Harrison, "Valuing Public Goods with the Contingent Valuation Method: A Critique of Kahneman and Knetsch", *Journal of Environmental Economics and Management*, Vol. 23, No. 3, November 1992.

[7] W. Michael Hanemann, "Valuing the Environment through Contingent Valuation", *The Journal of Economic Perspectives*, Vol. 8, No. 4, February 1994.

[8] Diane P. Dupont, "CVM Embedding Effects When There are Active, Potentially Active and Passive Users of Environmental Goods", *Environmental and Resource Economics*, Vol. 25, No. 3, July 2003.

[9] W. Michael Hanemann, "Valuing the Environment through Contingent Valuation", *The Journal of Economic Perspectives*, Vol. 8, No. 4, February 1994.

[10] Richard T. Carson and Robert Cameron Mitchell, "Sequencing and Nesting in Contingent Valuation Surveys", *Journal of Environmental Economics and Management*, Vol. 28, No. 2, March 1995.

入和地理（Geographical）范围嵌入。① 目前，嵌入效应问题研究已涉及森林②、河流③、湖泊④、湿地⑤、自然公园⑥、荒野区域⑦、水质⑧、生物多样性⑨、环境物品组合⑩、可再生能源⑪、交通碳减排⑫、健康风险⑬、

---

① Daniel Kahneman and Jack L. Knetsch, "Valuing Public Goods: The Purchase of Moral Satisfaction", *Journal of Environmental Economics and Management*, Vol. 22, No. 1, January 1992; Richard T. Carson and Robert Cameron Mitchell, "Sequencing and Nesting in Contingent Valuation Surveys", *Journal of Environmental Economics and Management*, Vol. 28, No. 2, March 1995; Ian J. Bateman, et al., *Visible Choice Sets and Scope Sensitivity: An Experimental and Field Test of Study Design Effects upon Nested Contingent Values*, UK: The Centre for Social and Economic Research on the Global Environmental (CSERGE), University of East Anglia, Working Paper EDM, NO. 01 – 01, 2001, pp. 4 – 7; Ian J. Bateman, et al., "On Visible Choice Sets and Scope Sensitivity", *Journal of Environmental Economics and Management*, Vol. 47, No. 1, January 2004.

② Christopher Giguere, et al., "Valuing Hemlock Woolly Adelgid Control in Public Forests: Scope Effects with Attribute Nonattendance", *Land Economics*, Vol. 96, No. 1, February 2020.

③ R. Pinto, et al., "Valuing the Non – market Benefits of Estuarine Ecosystem Services in a River Basin Context: Testing Sensitivity to Scope and Scale", *Estuarine, Coastal and Shelf Science*, Vol. 169, February 2016.

④ Ian J. Bateman, et al., "Economic Valuation of Policies for Managing Acidity in Remote Mountain Lakes: Examining Validity through Scope Sensitivity Testing", *Aquatic Sciences*, Vol. 67, No. 3, September 2005.

⑤ Ioanna Grammatikopoulou and Søren Bøye Olsen, "Accounting Protesting and Warm Glow Bidding in Contingent Valuation Surveys Considering the Management of Environmental Goods: An Empirical Case Study Assessing the Value of Protecting a Narura 2000 Wetland Area in Greece", *Journal of Environmental Management*, Vol. 130, November 2013.

⑥ Vito Frontuto, et al., "Earmarking Conservation: Further Inquiry on Scope Effects in Stated Preference Methods Applied to Nature – based Tourism", *Tourism Management*, Vol. 60, June 2017.

⑦ Peter A. Diamond and Jerry A. Hausman, *On Contingent Valuation Measurement of Nonuse Values. In Hausman J. A. (Ed.) Contingent Valuation: A Critical Assessment*, UK: Bingley: Emerald Group Publishing Limited, 1993, pp. 3 – 38.

⑧ Roy Brouwer, et al., "Economic Valuation of Groundwater Protection Using a Groundwater Quality Ladder Based on Chemical Threshold Levels", *Ecological Indicators*, Vol. 88, May 2018.

⑨ Elena Ojea and Maria L. Loureiro, "Identifying the Scope Effect on a Meta – analysis of Biodiversity Valuation Studies", *Resource and Energy Economics*, Vol. 33, No. 3, September 2011.

⑩ Henrik Svedsäter, "Contingent Valuation of Global Environmental Resources: Test of Perfect and Regular Embedding", *Journal of Economic Psychology*, Vol. 21, No. 6, December 2000.

⑪ Pallab Mozumder, et al., "Consumers' Preference for Renewable Energy in the Southwest USA", *Energy Economics*, Vol. 33, No. 6, November 2011.

⑫ Hilary Ndambiri, et al., "Scope Effects of Respondent Uncertainty in Contingent Valuation: Evidence from Motorized Emission Reductions in the City of Nairobi, Kenya", *Journal of Environmental Planning and Management*, Vol. 60, No. 1, January 2017.

⑬ Ian J. Bateman and Roy Brouwer, "Consistency and Construction in Stated WTP for Health Risk Reductions: A Novel Scope – sensitivity Test", *Resource and Energy Economics*, Vol. 28, No. 3, August 2006.

疫苗①、食品②等多个领域。关于嵌入效应问题的研究成果主要集中在，从边际效应递减③、收入效应④、调查设计或执行能力缺陷⑤、替代效应⑥、温情效应⑦等方面，来解释或验证嵌入效应问题。目前，从嵌入效应问题研究已有的典型案例来看（见表1.4）：研究成果主要集中在

---

① Alan Shiell and Lisa Gold, "Contingent Valuation in Health Care and the Persistence of Embedding Effects without the Warm Glow", *Journal of Economic Psychology*, Vol. 23, No. 2, April 2002.

② Maria L. Loureiro, et al., "Do Experimental Auction Estimates Pass the Scope Test?", *Journal of Economic Psychology*, Vol. 37, No. 4, August 2013.

③ John B. Loomis, et al., "Some Empirical Evidence on Embedding Effects in Contingent Valuation of Forest Protection", *Journal of Environmental Economics and Management*, Vol. 25, No. 1, July 1993; Kimberly Rollins and Audrey Lyke, "The Case for Diminishing Marginal Existence Values", *Journal of Environmental Economics and Management*, Vol. 36, No. 3, November 1998; R. Pinto, et al., "Valuing the Non-market Benefits of Estuarine Ecosystem Services in a River Basin Context: Testing Sensitivity to Scope and Scale", *Estuarine, Coastal and Shelf Science*, Vol. 169, February 2016.

④ Alan Shiell and Lisa Gold, "Contingent Valuation in Health Care and the Persistence of Embedding Effects Without the Warm Glow", *Journal of Economic Psychology*, Vol. 23, No. 2, April 2002; Neil A. Powe and Ian J. Bateman, "Investigating Insensitivity to Scope: A Split-sample Test of Perceived Scheme Realism", *Land Economics*, Vol. 80, No. 2, May 2004.

⑤ Richard T. Carson and Robert C. Mitchell, "The Issue of Scope in Contingent Valuation Studies", *American Journal of Agricultural Economics*, Vol. 75, No. 5, December 1993; Kevin J. Boyle, et al., "An Investigation of Part-whole Biases in Contingent-valuation Studies", *Journal of Environmental Economics and Management*, Vol. 27, No. 1, July 1994; Mikołaj Czajkowski and Nick Hanley, "Using Labels to Investigate Scope Effects in Stated Preference Methods", *Environmental and Resource Economics*, Vol. 44, No. 4, December 2009; Elena Ojea and Maria L. Loureiro, "Valuing the Recovery of Overexploited Fish Stocks in the Context of Existence and Option Values", *Marine Policy*, Vol. 34, No. 3, May 2010.

⑥ Jennifer Pate and John B. Loomis, "The Effect of Distance on Willingness to Pay Values: A Case Study of Wetlands and Salmon in California", *Ecological Economics*, Vol. 20, No. 3, March 1997; Paulo A. L. D. Nunes and Erik Schokkaert, "Identifying the Warm Glow Effect in Contingent Valuation", *Journal of Environmental Economics and Management*, Vol. 45, No. 2, March 2003; Sisse Liv Jørgensen, et al., "Spatially Induced Disparities in Users' and Non-users' WTP for Water Quality Improvements: Testing the Effect of Multiple Substitutes and Distance Decay", *Ecological Economics*, Vol. 92, August 2013.

⑦ Daniel Kahneman and Jack L. Knetsch, "Valuing Public Goods: The Purchase of Moral Satisfaction", *Journal of Environmental Economics and Management*, Vol. 22, No. 1, January 1992; S. M. Chilton and W. G. Hutchinson, "A Note on the Warm Glow of Giving and Scope Sensitivity in Contingent Valuation Studies", *Journal of Economic Psychology*, Vol. 21, No. 4, August 2000; Paulo A. L. D. Nunes and Erik Schokkaert, "Identifying the Warm Glow Effect in Contingent Valuation", *Journal of Environmental Economics and Management*, Vol. 45, No. 2, March 2003; Ioanna Grammatikopoulou and Søren Bøye Olsen, "Accounting Protesting and Warm Glow Bidding in Contingent Valuation Surveys Considering the Management of Environmental Goods: An Empirical Case Study Assessing the Value of Protecting a Natura 2000 Wetland Area in Greece", *Journal of Environmental Management*, Vol. 130, November 2013; Melville Saayman, et al., "Willingness to Pay: Who are the Cheap Talkers?", *Annals of Tourism Research*, Vol. 56, January 2016.

表1.4　　　　　国内外关于嵌入效应问题研究典型案例①

作者（年份）	估值内容	选择对象
Boyle et al. （1994）	美国蒙大拿五条河流保护生态基流	河流
Hanley et al. （2003）	英国泰晤士提高河流流量	
张翼飞（2012）	中国上海市城市内河生态恢复	

---

① Kevin J. Boyle, et al., "An Investigation of Part – whole Biases in Contingent – valuation Studies", *Journal of Environmental Economics and Management*, Vol. 27, No. 1, July 1994; Nick Hanley, et al., "Aggregating the Benefits of Environmental Improvements: Distance – decay Functions for Use and Non – use Values", *Journal of Environmental Management*, Vol. 68, No. 3, July 2003; 张翼飞:《CVM研究中支付意愿问卷"内容依赖性"的实证研究——以上海城市内河生态恢复CVM评估为例》,《中国人口·资源与环境》2012年第6期; Sisse Liv Jørgensen, et al., "Spatially Induced Disparities in Users' and Non – users' WTP for Water Quality Improvements: Testing the Effect of Multiple Substitutes and Distance Decay", *Ecological Economics*, Vol. 92, August 2013; R. Pinto, et al., "Valuing the Non – market Benefits of Estuarine Ecosystem Services in a River Basin Context: Testing Sensitivity to Scope and Scale", *Estuarine, Coastal and Shelf Science*, Vol. 169, February 2016; Jennifer Pate and John B. Loomis, "The Effect of Distance on Willingness to Pay Values: A Case Study of Wetlands and Salmon in California", *Ecological Economics*, Vol. 20, No. 3, March 1997; Neil A. Powe and Ian J. Bateman, "Investigating Insensitivity to Scope: A Split – sample Test of Perceived Scheme Realism", *Land Economics*, Vol. 80, No. 2, May 2004; Ioanna Grammatikopoulou and Søren Bøye Olsen, "Accounting Protesting and Warm Glow Bidding in Contingent Valuation Surveys Considering the Management of Environmental Goods: An Empirical Case Study Assessing the Value of Protecting a Natura 2000 Wetland Area in Greece", *Journal of Environmental Management*, Vol. 130, November 2013; Kimberly Rollins and Audrey Lyke, "The Case for Diminishing Marginal Existence Values", *Journal of Environmental Economics and Management*, Vol. 36, No. 3, November 1998; Paulo A. L. D. Nunes and Erik Schokkaert, "Identifying the Warm Glow Effect in Contingent Valuation", *Journal of Environmental Economics and Management*, Vol. 45, No. 2, March 2003; Vito Frontuto, et al., "Earmarking Conservation: Further Inquiry on Scope Effects in Stated Preference Methods Applied to Nature – based Tourism", *Tourism Management*, Vol. 60, June 2017; Alan Shiell and Lisa Gold, "Contingent Valuation in Health Care and the Persistence of Embedding Effects without the Warm Glow", *Journal of Economic Psychology*, Vol. 23, No. 2, April 2002; D. Gyrd – Hansen, et al., "Scope Insensitivity in Contingent Valuation Studies of Health Care Services: Should We Ask Twice?", *Health Economics*, Vol. 21, No. 2, February 2012; Ian J. Bateman and Roy Brouwer, "Consistency and Construction in Stated WTP for Health Risk Reductions: A Novel Scope – sensitivity Test", *Resource and Energy Economics*, Vol. 28, No. 3, August 2006; John B. Loomis, et al., "Some Empirical Evidence on Embedding Effects in Contingent Valuation of Forest Protection", *Journal of Environmental Economics and Management*, Vol. 25, No. 1, July 1993; 阮氏春香等:《条件价值评估法在森林生态旅游非使用价值评估中范围效应的研究》,《南京林业大学学报》（自然科学版）2013年第1期; John C. Whitehead, "Albemarle – Pamlico Sounds Revealed and Stated Preference Data", *Data in Brief*, Vol. 3, June 2015; Pallab Mozumder, et al., "Consumers' Preference for Renewable Energy in the Southwest USA", *Energy Economics*, Vol. 33, No. 6, November 2011; Maria L. Loureiro, et al., "Do Experimental Auction Estimates Pass the Scope Test?", *Journal of Economic Psychology*, Vol. 37, No. 4, August 2013.

续表

作者（年份）	估值内容	选择对象
Jørgensen et al.（2013）	丹麦欧登塞河改善河流水质	河流
Pinto et al.（2016）	葡萄牙蒙德古河提高河流水质	
Pate & Loomis（1997）	美国加利福尼亚湿地和野生动物保护	湿地
Powe & Bateman（2004）	英国布罗德兰湿地保护	
Grammatikopoulou & Olsen（2013）	希腊伯罗奔尼撒半岛湿地保护	
Rollins & Lyke（1998）	加拿大偏远十个荒野公园保护	自然公园
Nunes & Schokkaert（2003）	葡萄牙阿连特茹自然公园保护	
Frontuto et al.（2017）	意大利大帕拉迪索国家公园四种蹄类动物保护	
Shiell & Gold（2002）	英国接种传染病疫苗	健康
Gyrd-Hansen et al.（2012）	丹麦减少心血管疾病	
Bateman & Brouwer（2006）	新西兰降低皮肤癌	
Loomis et al.（1993）	澳大利亚东南部森林保护	森林
阮氏春香和温作民（2013）	越南巴为国家森林公园旅游资源保护	
Whitehead（2015）	美国北卡罗来纳州阿尔伯马尔湾和帕姆利科湾水质改善	海湾
Mozumder et al.（2011）	美国西南部新墨西哥州可再生能源项目	可再生能源
Loureiro et al.（2013）	墨西哥腌制火腿	商品

国外，国内关于嵌入效应问题的研究成果较少；研究选择河流、湿地、自然公园和森林作为研究对象的成果较多，其中，选择河流作为研究对象的成果最多。

二 嵌入效应问题文献检索分析

在"Web of Science"数据库中，通过检索相关主题词（国际文献检索方式："Web of Science"—高级检索—TS＝"contingent valuation"—精练依据：语种（English）；以此为基础，再根据研究需要分别检索。如检索主题为"有效性"的国际文献，检索方式："Web of Science"—高级检索—TS＝"contingent valuation"—精练依据：语种：（English）AND 主题：（validity）；其他检索类似；获取国际文献对嵌入效应问题相关研究的基本信息（时间截至：2020年5月8日）。同时，以此为基础，进一步检索大陆及港澳学者国际文献检索方式："Web of Science"—高级检索—TS＝"contingent valuation"—精练依据：语种（English）AND 国家/地区：（PEOPLES R CHINA OR CHINA）；其他与"国际文献检索方式"类似；获取大陆及港澳学者发表的国际文献对嵌入效应问题相关研究的基本信息（时间截至：2020年5月8日）。在"中国知网（CNKI）"数据库中，通过检索相关主题词（国内文献检索方式："中国知网（CNKI）"—高级检索—期刊—主题："contingent valuation"并且全文："支付意愿"或含"补偿意愿"，剔除掉不相关文献。"contingent valuation"在国内翻译不统一，经过反复尝试，最终选择的这种检索方法比较适合。获取中文文献对嵌入效应问题相关研究的基本信息（时间截至：2020年5月8日）。检索发现研究有以下几个特点（见表1.5）：①在"Web of Science"数据库中，英文国际文献量已超过6000篇；在"中国知网（CNKI）"数据库中，中文期刊文献量已超过600篇。②在两个数据库中，大陆及港澳学者中英文文献量已超过1000篇（未包含"中国知网（CNKI）"中的学位论文、会议论文等文献；运用"国内文献检索方式"检索到1073篇文献，除了包含648篇期刊论文外，还包含283篇硕士学位论文、98篇博士学位论文和44篇其他文献，时间截至：2020年5月8日）；但成果主要是关于CVM的案例应用，研究很少涉及CVM方法有效性和可靠性的验证与改进，如有效性或可靠性检验、范围反应敏感性或充分性等。③嵌入效应问题相关研究主要包括：嵌入效应问题相关概念、有效性或可靠性检验、范围反应敏感性或充分性、嵌入效应问题各种视角（经济学视角、心理学视角、设计与执行视角）研究与解释等。

表1.5　　　　　　　　　　文献检索结果

项目	Web of Science 数据库			中国知网（CNKI）数据库	
	主题	总文献量	大陆及港澳文献量	主题	文献量
有效性和可靠性、范围问题	contingent valuation	6004	452	contingent valuation	648
	validity	466	18	有效性	14
	reliability	236	11	可靠性	11

续表

项目	Web of Science 数据库			中国知网（CNKI）数据库	
	主题	总文献量	大陆及港澳文献量	主题	文献量
有效性和可靠性、范围问题	scope	238	11	范围	2
	issue/problem of scope	42/29	1/3	范围问题	0
	embedding	63	1	嵌入效应	1
	sequence	41	3	顺序效应	2
	symbolic	11	0	象征偏差	0
	part–whole	10	0	部分—整体偏差	1
	disaggregation	4	0	分解偏差	0
	sub–additivity	1	0	次可加效应	0
有效性检验、可靠性检验	validity test	216	2	有效性检验	4
	reliability test	92	2	可靠性检验	4
	consistency test	46	1	一致性检验	0
	economic significance	39	5	经济显著性	0
	economic intuition	6	0	经济直觉	0
	scope test	103	2	范围检验	0
	adding–up test	8	0	加总检验	0
	proportionality	4	0	比例标准	0
范围反应敏感性、范围反应充分性	scope sensitivity	85	2	范围敏感	0
	scope insensitivity	37	1	范围不敏感	0
	adequate	64	4	充分	0
	adequate response	12	0	充分反应	0
	adequacy	9	0	充分性	0
	plausible	24	2	合理	0
	plausible response	9	0	合理反应	0
	plausibility	6	0	合理性	0
经济学视角研究	income effect	296	41	收入效应	2
	substitution	68	5	替代效应	2
	marginal utility	66	3	边际效应	2
	budget constraint	30	0	预算限制	0
	complementarity	11	0	补偿效应	0
	satiation	2	0	饱和	0

续表

项目	Web of Science 数据库			中国知网（CNKI）数据库	
	主题	总文献量	大陆及港澳文献量	主题	文献量
心理学视角研究：温情效应	purchase model	139	6	购买模型	0
	contribution model	98	9	贡献模型	0
	warm glow	45	0	温情效应	0
	moral satisfaction	4	0	道德满足	0
心理学视角研究：社会心理学因素	social psychological theory	20	0	社会心理学理论	0
	behavioral/behavioural	193/69	16/5	行为	13
	psychological	111	6	心理	5
	cognitive	77	6	认知	44
	attitudinal	55	5	态度	11
	emotional	29	1	情感	4
	affective	15	1	感情	1
心理学视角研究：其他	mental model	19	0	心理模型	0
	uncertainty	370	12	不确定性	7
	flagship	11	1	旗舰物种	0
	label	122	9	标签效应	0
设计与执行视角研究	design	1082	78	设计	30
	implementation	278	18	执行/实施	0/3

第二章

理论基础

第一节 非使用价值估值比较研究理论基础

一 海洋旅游资源非使用价值

非使用价值概念首先由 Krutilla 提出，他观察到人们仅仅通过知道自然界存在就能获得效用。[①] Carson 等领导的埃克森—瓦尔德兹损害评估可能是最著名的非使用价值评估研究，它证实了人们愿意为他们可能从未见过或从未使用的资源支付。[②] 相应地，对于海洋旅游资源来讲，其非使用价值主要涉及人们的偏好，且与非使用满足收益有关，具体包括存在价值（Existence Value）、遗赠价值（Bequest Value）和选择价值（Option Value）。[③] 当前，尽管对于海洋旅游资源非使用价值包

[①] John V. Krutilla, "Conservation Reconsidered", *The American Economic Review*, Vol. 57, No. 4, September 1967.

[②] Tanya O'Garra, "Bequest Values for Marine Resources: How Important for Indigenous Communities in Less – developed Economies?", *Environmental and Resource Economics*, Vol. 44, No. 2, October 2009.

[③] Annika Batel, et al., "Valuing Visitor Willingness to Pay for Marine Conservation: The Case of the Proposed Cres – Lošinj Marine Protected Area, Croatia", *Ocean & Coastal Management*, Vol. 95, July 2014; S. Marzetti, et al., "Visitors' Awareness of ICZM and WTP for Beach Preservation in Four European Mediterranean Regions", *Marine Policy*, Vol. 63, January 2016; Luke Fitzpatrick, et al., "Threshold Effects in Meta – analyses with Application to Benefit Transfer for Coral Reef Valuation", *Ecological Economics*, Vol. 133, March 2017.

含存在价值和遗赠价值①等已形成共识，但对于选择价值是否应该归为海洋旅游资源的非使用价值，则仍存在一定分歧。② 有部分研究认为，应将选择价值归为海洋旅游资源的使用价值③，但主流研究则多将选择价值归为海洋旅游资源的非使用价值④，即海洋旅游资源的非使用价值包含存在价值、遗赠价值和选择价值⑤。也有研究将非使用价值分为利他价值、遗赠价值和存在价值⑥，研究考虑了为当代其他人的利他动机⑦，未考虑选择价值。

从概念上看，海洋旅游资源非使用价值是指其可持续存在、子孙后代使用或自己未来使用的价值，分别对应于存在价值、遗赠价值和选择

---

① A. Myrick Freeman III, et al., *The Measurement of Environmental and Resource Values: Theory and Measure* (2nd ed.), Washington D C: Resource for the Future Press, 2003; Paulo A. L. D. Nunes and Jeroen C. J. M. van den Bergh, "Can People Value Protection Against Invasive Marine Species? Evidence from a Joint TC – CV Survey in the Netherlands", *Environmental and Resource Economics*, Vol. 28, No. 4, August 2004; Tanya O'Garra, "Bequest Values for Marine Resources: How Important for Indigenous Communities in Less – developed Economies?", *Environmental and Resource Economics*, Vol. 44, No. 2, October 2009; Marina Farr, et al., "The Non – consumptive (tourism) 'Value' of Marine Species in the Northern Section of the Great Barrier Reef", *Marine Policy*, Vol. 43, January 2014.

② Marina Farr, et al., "The Non – consumptive (tourism) 'Value' of Marine Species in the Northern Section of the Great Barrier Reef", *Marine Policy*, Vol. 43, January 2014.

③ Niels Jobstvogt, et al., "Looking Below the Surface: The Cultural Ecosystem Service Values of UK Marine Protected Areas (MPAs)", *Ecosystem Services*, Vol. 10, December 2014.

④ Rodelio F. Subade, "Mechanisms to Capture Economic Values of Marine Biodiversity: The Case of Tubbataha Reefs UNESCO World Heritage Site, Philippines", *Marine Policy*, Vol. 31, No. 2, March 2007.

⑤ Choong – Ki Lee and Sang – Yoel Han, "Estimating the Use and Preservation Values of National Parks' Tourism Resources Using a Contingent Valuation Method", *Tourism Management*, Vol. 23, No. 5, October 2002; Adriana Ressurreição, et al., "Different Cultures, Different Values: The Role of Cultural Variation in Public's WTP for Marine Species Conservation", *Biological Conservation*, Vol. 145, No. 1, January 2012; Annika Batel, et al., "Valuing Visitor Willingness to Pay for Marine Conservation: The Case of the Proposed Cres – Lošinj Marine Protected Area, Croatia", *Ocean & Coastal Management*, Vol. 95, July 2014; S. Marzetti, et al., "Visitors' Awareness of ICZM and WTP for Beach Preservation in four European Mediterranean Regions", *Marine Policy*, Vol. 63, January 2016.

⑥ Niels Jobstvogt, et al., "Looking Below the Surface: The Cultural Ecosystem Service Values of UK Marine Protected Areas (MPAs)", *Ecosystem Services*, Vol. 10, December 2014.

⑦ Matthew J. Kotchen and Stephen D. Reiling, "Environmental Attitudes, Motivations, and Contingent Valuation of Nonuse Values: A Case Study Involving Endangered Species", *Ecological Economics*, Vol. 32, No. 1, January 2000.

价值①；具体地，存在价值是指保护海洋旅游资源的职责或责任感，被定义为保护海洋旅游资源永续存在的支付意愿；遗赠价值是指为未来一代保护海洋旅游资源的重要性，被定义为将海洋旅游资源遗赠给后代而产生满足感的支付意愿；而选择价值实则是指自己等利益相关者想有未来使用海洋旅游资源的选择，可被定义为保持可能未来使用机会的支付意愿②。与主流观点相一致，本书研究中海洋旅游资源非使用价值具体包含存在价值、遗赠价值和选择价值三种。

二 海洋旅游资源类型

（一）海洋旅游资源选取

近年来，通过到辽宁、山东、江苏、浙江、上海、福建、广西、广东、海南9个省（市、区）的主要旅游型海岛及主要沿海旅游城市进行实地调研发现，在我国大陆地区的海洋旅游资源中，海滩、海洋地质遗迹、海洋文化和珊瑚礁四种典型海洋旅游资源（见表2.1）的旅游业发展已形成规模。目前，我国大陆地区的海洋生物旅游资源开发，主要集中在一些沿海城市及少数海岛的海洋世界场馆内，海洋动物为人工饲养。现在已开发的野生海洋生物旅游，主要是庙岛群岛、海驴岛等少数海岛开发的乘船观看海岛旅游，庙岛群岛也开发了观看野生斑点海豹的海上旅游航线；但是，这些开发的野生海洋生物旅游均未形成规模，所以，本书研究未考虑在国外研究较多的海洋生物旅游资源。同时，为了能够更好地选择具有代表性的案例地和为研究问卷初稿设计做准备，研究负责人实地调研了我国四种典型海洋旅游资源（海滩、海洋地质遗

---

① Ronald J. Sutherland and Richard G. Walsh, "Effect of Distance on the Preservation Value of Water Quality", *Land Economics*, Vol. 61, No. 3, August 1985; Jennifer Pate and John B. Loomis, "The Effect of Distance on Willingness to Pay Values: A Case Study of Wetlands and Salmon in California", *Ecological Economics*, Vol. 20, No. 3, March 1997; Luke Fitzpatrick, et al., "Threshold Effects in Meta–analyses with Application to Benefit Transfer for Coral Reef Valuation", *Ecological Economics*, Vol. 133, March 2017.

② A. Myrick Freeman Ⅲ, et al., *The Measurement of Environmental and Resource Values: Theory and Measure* (2nd ed.), Washington DC: Resource for the Future Press, 2003; Anatoli Togridou, et al., "Determinants of Visitors' Willingness to Pay for the National Marine Park of Zakynthos, Greece", *Ecological Economics*, Vol. 60, No. 1, November 2006; S. Marzetti, et al., "Visitors' Awareness of ICZM and WTP for Beach Preservation in four European Mediterranean Regions", *Marine Policy*, Vol. 63, January 2016.

迹、海洋文化和珊瑚礁）具有代表性的旅游目的地。2017年，调研的旅游目的地具体包括：①海滩旅游资源。辽宁大连（含长山列岛），山东庙岛群岛和青岛，浙江舟山群岛，福建厦门（含鼓浪屿），广西北海（含涠洲岛），广东川山群岛、珠海（含万山群岛）和海陵岛，海南三亚（含西岛、蜈支洲岛）和陵水分界洲岛等海岛、群岛或沿海城市的主要海水浴场。②海洋地质遗迹旅游资源。辽宁大连（大连滨海国家地质公园）、山东庙岛群岛（山东长山列岛国家地质公园）和广西涠洲岛（广西北海涠洲岛火山国家地质公园）等典型海洋地质遗迹景观。③海洋文化旅游资源。山东刘公岛（甲午战争遗址）、浙江舟山群岛（普陀山观音菩萨道场、朱家尖国际沙雕艺术广场、桃花岛射雕英雄传影城）、福建湄洲岛（湄洲妈祖祖庙）和鼓浪屿（世界文化遗产）、广西涠洲岛（圣堂景区）、广东海陵岛（南海Ⅰ号沉船博物馆）和海南三亚（南山文化旅游区和南山大小洞天旅游区）等主要海洋文化旅游资源景区。④珊瑚礁旅游资源。海南三亚及陵水（海南三亚珊瑚礁国家级自然保护区、蜈支洲岛和分界洲岛）和广东徐闻县（广东徐闻珊瑚礁国家级自然保护区）等典型珊瑚礁潜水旅游区或珊瑚礁保护区。

表 2.1　　　　　　　　　　　海洋旅游资源类型

名称	大类	主类	亚类	基本类型
海滩	自然旅游资源	A 地文景观	AA 综合自然旅游地	AAD 滩地型旅游地
		A 地文景观	AC 地质地貌过程形迹	ACN 岸滩
海洋地质遗迹	自然旅游资源	A 地文景观	AA 综合自然旅游地	AAF 自然标志地
		A 地文景观	AB 沉积与构造	ABA 断层景观 ABB 褶曲景观
		A 地文景观	AC 地质地貌过程形迹	ACE 奇特与象形山石 ACF 岩壁与岩缝
海洋文化	人文旅游资源	F 建筑与设施	FA 综合人文旅游地	FAC 宗教与祭祀活动场所 FAK 景物观赏点
		F 建筑与设施	FC 景观建筑与附属型建筑	FCK 建筑小品
珊瑚礁	自然旅游资源	A 地文景观	AE 岛礁	AEB 岩礁
		C 生物景观	CD 野生动物栖息地	CDA 水生动物栖息地

（二）海洋旅游资源分类

我国大陆地区有 11 个沿海省（市、区），大陆岸线总长度 18000 千米，岛屿岸线总长度 14000 千米，具有非常丰富的海滩旅游资源。我国多数沿海旅游城市和旅游型海岛具有较大型的海水浴场。相对于海滩旅游资源的广泛分布，我国大陆地区的海洋地质遗迹、海洋文化和珊瑚礁旅游资源相对稀缺，只在一些特定的区域有所分布，形成旅游景区（点），所以，海洋地质遗迹、海洋文化和珊瑚礁旅游资源与海滩旅游资源相比，是相对稀缺型旅游资源。

1. 海洋地质遗迹资源

我国大陆地区涉及海洋或临海的国家地质公园主要包括：辽宁大连滨海国家地质公园、河北秦皇岛柳江国家地质公园、山东长山列岛国家地质公园、山东东营黄河三角洲国家地质公园、上海崇明岛国家地质公园、浙江雁荡山世界地质公园、浙江临海国家地质公园、福建平潭国家地质公园、福建宁德三都澳国家地质公园、福建晋江深沪湾国家地质公园、福建漳州滨海火山国家地质公园、福建福鼎太姥山国家地质公园、广西北海涠洲岛火山国家地质公园、广东深圳大鹏半岛国家地质公园、广东湛江湖光岩国家地质公园和海南海口石山火山群国家地质公园（依据中国地质科学院网站的《第八批国家地质公园资格名单》和《中国的国家地质公园》整理）。这些国家地质公园是我国大陆地区主要的海洋地质遗迹旅游资源。

2. 海洋文化资源

我国大陆地区涉及海洋文化的主要景区包括：山东威海刘公岛景区（甲午战争遗址）、山东青岛崂山景区（道教文化、佛教文化）、烟台市蓬莱阁旅游区（三仙山——八仙过海）（古建群、神仙文化）、舟山群岛普陀山风景名胜区（佛教文化）、舟山群岛桃花岛风景旅游区（海洋影视文化）、舟山群岛朱家尖景区（海洋沙雕艺术文化）、莆田湄洲岛国家旅游度假（妈祖文化）、厦门市鼓浪屿风景名胜区（国际历史社区）、北海涠洲岛圣堂景区（天主教文化）、阳江市海陵岛大角湾海上丝路旅游区（南宋沉船文化）、三亚市南山文化旅游区（佛教文化）和三亚市南山大小洞天旅游区（道教文化）（依据中华人民共和国文化和旅游部、浙江省旅游局、福建省旅游发展委员会和广西壮族自治区旅游发展委员会等官方网站上的资料整理)。

3. 珊瑚礁资源

我国大陆地区涉及珊瑚礁的自然保护区主要包括：广东徐闻珊瑚礁国家级自然保护区、海南三亚珊瑚礁国家级自然保护区、海南铜鼓岭国家级自然保护区（主要保护：珊瑚礁、热带季雨矮林及野生动物）、福建东山珊瑚礁省级自然保护区、广东珠海庙湾珊瑚市级自然保护区、海南西南中沙群岛省级自然保护区（主要保护：海龟、玳瑁、虎斑贝及珊瑚礁）、海南白蝶贝省级自然保护区（主要保护：白蝶贝及其生境、珊瑚礁生态系统）和海南儋州磷枪石岛珊瑚礁县级自然保护区（依据中华人民共和国生态环境部网站的《2015年全国自然保护区名录》整理）。目前，我国大陆地区珊瑚礁旅游发展形成规模的旅游景区主要集中在海南三亚珊瑚礁国家级自然保护区（外围）的亚龙湾、大东海和西岛，海南三亚蜈支洲岛和海南陵水分界洲岛。

结合《旅游资源分类、调查与评价》（GBT 18972—2003）与实地调研情况，本书研究选取我国四种典型海洋旅游资源——海滩、海洋地质遗迹、海洋文化和珊瑚礁为研究对象，并基于研究目的对其进行再归类。如表2.2所示，首先，从属性角度分为两大类，即将海洋文化归为海洋人文旅游资源，将海滩、海洋地质遗迹和珊瑚礁统归为海洋自然旅游资源。其次，从资源稀缺性角度分为两大类，即将海洋地质遗迹、海洋文化和珊瑚礁划归为海洋相对稀缺型旅游资源，将海滩划归为海洋相对充裕型旅游资源。

表2.2　　　　　　　　海洋旅游资源分类

典型海洋旅游资源	分类角度		基本构成
	资源属性	资源稀缺性	
海滩	自然旅游资源	相对充裕型旅游资源	滩地型旅游地、岸滩
海洋地质遗迹	自然旅游资源	相对稀缺型旅游资源	自然标志地、断层景观、褶曲景观、奇特与象形山石、岩壁与岩缝
海洋文化	人文旅游资源	相对稀缺型旅游资源	宗教与祭祀活动场所、景物观赏点、建筑小品
珊瑚礁	自然旅游资源	相对稀缺型旅游资源	岩礁、水生动物栖息地

三 非使用价值估值比较研究基本框架

本书研究主要从四方面对不同类型资源的 WTP 进行比较（图 2.1）：①同一案例地相对稀缺型与相对充裕型旅游资源平均 WTP 的比较研究；②不同案例地相对稀缺型旅游资源之间平均 WTP 的比较研究；③不同案例地相对充裕型旅游资源之间平均 WTP 的比较研究；④不同案例地或同一案例地海洋人文旅游资源与海洋自然旅游资源平均 WTP 的比较研究。其中，A、B 和 C 分别代表案例地 A、B 和 C；$\overline{WTP}^A_{beach}$、$\overline{WTP}^B_{beach}$、$\overline{WTP}^C_{beach}$ 分别表示受访者对 A 地、B 地和 C 地海滩旅游资源的平均 WTP；$\overline{WTP}^A_{maritimegeo-herita}$、$\overline{WTP}^B_{maritimecultures}$、$\overline{WTP}^C_{coralreef}$ 分别表示受访者对 A 地海洋地质遗迹旅游资源、B 地海洋文化旅游资源和 C 地珊瑚礁旅游资源的平均 WTP。

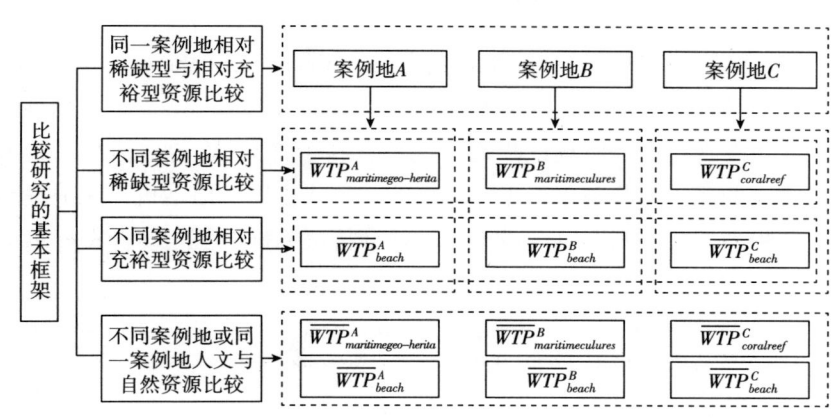

图 2.1 比较研究的基本框架

第二节 嵌入效应问题研究理论基础

一 嵌入效应问题发现与争论

嵌入效应问题（The Issue of Embedding Effect）包含两方面含义：一方面含义是范围反应敏感性（The Sensitivity of Response to Scope）问题，分为范围敏感（Scope Sensitivity）和范围不敏感（Scope Insensitivity）；另一方面含义是范围反应充分性（The Adequacy of Response to Scope）问题，分为充分反应（Adequate Response）和不充分反应（Inadequate Response）。Randall 等在研究芝加哥居民对空气质量改善的 WTP 中首次报

告了范围不敏感问题,他们推测嵌入效应问题能通过涉及替代效应、预算约束等标准经济相互作用来解释①;Kahneman 在研究加拿大安大略省湖泊渔业资源保护估值比较时,也较早地发现了范围不敏感问题②;接着,Kahneman 和 Knetsch 研究发现,公共物品作为更具包容性公共物品的组成部分被估值的 WTP 比其单独被估值的 WTP 低③;Desvousges 等研究发现,保护 2000 只、20000 只或 200000 只同种类的迁徙水鸟,WTP 差异不大④。Kahneman 和 Knetsch、Desvousges 等一些著名而有争议性研究成果的发表和埃克森—瓦尔迪兹油轮泄漏事件(The Exxon – Valdez oil Spill)⑤,改变了学者们对嵌入效应问题的"冷漠",标志着对 CVM 有效性(Validity)和可靠性(Reliability)持续争论的开始⑥。

这场嵌入效应问题的持续争论涉及四个核心理论问题:①受访者通过 CVM 表达的选择是符合经济理论预期(Economic – theoretic Expectations)还是符合心理学选择模型(Psychological Choice Models),如果响应模式被发现符合经济理论预期,这将有利于将 CVM 的评估结果纳入公共政策的成本—收益分析中;如果响应模式主要突出动机,无关提问的公共物品变化,则不符合成本—收益分析决策框架⑦。②CVM 揭示的

---

① Alan Randall, et al., *The Structure of Contingent Markets: Some Results of a Recent Experiment*. Presented to the Annual Meeting of the American Economic Association, Washington D. C., 1981.
② Daniel Kahneman, *Comments. In Brookshire D, Cummings R G, Schulze W D. (Eds.). Valuing Environmental Goods: An Assessment of the Contingent Valuation Method*, Totowa, New Jersey: Rowman & Littlefield, 1986, pp. 61 – 62.
③ Daniel Kahneman and Jack L. Knetsch, "Valuing Public Goods: The Purchase of Moral Satisfaction", *Journal of Environmental Economics and Management*, Vol. 22, No. 1, January 1992.
④ William Desvousges, et al., *Measuring Natural Resource Damages with Contingent Valuation: Tests of Validity and Reliability*, UK: Bingley: Emerald Group Publishing Limited, 1993, pp. 91 – 164.
⑤ Richard T. Carson, et al., *A Contingent Valuation Study of Lost Passive Use Values Resulting from the Exxon Valdez Oil Spill*, Germany: University Library of Munich, 1992, pp. 80 – 125.
⑥ V. Kerry Smith, "Nonmarket Valuation of Environmental Resources: An Interpretative Appraisal", *Land Economics*, Vol. 69, No. 1, February 1993; V. Kerry Smith and Laura L. Osborne, "Do Contingent Valuation Estimates Pass a 'Scope' Test? A Meta – analysis", *Journal of Environmental Economics and Management*, Vol. 31, No. 3, November 1996; Richard T. Carson, et al., "Contingent Valuation: Controversies and Evidence", *Environmental and Resource Economics*, Vol. 19, No. 2, June 2001.
⑦ Ian J. Bateman, et al., "Economic Valuation of Policies for Managing Acidity in Remote Mountain Lakes: Examining Validity through Scope Sensitivity Testing", *Aquatic Sciences*, Vol. 67, No. 3, September 2005.

消费者偏好是否符合新古典经济学关于偏好是定义完好的和不变的基本假设①。③CVM 结果是否通过内部一致性检验（Internal Consistency Tests）②。④如何判断 WTP 的变化对范围反应的经济显著性（Economic Significance）③。当 CVM 被应用到使用价值（Use Value）占主导的熟悉公共物品估值时，能够产生结构有效性（Construct Validity）估计④；但是，当 CVM 被应用到非使用价值（Non-use Value）占主导的公共物品估值时，通常受访者没有待估公共物品的选择经验和认知，则产生了众多冲突的观点⑤；其中有几项研究得出，CVM 调查的受访者

---

① Kevin J. Boyle, et al., "An Investigation of Part-whole Biases in Contingent-valuation Studies", *Journal of Environmental Economics and Management*, Vol. 27, No. 1, July 1994.

② Peter A. Diamond and Jerry A. Hausman, "Contingent Valuation: Is Some Number Better than no Number?", *The Journal of Economic Perspectives*, Vol. 8, No. 4, Fall 1994.

③ John C. Whitehead, "Plausible Responsiveness to Scope in Contingent Valuation", *Ecological Economics*, Vol. 128, August 2016.

④ Richard T. Carson and Robert C. Mitchell, "The Issue of Scope in Contingent Valuation Studies", *American Journal of Agricultural Economics*, Vol. 75, No. 5, December 1993; Ronald G. Cummings and Glenn W. Harrison, "The Measurement and Decomposition of Nonuse Values: A Critical Review", *Environmental and Resource Economics*, Vol. 5, No. 3, April 1995; Richard T. Carson, et al., "Contingent Valuation and Revealed Preference Methodologies: Comparing the Estimates for Quasi-public Goods", *Land Economics*, Vol. 72, No. 1, February 1996; V. Kerry Smith and Laura L. Osborne, "Do Contingent Valuation Estimates Pass a 'Scope' Test? A Meta-analysis", *Journal of Environmental Economics and Management*, Vol. 31, No. 3, November 1996.

⑤ Robert Cameron Mitchell and Richard T. Carson, *Using Surveys to Value Public Goods: The Contingent Valuation Method*, Washington: Resources for the Future, 1989, pp. 107 – 126; V. Kerry Smith, "Arbitrary Values, Good Causes, and Premature Verdicts", *Journal of Environmental Economics and Management*, Vol. 22, No. 1, January 1992; Richard C. Bishop and Michael P. Welsh, "Existence Values in Benefit-cost Analysis and Damage Assessment", *Land Economics*, Vol. 68, No. 4, November 1992; Raymond J. Kopp, "Why Existence Value Should be Included in Cost-benefit Analysis", *Journal of Policy Analysis and Management*, Vol. 11, No. 1, December 1992; W. Michael Hanemann, "Valuing the Environment through Contingent Valuation", *The Journal of Economic Perspectives*, Vol. 8, No. 4, February 1994; Peter A. Diamond and Jerry A. Hausman, "Contingent Valuation: Is Some Number Better than no Number?", *The Journal of Economic Perspectives*, Vol. 8, No. 4, Fall 1994; Ronald G. Cummings and Glenn W. Harrison, "Was the Ohio Court Well Informed in its Assessment of the Accuracy of the Contingent Valuation Method?", *Natural Resources Journal*, Vol. 34, No. 1, Winter 1994; Ronald G. Cummings and Glenn W. Harrison, "The Measurement and Decomposition of Nonuse Values: A Critical Review", *Environmental and Resource Economics*, Vol. 5, No. 3, April 1995.

对于不同范围的公共物品或者更具包容性的公共物品，陈述几乎相同的 *WTP*①。这些研究成果的出现，燃起了关于嵌入效应问题的激烈辩论，其中辩论的核心主要集中在道德满足/温情效应（Moral Satisfaction/Warm Glow）和更传统的经济商品价值动机（Economic – commodity Value Motivations）的相对重要性。② 嵌入效应问题被美国国家海洋和大气管理局（The National Oceanic and Atmospheric Administration，NOAA）专家小组称为"反对 CVM 可靠性的最重要内部论据"。③

二 结构效度检验

（一）范围检验和加总检验的含义

NOAA 专家小组建议，CVM 研究应进行内部一致性检验，评估结果与新古典经济理论预期的一致性；NOAA 推荐范围检验（Scope Test）作为评估 CVM 结果内部一致性的标准方法④。NOAA 专家小组建议的范围检验是一种结构效度检验（Construct Validity Test），基于"物品多

---

① Daniel Kahneman，*Comments. In Brookshire D，Cummings R G，Schulze W D．（Eds.）．Valuing Environmental Goods*：*An Assessment of the Contingent Valuation Method*，Totowa，New Jersey：Rowman & Littlefield，1986，pp. 61 – 62；Daniel Kahneman and Jack L. Knetsch，"Valuing Public Goods：The Purchase of Moral Satisfaction"，*Journal of Environmental Economics and Management*，Vol. 22，No. 1，January 1992；Peter A. Diamond，et al．，*Does Contingent Valuation Measure Preferences? Experimental Evidence. In Hausman J A（Ed.）．Contingent Valuation*：*A Critical Assessment*，UK：Bingley：Emerald Group Publishing Limited，1993，pp. 41 – 89；Kevin J. Boyle，et al．，"An Investigation of Part – whole Biases in Contingent – valuation Studies"，*Journal of Environmental Economics and Management*，Vol. 27，No. 1，July 1994.

② Ian J. Bateman，et al．，*Visible Choice Sets and Scope Sensitivity*：*An Experimental and Field Test of Study Design Effects upon Nested Contingent Values*，UK：The Centre for Social and Economic Research on the Global Environmental（CSERGE），University of East Anglia，Working Paper EDM，NO. 01 – 01，2001，pp. 4 – 7；Ian J. Bateman，et al．，"On Visible Choice Sets and Scope Sensitivity"，*Journal of Environmental Economics and Management*，Vol. 47，No. 1，January 2004.

③ Kenneth Arrow，et al．，"Report of the NOAA Panel on Contingent Valuation"，*Federal Register*，Vol. 58，No. 10，January 1993；Vito Frontuto，et al．，"Earmarking Conservation：Further Inquiry on Scope Effects in Stated Preference Methods Applied to Nature – based Tourism"，*Tourism Management*，Vol. 60，June 2017.

④ Kenneth Arrow，et al．，"Report of the NOAA Panel on Contingent Valuation"，*Federal Register*，Vol. 58，No. 10，January 1993.

优于少"的消费理论基本原则。① 范围检验分为内部范围检验（Internal Scope Test）和外部范围检验（External Scope Test）②，内部范围检验与配对样本（Paired Sample）对应，被 CVM 的批评者描述为弱检验（Weak Test），是衡量相同受访者在待估公共物品不同范围下的 *WTP* 变化；外部范围检验与分样本（Split Sample）对应，被描述为强检验（Strong Test），是衡量不同受访者在待估公共物品不同范围下的 *WTP* 变化。③ 内部范围检验和外部范围检验是一种互为补充的关系。④ Diamond 和 Hausman 也建议，CVM 研究应设计并执行内部一致性检验来评估结果的有效性和可靠性，特别是在非使用价值占主导地位的经济计量中尤其重要；他们推荐加总检验（Adding – up Test）方法。⑤ Diamond 等提出的加总检验也是一种结构效度检验。⑥ Diamond 等指出，标准效用理论（Standard Utility Theory）隐含着一种叫"加总条件"（Adding – up Condition）的关系，即第一件物品的 *WTP* 加上第二件物品在受访者已

---

① Kenneth Arrow, et al., "Report of the NOAA Panel on Contingent Valuation", *Federal Register*, Vol. 58, No. 10, January 1993; Brian R. Binger, et al., "Contingent Valuation Methodology in the Natural Resource Damage Regulatory Process: Choice Theory and the Embedding Phenomenon", *Natural Resources Journal*, Vol. 35, No. 3, July 1995; Nicolas Borzykowski, et al., "Scope Effects in Contingent Valuation: Does the Assumed Statistical Distribution of WTP Matter?", *Ecological Economics*, Vol. 144, February 2018.

② Richard T. Carson and Robert Cameron Mitchell, "Sequencing and Nesting in Contingent Valuation Surveys", *Journal of Environmental Economics and Management*, Vol. 28, No. 2, March 1995.

③ Richard T. Carson, et al., "Contingent Valuation: Controversies and Evidence", *Environmental and Resource Economics*, Vol. 19, No. 2, June 2001; Ian J. Bateman, et al., "On Visible Choice Sets and Scope Sensitivity", *Journal of Environmental Economics and Management*, Vol. 47, No. 1, January 2004.

④ Henrik Andersson and Mikael Svensson, "Cognitive Ability and Scale Bias in the Contingent Valuation Method: An Analysis of Willingness to Pay to Reduce Mortality Risk", *Environmental and Resource Economics*, Vol. 39, No. 4, April 2008; Hilary Ndambiri, et al., "Scope Effects of Respondent Uncertainty in Contingent Valuation: Evidence from Motorized Emission Reductions in the City of Nairobi, Kenya", *Journal of Environmental Planning and Management*, Vol. 60, No. 1, January 2017.

⑤ Peter A. Diamond and Jerry A. Hausman, *On Contingent Valuation Measurement of Nonuse Values. In Hausman J. A. (Ed.) Contingent Valuation: A Critical Assessment*, UK: Bingley: Emerald Group Publishing Limited, 1993, pp. 3 – 38; Peter A. Diamond and Jerry A. Hausman, "Contingent Valuation: Is Some Number better than no Number?", *The Journal of Economic Perspectives*, Vol. 8, No. 4, Fall 1994.

⑥ John C. Whitehead, "Plausible Responsiveness to Scope in Contingent Valuation", *Ecological Economics*, Vol. 128, August 2016.

经支付并得到第一件物品后的 WTP，必须等于受访者对两件物品结合的 WTP；并明确规定，加总检验是针对增量的收益（Incremental Benefits），在一定范围内存在的边际效应递减和替代效应被包含在估值中。① Desvousges 等统计分析了 CVM 实施范围检验的 109 个案例，其中 40 个检验通过、17 个检验没有通过、47 个检验结果混合和 5 个没有报告结果。② Whitehead 指出，目前非常少研究者选择利用加总检验，国际文献检索结果验证了这一点（见表 1.5）③；Desvousges 等的统计结果也验证了这一点，在这 109 个案例中，只有 3 个设计了增量加总检验，其中 1 个检验没有通过、1 个检验结果混合和 1 个没有报告结果。④ 目前，结构效度检验（范围检验或加总检验）面临的主要挑战是：如何判断对范围的反应是充分的（Adequate）或合理的（Plausible），即经济显著性（Economic Significance）问题。也就是，如何判断统计显著性差异与经济直觉（Economic Intuition）的一致性问题？⑤

（二）范围检验和加总检验的经济学基础

假设待估公共物品的最初供给水平和可支配收入分别为 X_0 和 y，待估公共物品的第一增加部分、第二增加部分分别为 b 和 c，待估公共物品的整体为 $a = b + c$；在独立估值时，受访者对待估公共物品整体、第一增加部分和第二增加部分 a、b 和 c 的支付意愿分别为 WTP_a、WTP_b 和 WTP_c；在已拥有待估公共物品第一增加部分 b 的情况下，对待估公共物品第二增加部分 c 的支付意愿为 $WTP_c \mid b$；个体偏好效用函数为 U。根据消费理论，对待估公共物品第一增加部分 b 的 WTP_b 有：$U(X_0, y) = U(X_0 + b, y - WTP_b)$；在已拥有待估公共物品第一增加部

---

① Peter A. Diamond, et al., *Does Contingent Valuation Measure Preferences? Experimental Evidence*. In Hausman J A (Ed.). *Contingent Valuation: A Critical Assessment*, UK: Bingley: Emerald Group Publishing Limited, 1993, pp. 41–89.

② William Desvousges, et al., "Adequate Responsiveness to Scope in Contingent Valuation", *Ecological Economics*, Vol. 84, December 2012.

③ John C. Whitehead, "Plausible Responsiveness to Scope in Contingent Valuation", *Ecological Economics*, Vol. 128, August 2016.

④ William Desvousges, et al., "Adequate Responsiveness to Scope in Contingent Valuation", *Ecological Economics*, Vol. 84, December 2012.

⑤ John C. Whitehead, "Plausible Responsiveness to Scope in Contingent Valuation", *Ecological Economics*, Vol. 128, August 2016.

分 b 的情况下，考虑存在替代效应和/或收入效应，对待估公共物品第二增加部分 c 的 $WTP_c \mid b$ 有：$U(X_0 + b, y - WTP_b) = U(X_0 + b + c, y - WTP_b - WTP_c \mid b)$；在田野实验中，通常不能调整收入效应，所以：$U(X_0 + b, y) = U(X_0 + b + c, y - WTP_c \mid b)$；对待估公共物品整体 a 的 WTP_a 有：$U(X_0, y) = U(X_0 + a, y - WTP_a)$。加总检验是验证是否：$WTP_a = WTP_b + WTP_c \mid b$；范围检验是验证是否：$WTP_c \mid b = WTP_a - WTP_b = WTP_c$，或 $WTP_b < WTP_a$。如果出现：①$WTP_a < WTP_b + WTP_c \mid b$，即待估公共物品各增加部分被估值的 WTP 之和超过其整体被估值的 WTP；②$WTP_c \mid b = WTP_a - WTP_b < WTP_c$，即待估特定公共物品作为更具包容性公共物品的组成部分被估值的 WTP 比其独立被估值的 WTP 低；③$WTP_b \approx WTP_a$，即待估公共物品部分被独立估值的 WTP 与其整体被估值的 WTP 相差不大。出现上述三种情况，表明存在嵌入效应问题。①

三 范围反应敏感性问题：经济学视角

许多学者从替代效应（Substitution Effect）、边际效应递减（Diminishing Marginal Utility）、饱和程度（The Degree of Satiation）、收入效应（Income Effect）/预算限制（Budget Constraint）及补偿效应（Complementarity Effect）等经济学相关理论视角，来研究范围反应敏感性问题。②

---

① Ian J. Bateman, et al., "Does Part – whole Bias Exist? An Experimental Investigation", *The Economic Journal*, Vol. 107, March 1997; John C. Whitehead, "Plausible Responsiveness to Scope in Contingent Valuation", *Ecological Economics*, Vol. 128, August 2016; Jonathan Baron, "Contingent Valuation: Flawed Logic?", *Science*, Vol. 357, No. 6349, July 2017.

② Alan Randall and John P. Hoehn, "Embedding in Market Demand Systems", *Journal of Environmental Economics and Management*, Vol. 30, No. 3, May 1996; Kimberly Rollins and Audrey Lyke, "The Case for Diminishing Marginal Existence Values", *Journal of Environmental Economics and Management*, Vol. 36, No. 3, November 1998; Paulo A. L. D. Nunes and Erik Schokkaert, "Identifying the Warm Glow Effect in Contingent Valuation", *Journal of Environmental Economics and Management*, Vol. 45, No. 2, March 2003; Neil A. Powe and Ian J. Bateman, "Investigating Insensitivity to Scope: A Split – sample Test of Perceived Scheme Realism", *Land Economics*, Vol. 80, No. 2, May 2004; Ioanna Grammatikopoulou and Søren Bøye Olsen, "Accounting Protesting and Warm Glow Bidding in Contingent Valuation Surveys Considering the Management of Environmental Goods: An Empirical Case Study Assessing the Value of Protecting a Natura 2000 Wetland Area in Greece", *Journal of Environmental Management*, Vol. 130, November 2013; William Desvousges, et al., "From Curious to Pragmatically Curious: Comment on 'from Hopeless to Curious? Thoughts on Hausman's 'Dubious to Hopeless' Critique of Contingent Valuation'", *Applied Economic Perspectives and Policy*, Vol. 38, No. 1, March 2016; Jeremy De Valck and John Rolfe, "Spatial Heterogeneity in Stated Preference Valuation: Status, Challenges and Road Ahead", *International Review of Environmental and Resource Economics*, Vol. 11, No. 4, August 2018.

（一）单一效应

1. 替代效应

因为公共物品的额外增加边际效应递减，替代品改变了待估公共物品的稀缺条件，进而会影响 WTP[①]；受访者对替代品信息相当敏感，关于替代品更多信息的受访者比信息少的受访者对估值的 WTP 更敏感，所以，合理的表达替代品信息非常重要。[②]

2. 边际效应递减

受访者对待估公共物品的低水平供给范围敏感，而高水平供给缺乏范围敏感，这正如理论指出的边际效应递减[③]；边际效应递减也解释了高存在价值（High Existence Values）的范围不敏感问题[④]。

3. 饱和程度

对于一个相对较大范围待估公共物品的 WTP 是否增加，将依靠受访者关于待估公共物品的供给水平是否饱和[⑤]；如果边际效应接近于零，范围间偏好趋近于水平[⑥]，个体效用趋于饱和，增加待估公共物品的供给水平将不增加个体效用[⑦]；所以，范围检验考虑边际 WTP 曲线

[①] Jeremy De Valck and John Rolfe, "Spatial Heterogeneity in Stated Preference Valuation: Status, Challenges and Road Ahead", *International Review of Environmental and Resource Economics*, Vol. 11, No. 4, August 2018.

[②] Thomas C. Brown, et al., "Does Better Information About the Good Avoid the Embedding Effect?", *Journal of Environmental Management*, Vol. 44, No. 1, May 1995; Thomas Brown and John W. Duffield, "Testing Part – whole Valuation Effects in Contingent Valuation of Instream Flow Protection", *Water Resources Research*, Vol. 31, No. 9, September 1995.

[③] Kimberly Rollins and Audrey Lyke, "The Case for Diminishing Marginal Existence Values", *Journal of Environmental Economics and Management*, Vol. 36, No. 3, November 1998.

[④] Kimberly Rollins and Audrey Lyke, "The Case for Diminishing Marginal Existence Values", *Journal of Environmental Economics and Management*, Vol. 36, No. 3, November 1998.

[⑤] S. M. Chilton and W. G. Hutchinson, "A Note on the Warm Glow of Giving and Scope Sensitivity in Contingent Valuation Studies", *Journal of Economic Psychology*, Vol. 21, No. 4, August 2000.

[⑥] Kevin J. Boyle, et al., "An Investigation of Part – whole Biases in Contingent – valuation Studies", *Journal of Environmental Economics and Management*, Vol. 27, No. 1, July 1994.

[⑦] Neil A. Powe and Ian J. Bateman, "Investigating Insensitivity to Scope: A Split – sample Test of Perceived Scheme Realism", *Land Economics*, Vol. 80, No. 2, May 2004.

上的位置非常重要。① 如 Rollins 和 Lyke 通过研究发现，受访者在保护四个公园后已接近饱和（Nearing Satiation），边际 WTP 增加值非常低。②

4. 收入效应/预算限制

通常，受访者的 WTP 只占收入的一小部分，收入效应应该很小；但是，由于多数家庭的收入已被预先承诺（Committed），真正可获得的任意可支配收入一般很小，尤其是如果被要求短期支付③；所以，收入效应/预算限制的影响可能相当大④，也会引起嵌入效应问题⑤。同时，待估公共物品的部分若免费提供将影响加总属性⑥，导致可能偏离精确的加总。⑦

（二）复合效应

1. 边际效应递减和替代效应交互作用

由于边际效应递减和替代效应存在，待估公共物品非增量部分的经济合理值不一定加总等于它们的组合值⑧；待估公共物品范围扩大的低增加值，也反映了公共物品间的替代效应和边际效应递减⑨。替代效应

---

① S. M. Chilton and W. G. Hutchinson, "A Qualitative Examination of How Respondents in a Contingent Valuation Study Rationalise their WTP Responses to an Increase in the Quantity of the Environmental Good", *Journal of Economic Psychology*, Vol. 24, No. 1, February 2003.

② Kimberly Rollins and Audrey Lyke, "The Case for Diminishing Marginal Existence Values", *Journal of Environmental Economics and Management*, Vol. 36, No. 3, November 1998.

③ Richard T. Carson, et al., "Contingent Valuation: Controversies and Evidence", *Environmental and Resource Economics*, Vol. 19, No. 2, June 2001.

④ Alan Randall and John P. Hoehn, "Embedding in Market Demand Systems", *Journal of Environmental Economics and Management*, Vol. 30, No. 3, May 1996.

⑤ Alan Shiell and Lisa Gold, "Contingent Valuation in Health Care and the Persistence of Embedding Effects without the Warm Glow", *Journal of Economic Psychology*, Vol. 23, No. 2, April 2002.

⑥ Levan Elbakidze and Rodolfo M. Nayga Jr., "The Adding-up Test in an Incentivized Value Elicitation Mechanism: The Role of the Income Effect", *Environmental and Resource Economics*, Vol. 71, No. 3, November 2018.

⑦ Peter A. Diamond and Jerry A. Hausman, "Contingent Valuation: Is Some Number Better than no Number?", *The Journal of Economic Perspectives*, Vol. 8, No. 4, Fall 1994.

⑧ Paulo A. L. D. Nunes and Erik Schokkaert, "Identifying the Warm Glow Effect in Contingent Valuation", *Journal of Environmental Economics and Management*, Vol. 45, No. 2, March 2003.

⑨ William Desvousges, et al., "Adequate Responsiveness to Scope in Contingent Valuation", *Ecological Economics*, Vol. 84, December 2012.

和边际效应递减的存在,限制了范围效应的大小,可能导致标准范围检验失败,这一观点被 Desvousges 等称为是自从引入范围检验以来出现的最重要认识之一。①

2. 替代效应和收入效应交互作用

如果提供多种待估公共物品的收益在局部均衡框架中(A Partial Equilibrium Framework)被独立估值后再加总,多种待估公共物品估值结果将被高估②,这一观点已经被延伸到解释嵌入效应问题③;替代效应和收入效应存在,意味着不能简单地将部分加总④;忽略替代效应和收入效应,将高估待估公共物品的总收益⑤;同时,这也意味着部分加总后的 WTP 高估符合经济理论。⑥

3. 替代效应和补偿效应交互作用

如果考虑替代效应和补偿效应,一些出现嵌入效应问题的案例可能与传统希克斯消费理论一致⑦;同时,替代效应和补偿效应存在,容易

---

① William Desvousges, et al., "From Curious to Pragmatically Curious: Comment on 'from Hopeless to Curious? Thoughts on Hausman's 'Dubious to Hopeless' Critique of Contingent Valuation'", *Applied Economic Perspectives and Policy*, Vol. 38, No. 1, March 2016.

② John P. Hoehn and Alan Randall, "Too Many Proposals Pass the Benefit Cost Test", *The American Economic Review*, Vol. 79, No. 3, June 1989.

③ Richard T. Carson and Robert Cameron Mitchell, "Sequencing and Nesting in Contingent Valuation Surveys", *Journal of Environmental Economics and Management*, Vol. 28, No. 2, March 1995.

④ Neil A. Powe and Ian J. Bateman, "Investigating Insensitivity to Scope: A Split–sample Test of Perceived Scheme Realism", *Land Economics*, Vol. 80, No. 2, May 2004.

⑤ William D. Schulze, et al., "Embedding and Calibration in Measuring Non–use Values", *Resource and Energy Economics*, Vol. 20, No. 2, June 1998.

⑥ Richard T. Carson and Robert C. Mitchell, "The Issue of Scope in Contingent Valuation Studies", *American Journal of Agricultural Economics*, Vol. 75, No. 5, December 1993; Richard T. Carson and Robert Cameron Mitchell, "Sequencing and Nesting in Contingent Valuation Surveys", *Journal of Environmental Economics and Management*, Vol. 28, No. 2, March 1995; Ian J. Bateman, et al., "Does Part–whole Bias Exist? An Experimental Investigation", *The Economic Journal*, Vol. 107, March 1997; M. Christie, "A Comparison of Alternative Contingent Valuation Elicitation Treatments for the Evaluation of Complex Environmental Policy", *Journal of Environmental Management*, Vol. 62, No. 3, July 2001.

⑦ Ian J. Bateman, et al., "Does Part–whole Bias Exist? An Experimental Investigation", *The Economic Journal*, Vol. 107, March 1997.

导致拒绝加总检验。①

四　范围反应敏感性问题：心理学视角

许多学者从温情效应/道德满足（Warm Glow/Moral Satisfaction）、社会心理学理论（Social Psychological Theory）、联合产品心理模型（Mental Models of Joint Products）、不确定性（Uncertainty）、旗舰物种效应（Flagship Species Effect）及标签效应（Label Effect）等心理学视角，来研究范围反应敏感性问题。②

（一）温情效应

1. 温情效应与 CVM

Kahneman 和 Knetsch 是第一个将温情效应与 CVM 联系在一起的学者；他们指出，如果存在温情效应动机（Warm Glow Motivations），*WTP* 代表通常的向慈善机构捐赠，无关描述的待估公共物品的变化，不是与所描述变化相关的个体偏好价值。③ 通过 CVM 引出的价值不是真正的

---

① Ioanna Grammatikopoulou and Søren Bøye Olsen, "Accounting Protesting and Warm Glow Bidding in Contingent Valuation Surveys Considering the Management of Environmental Goods: An Empirical Case Study Assessing the Value of Protecting a Natura 2000 Wetland Area in Greece", *Journal of Environmental Management*, Vol. 130, November 2013.

② Daniel Kahneman and Jack L. Knetsch, "Valuing Public Goods: The Purchase of Moral Satisfaction", *Journal of Environmental Economics and Management*, Vol. 22, No. 1, January 1992; William D. Schulze, et al., "Embedding and Calibration in Measuring Non – use Values", *Resource and Energy Economics*, Vol. 20, No. 2, June 1998; Paulo A. L. D. Nunes and Erik Schokkaert, "Identifying the Warm Glow Effect in Contingent Valuation", *Journal of Environmental Economics and Management*, Vol. 45, No. 2, March 2003; Thomas A. Heberlein, et al., "Rethinking the Scope Test as a Criterion for Validity in Contingent Valuation", *Journal of Environmental Economics and Management*, Vol. 50, No. 1, July 2005; Mikołaj Czajkowski and Nick Hanley, "Using Labels to Investigate Scope Effects in Stated Preference Methods", *Environmental and Resource Economics*, Vol. 44, No. 4, December 2009; James R. Meldrum, "Comparing Different Attitude Statements in Latent Class Models of Stated Preferences for Managing an Invasive Forest Pathogen", *Ecological Economics*, Vol. 120, December 2015; William Desvousges, et al., "From Curious to Pragmatically Curious: Comment on 'from Hopeless to Curious? Thoughts on Hausman's "Dubious to Hopeless" Critique of Contingent Valuation'", *Applied Economic Perspectives and Policy*, Vol. 38, No. 1, March 2016; Richard C. Bishop, "Warm Glow, Good Feelings, and Contingent Valuation", *Journal of Agricultural and Resource Economics*, Vol. 43, No. 3, September 2018; J. R. Molina, et al., "The Role of Flagship Species in the Economic Valuation of Wildfire Impacts: An Application to two Mediterranean Protected Areas", *Science of the Total Environment*, Vol. 675, July 2019.

③ Daniel Kahneman and Jack L. Knetsch, "Valuing Public Goods: The Purchase of Moral Satisfaction", *Journal of Environmental Economics and Management*, Vol. 22, No. 1, January 1992.

经济价值，而是产生于个体购买道德满足感（Purchase of Moral Satisfaction）[1]；购买道德满足作为解释不能被私人购买的待估公共物品的 *WTP* 尤其合理，即使这些待估公共物品具有使用价值。[2]

2. 贡献模型和购买模型

Kahneman 和他的同事们认为，有两个竞争模型（Competing Models）可以用于分析个体如何回答价值问题：贡献模型（Contribution Model）被认为更好地描述了受访者如何回答 CVM 的问题，从心理学视角来看，贡献模型假设个体把待估公共物品供给视为需要支持的原因，*WTP* 陈述表达对待估公共物品的一般态度或起因；表达一般态度的估值反应本身可能是内在满足（Intrinsic Satisfaction）和温情效应（Warm Glow Effects）的源泉，因此意味着对范围变化的敏感性普遍较低[3]；购买模型（Purchase Model）被认为是多数传统 CVM 文献的基础，陈述的 *WTP* 被解释为福利变化的有效衡量，购买模型强调获得精确划分的待估公共物品。[4]

3. 温情效应测度

Nunes 和 Schokkaert 认为，受访者的赠送行为源于自身的道德满足，温情效应对 *WTP* 有显著影响；嵌入效应问题并不一定意味着矛盾的行为，

---

[1] I Ritov and D. Kahneman., *How People Value the Environment: Attitudes Versus Economic Values. In: Bazerman M H, Messick D. M., Tenbrunzel A. E., et al. (Eds.). Environment, Ethics and Behaviour: The Psychology of Environmental Valuation and Degradation*, San Francisco, CA: The New Lexington Press, 1997.

[2] Daniel Kahneman and Jack L. Knetsch, "Valuing Public Goods: The Purchase of Moral Satisfaction", *Journal of Environmental Economics and Management*, Vol. 22, No. 1, January 1992.

[3] Daniel Kahneman and Jack L. Knetsch, "Valuing Public Goods: The Purchase of Moral Satisfaction", *Journal of Environmental Economics and Management*, Vol. 22, No. 1, January 1992; Daniel Kahneman, et al., "Stated Willingness to Pay for Public Goods: A Psychological Perspective", *Psychological Science*, Vol. 4, No. 5, September 1993; Daniel Kahneman and Ilana Ritov, "Determinants of Stated Willingness to Pay for Public Goods: A Study in the Headline Method", *Journal of Risk and Uncertainty*, Vol. 9, No. 1, July 1994; Donald Philip Green, et al., "How the Scope and Method of Public Funding Affect Willingness to Pay for Public Goods", *The Public Opinion Quarterly*, Vol. 58, No. 1, January 1994.

[4] Daniel Kahneman and Jack L. Knetsch, "Valuing Public Goods: The Purchase of Moral Satisfaction", *Journal of Environmental Economics and Management*, Vol. 22, No. 1, January 1992; Daniel Kahneman, et al., "Stated Willingness to Pay for Public Goods: A Psychological Perspective", *Psychological Science*, Vol. 4, No. 5, September 1993.

它能通过个体偏好中存在的稳定的和可度量的温情效应成分解释。[1] 个体偏好源于自利或者道德判断不要紧，CVM 的温情效应是可以容忍的事实[2]，并不意味着 CVM 无效[3]；并且，温情效应可以被测量。[4]

4. 温情效应与 WTP

Kahneman 和 Knetsch 认为，嵌入效应问题是源于购买道德满足；温情效应的边际效应递减迅速[5]，经常被用来解释嵌入效应问题。[6] Chilton 和 Hutchinson 从私人提供公共物品的捐赠理论视角，研究了 WTP 中没有温情效应（No Warm Glow）动机、部分温情效应（Partial Warm Glow）动机或完全温情效应（Complete Warm Glow）动机，将影响 WTP 的范围敏感性[7]；Bishop 则认为，温情效应只有在极端情况下

---

[1] Paulo A. L. D. Nunes and Erik Schokkaert, "Identifying the Warm Glow Effect in Contingent Valuation", *Journal of Environmental Economics and Management*, Vol. 45, No. 2, March 2003.

[2] Paulo A. L. D. Nunes and Erik Schokkaert, "Identifying the Warm Glow Effect in Contingent Valuation", *Journal of Environmental Economics and Management*, Vol. 45, No. 2, March 2003.

[3] Kunt Veisten, et al., "Scope Insensitivity in Contingent Valuation of Complex Environmental Amenities", *Journal of Environmental Management*, Vol. 73, No. 4, December 2004.

[4] Paulo A. L. D. Nunes and Erik Schokkaert, "Identifying the Warm Glow Effect in Contingent Valuation", *Journal of Environmental Economics and Management*, Vol. 45, No. 2, March 2003; Heidi Crumpler and Philip J. Grossman, "An Experimental Test of Warm Glow Giving", *Journal of Public Economics*, Vol. 92, No. 5 – 6, June 2008.

[5] William D. Schulze, et al., "Embedding and Calibration in Measuring Non – use Values", *Resource and Energy Economics*, Vol. 20, No. 2, June 1998; Paulo A. L. D. Nunes and Erik Schokkaert, "Identifying the Warm Glow Effect in Contingent Valuation", *Journal of Environmental Economics and Management*, Vol. 45, No. 2, March 2003.

[6] Paulo A. L. D. Nunes and Erik Schokkaert, "Identifying the Warm Glow Effect in Contingent Valuation", *Journal of Environmental Economics and Management*, Vol. 45, No. 2, March 2003; Ioanna Grammatikopoulou and Søren Bøye Olsen, "Accounting Protesting and Warm Glow Bidding in Contingent Valuation Surveys Considering the Management of Environmental Goods: An Empirical Case Study Assessing the Value of Protecting a Natura 2000 Wetland Area in Greece", *Journal of Environmental Management*, Vol. 130, November 2013.

[7] Susan M. Chilton and W. George Hutchinson, "Some Further Implications of Incorporating the Warm Glow of Giving into Welfare Measures: A Comment on the Use of Donation Mechanisms by Champ et al.", *Journal of Environmental Economics and Management*, Vol. 37, No. 2, March 1999; S. M. Chilton and W. G. Hutchinson, "A Note on the Warm Glow of Giving and Scope Sensitivity in Contingent Valuation Studies", *Journal of Economic Psychology*, Vol. 21, No. 4, August 2000.

才产生嵌入效应问题。

（二）社会心理学理论

1. 经济范围的扩展

Heberlein 等批评传统的范围检验只对比分样本的 WTP 均值/中位数，没有考虑超出经济范围（Beyond Economic Scope），从而经常忽略情感的（Affective）、认知的/态度的（Cognitive/Attitudinal）和行为的（Behavioral）范围；他们利用社会心理学理论（Social Psychological Theory）扩展了范围的定义，新范围包含两个维度的情感范围（Affective Scopes）和两个维度的认知范围（Cognitive Scopes），通过案例研究得出两条重要结论：当受访者对待估公共物品的部分知道（Know）更多、喜欢（Like）更多和有更多体验（Experience），他们很可能赋予待估公共物品的部分比整体更高的经济价值；当受访者对待估公共物品的整体和部分了解（Knowledge）、体验（Experience）和良好的态度（Well - formed Attitudes），WTP 的估值更可能是有效的（无论显示范围敏感或不敏感）。① 这些重要研究结论为从新的视角解释嵌入效应问题提供了依据。

2. 社会心理学因素与 WTP

受访者持有心理的和情感的信念（Psychological and Emotional Beliefs）能解释一些嵌入效应问题，态度影响（Attitudinal Influences）甚至可以解释负的范围效应（Negative Scope Effects）或过度嵌入效应（Over - embedding），但它们不会使 CVM 估计无效。② 如狼再引进计划出现了降低的 WTP，这种负范围可能与情感的和认知的范围（Affective and Cognitive Scopes）有关，反映人们的真实偏好。③ 许多研究试图将情感的、认知的、态度的和行为的等社会心理学因素变量与 WTP 的测

---

① Thomas A. Heberlein, et al., "Rethinking the Scope Test as a Criterion for Validity in Contingent Valuation", *Journal of Environmental Economics and Management*, Vol. 50, No. 1, July 2005.

② Thomas A. Heberlein, et al., "Rethinking the Scope Test as a Criterion for Validity in Contingent Valuation", *Journal of Environmental Economics and Management*, Vol. 50, No. 1, July 2005.

③ Thomas A. Heberlein, et al., "Rethinking the Scope Test as a Criterion for Validity in Contingent Valuation", *Journal of Environmental Economics and Management*, Vol. 50, No. 1, July 2005; Elena Ojea and Maria L. Loureiro, "Identifying the Scope Effect on a Meta - analysis of Biodiversity Valuation Studies", *Resource and Energy Economics*, Vol. 33, No. 3, September 2011.

度联系起来，提高实践中 CVM 的有效性和可靠性，探索解释嵌入效应问题。①

（三）联合产品心理模型

Schulze 等给出了联合产品心理模型思想的例子：挽救一个物种的唯一方法是通过挽救物种栖息地来挽救所有物种，这不仅提供了所有物种的价值，也提供了物种栖息地的价值，这一观点被心理学家称为心理模型（Mental Models）。② 受访者提供挽救一个物种的 WTP，事实上已经提供了挽救栖息地所有物种的 WTP；当再询问受访者挽救另一个物种 WTP 的增加值时，受访者的 WTP 增加值是零，因为他们已经为挽救第二个物种支付了。联合产品心理模型的联合性，将导致嵌入效应问题。③ 联合产品假设（The Joint Product Hypothesis）为解释存在的完全嵌入效应（公共物品与更具包容性公共物品被估值的 WTP 差异不大）提供了依据。④

（四）受访者和 CVM 方案不确定性

受访者不确定性是指受访者愿意为待估公共物品支付数额犹豫不决的状态（State of Indecisiveness）。⑤ 受访者不确定性会降低范围敏感性，

---

① Henrik Andersson and Mikael Svensson, "Cognitive Ability and Scale Bias in the Contingent Valuation Method: An Analysis of Willingness to Pay to Reduce Mortality Risk", *Environmental and Resource Economics*, Vol. 39, No. 4, April 2008; Andrea M. Leiter and Gerald J. Pruckner, "Proportionality of Willingness to Pay Small Changes in Risk: The Impact of Attitudinal Factors in Scope Tests", *Environmental and Resource Economics*, Vol. 42, No. 2, February 2009; Min Gong and Jonathan Baron, "The Generality of the Emotion Effect on Magnitude Sensitivity", *Journal of Economic Psychology*, Vol. 32, No. 1, February 2011; Elena Ojea and Maria L. Loureiro, "Identifying the Scope Effect on a Meta-analysis of Biodiversity Valuation Studies", *Resource and Energy Economics*, Vol. 33, No. 3, September 2011; James R. Meldrum, "Comparing Different Attitude Statements in Latent Class Models of Stated Preferences for Managing an Invasive Forest Pathogen", *Ecological Economics*, Vol. 120, December 2015.

② William D. Schulze, et al., "Embedding and Calibration in Measuring Non-use Values", *Resource and Energy Economics*, Vol. 20, No. 2, June 1998.

③ William D. Schulze, et al., "Embedding and Calibration in Measuring Non-use Values", *Resource and Energy Economics*, Vol. 20, No. 2, June 1998.

④ William D. Schulze, et al., "Embedding and Calibration in Measuring Non-use Values", *Resource and Energy Economics*, Vol. 20, No. 2, June 1998.

⑤ Hilary Ndambiri, et al., "Scope Effects of Respondent Uncertainty in Contingent Valuation: Evidence from Motorized Emission Reductions in the City of Nairobi, Kenya", *Journal of Environmental Planning and Management*, Vol. 60, No. 1, January 2017.

引起嵌入效应问题。① 另外，有一些学者从受访者对不同 CVM 方案是否可能被实施的现实性感知（Perceived Realism）视角，来研究嵌入效应问题。② 当受访者考虑待估公共物品更大的方案不太现实比更小的选择，将出现嵌入效应问题。③ 陈述的方案是否将被执行影响调查结果④，考虑调查方案将随之发生的受访者 WTP 高于没考虑的受访者。⑤

（五）旗舰物种效应和标签效应

Kontoleon 和 Swanson 研究考查了一种有魅力或旗舰物种在多大程度上能被用于促进更广泛的生物多样性保护，得出旗舰物种方法是生物多样性保护的一种重要工具。相对于大量不著名的物种，受访者对少数有魅力物种（Charismatic Species）存在偏好。⑥ 公众熟知的特定旗舰物种可能影响预算分配⑦，政府机构也展示了分配不同比例的保

---

① Hilary Ndambiri, et al., "Scope Effects of Respondent Uncertainty in Contingent Valuation: Evidence from Motorized Emission Reductions in the City of Nairobi, Kenya", *Journal of Environmental Planning and Management*, Vol. 60, No. 1, January 2017.

② Neil A. Powe and Ian J. Bateman, "Investigating Insensitivity to Scope: A Split–sample Test of Perceived Scheme Realism", *Land Economics*, Vol. 80, No. 2, May 2004.

③ Richard T. Carson and Robert Cameron Mitchell, "Sequencing and Nesting in Contingent Valuation Surveys", *Journal of Environmental Economics and Management*, Vol. 28, No. 2, March 1995; Neil A. Powe and Ian J. Bateman, "Investigating Insensitivity to Scope: A Split–sample Test of Perceived Scheme Realism", *Land Economics*, Vol. 80, No. 2, May 2004.

④ Pallab Mozumder, et al., "Consumers' Preference for Renewable Energy in the Southwest USA", *Energy Economics*, Vol. 33, No. 6, November 2011; William Desvousges, et al., "From Curious to Pragmatically Curious: Comment on 'from Hopeless to Curious? Thoughts on Hausman's "Dubious to Hopeless" Critique of Contingent Valuation'", *Applied Economic Perspectives and Policy*, Vol. 38, No. 1, March 2016.

⑤ Mani Nepal, et al., "Assessing Perceived Consequentiality: Evidence from a Contingent Valuation Survey on Global Climate Change", *International Journal of Ecological Economics and Statistics*, Vol. 14, No. P09, June 2009; Christian A. Vossler and Sharon B. Watson, "Understanding the Consequences of Consequentiality: Testing the Validity of Stated Preferences in the Field", *Journal of Economic Behavior & Organization*, Vol. 86, February 2013; Daniel R. Petrolia, et al., "America's Wetland? A National Survey of Willingness to Pay for Restoration of Louisiana's Coastal Wetlands", *Marine Resources Economics*, Vol. 29, No. 1, January 2014.

⑥ Andreas Kontoleon and Timothy Swanson, "The Willingness to Pay for Property Rights for the Giant Panda: Can a Charismatic Species be an Instrument for Nature Conservation?", *Land Economics*, Vol. 79, No. 4, November 2003.

⑦ J. R. Molina, et al., "The Role of Flagship Species in the Economic Valuation of Wildfire Impacts: An Application to two Mediterranean Protected Areas", *Science of the Total Environment*, Vol. 675, July 2019.

护基金给一小部分受欢迎的物种。① 受访者使用 CVM 赋予一组物种的 *WTP*，将与他们给予一组物种中的旗舰物种的 *WTP* 大致相同；这种旗舰物种效应存在，将会导致 CVM 估值出现嵌入效应问题。② Czajkowski 和 Hanley 研究发现，相对于一个包含相同保护水平但没有标签的待估公共物品，受访者对认可的、含有标签的待估公共物品将提供一个相对高的 *WTP*；这种标签效应存在，将会导致 CVM 估值出现嵌入效应问题。③

五　范围反应敏感性问题：调查设计与执行视角

许多学者从 CVM 传统调查设计与执行（Design and Implementation）、CVM 嵌入公共物品调查设计与执行及属性缺席（Attribute Nonattendance，ANA）、设备效应（Device Effects）、统计分布假设（The Statistical Distribution Assumption）等视角，来研究范围反应敏感性问题。④

（一）CVM 传统调查设计与执行

许多研究由于没有跟随 NOAA 准则，设计和执行可靠的 CVM 研究

---

① Vito Frontuto, et al., "Earmarking Conservation: Further Inquiry on Scope Effects in Stated Preference Methods Applied to Nature – based Tourism", *Tourism Management*, Vol. 60, June 2017.

② Piran C. L. White, et al., "Economic Values of Threatened Mammals in Britain: A Case Study of the Otter Lutra Lutra and the Water Vole Arvicola Terrestris", *Biological Conservation*, Vol. 82, No. 3, December 1997.

③ Mikołaj Czajkowski and Nick Hanley, "Using Labels to Investigate Scope Effects in Stated Preference Methods", *Environmental and Resource Economics*, Vol. 44, No. 4, December 2009.

④ Richard T. Carson and Robert C. Mitchell, "The Issue of Scope in Contingent Valuation Studies", *American Journal of Agricultural Economics*, Vol. 75, No. 5, December 1993; Richard T. Carson, et al., "Contingent Valuation: Controversies and Evidence", *Environmental and Resource Economics*, Vol. 19, No. 2, June 2001; Neil A. Powe and Ian J. Bateman, "Investigating Insensitivity to Scope: A Split – sample Test of Perceived Scheme Realism", *Land Economics*, Vol. 80, No. 2, May 2004; Elena Ojea and Maria L. Loureiro, "Valuing the Recovery of Overexploited Fish Stocks in the Context of Existence and Option Values", *Marine Policy*, Vol. 34, No. 3, May 2010; Nicolas Borzykowski, et al., "Scope Effects in Contingent Valuation: Does the Assumed Statistical Distribution of WTP Matter?", *Ecological Economics*, Vol. 144, February 2018; Magnus Aa. Skeie, et al., "Smartphone and Tablet Effects in Contingent Valuation Web Surveys – No Reason to Worry?", *Ecological Economics*, Vol. 165, November 2019; Christopher Giguere, et al., "Valuing Hemlock Woolly Adelgid Control in Public Forests: Scope Effects with Attribute Nonattendance", *Land Economics*, Vol. 96, No. 1, February 2020.

而受到批评。① 存在的问题主要包括：无效构建假想市场②，调查执行和抽样方法不正确、统计能力和信息提供质量不足、受访者不能理解调查问题等。③ 针对传统调查设计与执行问题，一些学者提出了处理方法：描述更大和更小的物品请受访者集中注意在更小的物品、使用地图和照片描述情景、简短说明、允许受访者修正投标值、使用绝对范围、调查中包含感知方案现实性问题等。④

（二）CVM 嵌入公共物品调查设计与执行

1. 自下而上方法和自上而下方法与 *WTP*

执行一次 CVM 调查研究同时评估嵌入公共物品（不同范围的公共物品），经常出现嵌入效应问题；而执行多次 CVM 调查研究成本又较高，更有效的选择是探索执行一次 CVM 调查研究同时评估嵌入公共物

---

① Kenneth Arrow, et al., "Report of the NOAA Panel on Contingent Valuation", *Federal Register*, Vol. 58, No. 10, January 1993.

② Richard T. Carson and Robert Cameron Mitchell, "Sequencing and Nesting in Contingent Valuation Surveys", *Journal of Environmental Economics and Management*, Vol. 28, No. 2, March 1995; Richard T. Carson, et al., "Contingent Valuation: Controversies and Evidence", *Environmental and Resource Economics*, Vol. 19, No. 2, June 2001; Mikołaj Czajkowski and Nick Hanley, "Using Labels to Investigate Scope Effects in Stated Preference Methods", *Environmental and Resource Economics*, Vol. 44, No. 4, December 2009.

③ W. George Hutchinson, et al., "Measuring Non-use Value of Environmental Goods Using the Contingent Valuation Method: Problems of Information and Cognition and the Application of Cognitive Questionnaire Design Methods", *Journal of Agricultural Economics*, Vol. 46, No. 1, January 1995; L. Venkatachalam, "The Contingent Valuation Method: A Review", *Environmental Impact Assessment Review*, Vol. 24, No. 1, January 2004; Kunt Veisten, et al., "Scope Insensitivity in Contingent Valuation of Complex Environmental Amenities", *Journal of Environmental Management*, Vol. 73, No. 4, December 2004; Elena Ojea and Maria L. Loureiro, "Valuing the Recovery of Overexploited Fish Stocks in the Context of Existence and Option Values", *Marine Policy*, Vol. 34, No. 3, May 2010.

④ Robert Cameron Mitchell and Richard T. Carson, *Using Surveys to Value Public Goods: The Contingent Valuation Method*, Washington: Resources for the Future, 1989, pp. 107-126; Kenneth Arrow, et al., "Report of the NOAA Panel on Contingent Valuation", *Federal Register*, Vol. 58, No. 10, January 1993; William D. Schulze, et al., "Embedding and Calibration in Measuring Non-use Values", *Resource and Energy Economics*, Vol. 20, No. 2, June 1998; Neil A. Powe and Ian J. Bateman, "Investigating Insensitivity to Scope: A Split-sample Test of Perceived Scheme Realism", *Land Economics*, Vol. 80, No. 2, May 2004; Elena Ojea and Maria L. Loureiro, "Identifying the Scope Effect on a Meta-analysis of Biodiversity Valuation Studies", *Resource and Energy Economics*, Vol. 33, No. 3, September 2011.

品的方法。① Carson 和 Mitchell 提出能同时评估嵌入公共物品所有组成部分的两种基本 *WTP* 引导策略：自下而上方法（Bottom – up Approach）和自上而下方法（Top – down Approach），自上而下方法又分为整体、部分分别独立估值和先对整体估值，再分配到每一个部分两种子方法。② 研究发现：部分独立估值的 *WTP* 与整体先估值、部分再估值的 *WTP* 一致，自上而下法的整体、部分分别独立估值方法提供了有效的和可靠的估计。③

2. 预先披露设计和逐步披露设计与 *WTP*

Powe 和 Bateman 提出了嵌入公共物品 *CVM* 同时估值的四个特征：数量范围或分类范围、包含列表（Inclusive List）或独立列表（Exclusive List）、自下而上列表（Bottom – up List）方向或自上而下列表（Top – down List）方向和预先披露（Advance Disclosure）设计或逐步披露（Stepwise Disclosure）设计四个方面。④ Bateman 等认为，嵌入公共物品同时估值，CVM 调查设计的列表方向（List Direction）和可见选择集（Visible Choice Set）变化，可能对范围敏感性有显著的影响；他们指出，Kahneman 和 Knetsch（引起嵌入效应问题争论的标志性文献）报告的检验是不完全的，因为他们没有考查列表方向和可见选择集变化对范围敏感性的作用。Bateman 等通过实验室实验和田野实验深入研究了分类嵌入公共物品采用独立列表估值、列表方向（自下而上列表或自上

---

① Thomas C. Brown and John W. Duffield, "Testing Part – whole Valuation Effects in Contingent Valuation of Instream Flow Protection", *Water Resources Research*, Vol. 31, No. 9, September 1995.

② Richard T. Carson and Robert Cameron Mitchell, "Sequencing and Nesting in Contingent Valuation Surveys", *Journal of Environmental Economics and Management*, Vol. 28, No. 2, March 1995.

③ John B. Loomis, et al., "Some Empirical Evidence on Embedding Effects in Contingent Valuation of Forest Protection", *Journal of Environmental Economics and Management*, Vol. 25, No. 1, July 1993; M. Christie, "A Comparison of Alternative Contingent Valuation Elicitation Treatments for the Evaluation of Complex Environmental Policy", *Journal of Environmental Management*, Vol. 62, No. 3, July 2001; Nick Hanley, et al., "Aggregating the Benefits of Environmental Improvements: Distance – decay Functions for Use and Non – use Values", *Journal of Environmental Management*, Vol. 68, No. 3, July 2003.

④ N. A. Powe and I. J. Bateman, "Ordering Effects in Nested 'Top – down' and 'Bottom – up' Contingent Valuation Designs", *Ecological Economics*, Vol. 45, No. 2, June 2003.

而下列表）和可见选择集（预先披露设计或逐步披露设计）对 *WTP* 的影响；实验结果表明：采用预先披露设计时，嵌入公共物品自下而上／自上而下列表方向的 *WTP* 估值结果均展现出了范围敏感性，符合理论预期；但采用逐步披露设计时，嵌入公共物品自下而上／自上而下列表方向对观察的范围敏感性影响非常大。[1]

（三）CVM 调查设计与执行最新成果

1. 属性缺席（ANA）

由于多种原因，当受访者忽略一个或多个选择属性产生 ANA。[2] Giguere 等通过研究考查生态、社会和处理方法（Treatment Method）三个属性，将 ANA 作为一个识别 CVM 受访者核心群体的因素，研究得出：当检验范围敏感性时，ANA 是一个重要因素，存在 ANA 可能引起范围（不敏感）问题。[3]

2. 设备效应

随着技术设备的发展，除了计算机外，智能手机和平板电脑被广泛应用，设备效应（Device Effects）将影响对范围反应的判断。[4] Skeie 等研究发现：智能手机和平板电脑与计算机相比，内部范围敏感程度差一些；智能手机受访者对四个顺序估值问题中的第一个 *WTP* 显著高，而平板电脑没有任何差异。[5]

3. 统计分布假设

WTP 估值对统计分布假设敏感是普遍认可的，*WTP* 估值的统计分

---

[1] Ian J. Bateman, et al., *Visible Choice Sets and Scope Sensitivity: An Experimental and Field Test of Study Design Effects upon Nested Contingent Values*, UK: The Centre for Social and Economic Research on the Global Environmental (CSERGE), University of East Anglia, Working Paper EDM, NO. 01-01, 2001, pp. 4-7; Ian J. Bateman, et al., "On Visible Choice Sets and Scope Sensitivity", *Journal of Environmental Economics and Management*, Vol. 47, No. 1, January 2004.

[2] Mohammed Hussen Alemu, et al., "Attending to the Reasons for Attribute Non-attendance in Choice Experiments", *Environmental and Resource Economics*, Vol. 54, No. 3, March 2013.

[3] Christopher Giguere, et al., "Valuing Hemlock Woolly Adelgid Control in Public Forests: Scope Effects with Attribute Nonattendance", *Land Economics*, Vol. 96, No. 1, February 2020.

[4] Magnus Aa. Skeie, et al., "Smartphone and Tablet Effects in Contingent Valuation Web Surveys – No Reason to Worry?", *Ecological Economics*, Vol. 165, November 2019.

[5] Magnus Aa. Skeie, et al., "Smartphone and Tablet Effects in Contingent Valuation Web Surveys – No Reason to Worry?", *Ecological Economics*, Vol. 165, November 2019.

布假设对范围敏感性影响很大。① 对于小样本量的 CVM 研究，非参数分析、Spike 模型或开放式格式（Open – ended Format），比经典参数二元选择分析更适合揭示范围效应；Borzykowski 等建议，系统应用几个 WTP 统计分布假设，检验范围效应和估值结果的合理性。②

六　范围反应充分性/合理性问题争论：结构效度检验面临的挑战

（一）NOAA 专家小组及其部分成员的观点

NOAA 专家小组要求，WTP 估值对范围作出充分反应（Adequate Responsive）。③ 最初 6 名 NOAA 专家小组中的 4 名专家提交了后续评论，澄清"充分反应"的含义；他们给出了充分的（Adequate）和合理的（Plausible）的解释：同义词（Synonyms）充分的（Adequate）包含充足的（Sufficient），而同义词合理的（Plausible）包含可信的（Believable）。④ Arrow 等注意到，统计显著差异与"合理反应"（Plausible Responsive）有明显差异，这不仅仅是简单孤立的统计上显著差异，也要求差异与经济直觉（Economic Intuition）一致。他们明确指出：统计显著反应不是我们导则中的充分反应检验，如果产生了对范围难以置信的反应迟钝（Implausibly Unresponsive），CVM 调查研究被判断为不可靠。⑤

（二）范围检验面临的挑战

范围检验面临的主要问题是事先确定何种程度的敏感性是适当的。⑥

---

① Nicolas Borzykowski, et al., "Scope Effects in Contingent Valuation: Does the Assumed Statistical Distribution of WTP Matter?", *Ecological Economics*, Vol. 144, February 2018.

② Nicolas Borzykowski, et al., "Scope Effects in Contingent Valuation: Does the Assumed Statistical Distribution of WTP Matter?", *Ecological Economics*, Vol. 144, February 2018.

③ Kenneth Arrow, et al., "Report of the NOAA Panel on Contingent Valuation", *Federal Register*, Vol. 58, No. 10, January 1993.

④ Kenneth Arrow, et al., *Comments on Proposed NOAA Scope Test. Appendix D of Comments on Proposed NOAA/DOI Regulations on Natural Resource Damage Assessment*, U.S.: Environmental Protection Agency, 1994, pp. D1 – D2.

⑤ Kenneth Arrow, et al., *Comments on Proposed NOAA Scope Test. Appendix D of Comments on Proposed NOAA/DOI Regulations on Natural Resource Damage Assessment*, U.S.: Environmental Protection Agency, 1994, pp. D1 – D2.

⑥ Ian J. Bateman and Roy Brouwer, "Consistency and Construction in Stated WTP for Health Risk Reductions: A Novel Scope – sensitivity Test", *Resource and Energy Economics*, Vol. 28, No. 3, August 2006.

因为我们不清楚什么应该是正确回答的先验预期——所有的结果都非常可行。[1] 尽管 CVM 的大多数支持者和批评者赞同范围敏感性作为接受 WTP 评估有效性的一个基本条件，但是，范围敏感性标准仍然存在争议。[2] 在边际 WTP 显著递减的情况下，WTP 变化与待估公共物品范围变化可能不是简单的线性关系[3]；所以，相关问题不是 CVM 估值结果是否通过了范围检验，而是证明 CVM 估值结果对范围充分反应[4]或经济学意义上显著。[5] 考虑范围充分性（Adequacy）或合理性（Plausibility）类似于，在经济学所有领域中，考虑统计显著性（Statistical Significance）外还应考虑经济显著性（Economic Significance）。[6] 对范围充分反应是一个经济显著性问题，范围反应不充分代表结果不可靠。[7] NOAA 专家小组担心对范围反应不充分的可能性，标准的范围检验没有解决这一问题，因为它检验的是显著性大小而不是充分性大小。[8] 反对简

---

[1] Ian J. Bateman, *Valid Value Estimates and Value Estimate Validation*: *Better Methods and Better Testing for Stated Preference Research*, Cheltenham UK: Edward Elgar Publishing, 2011, pp. 322 - 352.

[2] Mushtaq Ahmed Memon and Shunji Matsuoka, "Validity of Contingent Valuation Estimates from Developing Countries: Scope Sensitivity Analysis", *Environmental Economics and Policy Studies*, Vol. 5, No. 1, September 2002.

[3] Ian J. Bateman, et al., "Economic Valuation of Policies for Managing Acidity in Remote Mountain Lakes: Examining Validity through Scope Sensitivity Testing", *Aquatic Sciences*, Vol. 67, No. 3, September 2005.

[4] William Desvousges, et al., "Adequate Responsiveness to Scope in Contingent Valuation", *Ecological Economics*, Vol. 84, December 2012.

[5] Edoh Y. Amiran and Daniel A. Hagen, "The Scope Trials: Variation in Sensitivity to Scope and WTP with Directionally Bounded Utility Tunctions", *Journal of Environmental Economics and Management*, Vol. 59, No. 3, May 2010.

[6] John C. Whitehead, "Plausible Responsiveness to Scope in Contingent Valuation", *Ecological Economics*, Vol. 128, August 2016.

[7] Edoh Y. Amiran and Daniel A. Hagen, "The Scope Trials: Variation in Sensitivity to Scope and WTP with Directionally Bounded Utility Tunctions", *Journal of Environmental Economics and Management*, Vol. 59, No. 3, May 2010.

[8] William Desvousges, et al., "Adequate Responsiveness to Scope in Contingent Valuation", *Ecological Economics*, Vol. 84, December 2012; William Desvousges, et al., "From Curious to Pragmatically Curious: Comment on 'from Hopeless to Curious? Thoughts on Hausman's "Dubious to Hopeless" Critique of Contingent Valuation'", *Applied Economic Perspectives and Policy*, Vol. 38, No. 1, March 2016.

单的解释和过度依赖范围检验作为 CVM 研究有效性的唯一判断①,通过范围检验并不意味着反应是充分的,仅仅是指它不是零;而且,由于对范围反应很小是有合理理由的(如边际效应递减和替代效应),范围检验失败并不表示估计的反应不充足。② Amiran 和 Hagen 运用方向有界的(Directionally Bounded)新古典效应函数,评估传统的范围检验得出:不满足范围检验不应该作为拒绝 CVM 研究的依据,范围检验的结果应该更仔细地考虑,范围敏感度非常低可能是合理的。③

(三)加总检验面临的挑战

Desvousges 等考虑加总检验是一个充分性检验(Adequacy Test),它提供了关于范围反应充分性的信息。④ 为了解决 NOAA 专家组对范围变化充分反应的关切,在未来研究中,Desvousges 等推荐 Diamond 等的加总检验。⑤ 但是,加总检验很难通过,无论是对于公共物品还是私人物品。⑥ 已有研究得出,增量部分 WTP 估值之和远大于整体 WTP 估值,

---

① V. Kerry Smith and Laura L. Osborne, "Do Contingent Valuation Estimates Pass a 'Scope' Test? A Meta – analysis", *Journal of Environmental Economics and Management*, Vol. 31, No. 3, November 1996; Thomas A. Heberlein, et al., "Rethinking the Scope Test as a Criterion for Validity in Contingent Valuation", *Journal of Environmental Economics and Management*, Vol. 50, No. 1, July 2005.

② William Desvousges, et al., "Adequate Responsiveness to Scope in Contingent Valuation", *Ecological Economics*, Vol. 84, December 2012; William Desvousges, et al., "An Adding – up Test on Contingent Valuations of River and Lake Quality", *Land Economics*, Vol. 91, No. 3, August 2015.

③ Edoh Y. Amiran and Daniel A. Hagen, "The Scope Trials: Variation in Sensitivity to Scope and WTP with Directionally Bounded Utility Functions", *Journal of Environmental Economics and Management*, Vol. 59, No. 3, May 2010.

④ William Desvousges, et al., "Adequate Responsiveness to Scope in Contingent Valuation", *Ecological Economics*, Vol. 84, December 2012.

⑤ William Desvousges, et al., "An Adding – up Test on Contingent Valuations of River and Lake Quality", *Land Economics*, Vol. 91, No. 3, August 2015; William Desvousges, et al., "From Curious to Pragmatically Curious: Comment on 'from Hopeless to Curious? Thoughts on Hausman's "Dubious to Hopeless" Critique of Contingent Valuation'", *Applied Economic Perspectives and Policy*, Vol. 38, No. 1, March 2016.

⑥ Peter A. Diamond and Jerry A. Hausman, *On Contingent Valuation Measurement of Nonuse Values. In Hausman J. A. (Ed.) Contingent Valuation: A Critical Assessment*, UK: Bingley: Emerald Group Publishing Limited, 1993, pp. 3 – 38; Ian J. Bateman, et al., "Does Part – whole Bias Exist? An Experimental Investigation", *The Economic Journal*, Vol. 107, March 1997; William Desvousges, et al., "An Adding – up Test on Contingent Valuations of River and Lake Quality", *Land Economics*, Vol. 91, No. 3, August 2015.

甚至大3倍。① Whitehead 提出，对范围合理性反应是一个经济显著性问题，对合理性反应的检验是对经济显著性的检验，应该评估 WTP 变化的大小相对于范围变量变化的大小；这一思想与比例标准/理论相同。强比例标准（Strong Proportionality Criterion）和弱比例标准（Weak Proportionality Criterion）的争论，始于著名的埃克森—瓦尔迪兹漏油事件对自然资产损害评估。一些支持对范围反应强比例标准的专家认为，WTP 变化的大小应该高于范围变化的大小，或 WTP 的增长应该与范围的增长同比例；② 而支持对范围反应弱比例标准的专家则认为，WTP 应该随着范围的增长而增长，但不必同比例。③ 弱比例标准基于边际收益递减理论④，NOAA 专家小组支持弱比例标准⑤。Whitehead 认为加总检验对确定是否范围效应是合理的很少有用，他提出将范围弹性（Scope Elasticity）作为直接衡量经济显著性的方法，替代加总检验。⑥

七 再论范围反应充分性/合理性问题：未来研究的核心方向

（一）近期争论

近期，Bishop 等在世界顶尖期刊 Science 上，发表了英国石油公司泄漏事件（The BP Oil Spill）对自然资产损害评估的研究成果；他们通

---

① Jerry Hausman, "Contingent Valuation: From Dubious to Hopeless", *The Journal of Economic Perspective*, Vol. 26, No. 4, Fall 2012; William Desvousges, et al., "An Adding-up Test on Contingent Valuations of River and Lake Quality", *Land Economics*, Vol. 91, No. 3, August 2015.

② Peter A. Diamond, "Testing the Internal Consistency of Contingent Valuation Surveys", *Journal of Environmental Economics and Management*, Vol. 30, No. 3, May 1996; James K. Hammitt, "Evaluating Contingent Valuation of Environmental Health Risks: The Proportionality Test", *Association of Environmental and Resource Economists Newsletter*, Vol. 20, No. 1, January 2000.

③ V. Kerry Smith and Laura L. Osborne, "Do Contingent Valuation Estimates Pass a 'Scope' Test? A Meta-analysis", *Journal of Environmental Economics and Management*, Vol. 31, No. 3, November 1996; Mushtaq Ahmed Memon and Shunji Matsuoka, "Validity of Contingent Valuation Estimates from Developing Countries: Scope Sensitivity Analysis", *Environmental Economics and Policy Studies*, Vol. 5, No. 1, September 2002.

④ Mushtaq Ahmed Memon and Shunji Matsuoka, "Validity of Contingent Valuation Estimates from Developing Countries: Scope Sensitivity Analysis", *Environmental Economics and Policy Studies*, Vol. 5, No. 1, September 2002.

⑤ Kenneth Arrow, et al., "Report of the NOAA Panel on Contingent Valuation", *Federal Register*, Vol. 58, No. 10, January 1993.

⑥ John C. Whitehead, "Plausible Responsiveness to Scope in Contingent Valuation", *Ecological Economics*, Vol. 128, August 2016.

过设置避免更小的损害集合（The Smaller Set of Injuries）（第一个损害集合）和避免更大的损害集合（The Larger Set of Injuries）（包含第一个损害集合和第二个损害集合）两个范围，发现了为避免深水地平线石油泄漏（Deepwater Horizon Oil Spill）的 WTP 对范围充分敏感的证据。①Baron 在 Science 上发文，对 Bishop 等宣称的证明 WTP 对范围充分敏感（Adequate Sensitivity to Scope）的观点，提出质疑：为什么第二个损害集合不单独估值？他指出，已有研究发现：一个部分独立估值的 WTP 或两个部分作为一个整体估值的 WTP，远小于两个部分分别独立估值的 WTP 之和；运用 Bishop 等的方法，第二个损害集合的 WTP 低到了令人难以置信（Implausible）的 17 美元（第一个损害集合的 WTP 为 136 美元，第一个损害集合+第二个损害集合的 WTP 为 153 美元）。Baron 认为，Bishop 等关于 2010 年墨西哥湾石油泄漏研究，只考虑了范围检验而没有考虑加总检验的情况，进而对他们的研究方法和结论提出质疑。② Bishop 等在 Science 上发文回应，认为他们运用的方法是 NOAA 蓝带专家小组（The Blue Ribbon Panel）推荐的方法，能够判断受访者是否注意正在估值（变化）的细节；而 Baron 推荐的加总检验不在蓝带专家小组确定的一系列检验中；Bishop 等认为，Baron 讨论这一检验的逻辑实际上与经济理论不相符，他关于研究调查如何修改的建议似乎既不现实可行，也不具有科学价值。③

（二）争论背后的实质性问题

Bishop 等与 Baron 之间的争论，事实上反映了范围检验和加总检验两种方法，用于判断 WTP 估值变化对范围变化反应的充分性或合理性方面存在缺陷。避免更大的损害集合范围与避免更小的损害集合范围相差很大（Bishop 等文章中有详细描述），边际 WTP 增加值仅为 17 美元；WTP 估值变化相对于损害集合范围变化非常小，这就引起了 Baron 对

---

① Richard C. Bishop, et al., "Putting a Value on Injuries to Natural Assets: The BP Oil Spill", *Science*, Vol. 356, No. 6335, April 2017.

② Jonathan Baron, et al., "Contingent Valuation: Flawed Logic?", *Science*, Vol. 357, No. 6349, July 2017.

③ Richard C. Bishop, et al., "Contingent Valuation: Flawed Logic? —Response", *Science*, Vol. 357, No. 6349, July 2017.

Bishop 等基于范围检验方法的对范围充分敏感结论的质疑。Baron 建议 Bishop 等研究中补充的加总检验，因没有考虑物品间的互补效应、预算限制等因素①，同样面临无法用于判断 WTP 估值变化对范围变化反应的充分性或合理性问题。这场争论引出了目前嵌入效应问题研究的核心：随着待估公共物品范围的变化，WTP 应该变化多大？② 范围反应充分性或合理性持续存在争论③，学者尚未对"充分的"或"合理的"范围反应问题达成共识。④

（三）未来研究的方向

1. 应用领域差异

嵌入效应问题非常复杂，真实交易市场的私人商品、CVM 背景之外的决策研究（属性拆分效应、事件拆分效应），均发现了嵌入效应问题存在的案例，但目前研究主要集中在 CVM 领域。⑤ CVM 在许多领域被广泛应用，不同领域之间存在较大差异，如安全风险健康领域（公共或个人安全、交通事故、健康疾病等）与资源生态环境领域（自然资源、环境资源、生态资源、生物多样性等）；所以，很难能研究提出一个适合各领域的统一标准，用于判断 CVM 范围反应充分性或合理性问题。研究应考虑不同领域之间存在的差异性，分别研究提出相应的判断标准。

2. 经济范围扩展

CVM 是由两位诺贝尔经济学奖获得者阿罗（Arrow）和索洛（Solow）领衔的 NOAA 蓝带专家小组推荐的方法，他们提出了执行可靠的

---

① Richard C. Bishop, et al., "Contingent Valuation: Flawed Logic? —Response", *Science*, Vol. 357, No. 6349, July 2017.

② Richard C. Bishop, et al., "Putting a Value on Injuries to Natural Assets: The BP Oil Spill", *Science*, Vol. 356, No. 6335, April 2017.

③ David J. Chapman, et al., "On the Adequacy of Scope Test Results: Comments on Desvousges, Mathews, and Train", *Ecological Economics*, Vol. 130, October 2016; William Desvousges, et al., "Reply to on the Adequacy of Scope Test Results: Comments on Desvousges, Mathews, and Train", *Ecological Economics*, Vol. 130, October 2016.

④ Nicolas Borzykowski, et al., "Scope Effects in Contingent Valuation: Does the Assumed Statistical Distribution of WTP Matter?", *Ecological Economics*, Vol. 144, February 2018.

⑤ Maria L. Loureiro, et al., "Do Experimental Auction Estimates Pass the Scope Test?", *Journal of Economic Psychology*, Vol. 37, No. 4, August 2013.

CVM 研究的准则。NOAA 专家小组提出应论证 CVM 研究对范围反应的充分性，并提出对范围充分反应是 CVM 研究可靠性的一个重要标准；但是，NOAA 专家小组推荐的范围检验及其他学者推荐的加总检验等方法，在判断范围反应充分性或合理性方面，均存在争论与不足。同时，负范围、零范围[①]和微小范围反应[②]存在仍可能与现实相符；所以，范围检验等传统只考虑经济范围的方法，很难解释和解决这些现实中存在的嵌入效应问题。应研究扩展传统的经济范围，研究如何使新的范围涵盖经济范围、社会心理学各因素（情感、态度、认知或行为）范围及如何综合考虑其他心理学因素，建立判断范围反应充分性或合理性的新标准。

3. 调查设计与执行方案

具有嵌入关系（或嵌套关系）的公共物品在现实中非常普遍。公共物品的整体或部分均不是孤立存在的，它的整体与部分之间或整体与周围物品、环境之间经常存在一种嵌入关系。嵌入公共物品调查设计与执行方案对其估值非常关键，但目前只有少量研究专门涉及嵌入公共物品的调查设计与执行。研究应重点关注：范围嵌入方式、各部分属性信息描述策略、嵌入问卷投标值选取和间距、嵌入问卷调查方式、嵌入多估值问题（替代品、互补品、预算限制等）相关信息供给等。

4. CVM 与 CE 优势互补

更好地提供待估公共物品的属性信息，将更有利于受访者感知待估公共物品范围的变化。近几年，选择实验（Choice Experiment，CE）比 CVM 呈现出更受欢迎的趋势[③]，CE 比 CVM 具有的优势是能够提供更多的关于待估公共物品的属性信息。待估公共物品的属性信息是其重要的

---

① Vito Frontuto, et al., "Earmarking Conservation: Further Inquiry on Scope Effects in Stated Preference Methods Applied to Nature – based Tourism", *Tourism Management*, Vol. 60, June 2017.

② Edoh Y. Amiran and Daniel A. Hagen, "The Scope Trials: Variation in Sensitivity to Scope and WTP with Directionally Bounded Utility Functions", *Journal of Environmental Economics and Management*, Vol. 59, No. 3, May 2010.

③ Pierre – Alexandre Mahieu, et al., "Stated Preferences: A Unique Database Composed of 1657 Recent Published Articles in Journals Related to Agriculture, Environment, or Health", *Review of Agricultural, Food and Environmental Studies*, Vol. 98, No. 3, November 2017.

核心参数，属性缺席会引起嵌入效应问题。① 具有嵌入关系的待估公共物品较为复杂，不易准确描述各部分的属性信息。研究应思考如何将CVM与CE两种陈述性偏好方法的优势互补，探索建立准确描述嵌入公共物品属性信息的新方法，为更好地研究嵌入效应问题提供新思路。

5. 国内研究

国内运用CVM文献已达到1073篇（含硕博论文），但国内关于CVM主要是案例应用研究，而对CVM有效性和可靠性研究较为欠缺（见表1.5）；如NOAA建议CVM研究应进行范围检验，验证其结果与新古典经济理论预期的一致性，但国内研究基本没有进行这项工作；其他涉及CVM有效性和可靠性的核心问题，国内研究基本也没有涉及（见表1.5）。国内学者应加强CVM有效性和可靠性方面的研究，探索判断范围反应充分性或合理性的新方法。目前，更为重要的是在公共物品估值中，要充分考虑公共物品内部之间及公共物品与周围物品、环境之间的（数量或分类或地理）范围嵌入关系，详细研究制定待估公共物品估值的调查设计与执行方案。不能只是对存在的待估公共物品范围嵌入关系进行简单处理，将待估公共物品部分估值作为其整体估值，或将待估公共物品整体估值拆分成部分估值。

---

① Christopher Giguere, et al., "Valuing Hemlock Woolly Adelgid Control in Public Forests: Scope Effects with Attribute Nonattendance", *Land Economics*, Vol. 96, No. 1, February 2020.

第三章

数据来源

第一节 群岛案例地

一 案例地位置

在实地调研和前期研究的基础上,从研究目的、案例地地理区位、案例地旅游业发展水平、问卷调查可行性和调研经费等方面综合考虑,最终选择了黄渤海区—山东庙岛群岛、东海区—浙江舟山群岛和南海区—海南三亚及其附近岛屿(蜈支洲岛和西岛)三个典型的群岛海洋旅游目的地作为研究案例地。

二 庙岛群岛

庙岛群岛,又称长岛,县级海岛,地处山东省,位于黄渤海区。有大小岛屿151个,有居民海岛10个,总人口4.25万人;土地面积57平方公里,海域面积3541平方公里,海岸线长度188公里。2017年,庙岛群岛实现地区生产总值71.37亿元,旅游总收入44亿元,旅游接待人数385万人次。旅游业是庙岛群岛的核心支柱产业,2017年其旅游总收入与地区生产总值的比值达到了60.95%(地区生产总值是增加值,旅游总收入不是增加值;所以,旅游总收入与地区生产总值的比值,并不是占GDP的比例,但可以反映旅游业对当地经济发展的重要性。舟山群岛和三亚及其附近岛屿两个案例地的这一比值类似这种情况)。庙岛群岛待估海洋旅游资源包括海滩和海洋地质遗迹旅游资源(见表3.1)。

表 3.1　　　　　　　　庙岛群岛待估海洋旅游资源

旅游型海岛	资源类型	待估旅游资源
南长山岛	海滩	明珠广场海滩（长1000米）
	海洋地质遗迹	望夫礁景区、黄渤海分界线景区
北长山岛	海滩	月牙湾海滩（长约2000米）
	海洋地质遗迹	九丈崖景区、月牙湾景区
大黑山岛	海洋地质遗迹	龙爪山景区

三　舟山群岛

舟山群岛，又称舟山群岛新区，地市级海岛，地处浙江省，位于东海区。有大小岛屿1390个，户籍人口在50人以上的岛屿68个，常住人口116万人；土地面积1440.12平方公里，海域面积2.08万平方公里，海岸线长度2444公里。2017年，舟山群岛实现地区生产总值1219亿元，旅游总收入807亿元，旅游接待人数5507万人次。旅游业是舟山群岛三大核心产业之一，2017年其旅游总收入与地区生产总值的比值达到了66.18%。舟山群岛待估海洋旅游资源包括海滩和海洋文化旅游资源（见表3.2）。

表 3.2　　　　　　　　舟山群岛待估海洋旅游资源

旅游型海岛	资源类型	待估旅游资源
普陀山岛	海滩	百步沙海滩（长约660米）和千步沙海滩（长约1300米）
	海洋宗教文化	三大寺院（普济寺占地37000多平方米，建筑面积11400平方米；法雨寺占地33000多平方米，建筑面积9300平方米；慧济寺占地面积13000多平方米，建筑面积5500平方米）
朱家尖岛	海滩	南沙海滩（长约1000米）
	海洋沙雕艺术文化	沙雕艺术主题公园（长200米、宽50米，已连续举办十八届"中国舟山国际沙雕节"）
桃花岛	海滩	塔湾金沙海滩（长约1370米）
	海洋影视文化	射雕英雄传影视城（占地约200000平方米，主要建筑物包括黄药师庄、牛家村、归云庄、临安街、京城广场、南帝寺和东邪船埠）

续表

旅游型海岛	资源类型	待估旅游资源
岱山岛	海滩	鹿栏晴沙海滩（长约3600米）
泗礁山岛	海滩	南长涂海滩（长约2000米）和基湖海滩（长约2200米）

四 三亚及其附近岛屿

海南三亚，又称鹿城，地级市，地处海南省，位于南海区。全市土地面积1921.46平方公里，海域面积3500平方公里，海岸线长度263.29公里；有大小港湾19个，主要岛屿68个；常住人口76.42万人。2017年，三亚实现地区生产总值529.25亿元，旅游总收入406.17亿元，接待过夜游客1830.97万人次。旅游业是三亚的核心支柱产业，2017年其旅游总收入与地区生产总值的比值达到了76.74%。三亚及其附近岛屿待估海洋旅游资源包括海滩和珊瑚礁旅游资源（见表3.3）。

表3.3　　　　　三亚及其附近岛屿待估海洋旅游资源

旅游型海岛	资源类型	待估旅游资源
西岛	海滩	西岛海滩（长约500米）
西岛	珊瑚礁	西岛附近海域珊瑚礁的活珊瑚覆盖率约为36%，死珊瑚覆盖率约为7%
蜈支洲岛	海滩	蜈支洲岛海滩（长约1000米）
蜈支洲岛	珊瑚礁	蜈支洲岛附近海域珊瑚礁的活珊瑚覆盖率约为54%，死珊瑚覆盖率约为6%
亚龙湾	海滩	亚龙湾海滩（长约7000米）
亚龙湾	珊瑚礁	亚龙湾附近海域珊瑚礁的活珊瑚覆盖率约为35%，死珊瑚覆盖率约为39%
大东海	海滩	大东海海滩（长约1000米）
大东海	珊瑚礁	大东海附近海域珊瑚礁的活珊瑚覆盖率约为30%，死珊瑚覆盖率约为10%

第二节 调查问卷设计

调查问卷设计参照 NOAA 提出的非使用价值评估 15 条指导方针[1],并结合海洋旅游资源特征进行。

一 非使用价值引出方式

非使用价值引出方式主要有两种:一种是在询问受访者对保护公共物品使用价值和非使用价值总支付意愿的基础上,根据各项使用价值和非使用价值支付动机,拆分总支付意愿最终得出非使用价值[2];其缺陷在于,要求受访者能将总支付意愿分配到不同支付动机[3],但实际上受访者总支付意愿可能是由许多重叠或不同交互支付动机驱动,致使根据支付动机分割总支付意愿存在较大困难。[4] 另一种是直接评估受访者对保护公共物品非使用价值的支付意愿,该方法通过定义非使用价值,直接询问受访者对保护公共物品非使用价值的支付意愿,可有效避免因支付动机处理不当引发的研究偏差。[5] 本书研究采用后一种方法,直接调查受访者对保护海滩、海洋地质遗迹、海洋文化或珊瑚礁维持现有状态不下降,以使其可持续存在、子孙后代使用或自己未来使用的支

---

[1] Kenneth Arrow, et al., "Report of the NOAA Panel on Contingent Valuation", *Federal Register*, Vol. 58, No. 10, January 1993.

[2] Anatoli Togridou, et al., "Determinants of Visitors' Willingness to Pay for the National Marine Park of Zakynthos, Greece", *Ecological Economics*, Vol. 60, No. 1, November 2006; Adriana Ressurreição, et al., "Different Cultures, Different Values: The Role of Cultural Variation in Public's WTP for Marine Species Conservation", *Biological Conservation*, Vol. 145, No. 1, January 2012; Rodelio F. Subade and Herminia A. Francisco, "Do Non-users Value Coral Reefs? Economic Valuation of Conserving Tubbataha Reefs, Philippines", *Ecological Economics*, Vol. 102, June 2014.

[3] Tanya O'Garra, "Bequest Values for Marine Resources: How Important for Indigenous Communities in Less-developed Economies?", *Environmental and Resource Economics*, Vol. 44, No. 2, October 2009.

[4] Richard T. Carson, et al., *A Contingent Valuation Study of Lost Passive Use Values Resulting from the Exxon Valdez Oil Spill*, Germany: University Library of Munich, 1992, pp. 80-125; Ronald G. Cummings and Glenn W. Harrison, "The Measurement and Decomposition of Nonuse Values: A Critical Review", *Environmental and Resource Economics*, Vol. 5, No. 3, April 1995.

[5] Richard T. Carson, et al., *A Contingent Valuation Study of Lost Passive Use Values Resulting from the Exxon Valdez Oil Spill*, Germany: University Library of Munich, 1992, pp. 80-125.

付意愿。① 目前，在海洋旅游资源非市场经济价值评估领域，维持资源现有状态不下降是一种经常被选择的资源保护程度假想情景，如保护珊瑚礁当前状态②、保护当前数量海洋生物③、维持海滩现状④等。

二 偏差控制

（一）假想偏差

CVM 调查的一个重要问题就是假想偏差，在非使用价值评估中，通常不能避免假想估值问题的使用。⑤ 目前，控制假想偏差的方法主要有"廉价谈话"（Cheap Talk）⑥、确定性量表⑦和明确提醒受

---

① Mahfuzuddin Ahmed, et al., "Valuing Recreational and Conservation Benefits of Coral Reefs: The Case of Bolinao, Philippines" *Ocean & Coastal Management*, Vol. 50, No. 1 – 2, January 2007; A. Kontogianni, et al., "Service Providing Units, Existence Values and the Valuation of Endangered Species: A Methodological Test", *Ecological Economics*, Vol. 79, July 2012; Ivana Logar and Jeroen C. J. M. van den Bergh, "Respondent Uncertainty in Contingent Valuation of Preventing Beach Erosion: An Analysis with a Polychotomous Choice Question", *Journal of Environmental Management*, Vol. 113, December 2012; Murugadas Ramdas and Badaruddin Mohamed, "Impacts of Tourism on Environmental Attributes, Environmental Literacy and Willingness to Pay: A Conceptual and Theoretical Review", *Procedia – Social and Behavioral Sciences*, Vol. 144, August 2014.

② Mahfuzuddin Ahmed, et al., "Valuing Recreational and Conservation Benefits of Coral Reefs: The Case of Bolinao, Philippines" *Ocean & Coastal Management*, Vol. 50, No. 1 – 2, January 2007.

③ A. Kontogianni, et al., "Service Providing Units, Existence Values and the Valuation of Endangered Species: A Methodological Test", *Ecological Economics*, Vol. 79, July 2012.

④ Ivana Logar and Jeroen C. J. M. van den Bergh, "Respondent Uncertainty in Contingent Valuation of Preventing Beach Erosion: An Analysis with a Polychotomous Choice Question", *Journal of Environmental Management*, Vol. 113, December 2012.

⑤ P. C. Boxall, et al., "Analysis of the Economic Benefits Associated with the Recovery of Threatened Marine Mammal Species in the Canadian St. Lawrence Estuary", *Marine Policy*, Vol. 36, No. 1, January 2012; Ju – Yeon Kim, et al., "Comparing Willingness – to – pay between Residents and Non – residents when Correcting Hypothetical Bias: Case of Endangered Spotted Seal in South Korea", *Ecological Economics*, Vol. 78, June 2012.

⑥ John A. List, "Do Explicit Warnings Eliminate the Hypothetical Bias in Elicitation Procedures? Evidence from Field Auctions for Sportscards", *The American Economics Review*, Vol. 91, No. 5, December 2001; James J. Murphy, et al., "A Meta – analysis of Hypothetical Bias in Stated Preference Valuation", *Environmental and Resource Economics*, Vol. 30, No. 3, March 2005.

⑦ Rodelio F. Subade and Herminia A. Francisco, "Do Non – users Value Coral Reefs? Economic Valuation of Conserving Tubbataha Reefs, Philippines", *Ecological Economics*, Vol. 102, June 2014; Ivana Logar and Jeroen C. J. M. van den Bergh, "Respondent Uncertainty in Contingent Valuation of Preventing Beach Erosion: An Analysis with a Polychotomous Choice Question", *Journal of Environmental Management*, Vol. 113, December 2012.

访者①三种方法。本书研究选择了较简洁且可明确提醒受访者的方法控制假想偏差，具体为：在进行匿名调查时，调查人员在面对面调查时明确提醒受访者，想象假想表决为真实表决②、充分考虑家庭预算约束及因这项计划而额外新增的成本③和海滩、海洋地质遗迹、海洋文化或珊瑚礁其他替代品的存在④等。

（二）信息偏差

本书研究通过对调查人员进行严格培训，使调查人员掌握详细调研信息，再通过调查人员面对面向受访者讲解相关信息来控制信息偏差。在调查准备阶段，调查领队（教授）对7名调查人员（研究生）进行多次室内集中培训，详细讲解调查问卷涉及的各类信息；同时，在每一个案例地调查前，领队带领7名调查人员对案例地进行实地现场培训和资源考察，7名调查人员实地考察了正式调查拟选择的所有景区（游客）调查点和核心街区（居民）调查点。调查领队在各景区的实地现场，结合提前绘制的6幅海洋旅游资源简图（庙岛群岛、舟山群岛、三亚及其附近岛屿的海滩各1幅，庙岛群岛海洋地质遗迹、舟山群岛海洋文化和三亚及其附近岛屿珊瑚礁各1幅），向7名调查人员详细讲解研究选择的四类海洋旅游资源的范围和核心特征；同时，为了让调查人员更好地了解珊瑚礁旅游资源（在水下，地面看不见），在正式调查

---

① P. C. Boxall, et al., "Analysis of the Economic Benefits Associated with the Recovery of Threatened Marine Mammal Species in the Canadian St. Lawrence Estuary", *Marine Policy*, Vol. 36, No. 1, January 2012; Michelle Cazabon‐Mannette, et al., "Estimates of the Non‐market Value of Sea Turtles in Tobago Using Stated Preference Techniques", *Journal of Environmental Management*, Vol. 192, May 2017.

② James J. Murphy, et al., "A Meta‐analysis of Hypothetical Bias in Stated Preference Valuation", *Environmental and Resource Economics*, Vol. 30, No. 3, March 2005.

③ P. C. Boxall, et al., "Analysis of the Economic Benefits Associated with the Recovery of Threatened Marine Mammal Species in the Canadian St. Lawrence Estuary", *Marine Policy*, Vol. 36, No. 1, January 2012; Adriana Ressurreição, et al., "Different Cultures, Different Values: The Role of Cultural Variation in Public's WTP for Marine Species Conservation", *Biological Conservation*, Vol. 145, No. 1, January 2012.

④ Kenneth Arrow, et al., "Report of the NOAA Panel on Contingent Valuation", *Federal Register*, Vol. 58, No. 10, January 1993; Adriana Ressurreição, et al., "Different Cultures, Different Values: The Role of Cultural Variation in Public's WTP for Marine Species Conservation", *Biological Conservation*, Vol. 145, No. 1, January 2012.

前，每位调查人员在三亚西岛潜水基地分别进行了两次潜水，观看和熟悉珊瑚礁旅游资源。7 名调查人员经过前期的室内培训、实地现场培训和海洋旅游资源实地考察及每人 20 份问卷预练习调查，做好了充分的前期准备。正式调查时，调查人员结合简图向受访者详细讲解海洋旅游资源海滩、海洋地质遗迹、海洋文化或珊瑚礁的相关信息，有效地避免了信息偏差。

（三）抗议性反应偏差

本书研究通过设置一系列不愿意支付的原因，识别真零支付和抗议性支付反应[1]；被识别的抗议性支付反应，在进一步分析中被剔除[2]。同时，为避免强制性支付的抗议性和非使用价值连续支付的重复，本书研究选择在海洋旅游资源非市场经济价值评估领域被广泛采用的一次性自愿捐款的支付方式。[3]

（四）引导方式偏差

目前，在海洋旅游资源非市场经济价值评估领域，有关支付卡式、二分式和开放式三种投标值引导方式的研究成果均较多（见表1.3）。比较而言，二分式引导方式是在受访者对研究对象较为熟悉情况下所使用的一种引导方式，而当研究对象属于陌生或复杂待估物品时，二分式引导方式常因存在肯定性回答偏差而影响到研究结果的精确性，不仅如此，该方式往往需要较大样本量来支撑稳健模型的设定，限制性较高；开放式引导方式则是通过直接询问受访者对某物品或服务的最大支付意愿确

---

[1] Robert Cameron Mitchell and Richard T. Carson, *Using Surveys to Value Public Goods: The Contingent Valuation Method*, Washington: Resources for the Future, 1989, pp. 107 – 126; Kenneth Arrow, et al., "Report of the NOAA Panel on Contingent Valuation", *Federal Register*, Vol. 58, No. 10, January 1993.

[2] Robert Cameron Mitchell and Richard T. Carson, *Using Surveys to Value Public Goods: The Contingent Valuation Method*, Washington: Resources for the Future, 1989, pp. 107 – 126; Adriana Ressurreição, et al., "Economic Valuation of Species Loss in the Open Sea", *Ecological Economics*, Vol. 70, No. 4, February 2011.

[3] Michelle Cazabon – Mannette, et al., "Estimates of the Non – market Value of Sea Turtles in Tobago Using Stated Preference Techniques", *Journal of Environmental Management*, Vol. 192, May 2017; Niels Jobstvogt, et al., "Looking Below the Surface: The Cultural Ecosystem Service Values of UK Marine Protected Areas (MPAs)", *Ecosystem Services*, Vol. 10, December 2014; Stefania Tonin, "Economic Value of Marine Biodiversity Improvement in Coralligenous Habitats", *Ecological Indicators*, Vol. 85, February 2018.

定 WTP，通常存在受访者不反应或认知负担问题，甚至会出现受访者给出极端回答或夸大 WTP 的现象。与前两种引导方式相比，支付卡式引导方式一方面可通过避免肯定性回答，有效规避二分式引导方式存在的肯定性回答偏差和起点偏差问题，该引导方式在陌生或复杂待估物品 WTP 研究中应用较广[1]；另一方面，支付卡式引导方式可有效缓解受访者认知负担，从而降低不反应率和提高研究的高效性及精准性。[2] 不仅如此，支付卡式引导方式可收集更多 WTP 信息和拥有更低的实施成本[3]，尽管该方式存在锚定偏差和区间范围问题，但可以通过预调查和前期研究积累来弥补这些不足。[4] 综上所述，鉴于海洋旅游资源非使用价值这一研究对象属于复杂待估物品且支付卡式引导方式具有较强适用性和调研精准性这一事实，本书研究采用支付卡式引导方式获取受访者信息。

三 问卷结构、核心估值问题和支付卡式投标值

为便于比较，本书研究的三个案例地、四类资源均采用同样的调查方法和问卷结构[5]；同时为避免长问卷引起受访者应答疲劳和失去兴

---

[1] Adriana Ressurreição, et al., "Different Cultures, Different Values: The Role of Cultural Variation in Public's WTP for Marine Species Conservation", *Biological Conservation*, Vol. 145, No. 1, January 2012; Michelle Cazabon‑Mannette, et al., "Estimates of the Non‑market Value of Sea Turtles in Tobago Using Stated Preference Techniques", *Journal of Environmental Management*, Vol. 192, May 2017.

[2] Adriana Ressurreição, et al., "Different Cultures, Different Values: The Role of Cultural Variation in Public's WTP for Marine Species Conservation", *Biological Conservation*, Vol. 145, No. 1, January 2012; Abderraouf Dribek and Louinord Voltaire, "Contingent Valuation Analysis of Willingness to Pay for Beach Erosion Control through the Stabiplage Technique: A Study in Djerba (Tunisia)", *Marine Policy*, Vol. 86, December 2017; Stefania Tonin, "Citizens' Perspectives on Marine Protected Areas as a Governance Strategy to Effectively Preserve Marine Ecosystem Services and Biodiversity", *Ecosystem Services*, Vol. 34, December 2018.

[3] Emma Risén, et al., "Non‑market Values of Algae Beach‑cast Management‑study Site Trelleborg, Sweden", *Ocean & Coastal Management*, Vol. 140, May 2017.

[4] Adriana Ressurreição, et al., "Economic Valuation of Species Loss in the Open Sea", *Ecological Economics*, Vol. 70, No. 4, February 2011; Adriana Ressurreição, et al., "Different Cultures, Different Values: The Role of Cultural Variation in Public's WTP for Marine Species Conservation", *Biological Conservation*, Vol. 145, No. 1, January 2012.

[5] Adriana Ressurreição, et al., "Different Cultures, Different Values: The Role of Cultural Variation in Public's WTP for Marine Species Conservation", *Biological Conservation*, Vol. 145, No. 1, January 2012.

趣[①]而导致调研偏差，本书研究采用短问卷形式，具体分三部分：第一部分为海滩（海洋地质遗迹、海洋文化或珊瑚礁）旅游资源的研究范围和基本信息。第二部分为核心估值问题：①海滩资源核心估值问题为"台风等极端天气和旅游等人类活动将对（庙岛群岛、舟山群岛或三亚及其附近岛屿）海滩旅游资源造成严重影响，为保护（庙岛群岛、舟山群岛或三亚及其附近岛屿）海滩旅游资源，使其可持续存在、子孙后代使用或自己未来使用，设想成立一个海滩旅游资源保护基金，若该基金正在筹集资金阶段，您是否愿意通过一次性捐款的方式支持这项（庙岛群岛、舟山群岛或三亚及其附近岛屿）海滩旅游资源保护活动"。②海洋地质遗迹、海洋文化或珊瑚礁旅游资源核心估值问题为"（庙岛群岛问卷：旅游开发等人类活动及海水侵蚀、风化作用等自然活动；舟山群岛问卷：台风等极端天气和旅游等人类活动；三亚及其附近岛屿问卷：污水、泥沙、潜水旅游等人类活动）将对（海洋地质遗迹、海洋文化或珊瑚礁）旅游资源造成严重影响，为了保护（海洋地质遗迹、海洋文化或珊瑚礁）旅游资源，使其可持续存在、子孙后代使用或自己未来使用，设想成立一个（海洋地质遗迹、海洋文化或珊瑚礁）旅游资源保护基金，若该基金正在筹集资金阶段，您是否愿意通过一次性捐款的方式支持这项（海洋地质遗迹、海洋文化或珊瑚礁）旅游资源保护活动？"。第三部分为受访者性别、年龄、文化程度、家庭年收入和客源地等人口社会特征及可能存在的不愿意支付原因。

支付卡式投标值：1；2；5；10；20；30；50；60；80；100；120；150；200；300；400；500；600；800；1000；1500；2000。

第三节 调查实施

一 调查对象

CVM 的假想本质会面临定义样本抽样框（Sampling Frame）和目标

[①] Berta Martín-López, et al., "The Non-economic Motives behind the Willingness to Pay for Biodiversity Conservation", *Biological Conservation*, Vol. 139, No. 1-2, September 2007.

人群总体范围（Population Scope）等问题。① 因此，非使用价值评估确定目标人群的总体范围非常重要②，若处理不当，易出现总体选择偏差（Population Choice Bias）。③ 已有研究表明，非使用者往往不考虑收入约束④和易产生嵌入效应问题⑤，受访者对资源的认知水平与 CVM 评估有效性较为相关，一般对资源熟悉的受访者 WTP 更可靠。⑥ 相应地，本书研究将样本抽样目标人群的总体范围界定为庙岛群岛、舟山群岛或三亚及其附近岛屿的 18—65 周岁的当地（核心旅游型海岛和城镇）居民和游客。

二 调查地点和调查实施

首先，在游客调查样本选择中，因庙岛群岛、舟山群岛或三亚及其附近岛屿游客抽样框缺失，调查采取了核心景区随机选择样本的方法。为消除样本偏差，著名景区（如普陀山景区）的抽样频率更高；与此同时，为避免样本抽样偏差问题⑦，调查时间选为 2017 年 7—8 月，这

---

① Richard T. Carson, et al., "Contingent Valuation: Controversies and Evidence", *Environmental and Resource Economics*, Vol. 19, No. 2, June 2001; John Loomis, et al., "Improving Validity Experiments of Contingent Valuation Methods: Results of Efforts to Reduce the Disparity of Hypothetical and Actual Willingness to Pay", *Land Economics*, Vol. 72, No. 4, November 1996; Ju-Yeon Kim, et al., "Comparing Willingness-to-pay between Residents and Non-residents when Correcting Hypothetical Bias: Case of Endangered Spotted Seal in South Korea", *Ecological Economics*, Vol. 78, June 2012.

② V. Kerry Smith, "Nonmarket Valuation of Environmental Resources: An Interpretative Appraisal", *Land Economics*, Vol. 69, No. 1, February 1993; John B. Loomis, "How Large is the Extent of the Market for Public Goods: Evidence from a Nationwide Contingent Valuation Survey", *Applied Economics*, Vol. 28, No. 7, February 1996.

③ Robert Cameron Mitchell and Richard T. Carson, *Using Surveys to Value Public Goods: The Contingent Valuation Method*, Washington: Resources for the Future, 1989, pp. 107 – 126.

④ John C. Whitehead, et al., "Assessing the Validity and Reliability of Contingent Values: A Comparison of On-site Users, Off-site Users, and Non-users", *Journal of Environmental Economics and Management*, Vol. 29, No. 2, September 1995.

⑤ Kevin J. Boyle, et al., "An Investigation of Part-whole Biases in Contingent-Valuation Studies", *Journal of Environmental Economics and Management*, Vol. 27, No. 1, July 1994.

⑥ Massimo Paradiso and Antoenlla Trisorio, "The Effect of Knowledge on the Disparity Between Hypothetical and Real Willingness to Pay", *Applied Economics*, Vol. 33, No. 11, September 2001; John C. Whitehead, "Differentiating Use and Non-use Values with the Properties of the Variation Function", *Applied Economics Letters*, Vol. 2, No. 10, February 1995.

⑦ Juan C. Trujillo, et al., "Coral Reefs Under Threat in a Caribbean Marine Protected Area: Assessing Divers' Willingness to Pay Toward Conservation", *Marine Policy*, Vol. 68, June 2016.

是庙岛群岛、舟山群岛的旅游最旺季和三亚及其附近岛屿的潜水最佳时间。其次，居民调查点选择了三个案例地的核心街区和核心旅游型海岛，使得调查对象主要以核心旅游型海岛居民和城镇居民为主，且调查过程中主要采取在主要街道、商场、居民区等区域拦截调查的方法。①在综合考虑调查点分布、交通便利性、常住居民数量及游客量等基本信息的基础上，将问卷调查有效样本量的目标设定为：庙岛群岛 1400—1700 份，其中居民 400—500 份，游客 1000—1200 份；舟山群岛 2800—3100 份，其中居民 1200—1300 份，游客 1600—1800 份；三亚及其附近岛屿 2600—2900 份，其中居民 800—900 份，游客 1800—2000 份。即三个案例地共 6800—7700 份，其中居民 2400—2700 份，游客 4400—5000 份。

---

① Adriana Ressurreição, et al., "Different Cultures, Different Values: The Role of Cultural Variation in Public's WTP for Marine Species Conservation", *Biological Conservation*, Vol. 145, No. 1, January 2012.

第二篇 群岛旅游资源非使用价值估值比较研究

第四章
群岛旅游资源非使用价值估值比较 I

第一节 估值比较 I 计量经济模型

一 WTP 计算公式

使用支付卡式调查问卷询问受访者对于保护海滩、海洋地质遗迹、海洋文化或珊瑚礁海洋旅游资源非使用价值的支付意愿,受访者在一组有序的投标值中选出其最大支付意愿,则受访者真实支付意愿(WTP_i)位于所选择投标值(t_{li})和下一个较高投标值(t_{hi})之间,即 $t_{li} \leq WTP_i < t_{hi}$。[①] 常用支付卡式支付意愿的测度方法相应包括最小二乘法(Ordinary Least Square, OLS)和区间回归(Interval Regression, IR),前者是选取每个区间的中点值作为受访者真实支付意愿,并将其作为因变量进行最小二乘回归[②],事实上,尽管受访者真实支付意愿位于该区间内但并不一定等于中点值;后者则是以受访者真实支付意愿所在区间作

---

① Trudy Ann Cameron and Daniel D. Huppert, "OLS Versus ML Estimation of Non–market Resource Values with Payment Card Interval Data", *Journal of Environmental Economics and Management*, Vol. 17, No. 3, November 1989.

② Trudy Ann Cameron and Daniel D. Huppert, "OLS Versus ML Estimation of Non–market Resource Values with Payment Card Interval Data", *Journal of Environmental Economics and Management*, Vol. 17, No. 3, November 1989; Abderraouf Dribek and Louinord Voltaire, "Contingent Valuation Analysis of Willingness to Pay for Beach Erosion Control through the Stabiplage Technique: A Study in Djerba (Tunisia)", *Marine Policy*, Vol. 86, December 2017.

为因变量，利用最大似然估计进行参数估计，因此 IR 测度结果较 OLS 更加稳健，更适用于处理使用支付卡式调查问卷得到的数据。[1]

具体地，根据 Cameron 和 Huppert 的研究[2]，假设受访者对于保护某类海洋旅游资源非使用价值的真实支付意愿为 WTP_i，由于受访者支付意愿是非负的，且 CVM 调查得到的支付意愿分布通常是偏斜的，假设支付意愿为对数正态条件分布，则支付意愿函数为：

$$\log WTP_i = x'_i\beta + \varepsilon_i \tag{4-1}$$

式中，WTP_i 为受访者 i 的真实支付意愿；x_i 为自变量向量；β 为自变量回归系数向量；ε_i 为误差项且服从均值为 0、标准差为 σ 的正态分布。则受访者真实支付意愿位于某个特定区间的概率为：

$$\Pr(t_{li} < WTP_i < t_{hi}) = \Pr(\log t_{li} < \log WTP_i < \log t_{hi}) = \Pr[(\log t_{li} - x'_i\beta)/\sigma < z_i < (\log t_{hi} - x'_i\beta)/\sigma] \tag{4-2}$$

式中，t_{li} 和 t_{hi} 分别为区间下限和上限；z_i 为服从标准正态分布的随机变量，且式（4-2）可简写为：

$$\Pr(t_{li} < WTP_i < t_{hi}) = \Phi(z_{hi}) - \Phi(z_{li}) \tag{4-3}$$

式中，$\Phi(\cdot)$ 为标准正态累积分布函数，z_{li} 和 z_{hi} 分别为式（4-2）中的 $(\log t_{li} - x'_i\beta)/\sigma$ 和 $(\log t_{hi} - x'_i\beta)/\sigma$。$n$ 个独立样本的联合概率密度函数为未知参数 β 和 σ 的似然函数，且对数似然函数为：

$$\log L = \sum_{i=1}^{n} \log[\Phi(z_{hi}) - \Phi(z_{li})] \tag{4-4}$$

应用最大似然估计法（Maximum Likelihood Estimation，MLE）估计出 β 和 σ 值，根据给定 x_i，可求得受访者支付意愿的中位数和均值，计算公式为：

---

[1] Trudy Ann Cameron and Daniel D. Huppert, "OLS Versus ML Estimation of Non-market Resource Values with Payment Card Interval Data", *Journal of Environmental Economics and Management*, Vol. 17, No. 3, November 1989; Stefania Tonin, "Citizens' Perspectives on Marine Protected Areas as a Governance Strategy to Effectively Preserve Marine Ecosystem Services and Biodiversity", *Ecosystem Services*, Vol. 34, December 2018; Abderraouf Dribek and Louinord Voltaire, "Contingent Valuation Analysis of Willingness to Pay for Beach Erosion Control through the Stabiplage Technique: A Study in Djerba (Tunisia)", *Marine Policy*, Vol. 86, December 2017.

[2] Trudy Ann Cameron and Daniel D. Huppert, "OLS Versus ML Estimation of Non-market Resource Values with Payment Card Interval Data", *Journal of Environmental Economics and Management*, Vol. 17, No. 3, November 1989.

$$MedianWTP = \exp(x'_i\beta) \tag{4-5}$$

$$MedianWTP = \exp(x'_i\beta + \sigma^2/2) \tag{4-6}$$

依据庙岛群岛、舟山群岛和三亚及其附近岛屿居民和游客对保护海滩、海洋地质遗迹、海洋文化或珊瑚礁海洋旅游资源非使用价值的 WTP 数据，计算 WTP 的公式为：

$$\ln WTP_i = \alpha + \beta_1 Gender_i + \beta_2 Age_i + \beta_3 Ages_i + \beta_4 Education_i + \beta_5 \ln income_i \tag{4-7}$$

式中，α 为常数项；$Gender$ 为受访者的性别（虚拟变量：男 = 1，女 = 0）；Age 为受访者的年龄（2017 减去出生年）；$Ages$ 为受访者年龄的平方项除以 100；$Education$ 为受访者的学历水平（虚拟变量：受过高等教育（大专、本科、研究生）= 1，未受过高等教育（初中及以下、高中、中专、技校）= 0）；$\ln income$ 为受访者家庭年收入的自然对数（收入选取各个收入区间的中点值）。β_j（j = 1，2，3，4，5）为自变量的回归系数。另外，本书研究对于真零支付意愿，令 $t_{li} = 0$，$t_{hi} = bid_{min}$，bid_{min} 为支付卡中最小投标值；对于选择最大投标值 bid_{max} 的支付意愿，令 $t_{li} = bid_{max}$，$t_{hi} bid_{max} + 1$。

二 不同类型资源 WTP 的调整核算方法

$$\Delta\overline{WTP}_{M-N} = \overline{WTP}_M - \overline{WTP}_N = \Delta dr\,\overline{WTP}_{M-N} + \Delta sc\,\overline{WTP}_{M-N} \tag{4-8}$$

$$\Delta dr\,\overline{WTP}_{M-N} = [(\overline{WTP}_M - adj\,\overline{WTP}_{N-at-M}) + (adj\,\overline{WTP}_{M-at-N} - \overline{WTP}_N)]/2 \tag{4-9}$$

$$\Delta sc\,\overline{WTP}_{M-N} = [(adj\,\overline{WTP}_{N-at-M} - \overline{WTP}_N) + (\overline{WTP}_M - adj\,\overline{WTP}_{M-at-N})]/2 \tag{4-10}$$

式中，$\overline{WTP}_M$ 为受访者对 M 类资源的平均 WTP，$\overline{WTP}_N$ 为受访者对 N 类资源的平均 WTP，$\Delta\,\overline{WTP}_{M-N}$ 为 $\overline{WTP}_M$ 与 $\overline{WTP}_N$ 的差值；$adj\,\overline{WTP}_{N-at-M}$（或 $\overline{WTP}_{M-at-N}$）为运用 M（或 N）类资源的受访者人口社会特征调整的 N（或 M）类资源平均 WTP；$\Delta dr\,\overline{WTP}_{M-N}$ 为因资源类型不同（本研究不同案例地海滩之间比较时，考虑的是海滩长度的不同）而引起的平均 WTP 的差值，即资源类型对 WTP 的作用；$\Delta sc\,\overline{WTP}_{M-N}$ 为因样本人口社会特征差异而出现的平均 WTP 差值，即由不同案例地或同一案例地受访者人口社会特征（性别、年龄、学历、收入等）差异引起的 WTP 差值。进一步地，为确认 WTP 差值是由资源类型差异引发，还是由受访者人口社会特征差异导致，本书研究参考 Carson 和 Mitchell 及 Borzykowski 等关于 CVM 研究样本之间人口社会特征差异调整的思想，结合区间回归计量模型来调整 WTP。① 具体地，$adj\overline{WTP}_{N-at-M}$ 或 $adj\overline{WTP}_{M-at-N}$ 计算如下：①对 N（或 M）类海洋旅游资源样本调查数据进行区间回归，得出回归系数向量 β_N（或 β_M），用以表征受访者对 N（或 M）类海洋旅游资源的支付意愿情景；②选取 M（或 N）类海洋旅游资源样本的人口社会特征 x_{Mi}（或 x_{Ni}）作为参照标准；③将人口社会特征参照标准 x_{Mi}（或 x_{Ni}）与支付意愿情景 β_N（或 β_M）代入式（4-6），计算得出 $adj\overline{WTP}_{N-at-M}$（或 $adj\overline{WTP}_{M-at-N}$）。

三　分位数回归模型

分位数回归（Quantile Regression，QR）最早由 Koenker 和 Bassett 提出。② 在绝大多数回归模型都关注被解释变量的条件均值的情况时，分位数回归提供了对解释变量 X 和被解释变量 Y 的分位数之间线性关系的估计方法，与普通均值回归相比，分位数回归使用残差绝对值的加权平均作为最小化的目标函数，能避免受极端值的影响，适合具有异方差的模型，使回归结果更加稳健。分位数回归对被解释变量的条件分布刻画更加细致，能给出被解释变量条件分布的大体特征。每个分位点上的回归都被赋予条件分布上某个特殊点（中央或尾部）的一些特征；把不同的分位点回归集中起来就能提供一个关于被解释变量条件分布的更完整的统计特征描述。分位数回归并不要求很强的分布假设，在扰动项非正态分布的情形下，分位数估计量可能比最小二乘估计量更为有效。本书研究运用分位数回归刻画 WTP 与样本人口社会特征之间更为详细的关系。分位数回归模型：

---

① Trudy Ann Cameron and Daniel D. Huppert, "OLS Versus ML Estimation of Non–market Resource Values with Payment Card Interval Data", *Journal of Environmental Economics and Management*, Vol. 17, No. 3, November 1989; Stefania Tonin, "Citizens' Perspectives on Marine Protected Areas as a Governance Strategy to Effectively Preserve Marine Ecosystem Services and Biodiversity", *Ecosystem Services*, Vol. 34, December 2018.

② Roger Koenker and Gilbert Bassett, "Regression Quantiles", *Econometrica*, Vol. 46, January 1978.

$$WTP_i = X_i\beta_\theta + \mu_{i,\theta} \quad (4-11)$$

$$quant_\theta(WTP_i \mid X_i) = X_i\beta_\theta \quad (4-12)$$

式（4-11）和式（4-12）中，X_i 为解释变量的向量，β_θ 为各个解释变量的回归系数向量，$\mu_{i,\theta}$ 为误差项，$quant_\theta(WTP_i \mid X_i)$ 为给定 X_i 条件下的第 θ 分位数回归的 WTP_i，$0 < \theta < 1$。

为了求解样本第 θ 分位数回归，使用线性规划方法求解最小化残差绝对值的加权平均：

$$\min b_\theta \left[\sum_{i:WTP_i \geq X_i\beta_\theta}^{n} \theta \mid WTP_i - X_i\beta_\theta \mid + \sum_{i:WTP_i < X_i\beta_\theta}^{n} (1-\theta) \mid WTP_i - X_i\beta_\theta \mid \right] \quad (4-13)$$

式（4-13）中，b_θ 为 β_θ 估计量。

第二节 估值比较 I 描述性统计分析

一 有效样本量

正式调查共进行了 25 天，获得问卷 6264 份，有效问卷 6075 份且有效率达到 96.98%。具体为庙岛群岛调查持续 7 天，获得调查问卷 1706 份，有效问卷和有效率分别为 1679 份和 98.42%；舟山群岛正式调查持续 10 天，获得调查问卷 2182 份，有效问卷和有效率分别为 2089 份和 95.74%；三亚及其附近岛屿正式调查持续进行 8 天，获得调查问卷 2376 份，有效问卷和有效率分别为 2307 份和 97.10%（见表 4.1）。

表 4.1 调查点和有效样本分布

案例地	调查地点	海滩			海洋地质遗迹		
		居民和游客	居民	游客	居民和游客	居民	游客
黄渤海区—庙岛群岛	九丈崖景区	193	1	192	286	1	285
	月牙湾景区	193	4	189	284	0	284
	望夫礁景区	96	1	95	142	1	141
	南长山岛和北长山岛	189	188	1	280	277	3
	合计	671	194	477	992	279	713

续表

案例地	调查地点	海滩			海洋文化		
		居民和游客	居民	游客	居民和游客	居民	游客
东海区—舟山群岛	普陀山景区和普陀山岛	361	90	271	272	59	213
	朱家尖国际沙雕艺术广场景区和朱家尖岛	176	54	122	130	34	96
	桃花岛茅草屋码头和桃花岛	154	58	96	107	39	68
	岱山鹿栏晴沙景区和岱山岛	137	71	66	99	41	58
	嵊泗南长涂景区、基湖景区和泗礁山岛	189	89	100	121	63	58
	定海区和普陀区市区	178	176	2	135	135	0
	合计	1195	538	657	864	371	493

案例地	调查地点	海滩			珊瑚礁		
		居民和游客	居民	游客	居民和游客	居民	游客
南海区—三亚及其附近岛屿	亚龙湾景区	368	17	351	232	21	211
	大东海景区	196	15	181	126	13	113
	蜈支洲岛景区	241	21	220	120	10	110
	西岛景区	219	18	201	108	13	95
	三亚市区	340	339	1	337	336	1
	合计	1364	410	954	923	393	530

注：a. 表中有效样本未包含抗议性零支付样本；b. 庙岛群岛九丈崖、月牙湾、望夫礁、仙境源、林海和烽山六个核心景区位于南长山岛和北长山岛，居民抽样范围为两个核心旅游型海岛居民；c. 舟山群岛核心景区主要位于普陀山岛、朱家尖岛、桃花岛、岱山岛和泗礁山岛五个核心旅游型海岛，居民抽样范围为五个核心旅游型海岛居民和舟山群岛本岛（定海区和普陀区）市区主要街区居民；d. 三亚及其附近岛屿潜水和水上运动地点主要位于亚龙湾和大东海两个海湾、蜈支洲岛和西岛两个海岛，居民抽样范围主要为三亚市区内的新风街、金鸡岭街、吉祥街、凤凰路、榆亚路、河东路、解放路、迎宾路等主要街区的居民。

二 抗议性零支付

在6075份有效样本中存在零支付样本187份。通过不愿意支付原因和调查人员备注信息，判断抗议性零支付反应，并将对这类支付意愿不感兴趣、对旅游资源保护不感兴趣、不认可捐款方式或基金形式、认为跟自己没关系、认为景区管理有问题拒绝支付等不愿意支付原因界定为抗议性零支付反应，共计66份样本、占比为1.09%。本书研究进一步分析中剔除66份抗议性零支付反应样本，保留121份真零支付样本[1]，最终分析总样本量为6009份。

三 受访者人口社会特征

从样本的人口社会特征来看（见表4.2），在性别方面，居民受访者中女性略多，游客中男性略多；在平均年龄方面，居民和游客平均年龄分别低于37岁和36岁；在学历水平方面，居民平均学历为高中水平，游客平均学历则为大专水平；在收入方面，2016年居民和游客受访者平均家庭年收入分别在10万元和15万元左右。进一步结合不同案例地比较来看，庙岛群岛、舟山群岛和三亚及其附近岛屿的居民受访者平均学历和平均家庭年收入均明显低于对应案例地的游客受访者。此外，舟山群岛居民和游客平均家庭年收入均分别高于庙岛群岛、三亚及其附近岛屿的居民和游客；三亚及其附近岛屿居民和游客平均学历均分别高于庙岛群岛和舟山群岛的居民和游客；三亚及其附近岛屿居民受访者平均年龄均分别小于庙岛群岛和舟山群岛的居民；另外在性别方面，庙岛群岛和舟山群岛居民受访者中女性偏多，三亚及其附近岛屿居民受访者中则是男性偏多。

表4.2　样本人口社会特征平均值

案例地	统计样本量	性别	年龄（岁）	学历	家庭年收入（万元）
三个案例地	居民+游客（n=6009）	0.50	36	2.70	13.06
	居民（n=2185）	0.47	37	2.00	10.18
	游客（n=3824）	0.51	36	3.10	14.70
黄渤海区—庙岛群岛	居民+游客（n=1663）	0.48	38	2.70	12.37
	居民（n=473）	0.42	43	1.90	9.71
	游客（n=1190）	0.50	37	3.10	13.43

---

[1] Adriana Ressurreição, et al., "Economic Valuation of Species Loss in the Open Sea", *Ecological Economics*, Vol. 70, No. 4, February 2011.

续表

案例地	统计样本量	性别	年龄（岁）	学历	家庭年收入（万元）
东海区—舟山群岛	居民+游客（n=2059）	0.51	37	2.50	13.84
	居民（n=909）	0.45	39	2.00	10.97
	游客（n=1150）	0.55	35	3.00	16.12
南海区—三亚及其附近岛屿	居民+游客（n=2287）	0.50	34	2.80	12.85
	居民（n=803）	0.53	31	2.20	9.57
	游客（n=1484）	0.49	35	3.20	14.63

注：a. 性别：男=1，女=0；b. 学历：初中及以下=1，高中、中专和技校=2，大专=3，本科=4，研究生=5。

四 样本组间人口社会特征差异

运用 Mann–Whitney U 检验和 Kruskal–Wallis 检验方法，依次进行两个样本组之间差异显著性检验和三个样本组之间差异显著性检验。从检验结果来看，庙岛群岛、舟山群岛和三亚及其附近岛屿同一案例地内部两种资源样本组之间比较时，居民（或游客）受访者的人口社会特征差异较小；庙岛群岛、舟山群岛和三亚及其附近岛屿不同案例地两个样本组或三个样本组之间比较，居民（或游客）受访者的人口社会特征则差异较大（见表4.3）。

表4.3　　　　　样本组间人口社会特征差异显著性检验

比较项目	居民				游客			
	性别	年龄	学历	收入	性别	年龄	学历	收入
庙岛海滩与海洋地质遗迹	0.68 (−0.42)	0.53 (−0.63)	0.50 (−0.67)	0.59 (−0.54)	0.95 (−0.06)	0.01 (−2.51)	0.00 (−2.97)	0.64 (−0.47)
舟山海滩与海洋文化	0.54 (−0.61)	0.90 (−0.13)	0.08 (−1.77)	0.24 (−1.17)	0.63 (−0.49)	0.16 (−1.39)	0.67 (−0.43)	0.95 (−0.06)
三亚海滩与珊瑚礁	0.73 (−0.35)	0.32 (−0.99)	0.00 (−3.38)	0.26 (−1.13)	0.35 (−0.94)	0.97 (−0.03)	0.38 (−0.88)	0.85 (−0.20)

续表

比较项目	居民				游客			
	性别	年龄	学历	收入	性别	年龄	学历	收入
庙岛海洋地质遗迹、舟山海洋文化与三亚珊瑚礁	0.01 (9.79)	0.00 (178.50)	0.00 (44.76)	0.00 (21.50)	0.27 (2.62)	0.01 (8.57)	0.00 (13.17)	0.00 (25.66)
庙岛海滩、舟山海滩与三亚海滩	0.02 (7.44)	0.00 (164.21)	0.02 (7.67)	0.00 (51.41)	0.01 (10.25)	0.00 (38.09)	0.00 (21.01)	0.00 (29.89)
舟山海洋文化与庙岛海滩	0.50 (−0.67)	0.00 (−3.35)	0.63 (−0.49)	0.00 (−2.85)	0.15 (−1.46)	0.00 (−4.62)	0.78 (−0.28)	0.00 (−5.13)
舟山海洋文化与庙岛海洋地质遗迹	0.80 (−0.26)	0.00 (−4.74)	0.83 (−0.21)	0.04 (−2.11)	0.13 (−1.54)	0.00 (−2.84)	0.01 (−2.67)	0.00 (−5.00)
舟山海洋文化与舟山海滩	0.54 (−0.61)	0.90 (−0.13)	0.08 (−1.77)	0.24 (−1.17)	0.63 (−0.49)	0.16 (−1.39)	0.67 (−0.43)	0.95 (−0.06)
舟山海洋文化与三亚海滩	0.02 (−2.31)	0.00 (−10.08)	0.01 (−2.71)	0.00 (−5.45)	0.02 (−2.36)	0.47 (−0.73)	0.00 (−3.15)	0.00 (−3.58)
舟山海洋文化与三亚珊瑚礁	0.01 (−2.63)	0.00 (−9.47)	0.00 (−5.91)	0.00 (−4.67)	0.20 (−1.28)	0.49 (−0.69)	0.00 (−3.52)	0.00 (−3.24)

注：括号内数字 Mann – Whitney U 检验为 Z 值；Kruskal – Wallis 检验为卡方值。

五　投标值分布

从各投标值占比来看，庙岛群岛、舟山群岛和三亚及其附近岛屿三个案例地受访者的正支付意愿率处于 95.50%—99.30%，居民和游客选择 10 元、20 元、50 元、100 元和 200 元投标值均较多，且投标值主要集中在 200 元及以下。庙岛群岛海滩和海洋地质遗迹旅游资源的居民和游客选择投标值在 200 元及以下的样本占比分别为 88.20%、87.40% 和 84.20%、84.80%；舟山群岛海滩和海洋文化旅游资源的对应比例分别为 86.30%、83.00% 和 80.90%、77.70%；三亚及其附近岛屿海滩和珊瑚礁旅游资源的对应比例分别为 87.30%、84.30% 和 87.00%、85.80%（见表4.4）。

表 4.4　　　　　各投标值样本量占总样本量比例　　　　　单位:%

投标值区间（元）	庙岛群岛海滩		庙岛群岛海洋地质遗迹		舟山群岛海滩		舟山群岛海洋文化		三亚及其附近岛屿海滩		三亚及其附近岛屿珊瑚礁	
	居民	游客	居民	游客	居民	游客	居民	游客	居民	游客	居民	游客
0—1	2.60	0.80	0.70	1.30	4.50	2.40	3.80	2.20	1.50	1.70	0.80	2.10
1—2	3.10	1.90	1.40	1.10	0.90	1.80	1.40	0.80	2.70	1.30	2.00	1.90
2—5	0.50	1.70	1.40	0.30	0.60	0.30	0.80	0.60	2.00	0.50	0.80	0.90
5—10	3.10	2.90	0.40	3.40	1.90	2.70	2.20	2.00	3.20	2.60	3.10	2.30
10—20	11.30	16.40	8.60	10.70	11.20	9.40	8.90	5.90	13.20	10.30	8.40	10.90
20—30	7.20	5.70	5.40	5.20	8.20	5.50	7.00	5.90	8.80	7.20	10.40	6.60
30—50	4.10	2.90	2.50	1.70	3.40	1.20	3.00	1.00	3.70	2.50	2.80	1.30
50—60	12.90	15.30	11.50	13.50	14.50	10.80	11.30	9.30	13.20	14.20	14.50	14.50
60—80	1.00	0.60	0.70	0.00	0.60	0.00	0.00	0.00	0.50	0.10	0.30	0.60
80—100	0.50	0.80	0.40	0.70	0.00	0.50	0.30	0.60	1.20	0.20	1.30	0.00
100—120	30.90	30.60	40.90	35.30	29.70	33.00	29.90	28.60	29.00	31.60	33.10	30.00
120—150	0.50	0.00	0.00	0.00	0.20	0.20	0.00	0.30	0.70	0.00	0.30	0.20
150—200	0.00	0.40	0.40	0.30	1.10	1.80	0.80	1.00	1.00	0.80	0.50	0.90
200—300	10.30	7.30	10.00	10.70	9.30	12.60	11.30	17.40	6.80	11.10	8.90	13.60
300—400	2.10	1.50	1.80	3.10	3.20	3.70	3.20	5.70	1.50	2.20	2.50	1.90
400—500	0.00	0.00	0.40	0.00	0.00	0.20	0.50	0.00	0.00	0.00	0.30	0.20
500—600	5.20	5.50	3.90	5.10	4.80	6.10	8.40	8.10	4.60	6.70	4.10	5.10
600—800	1.00	0.40	1.10	1.00	0.60	0.90	1.60	1.00	1.50	0.70	0.80	0.60
800—1000	0.50	1.50	0.00	0.60	0.70	0.50	0.50	1.20	0.50	0.50	0.50	0.60
1000—1500	1.60	2.70	6.10	4.60	3.20	3.40	4.00	5.30	2.70	4.30	3.80	4.00
1500—2000	0.00	0.00	0.00	0.00	0.20	0.50	0.00	0.00	0.10	0.30	0.20	0.20
2000—2001	1.60	0.60	2.50	0.80	1.10	2.00	1.00	1.20	1.20	1.20	0.80	1.70

注：表中数据进行了四舍五入处理。

六　WTP 与人口社会特征分位数回归

WTP 与人口社会特征分位数回归各变量定义如表 4.5 所示。

表 4.5　　分位数回归各变量定义

变量类型	变量	定义
因变量	WTP	支付意愿区间中点值
自变量	Sex	性别：男 =1，女 =0
	Age	年龄：受访者 2017 年的年龄（单位：岁）
	Ages	年龄的平方项除以 100
	Edu	学历：受过高等教育 =1，未受过高等教育 =0
	Inc	收入：受访者 2016 年的年收入区间中点值（单位：万元）

对庙岛群岛海滩、庙岛群岛海洋地质遗迹、舟山群岛海滩、舟山群岛海洋文化、三亚及其附近岛屿海滩和三亚及其附近岛屿珊瑚礁居民样本数据和游客样本数据分别进行分位数回归，分位数回归模型选取 25%、50%、75% 和 90% 四个分位点进行分位数回归（见表 4.6 至表 4.11），根据各分位数回归结果可以发现不同分位点条件下受访者 WTP 与各人口社会特征之间的关系（见图 4.1 至图 4.12）。从总体来看，各案例地各类资源分位数回归最典型的规律为：收入变量的回归系数在多个分位数回归模型中都呈现出统计显著性，且除个别分位点外，收入变量回归系数均为正值，说明受访者的 WTP 与收入成正比，收入越高的受访者 WTP 越高。根据分位数回归系数图可以看出（见图 4.1 至图 4.12），收入变量的回归系数随着分位点的升高呈现递增趋势，表明收入变化对 WTP 较高的受访者影响更大。

表 4.6　　庙岛群岛海滩分位数回归结果

变量	居民				游客			
	QR_25	QR_50	QR_75	QR_90	QR_25	QR_50	QR_75	QR_90
Sex	7.88	-6.00	34.89	99.28	2.69	4.37	-1.62	-26.48
	(11.26)	(19.03)	(46.31)	(82.49)	(7.04)	(18.29)	(13.63)	(130.53)
Age	-0.29	-3.58	3.08	-15.34	-1.32	0.12	-12.34	-130.31**
	(3.66)	(6.26)	(8.82)	(21.97)	(2.54)	(4.77)	(18.06)	(52.81)
Ages	0.34	4.37	-2.67	22.83	1.05	-1.52	14.88	166.29**
	(4.22)	(7.30)	(10.54)	(29.92)	(2.89)	(6.11)	(23.79)	(69.24)

续表

变量	居民				游客			
	QR_25	QR_50	QR_75	QR_90	QR_25	QR_50	QR_75	QR_90
Edu	30.42*	-0.00	26.96	83.26	1.16	24.14	-12.45	-32.72
	(18.28)	(40.82)	(54.98)	(98.41)	(6.55)	(18.61)	(13.84)	(111.38)
Inc	1.73	9.80	29.01***	61.49***	0.01	0.56	7.04**	10.59
	(2.74)	(7.26)	(8.31)	(19.64)	(0.48)	(1.33)	(2.79)	(11.83)
$Intercept$	13.29	74.44	-137.41	22.81	55.02	84.04	315.44	2748.14***
	(76.44)	(122.25)	(184.20)	(403.19)	(55.26)	(84.64)	(339.29)	(981.21)
N	194	194	194	194	477	477	477	477
$Pseudo\ R^2$	0.02	0.03	0.18	0.34	0.00	0.01	0.02	0.04

注：括号内为自助法500次计算的标准误；$*p<0.1$，$**p<0.05$，$***p<0.01$。

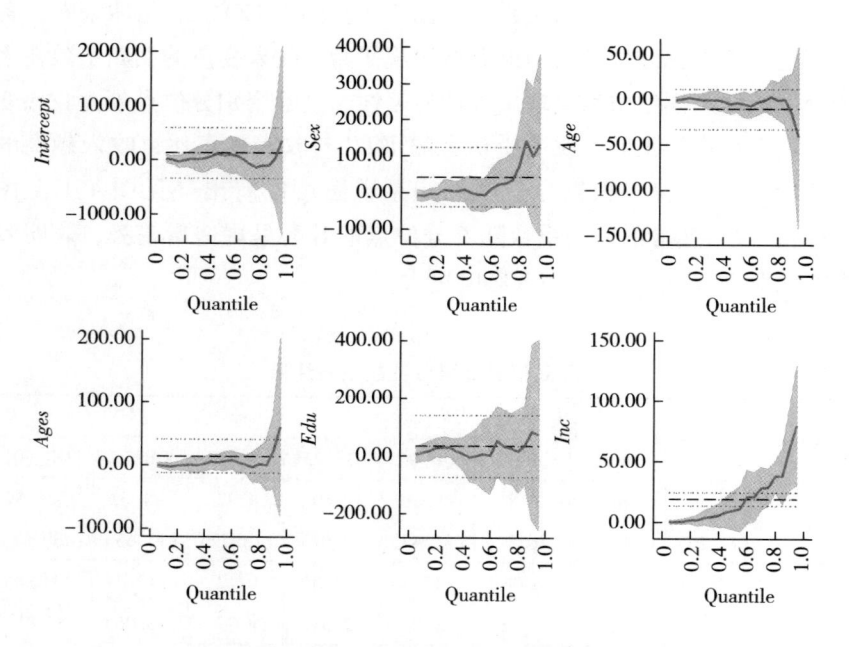

图4.1 庙岛群岛海滩（居民）分位数回归系数

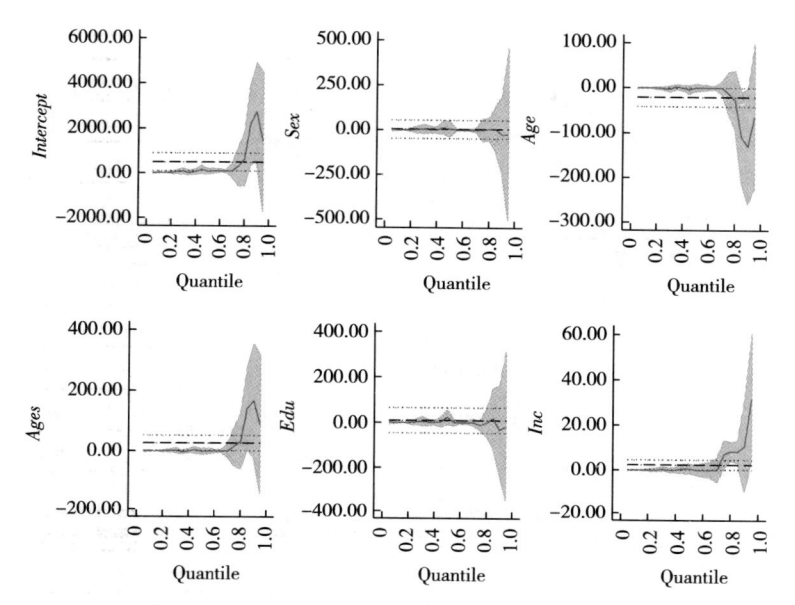

图 4.2　庙岛群岛海滩（游客）分位数回归系数

表 4.7　　　　　　庙岛群岛海洋地质遗迹分位数回归结果

变量	居民				游客			
	QR_25	QR_50	QR_75	QR_90	QR_25	QR_50	QR_75	QR_90
Sex	16.44	22.76	44.48	0.00	-8.20	0.00	17.76	208.47**
	(12.18)	(14.21)	(27.15)	(71.14)	(6.91)	(4.21)	(29.20)	(92.71)
Age	7.10	6.01	0.00	0.00	0.00	-0.00	-3.79	17.34
	(4.63)	(4.62)	(7.65)	(19.83)	(2.57)	(2.05)	(7.86)	(24.19)
Ages	-8.95*	-8.12	-0.00	-0.00	-0.00	0.00	4.63	-23.12
	(4.74)	(5.20)	(8.64)	(27.78)	(3.54)	(2.73)	(9.88)	(32.25)
Edu	21.37	38.22	44.48	447.32	27.30***	-0.00	6.66	29.14
	(22.69)	(25.63)	(63.10)	(282.08)	(8.84)	(12.70)	(22.06)	(67.94)
Inc	2.88*	7.43	44.48***	71.34***	0.90	-0.00	11.10***	23.00***
	(1.52)	(6.00)	(13.86)	(4.83)	(0.61)	(1.26)	(2.55)	(7.32)
Intercept	-101.73	-76.39	-134.65	-211.03	19.15	110.00***	114.44	-230.74
	(115.32)	(119.76)	(168.58)	(354.54)	(46.08)	(30.14)	(150.98)	(413.66)
N	279	279	279	279	713	713	713	713
Pseudo R^2	0.04	0.01	0.19	0.40	0.02	0.00	0.07	0.12

注：括号内为自助法 500 次计算的标准误；*$p<0.1$，**$p<0.05$，***$p<0.01$。

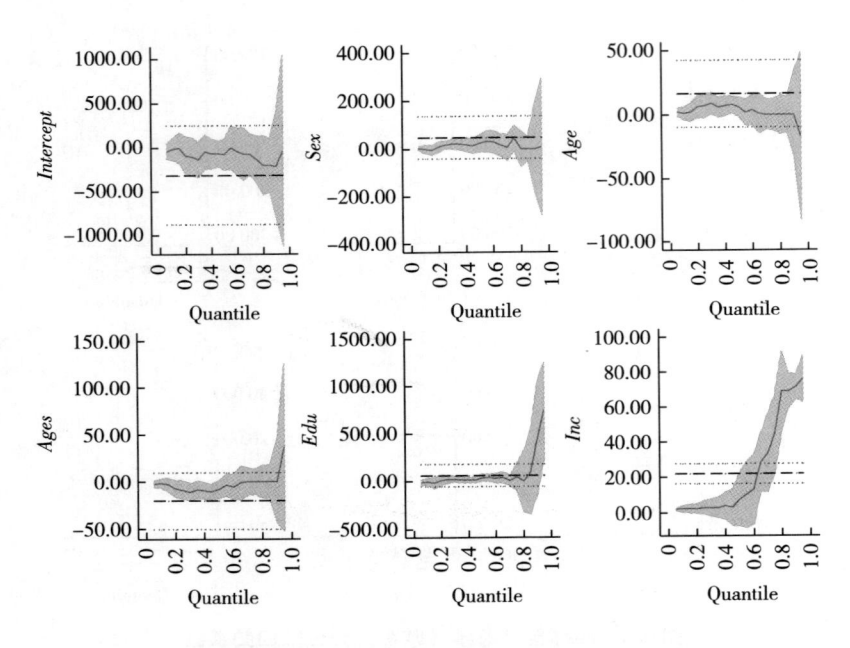

图 4.3 庙岛群岛海洋地质遗迹（居民）分位数回归系数

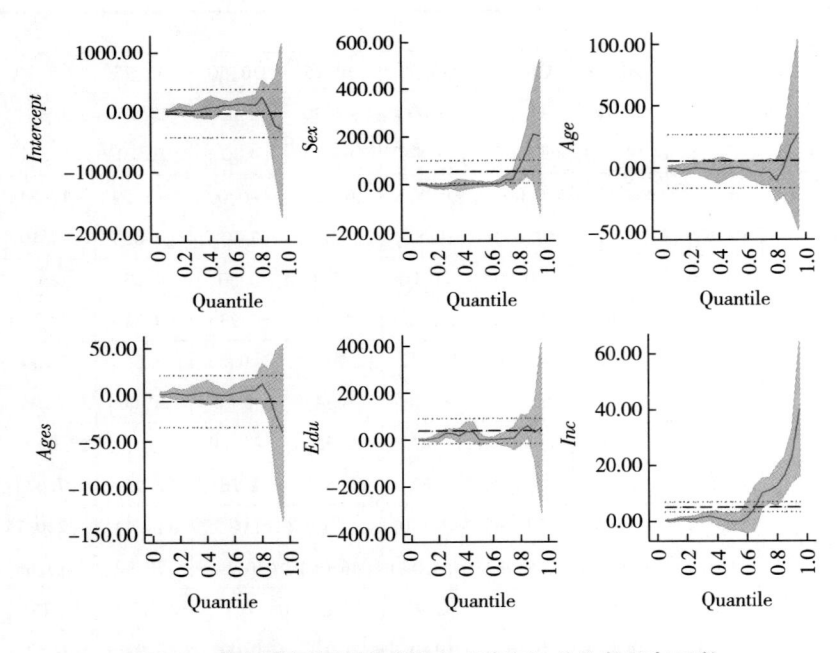

图 4.4 庙岛群岛海洋地质遗迹（游客）分位数回归系数

表 4.8　　　　　　　　舟山群岛海滩分位数回归结果

变量	居民				游客			
	QR_25	QR_50	QR_75	QR_90	QR_25	QR_50	QR_75	QR_90
Sex	7.15	11.08	8.14	3.77	6.18	-0.00	27.02	82.35
	(6.33)	(11.88)	(27.52)	(55.40)	(6.78)	(9.35)	(22.69)	(66.69)
Age	1.69	-1.95	-2.97	-28.64	2.07	-0.75	-5.61	-30.16
	(1.61)	(3.51)	(7.24)	(20.67)	(2.47)	(4.32)	(7.12)	(47.40)
$Ages$	-2.48	2.05	2.85	43.14	-1.74	1.30	6.76	35.48
	(1.91)	(4.28)	(9.44)	(29.96)	(3.41)	(5.56)	(9.07)	(65.68)
Edu	-4.46	19.20	27.38	106.32	15.85**	11.70	-8.51	-70.22
	(11.53)	(14.27)	(35.86)	(83.04)	(6.91)	(12.42)	(26.35)	(69.16)
Inc	2.67**	5.60	27.38***	39.31***	2.86***	6.07**	18.18***	36.37***
	(1.32)	(3.73)	(6.24)	(6.92)	(0.64)	(2.66)	(2.01)	(5.15)
$Intercept$	-20.84	61.08	9.11	398.24	-49.43	29.99	97.30	576.43
	(34.39)	(61.09)	(113.68)	(336.59)	(42.75)	(76.95)	(135.80)	(855.08)
N	538	538	538	538	657	657	657	657
$Pseudo\ R^2$	0.02	0.02	0.12	0.25	0.05	0.03	0.15	0.25

注：括号内为自助法 500 次计算的标准误；*$p<0.1$，**$p<0.05$，***$p<0.01$。

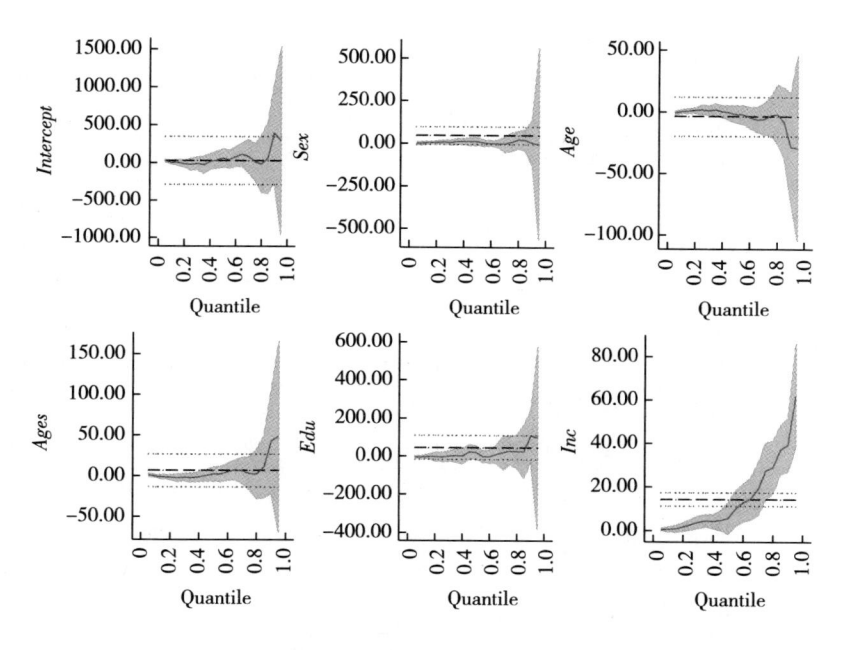

图 4.5　舟山群岛海滩（居民）分位数回归系数

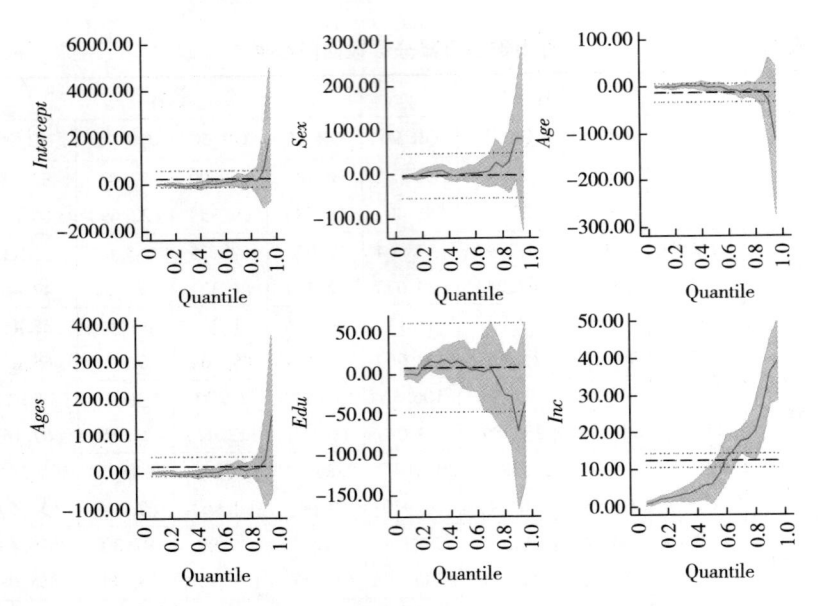

图 4.6　舟山群岛海滩（游客）分位数回归系数

表 4.9　　　　　　　　舟山群岛海洋文化分位数回归结果

变量	居民				游客			
	QR_25	QR_50	QR_75	QR_90	QR_25	QR_50	QR_75	QR_90
Sex	-15.32*	-27.85	0.00	-4.88	16.46	18.11	45.84	150.26*
	(8.93)	(16.91)	(36.43)	(108.62)	(15.59)	(17.10)	(28.11)	(84.25)
Age	0.93	-4.78	-0.00	24.77	-4.53	-3.74	-37.61*	-75.57
	(2.81)	(4.27)	(10.23)	(27.83)	(4.93)	(6.25)	(22.36)	(63.13)
Ages	-1.14	5.30	0.00	-34.54	5.83	4.37	50.18	103.19
	(3.33)	(5.44)	(12.76)	(34.03)	(6.50)	(8.71)	(30.82)	(90.94)
Edu	14.47	12.76	123.27	409.62	7.66	2.11	-7.39	138.12
	(15.68)	(23.34)	(79.85)	(259.17)	(14.40)	(15.89)	(28.48)	(89.01)
Inc	4.22***	10.65**	17.96***	17.45	1.82*	5.53**	17.53***	30.00***
	(1.26)	(4.22)	(2.96)	(10.86)	(1.05)	(2.62)	(2.70)	(6.77)
Intercept	-11.61	114.31	29.18	-80.83	107.08	127.04	697.19*	1303.36
	(59.28)	(78.10)	(191.03)	(516.69)	(92.26)	(108.02)	(388.05)	(1081.79)
N	371	371	371	371	493	493	493	493
Pseudo R^2	0.05	0.03	0.12	0.11	0.01	0.02	0.11	0.17

注：括号内为自助法 500 次计算的标准误；$*p<0.1$，$**p<0.05$，$***p<0.01$。

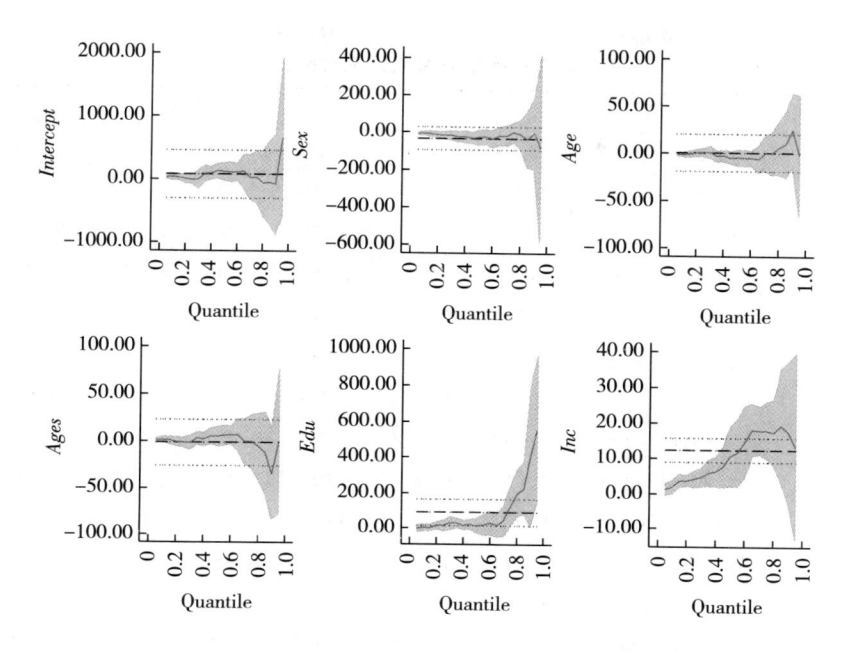

图 4.7　舟山群岛海洋文化（居民）分位数回归系数

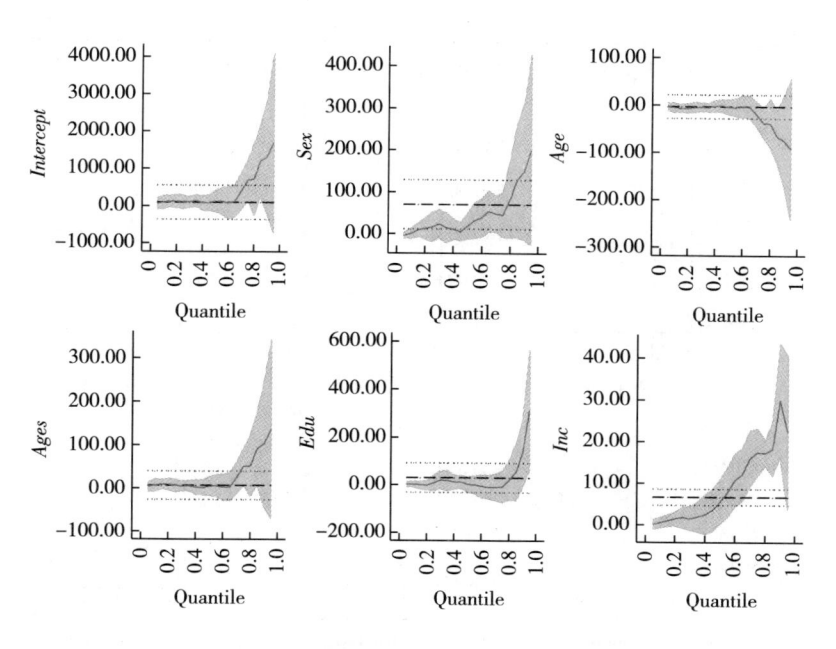

图 4.8　舟山群岛海洋文化（游客）分位数回归系数

表 4.10　三亚及其附近岛屿海滩分位数回归结果

变量	居民				游客			
	QR_25	QR_50	QR_75	QR_90	QR_25	QR_50	QR_75	QR_90
Sex	-1.65 (5.72)	0.19 (9.80)	0.71 (20.02)	55.75 (58.78)	-1.73 (4.45)	5.80 (8.91)	5.10 (16.85)	19.01 (70.06)
Age	-1.27 (2.26)	-8.52** (3.66)	-4.73 (4.74)	3.07 (13.70)	1.15 (1.42)	-1.38 (3.14)	-5.70 (5.53)	-1.27 (28.90)
Ages	0.75 (2.84)	8.53* (5.15)	5.33 (6.08)	-6.97 (16.10)	-1.65 (1.72)	0.69 (4.33)	6.57 (7.10)	-2.17 (41.58)
Edu	-2.47 (7.89)	-10.09 (12.99)	-6.12 (20.32)	-84.74 (61.88)	7.29 (6.02)	23.66** (11.07)	5.62 (18.02)	12.16 (81.21)
Inc	3.20*** (0.78)	8.33** (3.98)	27.41*** (7.58)	60.96*** (11.56)	2.49*** (0.81)	5.48*** (1.29)	13.72*** (1.87)	27.92*** (4.14)
Intercept	36.80 (45.43)	189.98*** (59.35)	63.38 (85.19)	-112.69 (274.70)	-12.78 (28.20)	48.21 (53.25)	139.04 (102.56)	150.50 (484.15)
N	410	410	410	410	954	954	954	954
Pseudo R^2	0.04	0.06	0.14	0.31	0.04	0.03	0.12	0.14

注：括号内为自助法 500 次计算的标准误；*$p<0.1$，**$p<0.05$，***$p<0.01$。

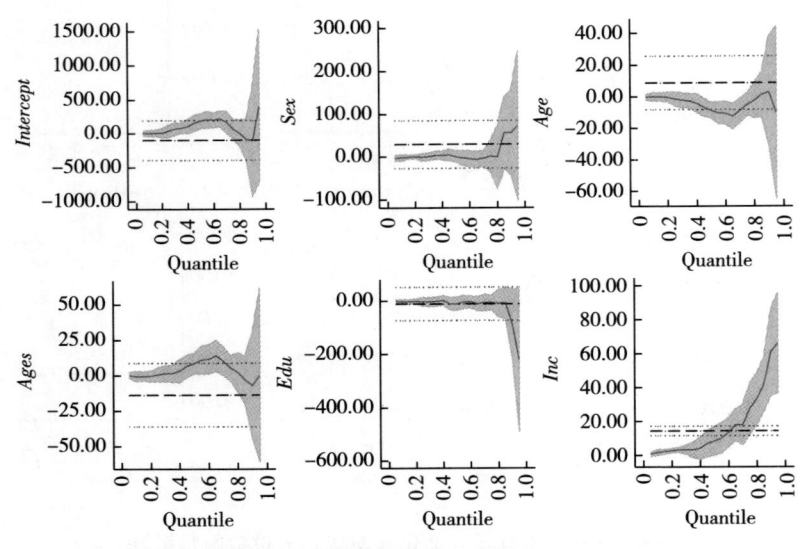

图 4.9　三亚及其附近岛屿海滩（居民）分位数回归系数

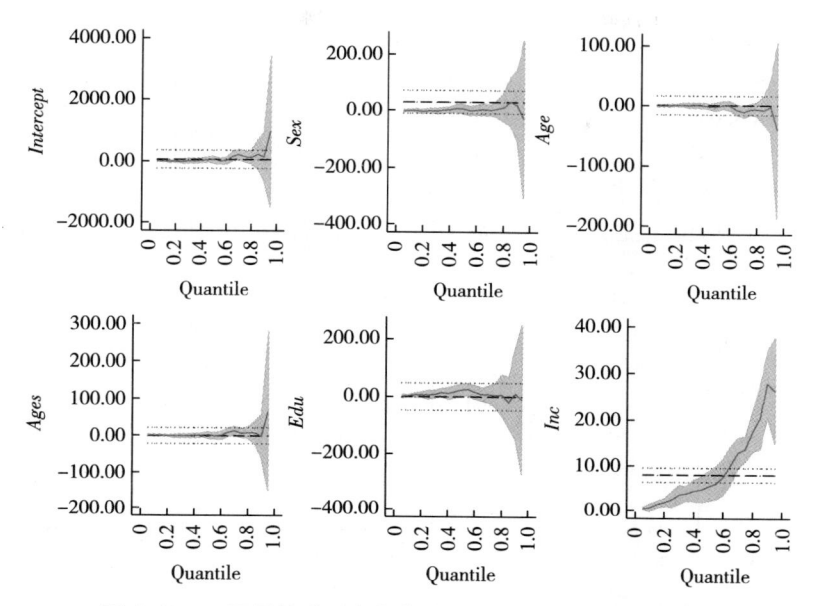

图 4.10　三亚及其附近岛屿海滩（游客）分位数回归系数

表 4.11　　　　三亚及其附近岛屿珊瑚礁分位数回归结果

变量	居民				游客			
	QR_25	QR_50	QR_75	QR_90	QR_25	QR_50	QR_75	QR_90
Sex	2.06	11.84	-0.00	24.93	-5.27	-11.68	-0.43	1.26
	(6.70)	(11.86)	(16.97)	(45.05)	(6.56)	(11.04)	(25.81)	(73.03)
Age	0.24	-5.79	-14.42*	-23.71	-2.87	-5.30	-35.67	-99.87**
	(2.73)	(5.17)	(7.56)	(17.47)	(2.91)	(6.55)	(27.49)	(42.72)
Ages	-0.86	6.78	16.70*	26.34	3.11	6.84	47.06	149.43**
	(3.65)	(6.94)	(9.55)	(22.70)	(3.60)	(9.00)	(40.07)	(64.54)
Edu	25.99**	10.84	-12.81	-32.93	0.76	24.28*	30.99	-69.83
	(10.13)	(15.08)	(22.92)	(50.15)	(8.63)	(13.98)	(35.11)	(86.03)
Inc	0.97	10.79*	29.52***	69.11***	3.06***	6.35***	12.45***	26.01***
	(2.31)	(5.53)	(9.14)	(9.50)	(1.04)	(1.87)	(3.30)	(5.57)
Intercept	19.58	102.48	233.30*	281.16	68.64	103.54	659.90	1765.49**
	(50.16)	(75.31)	(131.89)	(334.38)	(59.57)	(118.83)	(457.94)	(702.73)
N	393	393	393	393	530	530	530	530
Pseudo R^2	0.03	0.03	0.17	0.36	0.05	0.04	0.11	0.19

注：括号内为自助法 500 次计算的标准误；*$p<0.1$，**$p<0.05$，***$p<0.01$。

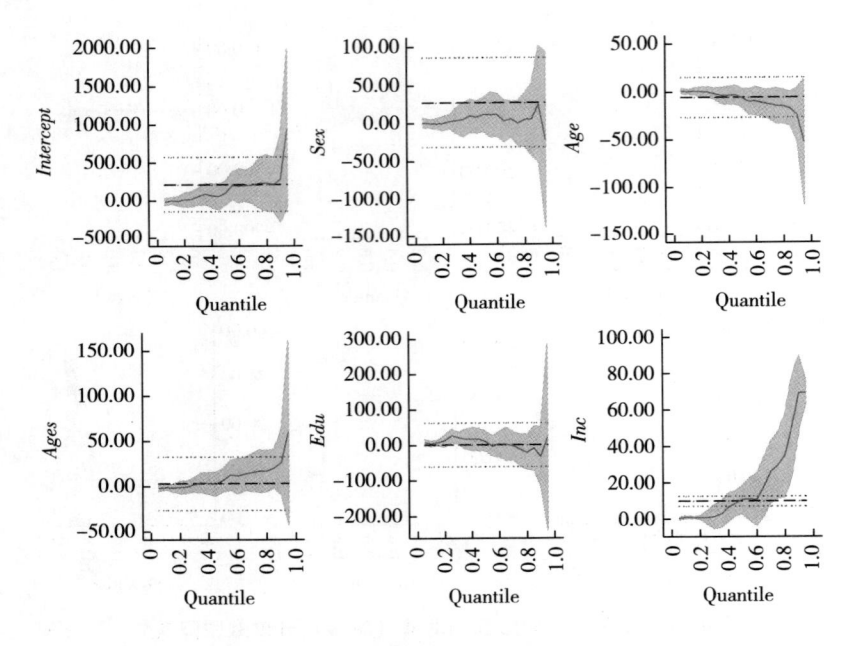

图 4.11　三亚及其附近岛屿珊瑚礁（居民）分位数回归系数

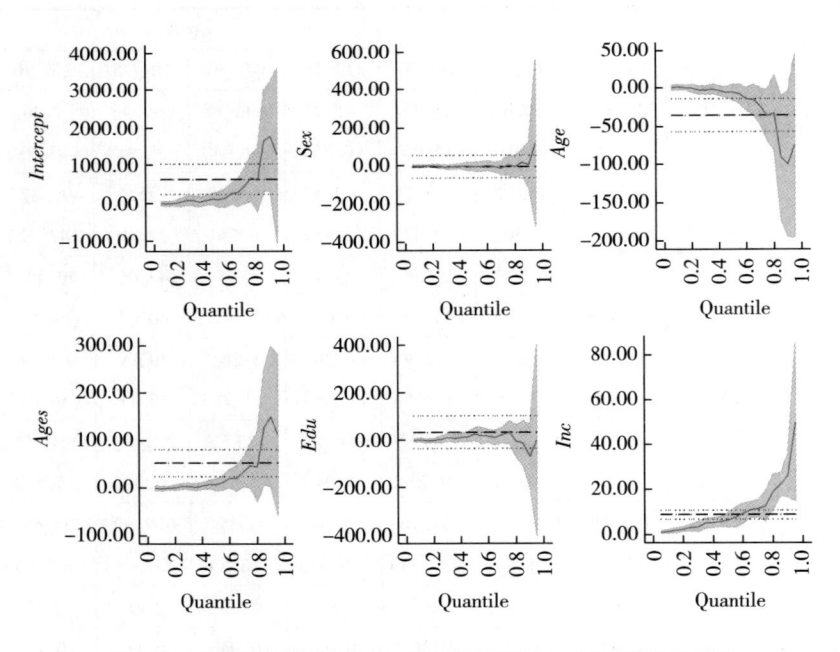

图 4.12　三亚及其附近岛屿珊瑚礁（游客）分位数回归系数

第三节　估值比较 I 结果分析

一　WTP 差异性分析

从区间回归结果来看，公众对保护海洋旅游资源非使用价值具有显著的 WTP，受访者对各类海洋旅游资源非使用价值的平均 WTP 处于 187.85—353.63 元；同时，家庭年收入对各 WTP 均具有显著影响，显示出受访者对待 WTP 的严肃性[①]（见表 4.12）。

从庙岛群岛、舟山群岛和三亚及其附近岛屿内部比较来看，庙岛群岛海滩和海洋地质遗迹的居民平均 WTP 均分别大于其游客平均 WTP，而舟山群岛海滩和海洋文化、三亚及其附近岛屿海滩和珊瑚礁的居民平均 WTP 均分别小于其游客平均 WTP；庙岛群岛海洋地质遗迹与海滩、舟山群岛海洋文化与海滩、三亚及其附近岛屿珊瑚礁与海滩，均表现出海洋相对稀缺型旅游资源的居民（或游客）平均 WTP 大于海洋相对充裕型旅游资源的居民（或游客）平均 WTP。

从庙岛群岛、舟山群岛和三亚及其附近岛屿案例地之间比较来看，舟山群岛海洋文化的居民（或游客）平均 WTP 分别大于庙岛群岛海洋地质遗迹和三亚及其附近岛屿珊瑚礁的居民（或游客）平均 WTP；舟山群岛海滩的居民（或游客）平均 WTP 分别大于庙岛群岛和三亚及其附近岛屿海滩的居民（或游客）平均 WTP；海洋文化旅游资源的居民（或游客）平均 WTP 大于海洋自然旅游资源的居民（或游客）平均 WTP。

由此可见，不同类型的海洋旅游资源平均 WTP 之间存在显著差异，而这种差异又可进一步划分为受访者样本人口社会特征差异引起的平均 WTP 差值（$\Delta sc\ \overline{WTP}_{M-N}$）和不同资源类型引起的平均 WTP 差值（$\Delta dr\ \overline{WTP}_{M-N}$）。

[①] John B. Loomis and Armando González-Cabán, "A Willingness-to-pay Function for Protecting Acres of Spotted Owl Habitat from Fire", *Ecological Economics*, Vol. 25, No. 3, June 1998.

表 4.12　　区间回归结果

变量	庙岛群岛海滩		庙岛群岛海洋地质遗迹	
	居民	游客	居民	游客
Gender	-0.09(0.24)	0.08(0.13)	0.16(0.15)	0.01(0.10)
Age	-0.02(0.06)	-0.08(0.05)	0.10*(0.05)	-0.06(0.04)
Ages	0.02(0.08)	0.09(0.07)	-0.12**(0.06)	0.08(0.05)
Education	0.28(0.29)	-0.01(0.14)	0.09(0.22)	0.10(0.12)
Lnincome	1.03***(0.26)	0.43***(0.15)	1.12***(0.15)	0.71***(0.09)
Constant	-7.09**(2.90)	0.78(1.65)	-10.03***(1.98)	-2.69**(1.11)
Lnsigma	0.39***(0.07)	0.36***(0.04)	0.21***(0.06)	0.30***(0.04)
Median	77.15[63.72]	67.45[20.57]	128.15[122.10]	95.75[56.17]
Mean	231.51[191.22]	187.85[57.30]	274.49[261.53]	236.98[139.01]
N	194	477	279	713
Log pseudolikelihood	-601.52	-1441.57	-863.79	-2165.71
Wald χ^2	19.94	11.13	81.35	73.70
Prob > χ^2	0.00	0.05	0.00	0.00
变量	舟山群岛海滩		舟山群岛海洋文化	
	居民	游客	居民	游客
Gender	0.06(0.14)	-0.10(0.11)	-0.40**(0.17)	0.15(0.13)
Age	-0.01(0.04)	-0.02(0.06)	0.00(0.06)	-0.09*(0.05)
Ages	0.01(0.06)	0.02(0.08)	-0.01(0.07)	0.11*(0.07)
Education	-0.08(0.18)	0.02(0.13)	0.24(0.21)	0.01(0.14)
Lnincome	1.01***(0.14)	1.06***(0.09)	1.02***(0.15)	0.77***(0.11)
Constant	-6.97***(1.65)	-7.71***(1.40)	-6.99***(1.81)	-2.54*(1.45)
Lnsigma	0.43***(0.05)	0.35***(0.04)	0.43***(0.05)	0.35***(0.05)
Median	80.04[61.81]	114.14[110.24]	102.48[94.25]	128.86[83.64]
Mean	258.79[199.87]	313.19[302.48]	335.75[308.80]	353.63[229.53]
N	538	657	371	493
Log pseudolikelihood	-1670.68	-2060.39	-1154.23	-1517.41
Wald χ^2	64.21	142.78	63.61	54.82
Prob > χ^2	0.00	0.00	0.00	0.00

续表

变量	三亚及其附近岛屿海滩		三亚及其附近岛屿珊瑚礁	
	居民	游客	居民	游客
$Gender$	-0.07(0.14)	-0.05(0.09)	0.06(0.13)	-0.10(0.12)
Age	-0.05(0.04)	-0.03(0.04)	-0.05(0.05)	-0.08(0.05)
$Ages$	0.04(0.06)	0.03(0.05)	0.05(0.07)	0.11*(0.06)
$Education$	-0.09(0.15)	0.14(0.11)	0.10(0.13)	-0.05(0.15)
$Lnincome$	1.04***(0.12)	0.90***(0.08)	1.10***(0.15)	1.04***(0.09)
$Constant$	-6.30***(1.51)	-5.53***(0.91)	-6.93***(1.75)	-6.26***(1.40)
$Lnsigma$	0.35***(0.05)	0.30***(0.03)	0.23***(0.05)	0.35***(0.04)
$Median$	80.28[93.76]	101.97[80.93]	101.45[144.60]	102.74[105.77]
$Mean$	220.29[257.29]	255.00[202.39]	222.07[316.53]	279.48[287.72]
N	410	954	393	530
$Log\ pseudolikelihood$	-1240.90	-2902.77	-1160.78	-1638.19
$Wald\ \chi^2$	78.45	177.12	68.38	126.41
$Prob > \chi^2$	0.00	0.00	0.00	0.00

注：a. 圆括号内的数字为稳健标准误；b. 方括号内的数字为标准差；c. $*p<0.1$，$**p<0.05$，$***p<0.01$；d. 为了检验是否存在遗漏变量偏差，游客样本的计量模型分析也考虑了加入"地理距离"和"客源地特征"两个变量，计算的各类资源 WTP 与未加入这两个变量计算的各类资源的 WTP 差异较小，不存在遗漏变量偏差，所以，为了保证游客样本和居民样本的计算结果具有可比性，本研究计算各类资源 WTP 的计量模型均未考虑"地理距离"和"客源地特征"两个变量。

二 基于资源类型的 WTP 测度

运用 $adj\overline{WTP}_{N-at-M}$ 和 $adj\overline{WTP}_{M-at-N}$ 调整方法，对庙岛群岛、舟山群岛和三亚及其附近岛屿案例地内部和三个案例地之间，海洋旅游资源的居民（或游客）平均 WTP 进行调整，剔除因居民（或游客）样本人口社会特征差异引起的 WTP 差值（$\Delta sc\overline{WTP}_{M-N}$）。同一案例地两种资源之间居民（或游客）样本人口社会特征的差异较小（见表 4.3），得出各调整后的平均 WTP 与其原值间的差值（$adj\overline{WTP}_{N-at-M} - \overline{WTP}_N$ 或 $\overline{WTP}_M - adj\overline{WTP}_{M-at-N}$）均较小；不同案例地居民（或游客）样本人口社会特征的差异较大（见表 4.3），得出各调整后的平均 WTP 与其原值间的差值（$adj\overline{WTP}_{N-at-M} - \overline{WTP}_N$ 或 $\overline{WTP}_M - adj\overline{WTP}_{M-at-N}$）均较大。

同一案例地两种资源之间比较时，如表 4.13 中 $\Delta dr\overline{WTP}_{M-N}$ 值所示，三个案例地均表现出海洋相对稀缺型旅游资源的居民（或游客）平均 WTP 大于对海洋相对充裕型旅游资源的平均 WTP。不同案例地海洋相对稀缺型旅游资源之间比较则表现为，海洋文化旅游资源的居民（或游客）平均 WTP 大于珊瑚礁旅游资源和海洋地质遗迹旅游资源的平均 WTP，且游客平均 WTP 排序相应为舟山群岛海洋文化 > 三亚及其附近岛屿珊瑚礁 > 庙岛群岛海洋地质遗迹，居民平均 WTP 的排序则为舟山群岛海洋文化 > 庙岛群岛海洋地质遗迹 > 三亚及其附近岛屿珊瑚礁（见表 4.14）。

不同案例地海洋相对充裕型旅游资源之间比较时，游客平均 WTP 的高低则与待估海滩长度之和的长短一致（见表 3.1 至表 3.3），即游客平均 WTP 表现为舟山群岛海滩 > 三亚及其附近岛屿海滩 > 庙岛群岛海滩；不仅如此，待估海滩长度之和也影响了舟山群岛、三亚及其附近岛屿居民平均 WTP 高低，即居民平均 WTP 表现为庙岛群岛海滩 > 舟山群岛海滩 > 三亚及其附近岛屿海滩（见表 4.15）。不同案例地或同一案例地海洋人文旅游资源与自然旅游资源比较时则表现为，海洋人文旅游资源的居民（或游客）平均 WTP 均大于海洋自然旅游资源的平均 WTP（见表 4.16）。

表 4.13 同一案例地海洋相对稀缺型与相对充裕型旅游资源比较

计算项目	庙岛群岛		舟山群岛		三亚及其附近岛屿	
	居民	游客	居民	游客	居民	游客
相对稀缺型资源—原值	274.49	236.98	335.75	353.63	222.07	279.48
相对稀缺型资源—调整值（相对充裕型为参照）	243.32	228.98	346.16	357.67	219.62	281.99
相对充裕型资源—原值	231.51	187.85	258.79	313.19	220.29	255.00
相对充裕型资源—调整值（相对稀缺型为参照）	254.72	191.59	249.45	319.83	216.71	251.28
相对稀缺型与相对充裕型差值（相对稀缺型为参照）	19.77	45.39	86.30	33.80	5.36	28.20

续表

计算项目	庙岛群岛		舟山群岛		三亚及其附近岛屿	
	居民	游客	居民	游客	居民	游客
相对稀缺型与相对充裕型差值（相对充裕型为参照）	11.81	41.13	87.37	44.48	-0.67	26.99
$\Delta dr \overline{WTP}_{M-N}$（相对稀缺型与相对充裕型资源）	15.79	43.26	86.84	39.14	2.35	27.60

注：a. 庙岛群岛、舟山群岛和三亚及其附近岛屿相对稀缺型旅游资源分别为海洋地质遗迹、海洋文化和珊瑚礁，相对充裕型旅游资源为海滩；b. 原值为式（4-8）中的 $\overline{WTP}_M$ 或 $\overline{WTP}_N$；c. 调整值为式（4-9）或式（4-10）中的 $adj\overline{WTP}_{N-at-M}$ 或 $adj\overline{WTP}_{M-at-N}$；d. 差值为式（4-9）中的 $\overline{WTP}_M - adj\overline{WTP}_{N-at-M}$ 或 $adj\overline{WTP}_{M-at-N} - \overline{WTP}_N$。

表 4.14　不同案例地海洋相对稀缺型旅游资源之间比较结果

计算项目	居民	游客
庙岛群岛海洋地质遗迹——原值	274.49	236.98
庙岛群岛海洋地质遗迹——调整值（舟山群岛海洋文化参照）	301.72	269.25
庙岛群岛海洋地质遗迹——调整值（三亚及其附近岛屿珊瑚礁参照）	262.68	250.57
舟山群岛海洋文化——原值	335.75	353.63
舟山群岛海洋文化——调整值（庙岛群岛海洋地质遗迹参照）	299.78	301.08
舟山群岛海洋文化——调整值（三亚及其附近岛屿珊瑚礁参照）	310.48	324.98
三亚及其附近岛屿珊瑚礁——原值	222.07	279.48
三亚及其附近岛屿珊瑚礁——调整值（庙岛群岛海洋地质遗迹参照）	194.35	258.07
三亚及其附近岛屿珊瑚礁——调整值（舟山群岛海洋文化参照）	216.06	314.14
舟山群岛海洋文化与庙岛群岛海洋地质遗迹差值（舟山群岛海洋文化参照）	34.03	84.38
舟山群岛海洋文化与庙岛群岛海洋地质遗迹差值（庙岛群岛海洋地质遗迹参照）	25.29	64.10
舟山群岛海洋文化与三亚及其附近岛屿珊瑚礁差值（舟山群岛海洋文化参照）	119.69	39.49
舟山群岛海洋文化与三亚及其附近岛屿珊瑚礁差值（三亚及其附近岛屿珊瑚礁参照）	88.41	45.50
三亚及其附近岛屿珊瑚礁与庙岛群岛海洋地质遗迹差值（三亚及其附近岛屿珊瑚礁参照）	-40.61	28.91

续表

计算项目	居民	游客
三亚及其附近岛屿珊瑚礁与庙岛群岛海洋地质遗迹差值（庙岛群岛海洋地质遗迹参照）	-80.14	21.09
$\Delta dr\,\overline{WTP}_{M-N}$（舟山群岛海洋文化与庙岛群岛海洋地质遗迹）	29.66	74.24
$\Delta dr\,\overline{WTP}_{M-N}$（舟山群岛海洋文化与三亚及其附近岛屿珊瑚礁）	104.05	42.50
$\Delta dr\,\overline{WTP}_{M-N}$（三亚及其附近岛屿珊瑚礁与庙岛群岛海洋地质遗迹）	-60.38	25.00

注：原值、调整值和差值的含义同表 4.13 的备注。

表 4.15　不同案例地海洋相对充裕型旅游资源之间比较结果

计算项目	居民	游客
庙岛群岛海滩——原值	231.51	187.85
庙岛群岛海滩——调整值（舟山群岛海滩参照）	293.43	214.91
庙岛群岛海滩——调整值（三亚及其附近岛屿海滩参照）	257.54	202.19
舟山群岛海滩——原值	258.79	313.19
舟山群岛海滩——调整值（庙岛群岛海滩参照）	212.73	252.29
舟山群岛海滩——调整值（三亚及其附近岛屿海滩参照）	233.92	287.58
三亚及其附近岛屿海滩——原值	220.29	255.00
三亚及其附近岛屿海滩——调整值（庙岛群岛海滩参照）	176.71	222.62
三亚及其附近岛屿海滩——调整值（舟山群岛海滩参照）	220.68	273.32
舟山群岛海滩与庙岛群岛海滩差值（舟山群岛海滩参照）	-34.64	98.28
舟山群岛海滩与庙岛群岛海滩差值（庙岛群岛海滩参照）	-18.78	64.44
舟山群岛海滩与三亚及其附近岛屿海滩差值（舟山群岛海滩参照）	38.11	39.87
舟山群岛海滩与三亚及其附近岛屿海滩差值（三亚及其附近岛屿海滩参照）	13.63	32.58
三亚及其附近岛屿海滩与庙岛群岛海滩差值（三亚及其附近岛屿海滩参照）	-37.25	52.81
三亚及其附近岛屿海滩与庙岛群岛海滩差值（庙岛群岛海滩参照）	-54.80	34.77
$\Delta dr\,\overline{WTP}_{M-N}$（舟山群岛海滩与庙岛群岛海滩）	-26.71	81.36
$\Delta dr\,\overline{WTP}_{M-N}$（舟山群岛海滩与三亚及其附近岛屿海滩）	25.87	36.23
$\Delta dr\,\overline{WTP}_{M-N}$（三亚及其附近岛屿海滩与庙岛群岛海滩）	-46.03	43.79

注：原值、调整值和差值的含义同表 4.13 的备注。

表 4.16　不同案例地或同一案例地海洋人文与自然旅游资源比较结果

计算项目	居民	游客
舟山群岛海洋文化——原值	335.75	353.63
舟山群岛海洋文化——调整值（庙岛群岛海滩参照）	275.05	291.48
舟山群岛海洋文化——调整值（庙岛群岛海洋地质遗迹参照）	299.78	301.08
舟山群岛海洋文化——调整值（舟山群岛海滩参照）	346.16	357.67
舟山群岛海洋文化——调整值（三亚及其附近岛屿海滩参照）	300.66	325.73
舟山群岛海洋文化——调整值（三亚及其附近岛屿珊瑚礁参照）	310.48	324.98
庙岛群岛海滩——原值	231.51	187.85
庙岛群岛海滩——调整值（舟山群岛海洋文化参照）	279.61	212.07
庙岛群岛海洋地质遗迹——原值	274.49	236.98
庙岛群岛海洋地质遗迹——调整值（舟山群岛海洋文化参照）	301.72	269.25
舟山群岛海滩——原值	258.79	313.19
舟山群岛海滩——调整值（舟山群岛海洋文化参照）	249.45	319.83
三亚及其附近岛屿海滩——原值	220.29	255.00
三亚及其附近岛屿海滩——调整值（舟山群岛海洋文化参照）	211.55	275.81
三亚及其附近岛屿珊瑚礁——原值	222.07	279.48
三亚及其附近岛屿珊瑚礁——调整值（舟山群岛海洋文化参照）	216.06	314.14
舟山群岛海洋文化与庙岛群岛海滩差值（舟山群岛海洋文化参照）	56.14	141.56
舟山群岛海洋文化与庙岛群岛海滩差值（庙岛群岛海滩参照）	43.54	103.63
舟山群岛海洋文化与庙岛群岛海洋地质遗迹差值（舟山群岛海洋文化参照）	34.03	84.38
舟山群岛海洋文化与庙岛群岛海洋地质遗迹差值（庙岛群岛海洋地质遗迹参照）	25.29	64.10
舟山群岛海洋文化与舟山群岛海滩差值（舟山群岛海洋文化参照）	86.30	33.80
舟山群岛海洋文化与舟山群岛海滩差值（舟山群岛海滩参照）	87.37	44.48
舟山群岛海洋文化与三亚及其附近岛屿海滩差值（舟山群岛海洋文化参照）	124.20	77.82
舟山群岛海洋文化与三亚及其附近岛屿海滩差值（三亚及其附近岛屿海滩参照）	80.37	70.73
舟山群岛海洋文化与三亚及其附近岛屿珊瑚礁差值（舟山群岛海洋文化参照）	119.69	39.49
舟山群岛海洋文化与三亚及其附近岛屿珊瑚礁差值（三亚及其附近岛屿珊瑚礁参照）	88.41	45.50

续表

计算项目	居民	游客
$\Delta dr\,\overline{WTP}_{M-N}$（舟山群岛海洋文化与庙岛群岛海滩）	49.84	122.60
$\Delta dr\,\overline{WTP}_{M-N}$（舟山群岛海洋文化与庙岛群岛海洋地质遗迹）	29.66	74.24
$\Delta dr\,\overline{WTP}_{M-N}$（舟山群岛海洋文化与舟山群岛海滩）	86.84	39.14
$\Delta dr\,\overline{WTP}_{M-N}$（舟山群岛海洋文化与三亚及其附近岛屿海滩）	102.29	74.28
$\Delta dr\,\overline{WTP}_{M-N}$（舟山群岛海洋文化与三亚及其附近岛屿珊瑚礁）	104.05	42.50

注：原值、调整值和差值的含义同表4.13的备注。

三 结果稳健性分析

同一案例地两种资源之间比较时，庙岛群岛、舟山群岛和三亚及其附近岛屿三个案例地均表现出：海洋相对稀缺型旅游资源（海洋地质遗迹、海洋文化或珊瑚礁）的居民（或游客）平均 WTP 大于海洋相对充裕型旅游资源（海滩）。庙岛群岛、舟山群岛和三亚及其附近岛屿三个案例地相互独立，评估结果互相验证；同时，这一结果与公众偏向于把保护资金分配给可爱的和有魅力的物种的研究结论[1]较为相似（见表4.13）。

不同案例地海洋相对充裕型旅游资源之间比较时，游客平均 WTP 表现出：舟山群岛海滩＞三亚及其附近岛屿海滩＞庙岛群岛海滩。这一评估结果与三个案例地待估海滩长度之和长短排序完全一致：舟山群岛待估海滩（长度之和约12千米）＞三亚及其附近岛屿待估海滩（长度之和约10千米）＞庙岛群岛待估海滩（长度之和约3千米）；不仅如此，该评估结果与 Castaño – Isaza 等关于海滩旅游资源的研究结论相似（见表4.15）。[2]

不同案例地海洋相对稀缺型旅游资源之间、不同案例地或同一案例

---

[1] Adriana Ressurreição, et al., "Economic Valuation of Species Loss in the Open Sea", *Ecological Economics*, Vol. 70, No. 4, February 2011; P. C. Boxall, et al., "Analysis of the Economic Benefits Associated with the Recovery of Threatened Marine Mammal Species in the Canadian St. Lawrence Estuary", *Marine Policy*, Vol. 36, No. 1, January 2012.

[2] Juliana Castaño – Isaza, et al., "Valuing Beaches to Develop Payment for Ecosystem Services Schemes in Colombia's Seaflower Marine Protected Area", *Ecosystem Services*, Vol. 11, February 2015.

地海洋人文旅游资源与自然旅游资源比较均表现出，海洋文化旅游资源的居民（或游客）平均 WTP 大于珊瑚礁旅游资源和海洋地质遗迹旅游资源的居民（或游客）平均 WTP；海洋人文旅游资源的平均 WTP 大于海洋自然旅游资源的平均 WTP。居民和游客受访者相互独立，评估结果互相验证（见表4.14、表4.16）。

庙岛群岛属于小岛屿案例地，庙岛群岛居民受访者与待估旅游资源分布范围均较小。居民受访者分布在景区周边区域，与待估旅游资源联系紧密，庙岛群岛居民平均 WTP 较高。[①] 庙岛群岛居民对海滩和海洋地质遗迹的平均 WTP 均大于游客（见表4.12）；不同案例地相对稀缺型（或充裕型）旅游资源之间比较，庙岛群岛居民受访者则表现出与其游客受访者不一致的评估结果：庙岛群岛海洋地质遗迹居民平均 WTP 大于三亚及其附近岛屿珊瑚礁居民平均 WTP（见表4.14）；庙岛群岛海滩居民平均 WTP 大于舟山群岛海滩、三亚及其附近岛屿海滩的居民平均 WTP（见表4.15）。舟山群岛和三亚及其附近岛屿居民受访者的分布范围远大于待估旅游资源的分布范围，居民受访者居住在景区之外更大范围的区域，舟山群岛和三亚及其附近岛屿居民受访者并未表现出像庙岛群岛居民受访者一样相对较高的平均 WTP（依据舟山群岛新区统计信息网和三亚市统计局网站资料可知，浙江舟山常住人口为116万人、海南三亚常住人口为76.42万人，舟山群岛和三亚及其附近岛屿居民样本可选择的抽样范围较大）。舟山群岛居民受访者对海滩和海洋文化、三亚及其附近岛屿居民受访者对海滩和珊瑚礁的平均 WTP 均分别低于其游客受访者对两种资源的平均 WTP（见表4.12）；不同案例地相对稀缺型（或充裕型）旅游资源之间比较时，舟山群岛和三亚及其附近岛屿居民受访者均表现出与其游客受访者一致的评估结果：舟山群岛海洋文化居民平均 WTP 大于三亚及其附近岛屿珊瑚礁居民平均 WTP（见表4.14）；舟山群岛海滩居民平均 WTP 大于三亚及其附近岛屿海滩居民平均 WTP（见表4.15）。像庙岛群岛这样陆地面积比较小、人口比较少的小岛屿案例地，当地海岛居民世代对海洋资源的依赖性较强，所以，庙

[①] R. Brouwer, et al., "Public Willingness to Pay for Alternative Management Regimes of Remote Marine Protected Areas in the North Sea", *Marine Policy*, Vol. 68, June 2016.

岛群岛居民表现出对保护本岛海滩旅游资源和海洋地质遗迹旅游资源非使用价值的 WTP 较高（依据长岛县人民政府网站和《长岛县统计年鉴》（未公开出版）资料可知，庙岛群岛总人口为 4.25 万人，居民样本抽样选择的南长山岛和北长山岛总人口为 2.49 万人）。研究认为，这是一种正常现象而并不属于 CVM 中的策略性偏差（Strategic Bias）。该结论与 O'Garra 关于对低收入国家斐济维提岛的研究较一致，正因当地居民对资源使用存在较高依赖性和较强的管理意识，愿意将本地资源遗赠给后代，使得当地居民对保护维提岛纳瓦卡夫社区附近海洋资源非使用价值（遗赠价值）表现出较高的支付意愿。[1]

第四节　估值比较 I 结论

公众对保护海洋旅游资源非使用价值的意愿非常强，有 96.92% 的受访者具有正 WTP；受访者对各海洋旅游资源非使用价值的平均 WTP 处于 187.85—353.63 元。此外，不同类型海洋旅游资源非使用价值的 WTP 表现出明显的差异性，一方面，公众对保护海洋相对稀缺型旅游资源（海洋地质遗迹、海洋文化或珊瑚礁）的平均 WTP 高于对保护海洋相对充裕型旅游资源（海滩）的平均 WTP。相比海滩，海洋地质遗迹、海洋文化和珊瑚礁较为独特，具有明显的区域异质性，公众对较为独特的资源具有更高的支付意愿。[2] 另一方面，公众对保护海洋文化旅游资源的平均 WTP 高于对保护海洋自然旅游资源（海滩、海洋地质遗迹、珊瑚礁）的平均 WTP。相比海洋自然旅游资源，海洋文化旅游资源具有独特的历史文化价值，这与公众重视对子孙后代的文化传承以确

---

[1] Tanya O'Garra, "Bequest Values for Marine Resources: How Important for Indigenous Communities in Less-developed Economies?", *Environmental and Resource Economics*, Vol. 44, No. 2, October 2009.

[2] Allan Provins, et al., "Valuation of the Historic Environment: The Scope for Using Economic Valuation Evidence in the Appraisal of Heritage-related Projects", *Progress in Planning*, Vol. 69, No. 4, May 2008.

保社会文化的可持续性有关。①

评估结果表明，公众不但能够感知到海洋旅游资源非使用价值的存在，而且还能够识别出不同类型的海洋旅游资源具有不同非使用价值，这不仅为海洋旅游资源非使用价值在我国的存在提供了实验证据，也为包含非使用价值的海洋旅游资源保护或恢复工程成本—收益分析在中国的应用起到推进作用，只有将海洋旅游资源非使用价值纳入到成本—收益分析中，才能在对保护或恢复工程进行合理分析的基础上制定针对性保护政策。

---

① Kirsten L. L. Oleson, et al., "Cultural Bequest Values for Ecosystem Service Flows among Indigenous Fishers: A Discrete Choice Experiment Validated with Mixed Methods", *Ecological Economics*, Vol. 114, June 2015.

第五章

群岛旅游资源非使用价值估值比较 II

第一节 估值比较 II WTP 计算公式

本书研究运用 OLS 和 IR 计算受访者 WTP 公式为:

$$\ln WTP_i = \alpha + \beta_1 sex_i + \beta_2 age_i + \beta_3 ages_i + \beta_4 edu_i + \beta_5 \ln inc_i + \beta_6 region1_i + \beta_7 region2_i + \beta_8 region3_i \qquad (5-1)$$

式 (5-1) 中,α 为常数项;$\beta_j (j=1,2,3,4,5,6,7,8)$ 为回归系数;其他变量含义如表 5.1 所示。

表 5.1　　　　　　　　　解释变量

变量	赋值
sex 为性别,虚拟变量	男 = 1,女 = 0
age 为年龄	2017 减去出生年
$ages$ 为年龄平方项	除以 100
edu 为学历水平,虚拟变量	受过高等教育(大专、本科、研究生)= 1,未受过高等教育(初中及以下、高中、中专、技校)= 0
$lninc$ 为家庭年收入自然对数	家庭年收入选取各个收入区间中点值

续表

变量	赋值
region 为客源地，region 1、region 2 和 region 3 分别为短途客源地、中途客源地和长途客源地，虚拟变量，居民为参照组	短途客源地游客 = 1，其他 = 0
	中途客源地游客 = 1，其他 = 0
	长途客源地游客 = 1，其他 = 0

注：庙岛群岛短途客源地为山东，中途客源地为北京、天津和河北，长途客源地为大陆其他省（市、区）；舟山群岛短途客源地为浙江，中途客源地为上海、江苏和安徽，长途客源地为大陆其他省（市、区）；三亚及其附近岛屿短途客源地为海南、广东、广西、湖南、贵州、云南、福建、江西，中途客源地为四川、重庆、湖北、安徽、浙江、上海、江苏，长途客源地为大陆其他省（市、区）。

第二节　估值比较 II 描述性统计分析

一　样本量

调查共获得有效问卷 6492 份，其中包含真零支付问卷 124 份，抗议性零支付问卷 66 份。庙岛群岛共获得有效问卷 1679 份，其中包含真零支付问卷 20 份和抗议性零支付问卷 16 份；舟山群岛共获得有效问卷 2089 份，其中包含真零支付问卷 65 份和抗议性零支付问卷 30 份；三亚及其附近岛屿共获得有效问卷 2724 份，其中包含真零支付问卷 39 份和抗议性零支付问卷 20 份。本书研究分析中剔除了 66 份抗议性零支付反应样本，包含了 124 份真零支付样本，分析样本总计 6426 份。

二　受访者人口社会特征

庙岛群岛、舟山群岛和三亚及其附近岛屿三个案例地海滩、海洋地质遗迹、海洋文化、珊瑚礁等各组样本受访者的人口社会特征如表 5.2 所示。本书研究运用 Mann – Whitney U 检验方法，进行两组海洋旅游资源样本之间受访者人口社会特征差异显著性检验；运用 Kruskal – Wallis 检验方法，进行三组海洋旅游资源样本之间受访者人口社会特征差异显著性检验。各组样本之间的差异显著性检验结果如表 5.3 所示。

表 5.2　　　　　　　　　　样本人口社会特征均值

案例地	资源类型	样本量	性别	年龄(岁)	学历	家庭年收入(万元)	居民比例(%)	短途游客比例(%)	中途游客比例(%)	长途游客比例(%)
黄渤海区—庙岛群岛	海滩	671	0.47	39	0.51	11.89	28.91	26.83	22.21	22.06
	海洋地质遗迹	992	0.48	38	0.58	12.70	28.13	24.50	23.99	23.39
东海区—舟山群岛	海滩	1195	0.51	37	0.47	13.79	45.02	21.09	17.91	15.98
	海洋文化	864	0.50	37	0.47	13.92	42.94	20.72	18.87	17.48
南海区—三亚及其附近岛屿	海滩	1364	0.49	34	0.60	13.15	30.06	26.17	18.62	25.15
	珊瑚礁	1340	0.57	33	0.66	13.86	29.33	23.88	22.46	24.33

表 5.3　　　　　样本组间人口社会特征差异显著性检验

比较内容	性别	年龄	学历	收入
庙岛群岛海滩与庙岛群岛海洋地质遗迹	-0.30	-1.62	-3.02***	-0.88
舟山群岛海滩与舟山群岛海洋文化	-0.67	-0.52	-0.27	-0.39
三亚及其附近岛屿海滩与三亚及其附近岛屿珊瑚礁	-3.88***	-1.84*	-3.47***	-2.70***
庙岛群岛海滩、舟山群岛海滩与三亚及其附近岛屿海滩	3.10	112.13***	45.73***	30.50***
庙岛群岛海洋地质遗迹、舟山群岛海洋文化与三亚及其附近岛屿珊瑚礁	19.50***	157.92***	78.05***	12.78***

注：Mann - Whitney U 检验为 Z 值；Kruskal - Wallis 检验为卡方值；*$p<0.1$，**$p<0.05$，***$p<0.01$。

三　受访者 WTP 分布

庙岛群岛海滩和海洋地质遗迹受访者的正支付意愿率分别为 98.70% 和 98.90%，受访者选择投标值 200 元及以下的比例分别为 87.60% 和 84.70%；舟山群岛海滩和海洋文化受访者的正支付意愿率分别为 96.70% 和 97.10%，受访者选择投标值 200 元及以下的比例分别为 84.40% 和 79.10%；三亚及其附近岛屿海滩和珊瑚礁受访者的正支付意愿率分别为 98.40% 和 98.70%，受访者选择投标值 200 元及以下的比例分别为 85.20% 和 84.90%（见表 5.4）。同时，三个案例地受访者选择 10 元、50 元、100 元和 200 元投标值的均较多（见表 5.4）。

表5.4　　　　　　三个案例地区间投标值累计百分比　　　　单位:%

区间投标值（元）	庙岛群岛		舟山群岛		三亚及其附近岛屿	
	MD 海滩	MD 海洋地质遗迹	ZS 海滩	ZS 海洋文化	SY 海滩	SY 珊瑚礁
0—1	1.30	1.10	3.30	2.90	1.60	1.30
1—2	3.60	2.30	4.80	3.90	3.30	2.90
2—5	4.90	2.90	5.20	4.60	4.30	3.50
5—10	7.90	5.40	7.50	6.70	7.00	6.10
10—20	22.80	15.50	17.70	13.90	18.20	15.00
20—30	28.90	20.80	24.40	20.30	25.90	22.20
30—50	32.20	22.70	26.60	22.80	28.70	24.30
50—60	46.80	35.60	39.10	33.00	42.60	38.70
60—80	47.50	36.40	39.70	33.10	42.80	39.00
80—100	48.30	37.00	40.10	33.60	43.30	39.50
100—120	79.00	73.90	71.60	62.70	74.10	71.00
120—150	79.10	73.90	71.80	63.30	74.50	71.30
150—200	79.40	74.20	73.30	64.20	75.40	72.00
200—300	87.60	84.70	84.40	79.10	85.20	84.90
300—400	89.30	87.40	87.90	83.70	87.20	87.40
400—500	89.60	87.50	87.90	83.90	87.20	87.40
500—600	94.90	92.20	93.50	92.20	93.30	92.90
600—800	95.50	93.20	94.20	93.40	94.20	93.70
800—1000	96.70	93.60	94.80	94.30	94.90	94.30
1000—1500	99.10	98.70	98.10	99.10	98.80	98.50
1500—2000	99.10	98.70	98.40	99.10	98.80	98.70
2000—2001	100.00	100.00	100.00	100.00	100.00	100.00

四 异方差和多重共线性检验

运用怀特检验（White Test）和方差膨胀因子（Variance Inflation Factor, VIF）考察数据异方差和多重共线性问题。对庙岛群岛海滩、庙岛群岛海洋地质遗迹、舟山群岛海滩、舟山群岛海洋文化、三亚及其附近岛屿海滩和三亚及其附近岛屿珊瑚礁的居民和游客合并数据进行异方差检验，P值均等于0.00，强烈拒绝同方差的原假设，这六组样本数据存在异方差（见表5.5），故采用稳健标准误。对庙岛群岛海滩、庙岛群岛海洋地质遗迹、舟山群岛海滩、舟山群岛海洋文化、三亚及其附近岛屿海滩和三亚及其附近岛屿珊瑚礁的居民和游客合并数据进行多重共线性检验，年龄和年龄的平方项的VIF值大于10，存在共线性；其他解释变量的VIF值均远小于10，不存在多重共线性（见表5.6）。

表 5.5　　　　　　　　　异方差检验

案例地	资源类型	Source	Chi2	df	P
庙岛群岛	海滩	heteroskedasticity	68.56	23	0.00
	海洋地质遗迹	heteroskedasticity	119.66	23	0.00
舟山群岛	海滩	heteroskedasticity	204.71	23	0.00
	海洋文化	heteroskedasticity	70.47	23	0.00
三亚及其附近岛屿	海滩	heteroskedasticity	103.44	23	0.00
	珊瑚礁	heteroskedasticity	193.12	23	0.00

表 5.6　　　　　　　　　多重共线性检验

庙岛群岛海滩			庙岛群岛海洋地质遗迹		
变量	VIF	1/VIF	变量	VIF	1/VIF
age	47.31	0.02	age	43.88	0.02
ages	46.47	0.02	ages	42.84	0.02
edu	1.30	0.77	edu	1.40	0.72
resp	1.29	0.78	resp	1.38	0.72
inc	1.05	0.96	inc	1.06	0.94
sex	1.02	0.98	sex	1.01	0.99
Mean VIF	16.40	—	Mean VIF	15.26	—

续表

舟山群岛海滩			舟山群岛海洋文化		
变量	VIF	1/VIF	变量	VIF	1/VIF
age	45.66	0.02	age	45.93	0.02
ages	45.64	0.02	ages	45.46	0.02
edu	1.32	0.76	edu	1.29	0.77
resp	1.20	0.84	resp	1.26	0.79
inc	1.10	0.91	inc	1.08	0.93
sex	1.04	0.96	sex	1.03	0.97
Mean VIF	15.99	—	Mean VIF	16.01	—

三亚及其附近岛屿海滩			三亚及其附近岛屿珊瑚礁		
变量	VIF	1/VIF	变量	VIF	1/VIF
age	40.80	0.02	age	42.18	0.02
ages	40.31	0.02	ages	42.13	0.02
edu	1.38	0.73	edu	1.24	0.80
resp	1.29	0.78	resp	1.22	0.82
inc	1.07	0.94	inc	1.07	0.94
sex	1.03	0.98	sex	1.02	0.98
Mean VIF	14.31	—	Mean VIF	14.81	—

五　WTP 与人口社会特征分位数回归

WTP 与人口社会特征分位数回归各变量定义如表 5.7 所示。

表 5.7　　　　　　　　分位数回归各变量定义

变量类型	变量	定义
因变量	WTP	支付意愿区间中点值
自变量	Sex	性别：男 = 1，女 = 0
	Age	年龄：受访者 2017 年的年龄（单位：岁）
	Ages	年龄的平方项除以 100
	Edu	学历：受过高等教育 = 1，未受过高等教育 = 0
	Inc	收入：受访者 2016 年的年收入区间中点值（单位：万元）
	Resp	受访者类型：游客 = 1，居民 = 0

对庙岛群岛海滩、庙岛群岛海洋地质遗迹、舟山群岛海滩、舟山群岛海洋文化、三亚及其附近岛屿海滩和三亚及其附近岛屿珊瑚礁的居民和游客样本数据分别进行分位数回归，分位数回归模型选取25%、50%、75%和90%四个分位点进行分位数回归（见表5.8至表5.10），根据各分位数回归结果可以发现不同分位点条件下受访者WTP与各人口社会特征之间的关系（见图5.1至图5.6）。从总体来看，各案例地各类资源分位数回归最典型的规律为：收入变量的回归系数在多个分位数回归模型中都呈现出统计显著性，且除个别分位点外，收入变量回归系数均为正值，说明受访者的WTP与收入成正比，收入越高的受访者WTP越高。根据分位数回归系数图可以看出（见图5.1至图5.6），收入变量的回归系数随着分位点的升高呈现递增趋势，表明收入变化对WTP较高的受访者影响更大。

表5.8　　　　　　　　　　庙岛群岛分位数回归结果

变量	海滩				海洋地质遗迹			
	QR_25	QR_50	QR_75	QR_90	QR_25	QR_50	QR_75	QR_90
Sex	0.00	8.98	11.01	20.43	-2.64	-0.00	22.66	221.78**
	(5.09)	(14.00)	(14.99)	(75.80)	(5.51)	(3.67)	(19.82)	(90.38)
Age	-0.00	-2.19	-13.73	-70.56*	2.48	-0.00	-0.80	3.21
	(2.10)	(4.42)	(8.88)	(37.16)	(1.56)	(1.87)	(5.08)	(18.96)
Ages	0.00	1.51	15.69	88.21*	-3.91**	0.00	-0.43	-4.96
	(2.36)	(5.44)	(10.66)	(48.19)	(1.85)	(2.58)	(6.17)	(23.04)
Edu	10.00	18.54	-12.18	57.34	24.14***	0.00	14.47	27.82
	(6.98)	(17.09)	(20.04)	(82.93)	(7.79)	(8.60)	(19.38)	(71.94)
Inc	0.00	1.08	8.65***	32.91***	1.32**	-0.00	14.69***	34.36***
	(0.55)	(1.58)	(2.51)	(8.75)	(0.56)	(1.32)	(3.05)	(10.13)
Resp	-10.00	-20.46	-19.66	-26.63	-36.93***	-0.00	-45.51**	-199.19
	(6.51)	(15.78)	(24.48)	(78.42)	(8.20)	(11.81)	(20.55)	(130.25)
Intercept	25.00	139.10*	359.25**	1375.58*	16.75	110.00***	94.66	112.89
	(46.36)	(77.28)	(179.29)	(720.88)	(35.97)	(39.20)	(98.61)	(393.42)
N	671	671	671	671	992	992	992	992
Pseudo R^2	0.00	0.00	0.03	0.10	0.02	0.00	0.08	0.16

注：括号内为自助法500次计算的标准误；$*p<0.1$，$**p<0.05$，$***p<0.01$。

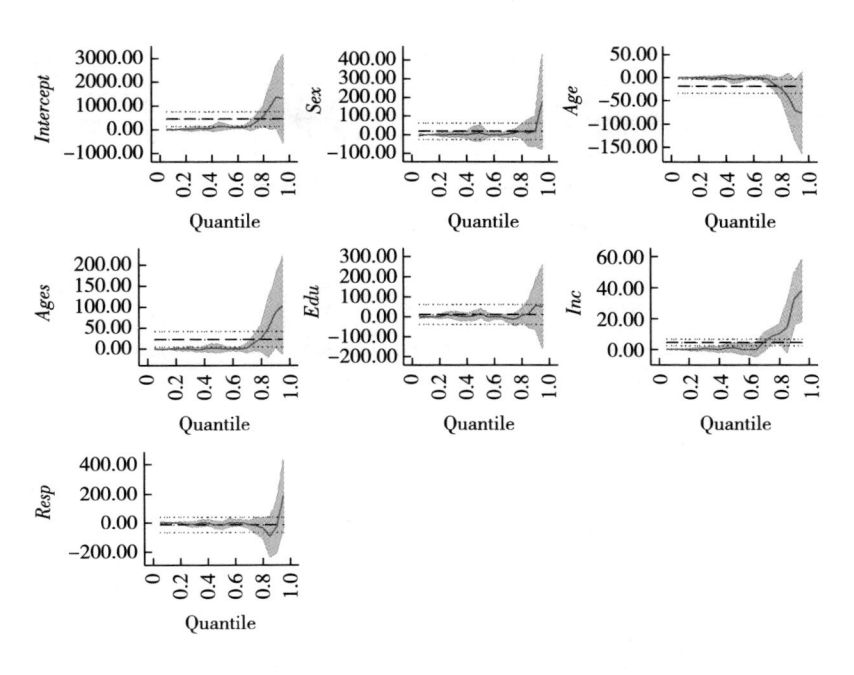

图 5.1 庙岛群岛海滩分位数回归系数

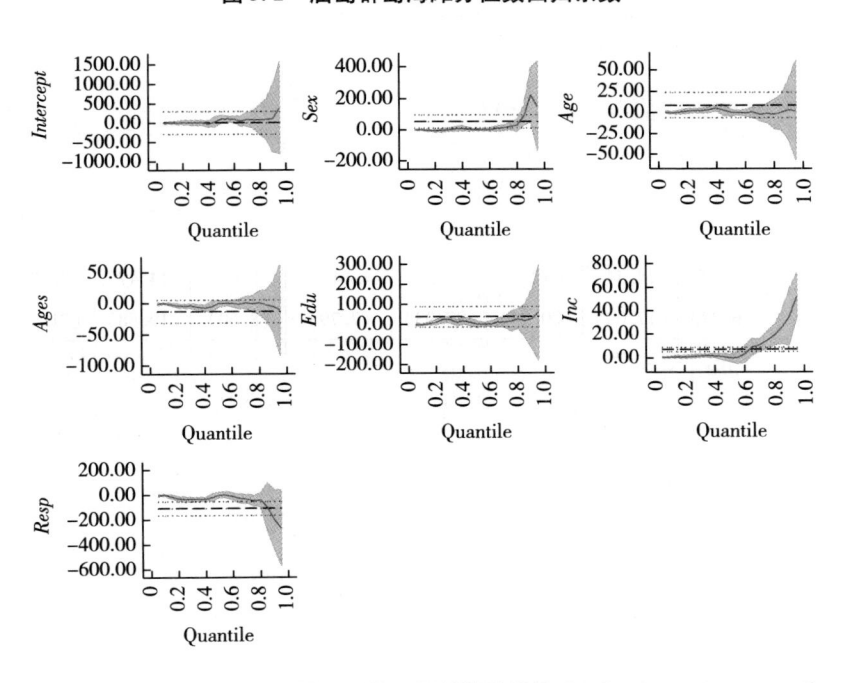

图 5.2 庙岛群岛海洋地质遗迹分位数回归系数

表 5.9　　　　　　　　舟山群岛分位数回归结果

变量	海滩				海洋文化			
	QR_25	QR_50	QR_75	QR_90	QR_25	QR_50	QR_75	QR_90
Sex	5.07	4.63	16.67	25.01	-4.46	0.03	32.10	108.37
	(4.86)	(7.59)	(17.01)	(45.32)	(8.05)	(9.20)	(23.08)	(68.73)
Age	1.93	-2.07	-3.07	-27.15	-0.82	-3.45	-11.85	-13.21
	(1.30)	(2.71)	(4.55)	(20.04)	(2.67)	(3.12)	(10.13)	(20.28)
$Ages$	-2.39	2.41	3.63	40.72	0.61	4.08	14.33	15.47
	(1.67)	(3.36)	(5.87)	(27.96)	(3.39)	(4.16)	(12.44)	(26.51)
Edu	5.92	9.91	5.54	32.21	5.96	7.17	13.96	143.70
	(7.21)	(9.68)	(21.48)	(48.78)	(10.79)	(10.21)	(28.37)	(91.72)
Inc	3.10***	6.21***	18.15***	38.75***	2.56***	5.52**	17.86***	29.00***
	(0.60)	(1.93)	(2.22)	(3.64)	(0.85)	(2.46)	(1.52)	(5.75)
$Resp$	1.84	0.18	-21.31	-24.61	10.36	0.56	-30.64	-135.75*
	(5.50)	(8.88)	(21.03)	(42.18)	(8.13)	(9.68)	(26.00)	(75.20)
$Intercept$	-35.97	58.84	67.92	387.92	35.04	121.63**	271.62	396.68
	(23.45)	(48.85)	(77.13)	(354.28)	(51.17)	(53.57)	(197.14)	(364.50)
N	1195	1195	1195	1195	864	864	864	864
$Pseudo\ R^2$	0.04	0.03	0.14	0.25	0.02	0.02	0.11	0.13

注：括号内为自助法 500 次计算的标准误；$*p<0.1$，$**p<0.05$，$***p<0.01$。

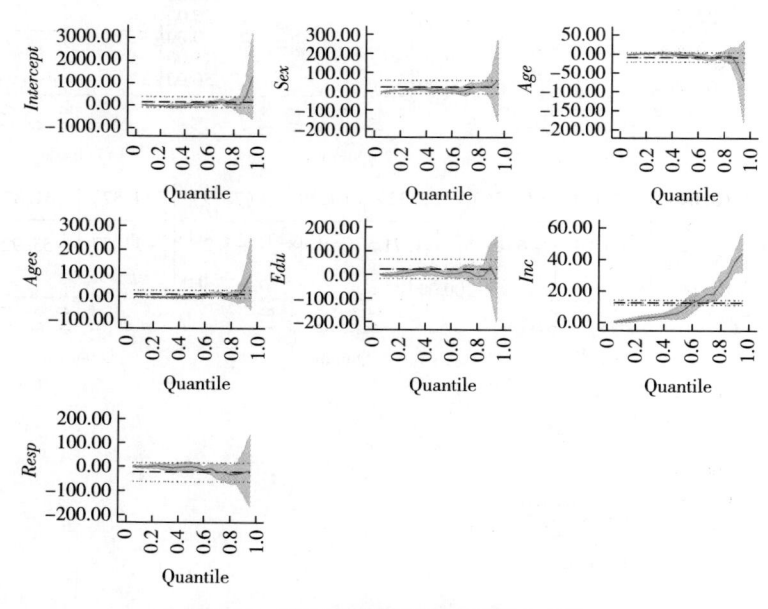

图 5.3　舟山群岛海滩分位数回归系数

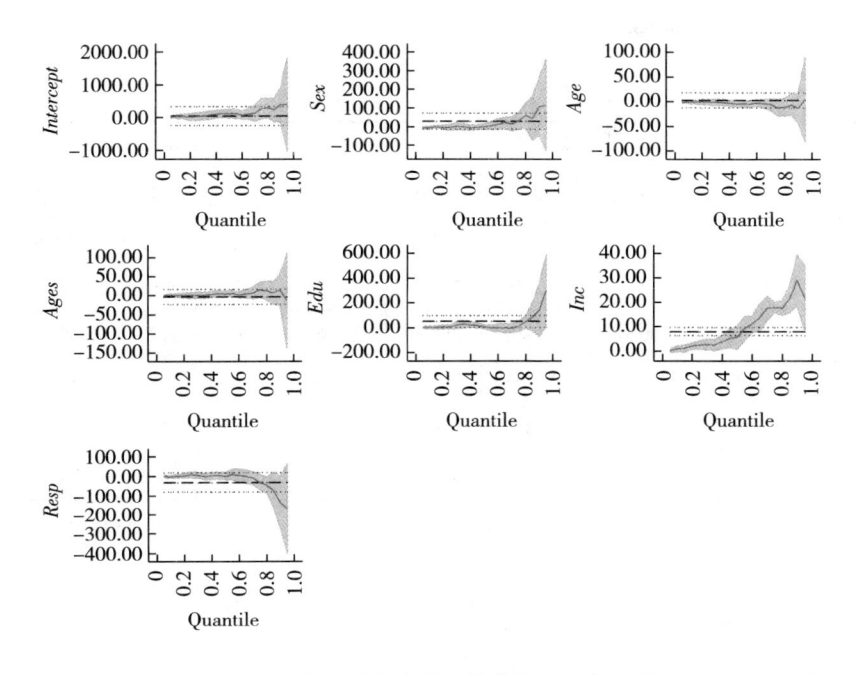

图 5.4　舟山群岛海洋文化分位数回归系数

表 5.10　三亚及其附近岛屿分位数回归结果

变量	海滩				珊瑚礁			
	QR_25	QR_50	QR_75	QR_90	QR_25	QR_50	QR_75	QR_90
Sex	−2.82	2.74	1.23	30.45	5.22	9.93	17.66	15.72
	(3.64)	(7.43)	(11.56)	(52.32)	(4.49)	(7.99)	(14.87)	(41.87)
Age	−0.01	−3.04	−6.19*	−1.71	−0.48	−3.25	−11.57	−55.92*
	(1.09)	(2.67)	(3.46)	(14.16)	(1.76)	(2.98)	(9.01)	(30.27)
Ages	−0.45	2.33	7.16*	−1.94	0.24	4.23	15.03	78.54*
	(1.31)	(3.51)	(4.33)	(17.67)	(2.30)	(4.15)	(12.72)	(46.81)
Edu	4.94	11.43	2.68	4.26	14.15*	17.14*	7.59	−51.88
	(4.63)	(10.10)	(12.44)	(66.00)	(7.46)	(9.24)	(18.36)	(51.47)
Inc	2.64***	6.11***	15.66***	28.89***	2.28***	6.38***	17.66***	31.33***
	(0.62)	(1.33)	(1.87)	(3.36)	(0.72)	(1.60)	(3.20)	(4.43)

续表

变量	海滩				珊瑚礁			
	QR_25	QR_50	QR_75	QR_90	QR_25	QR_50	QR_75	QR_90
Resp	2.35	-3.77	-9.70	-15.44	-3.68	-28.95***	-19.08	29.62
	(3.54)	(8.74)	(12.58)	(71.89)	(5.32)	(8.73)	(16.95)	(46.54)
Intercept	11.52	90.05*	146.86**	159.80	23.08	88.32*	217.19	1020.94**
	(22.45)	(46.55)	(59.38)	(262.71)	(31.58)	(49.39)	(150.32)	(463.25)
N	1364	1364	1364	1364	1340	1340	1340	1340
Pseudo R²	0.04	0.04	0.14	0.17	0.04	0.03	0.12	0.21

注：括号内为自助法 500 次计算的标准误；*$p<0.1$，**$p<0.05$，***$p<0.01$。

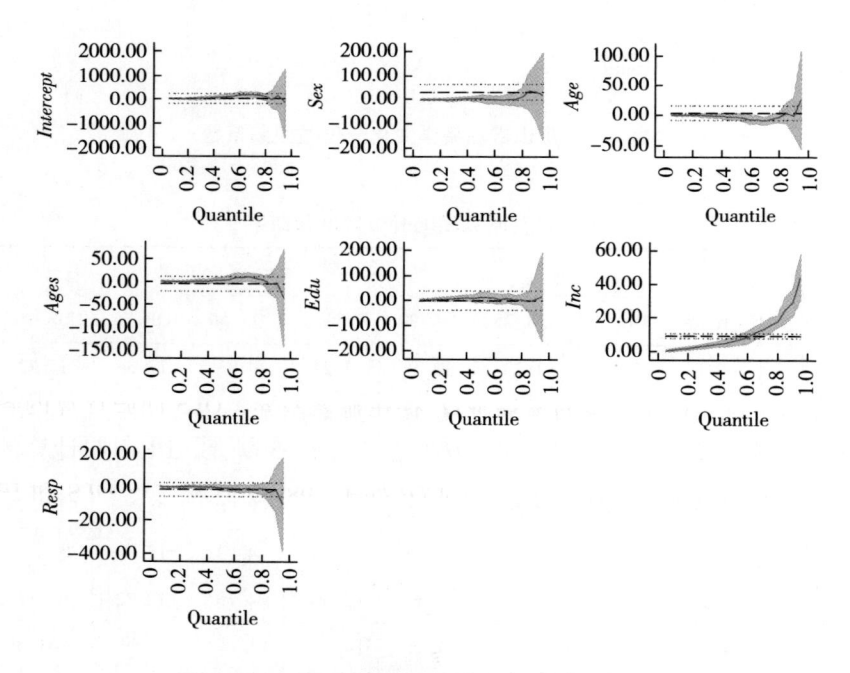

图 5.5　三亚及其附近岛屿海滩分位数回归系数

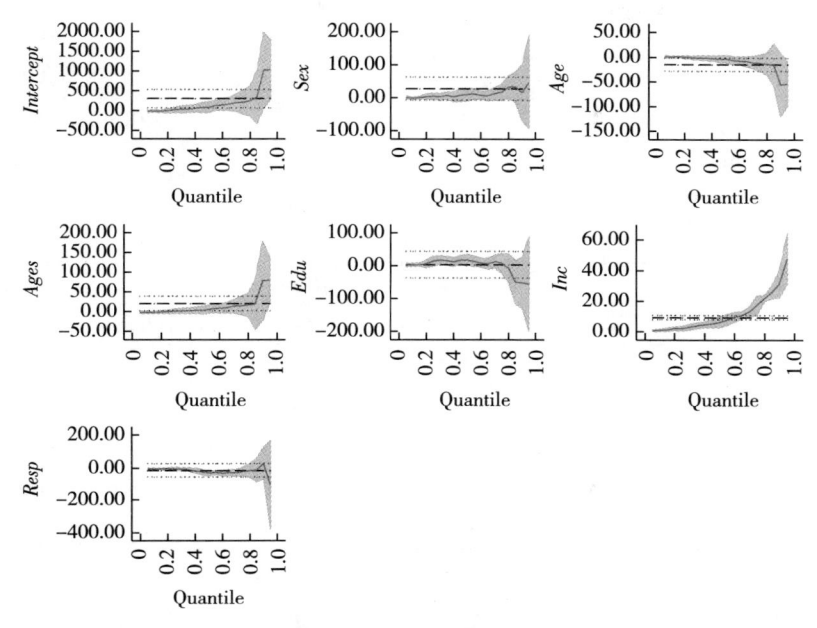

图 5.6　三亚及其附近岛屿珊瑚礁分位数回归系数

第三节　估值比较Ⅱ结果分析

一　OLS 和 IR 回归结果

OLS 和 IR 回归结果表明（见表 5.11 至表 5.13），受访者对各种海洋旅游资源非使用价值的平均 WTP 存在显著差异，OLS 回归计算的各海洋旅游资源非使用价值平均 WTP 处于 205—369 元，IR 回归计算的各海洋旅游资源非使用价值平均 WTP 处于 198—350 元。将 OLS 和 IR 两种回归计算结果取均值得出，各海洋旅游资源非使用价值平均 WTP 处于 201—359 元（本书研究取两种回归结果的均值进行分析）。

表 5.11　　　　　　　　庙岛群岛回归结果

变量	海滩		变量	海洋地质遗迹	
	OLS	IR		OLS	IR
Sex	0.03	0.03	Sex	0.04	0.04
Age	−0.06	−0.06	Age	0.02	0.02

续表

变量	海滩		变量	海洋地质遗迹	
	OLS	IR		OLS	IR
Ages	0.06	0.06	*Ages*	-0.03	-0.03
Edu	0.05	0.05	*Edu*	0.06	0.06
Lninc	0.56***	0.57***	*Lninc*	0.82***	0.82***
*Region*1	-0.13	-0.14	*Region*1	-0.25*	-0.25*
*Region*2	-0.12	-0.13	*Region*2	-0.60***	-0.60***
*Region*3	-0.26	-0.26	*Region*3	-0.46***	-0.46***
Constant	-0.91	-0.93	*Constant*	-5.02***	-4.99***
Sigma	1.47	1.46	*Sigma*	1.34	1.32
N	671	671	*N*	992	992
$R^2/Log\ pseudolikelihood$	0.05	-2047.19	$R^2/Log\ pseudolikelihood$	0.13	-3033.40
$F/Wald\ \chi^2$	3.01	24.41	$F/Wald\ \chi^2$	17.17	138.92
$Prob>F/Prob>\chi^2$	0.00	0.00	$Prob>F/Prob>\chi^2$	0.00	0.00
Median	69.46	68.79	*Median*	104.31	103.48
Mean	204.56	198.12	*Mean*	255.41	246.94
Median at ZS 海滩	80.12	79.42	*Median at ZS* 海洋文化	119.82	118.87
Mean at ZS 海滩	235.96	228.75	*Mean at ZS* 海洋文化	293.40	283.65
Median at SY 海滩	76.86	76.14	*Median at SY* 珊瑚礁	114.05	113.25
Mean at SY 海滩	226.35	219.28	*Mean at SY* 珊瑚礁	279.26	270.25
Median at MD 海洋地质遗迹	72.00	71.32	*Median at MD* 海滩	99.43	98.61
Mean at MD 海洋地质遗迹	212.04	205.43	*Mean at MD* 海滩	243.47	235.32

注：稳健标准误；$*p<0.1$，$**p<0.05$，$***p<0.01$；"at ZS 海滩"表示将庙岛群岛海滩支付情景各系数，代入舟山群岛海滩受访者人口社会特征，计算的庙岛群岛海滩 WTP 调整值；其他关于"at"的含义与此类似。

表 5.12　　　　　　　　舟山群岛回归结果

变量	海滩		变量	海洋文化	
	OLS	IR		OLS	IR
Sex	-0.04	-0.03	*Sex*	-0.09	-0.08
Age	-0.01	-0.01	*Age*	-0.04	-0.04
Ages	0.01	0.01	*Ages*	0.03	0.03

续表

变量	海滩		变量	海洋文化	
	OLS	IR		OLS	IR
Edu	-0.02	-0.01	Edu	0.09	0.09
$Lninc$	1.06***	1.06***	$Lninc$	0.88***	0.88***
$Region1$	-0.07	-0.08	$Region1$	0.01	0.00
$Region2$	-0.10	-0.11	$Region2$	-0.19	-0.19
$Region3$	0.04	0.03	$Region3$	0.07	0.06
$Constant$	-7.62***	-7.62***	$Constant$	-4.81***	-4.78***
$Sigma$	1.50	1.47	$Sigma$	1.51	1.48
N	1195	1195	N	864	864
$R^2/Log\ pseudolikelihood$	0.16	-3733.01	$R^2/Log\ pseudolikelihood$	0.12	-2677.88
$F/Wald\ \chi^2$	26.13	213.76	$F/Wald\ \chi^2$	14.40	117.37
$Prob>F/Prob>\chi^2$	0.00	0.00	$Prob>F/Prob>\chi^2$	0.00	0.00
$Median$	98.95	98.52	$Median$	117.69	116.96
$Mean$	304.55	290.91	$Mean$	368.72	350.26
$Median\ at\ MD$ 海滩	84.64	84.18	$Median\ at\ MD$ 海洋地质遗迹	106.97	106.36
$Mean\ at\ MD$ 海滩	260.51	248.55	$Mean\ at\ MD$ 海洋地质遗迹	335.15	318.51
$Median\ at\ SY$ 海滩	94.93	94.44	$Median\ at\ SY$ 珊瑚礁	121.58	120.86
$Mean\ at\ SY$ 海滩	292.19	278.85	$Mean\ at\ SY$ 珊瑚礁	380.92	361.94
$Median\ at\ ZS$ 海洋文化	99.97	99.49	$Median\ at\ ZS$ 海滩	118.29	117.60
$Mean\ at\ ZS$ 海洋文化	307.69	293.75	$Mean\ at\ ZS$ 海滩	370.60	352.16

注：稳健标准误；*$p<0.1$，**$p<0.05$，***$p<0.01$；关于"at"的含义同表5.11。

表5.13　　　　　　　　三亚及其附近岛屿回归结果

变量	海滩		变量	珊瑚礁	
	OLS	IR		OLS	IR
Sex	-0.06	-0.06	Sex	0.07	0.07
Age	-0.04	-0.04	Age	-0.05*	-0.05*
$Ages$	0.03	0.03	$Ages$	0.06	0.06
Edu	0.07	0.07	Edu	0.05	0.06

续表

变量	海滩		变量	珊瑚礁	
	OLS	IR		OLS	IR
$Lninc$	0.94***	0.94***	$Lninc$	1.00***	1.00***
$Region1$	-0.05	-0.05	$Region1$	-0.31***	-0.31***
$Region2$	-0.10	-0.10	$Region2$	-0.21*	-0.21**
$Region3$	-0.01	-0.01	$Region3$	-0.22**	-0.23**
$Constant$	-5.55***	-5.58***	$Constant$	-5.98***	-5.99***
$Sigma$	1.39	1.38	$Sigma$	1.33	1.31
N	1364	1364	N	1340	1340
$R^2/Log\ pseudolikelihood$	0.17	-4146.64	$R^2/Log\ pseudolikelihood$	0.19	-4065.12
$F/Wald\ \chi^2$	33.17	268.42	$F/Wald\ \chi^2$	37.46	301.87
$Prob>F/Prob>\chi^2$	0.00	0.00	$Prob>F/Prob>\chi^2$	0.00	0.00
$Median$	96.02	95.29	$Median$	111.18	110.39
$Mean$	253.84	245.88	$Mean$	270.57	261.64
$Median\ at\ MD$ 海滩	83.00	82.33	$Median\ at\ MD$ 海洋地质遗迹	98.95	98.20
$Mean\ at\ MD$ 海滩	219.43	212.43	$Mean\ at\ MD$ 海洋地质遗迹	240.81	232.75
$Median\ at\ ZS$ 海滩	98.51	97.70	$Median\ at\ ZS$ 海洋文化	111.55	110.65
$Mean\ at\ ZS$ 海滩	260.42	252.10	$Mean\ at\ ZS$ 海洋文化	271.46	262.25
$Median\ at\ SY$ 珊瑚礁	101.27	100.52	$Median\ at\ SY$ 海滩	104.60	103.82
$Mean\ at\ SY$ 珊瑚礁	267.73	259.38	$Mean\ at\ SY$ 海滩	254.56	246.07

注：稳健标准误；*$p<0.1$，**$p<0.05$，***$p<0.01$；关于"at"的含义同表5.11。

二 支付意愿偏好分析

同一案例地两种海洋旅游资源比较时，庙岛群岛海滩平均 WTP < 海洋地质遗迹平均 WTP、舟山群岛海滩平均 WTP < 海洋文化平均 WTP、三亚及其附近岛屿海滩平均 WTP < 珊瑚礁平均 WTP，三个案例地均表现出海滩平均 WTP 小于同一案例地另一种海洋旅游资源平均 WTP（见图5.7）。因同一案例地两种海洋旅游资源样本组受访者的性别、年龄、学历、收入等人口社会特征存在差异（见表5.3），本书借鉴Borzykowski 等关于 CVM 样本组之间人口社会特征差异的调整思想，对同一案例

地两种海洋旅游资源的平均 WTP 进行调整，消除样本组之间受访者人口社会特征差异对平均 WTP 差异的影响。[①] 调整后的结果仍表现出海滩平均 WTP 相对较小（见图 5.8）。这一结果表明，受访者对海洋相对充裕型旅游资源（海滩）的 WTP 较低，而对海洋相对稀缺型旅游资源（海洋地质遗迹、海洋文化、珊瑚礁）的 WTP 较高。

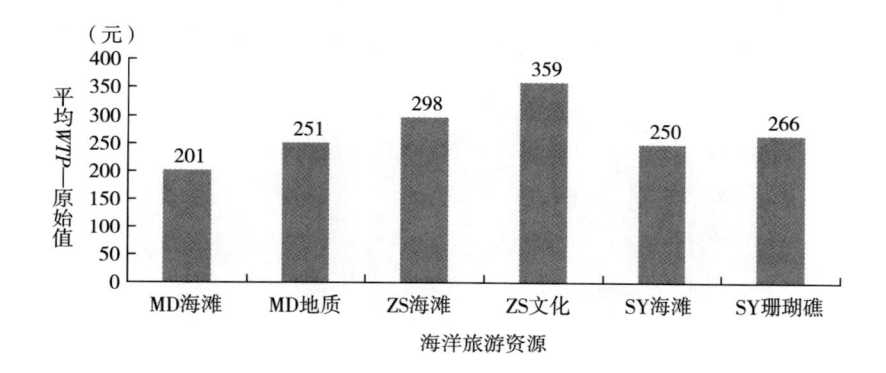

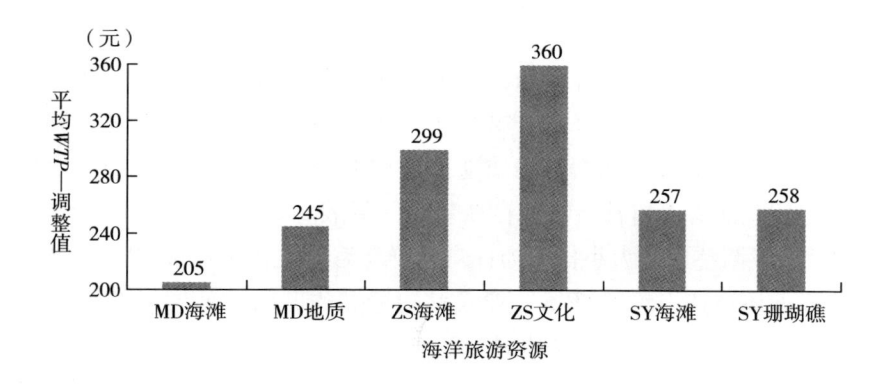

图 5.7 平均 WTP—原始值

图 5.8 平均 WTP—调整值 I

[①] Nicolas Borzykowski, et al., "Scope Effects in Contingent Valuation: Does the Assumed Statistical Distribution of WTP Matter?", *Ecological Economics*, Vol. 144, February 2018.

不同案例地同一种海洋旅游资源（海滩）比较时，庙岛群岛海滩平均WTP<三亚及其附近岛屿海滩平均WTP<舟山群岛海滩平均WTP（见图5.7）。因三个样本组之间受访者人口社会特征存在差异（见表5.3），对各平均WTP进行调整①，三个案例地海滩旅游资源平均WTP调整后的大小排序与调整前的大小排序一致（见图5.9）；同时，这一大小排序也与三个案例地待估海滩长度之和的长短排序一致。这一结果表明，受访者对海滩WTP大小与待估海滩长度之和的长短呈现正相关。

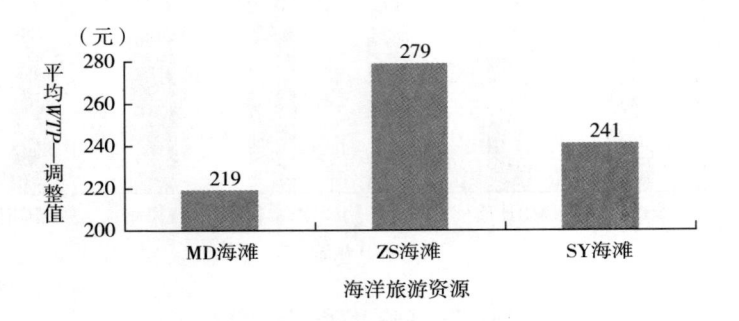

图5.9　平均WTP—调整值Ⅱ

不同案例地不同种海洋旅游资源（海洋地质遗迹、海洋文化、珊瑚礁）比较时，舟山群岛海洋文化平均WTP>三亚及其附近岛屿珊瑚礁平均WTP>庙岛群岛海洋地质遗迹平均WTP（见图5.7）。因三个样本组之间受访者人口社会特征存在差异（见表5.3），对各平均WTP进行调整②，调整后的大小排序为：舟山群岛海洋文化平均WTP>庙岛群岛海洋地质遗迹平均WTP>三亚及其附近岛屿珊瑚礁平均WTP（见图5.10）。这一结果表明，受访者对海洋人文旅游资源（海洋文化）的WTP大于对海洋自然旅游资源（海洋地质遗迹、珊瑚礁）的WTP，也大于对海滩旅游资源的WTP。

---

① Nicolas Borzykowski, et al., "Scope Effects in Contingent Valuation: Does the Assumed Statistical Distribution of WTP Matter?", *Ecological Economics*, Vol. 144, February 2018.

② Nicolas Borzykowski, et al., "Scope Effects in Contingent Valuation: Does the Assumed Statistical Distribution of WTP Matter?", *Ecological Economics*, Vol. 144, February 2018.

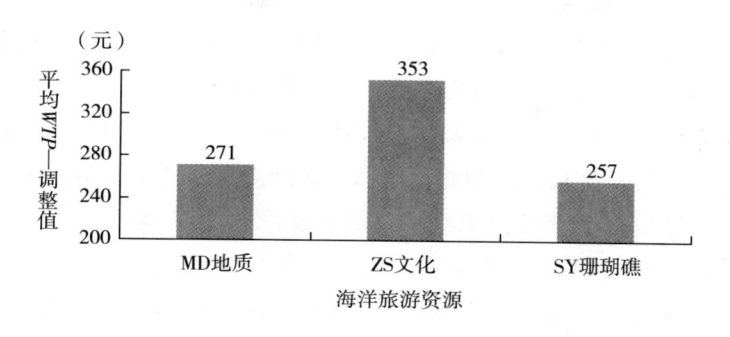

（元）
360 ┤   353
340 ┤
320 ┤
300 ┤
280 ┤ 271
260 ┤   257
240 ┤
220 ┤
200 ┤
         MD地质   ZS文化   SY珊瑚礁
               海洋旅游资源

平均WTP—调整值

图 5.10　平均 *WTP*—调整值Ⅲ

第四节　估值比较Ⅱ结论及进一步分析

公众保护海洋旅游资源非使用价值支付意愿偏好存在显著差异，平均 *WTP* 处于 201—359 元。在消除样本组之间受访者人口社会特征差异影响后，公众表现为：海洋相对稀缺型旅游资源（海洋地质遗迹、海洋文化或珊瑚礁）与海洋相对充裕型旅游资源（海滩）比较，公众更偏爱海洋相对稀缺型旅游资源（平均 *WTP* 更高）；海洋人文旅游资源（海洋文化）与海洋自然旅游资源（海滩、海洋地质遗迹或珊瑚礁）比较，公众更偏爱海洋人文旅游资源（平均 *WTP* 更高）；数量相对较多海洋旅游资源（较长海滩）与数量相对较少海洋旅游资源（较短海滩）比较，公众更偏爱数量相对较多海洋旅游资源（平均 *WTP* 更高）。本书揭示了我国公众保护海洋旅游资源非使用价值的偏好，为在我国海洋旅游资源保护或恢复工程成本—收益分析中考虑非使用价值起到了推进作用。

收入是 *WTP* 的最重要影响因素。将庙岛群岛、舟山群岛和三亚及其附近岛屿三个案例地居民受访者的 2016 年平均家庭收入分别与三个案例地城镇常住居民的 2016 年平均家庭收入进行比较，判断居民受访者调查样本的代表性。通过比较得知，三个案例地居民受访者调查样本具有较好的代表性：①2016 年，庙岛群岛（长岛县）城镇常住居民人均可支配收入为 3.06 万元，平均每个家庭的人口为 2.71 人（依据长岛县人民政府网站数据计算），得出庙岛群岛城镇常住居民的 2016 年平均家庭收入为 8.29 万元，比调查样本居民受访者的 2016 年平均家庭收入 9.71 万元低 14.62%，收入有差异。庙岛群岛有 10 个海岛有居民居住，居民调查样本选择的南长山岛为县城所在地，北长山岛为长岛县最富裕的海岛；同时，南长山岛和北长山岛是我国渔家乐的发源地，聚集着一千余家渔家乐（因有部分家庭未注册，渔家乐数量是访谈长岛县旅游局的估计数），旅游业主要集中在这两个海岛上；所以，庙岛群岛居民受访者与城镇常住居民的 2016 年平均家庭收入差异近 15% 属于正常。②2016 年，舟山群岛城镇常住居民人均可支配收入为 4.41 万元（不含财产收入），平均每个家庭的人口为 2.39 人（依据舟山群岛新区统计信息网数据计算），得出舟山群岛城镇常住居民的 2016 年平均家庭收入为 10.54 万元，比调查样本居民受访者的 2016 年平均家庭收入 10.97 万元低 3.92%，收入差异较小。③2016 年，三亚市城镇常住居民人均可支配收入为 2.75 万元（不含财产收入），平均每个家庭的人口为 3.75 人（依据三亚市统计局网站数据计算），得出三亚市城镇常住居民的 2016 年平均家庭收入为 10.30 万元，比调查样本居民受访者的 2016 年平均家庭收入 9.57 万元高 7.63%，收入差异较小。

案例地各客源地游客所占比例是判断游客样本代表性的重要依据。将庙岛群岛和舟山群岛各客源地样本量所占比例与项目组 2014—2015 年的较大样本量调研数据进行比较得知，庙岛群岛和舟山群岛各客源地样本量所占比例，与 2014—2015 年调研数据的各客源地样本量所占比例比较接近（见表 5.14），庙岛群岛和舟山群岛游客调查样本具有较好的代表性。将三亚及其附近岛屿主要客源地样本量所占比例大小，与三亚市旅游局统计的 2017 年节庆主要客源地排序比较得知，三亚及其附近岛屿游客调查样本具有较好的代表性（见表 5.14）。

通过分析可知，本书研究选取的居民和游客受访者样本具有较好的代表性；所以，评估结果能够较好地反映我国公众保护海洋旅游资源支付意愿的偏好，研究成果能够为海洋旅游资源保护或恢复工程的成本—收益分析提供参考借鉴。

表 5.14　　游客客源地比较

案例地	短中长途客源地	具体客源地	2014—2015年调查	2017年调查
黄渤海区—庙岛群岛	短途客源地	山东济南	10.03	7.90
	短途客源地	山东潍坊、淄博和烟台	14.81	12.27
	短途客源地	山东其他地区	18.17	15.38
	中途客源地	北京、天津和河北	27.13	32.52
	长途客源地	国内其他省（市、区）	29.85	31.93
	样本量		3538	1190
东海区—舟山群岛	短途客源地	浙江杭州	11.89	10.61
	短途客源地	浙江宁波	9.56	7.57
	短途客源地	浙江其他地区	17.85	19.30
	中途客源地	上海、江苏和安徽	30.01	32.78
	长途客源地	江西、福建、河南、湖南、湖北和山东	19.22	17.74
	长途客源地	国内其他省（市、区）	11.48	12.00
	样本量		5452	1150
南海区—海南三亚及其附近岛屿	短途客源地	广东	排进前五位	7.79
	短途客源地	湖南	排进前五位	6.58
	中途客源地	四川	排进前五位	6.05
	长途客源地	河南	排进前五位	5.73
	中途客源地	江苏	排进前五位	5.68
	短途客源地	广西	—	5.58
	中途客源地	湖北	—	5.16
	长途客源地	陕西	—	4.89
	长途客源地	北京	排进前五位	4.63
	短途客源地	海南	—	4.21
	短途客源地	贵州	—	3.73
	中途客源地	浙江	—	3.73
	短途客源地	江西	—	3.68
	长途客源地	黑龙江	—	3.63
	中途客源地	重庆	排进前五位	3.37
	长途客源地	河北	—	2.84

续表

案例地	短中长途客源地	具体客源地	2014—2015 年调查	2017 年调查
南海区—海南三亚及其附近岛屿	中途客源地	上海	排进前五位	2.74
	短中长途客源地	国内其他省（市、区）	—	19.98
	样本量		—	1901

注：2017 年 10 月 2—7 日 6 天中，每天三亚市接待国内游客排进前五位的省市有：广东、北京、上海、江苏、重庆、四川、湖南和河南。

第六章

群岛旅游资源非使用价值估值比较Ⅲ

第一节 估值比较Ⅲ模型与分类

一 定序 logit 模型

运用支付卡式引导方式询问游客受访者对保护海洋旅游资源非使用价值的 WTP，WTP 呈现 10 元、50 元、100 元和 200 元的多峰分布。为减少投标值设置偏差，本书研究选用定序 logit 模型进行计量分析。[1] 根据 WTP 的分布情况，设定一个分类定序变量 WTP_Ordinal，分三类：小于等于 50 元、大于 50 元且小于等于 100 元和大于 100 元，分别取值为 1、2 和 3。选用基于潜变量的定序 logit 模型（Ordered Logit Model）分析，建立回归模型：

$$WTP_i^* = x'_i \beta + \varepsilon_i \qquad (6-1)$$

式（6-1）中，WTP_i^* 为第 i 个受访者的潜在最大支付意愿，x_i 为解释变量向量，β 为回归系数向量，ε_i 为随机误差项并假设其服从逻辑

---

[1] Hilary Nixon and Jean-Daneil M. Saphores, "Financing Electronic Waste Recycling Californian Households' Willingness to Pay Advanced Recycling Fees", *Journal of Environmental Management*, Vol. 84, No. 4, September 2007; Elcin Akcura, "Mandatory Versus Voluntary Payment for Green Electricity", *Ecological Economics*, Vol. 116, August 2015; Chiradip Chatterjee, et al., "Willingness to Pay for Safe Drinking Water: A Contingent Valuation Study in Jacksonville, FL", *Journal of Environmental Management*, Vol. 203, December 2017.

分布。

$WTP\_Ordinal$ 变量与潜变量的关系：

$$WTP\_Ordinal_i = m \ if \ \tau_{m-1} < WTP_i^* \leq \tau_m, \ m=1,\cdots,J \quad (6-2)$$

式（6-2）中，τ_1 至 τ_{J-1} 为切点，并假设 $\tau_0 = -\infty$，$\tau_J = \infty$。

$WTP\_Ordinal$ 变量的观测值取值 m 的概率：

$$\Pr(WTP\_Ordinal_i = m) = F(\tau_m - x'_i\beta) - F(\tau_{m-1} - x'_i\beta) \quad (6-3)$$

式（6-3）中，F 为逻辑分布函数且随机误差项的方差为 $\pi^2/3$。

定序 logit 模型运用极大似然估计，对数似然函数：

$$\ln L = \sum_{i=1}^{n}\sum_{m=1}^{J} d_i^m \ln[\Pr(WTP\_Ordinal_i = m)] \quad (6-4)$$

式（6-4）中，d_i^m 为虚拟变量，当第 i 个受访者 $WTP\_Ordinal$ 变量的观测值取值为 m 时取 1，否则取 0。

基于预测概率的相关解释更加清晰有效，预测概率的计算公式：

$$\hat{\Pr}(WTP\_Ordinal_i = m) = F(\hat{\tau}_m - x'_i\hat{\beta}) - F(\hat{\tau}_{m-1} - x'_i\hat{\beta}) \quad (6-5)$$

定序 logit 模型的前提假设是满足比例比数假设（Proportional Odds Assumption），即自变量的回归系数在 $WTP\_Ordinal$ 变量的不同的分割间是不变的。比例比数假设的检验方法有 Brant 检验和得分检验。如果违反比例比数假设，广义定序 logit 模型（Generalized Ordered Logit Model）是一个可供选择的替代方案。

二 资源分类

研究选取四种典型海洋旅游资源作为研究对象，即黄渤海区——庙岛群岛的海滩旅游资源和海洋地质遗迹旅游资源、东海区——舟山群岛的海滩旅游资源和海洋文化旅游资源、南海区——三亚及其附近岛屿的海滩旅游资源和珊瑚礁旅游资源。参照图 2.1，从旅游资源的属性角度和稀缺性角度，将四种典型海洋旅游资源进行分类（见图 6.1）。以图 2.1 和图 6.1 设计思路为依据，本书研究从四个方面进行估值比较研究：①同一个案例地内部之间，游客受访者对保护相对充裕型旅游资源与相对稀缺型旅游资源非使用价值 WTP 的差异比较，即庙岛群岛的海滩旅游资源与海洋地质遗迹旅游资源的比较（MB 与 MG 比较）、舟山群岛的海滩旅游资源与海洋文化旅游资源的比较（ZB 与 ZC 比较）、三亚及其附近岛屿的海滩旅游资源与珊瑚礁旅游资源的比较（SB 与 SC 比较）；

②不同案例地之间，游客受访者对保护相对稀缺型旅游资源非使用价值WTP的差异比较，即庙岛群岛的海洋地质遗迹旅游资源、舟山群岛的海洋文化旅游资源与三亚及其附近岛屿的珊瑚礁旅游资源之间的比较（MG、ZC与SC比较）；③不同案例地之间，游客受访者对保护相对充裕型旅游资源非使用价值WTP的差异比较，即庙岛群岛的海滩旅游资源、舟山群岛的海滩旅游资源与三亚及其附近岛屿的海滩旅游资源之间的比较（MB、ZB与SB比较）；④不同案例地或同一案例地之间，游客受访者对保护海洋人文旅游资源与海洋自然旅游资源非使用价值WTP的差异比较，即舟山群岛的海洋文化旅游资源与其他海洋自然旅游资源的比较（ZC与MB、MG、ZB、SB、SC比较）。

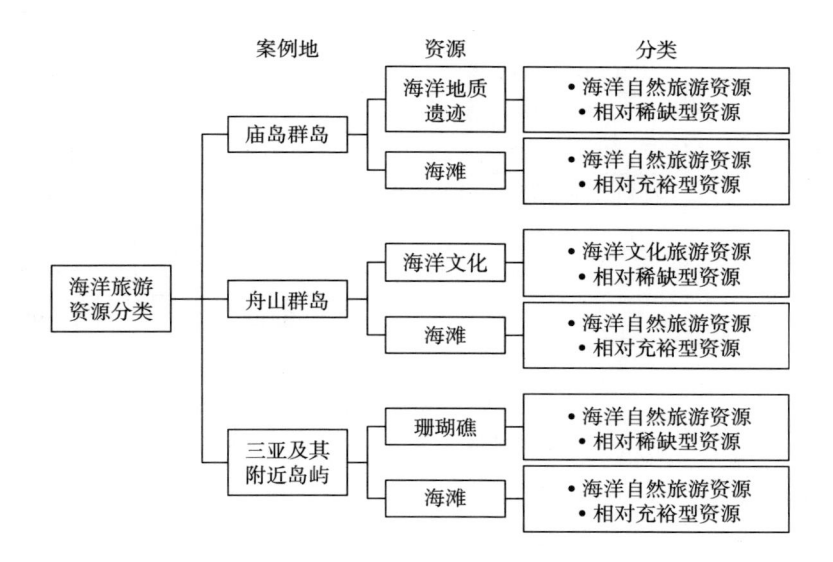

图6.1 海洋旅游资源分类

第二节 估值比较Ⅲ描述性统计分析

一 样本分布

庙岛群岛、舟山群岛和三亚及其附近岛屿三个案例地共获得调查问卷4449份，其中有效问卷4289份，有效率96.40%；抗议性零支付样本 48 份，在进一步分析中剔除，最终分析样本 4241 份。有效样本分布如表 6.1 所示。

表 6.1 有效样本分布

案例地	调查地点	海洋地质遗迹（MG）	海滩（MB）
黄渤海区—庙岛群岛	九丈崖景区	285	192
	月牙湾景区	284	189
	望夫礁景区	141	95
	其他	3	1
	合计	713	477
案例地	调查地点	海洋文化（ZC）	海滩（ZB）
东海区—舟山群岛	普陀山景区	213	271
	朱家尖国际沙雕艺术广场景区	96	122
	桃花岛茅草屋码头	68	96
	岱山岛鹿栏晴沙景区	58	66
	泗礁山岛南长涂景区和基湖景区	58	100
	其他	0	2
	合计	493	657
案例地	调查地点	珊瑚礁（SC）	海滩（SB）
南海区—三亚及其附近岛屿	西岛景区	205	201
	蜈支洲岛景区	236	220
	亚龙湾景区	326	351
	大东海景区	179	181
	其他	1	1
	合计	947	954

注：未包含抗议性零样本。

二 样本人口社会特征分析

各样本组的人口社会特征如表 6.2 所示。庙岛群岛的海滩旅游资源样本中，男女比例基本相当，平均年龄不足 38 岁，近 2/3 的游客受过高等教育，平均年收入接近 13 万元；海洋地质遗迹样本中，男女比例基本相当，平均年龄略高于 36 岁，受过高等教育的游客比例超过

70%，平均年收入不足 14 万元。舟山群岛的海滩旅游资源和海洋文化旅游资源样本中，男性游客偏多，平均年龄 35 岁左右，近 2/3 的游客受过高等教育，平均年收入 16 万元左右。三亚及其附近岛屿的海滩旅游资源样本中，女性游客略多，平均年龄高于 35 岁，受过高等教育的游客比例超过 70%，平均年收入不足 15 万元；珊瑚礁旅游资源样本中，男性游客居多，平均年龄约为 34 岁，受过高等教育的游客比例接近 80%，平均年收入不足 16 万元。

由表 6.2 可知，各样本组的人口社会特征存在差异，同一案例地的样本组间人口社会特征差异较小，而不同案例地的样本组间人口社会特征差异较大。其中，庙岛群岛游客的平均年龄大于舟山群岛游客和三亚及其附近岛屿游客，舟山群岛游客的平均年收入大于庙岛群岛游客和三亚及其附近岛屿游客，三亚及其附近岛屿游客的平均受教育年限高于庙岛群岛游客和舟山群岛游客。

表 6.2　　　　　　　　　　样本人口社会特征

样本组	性别		年龄		学历		收入（万元）	
	均值	标准差	均值	标准差	均值	标准差	均值	标准差
庙岛群岛（N=1190）	0.50	0.50	36.76	7.87	0.69	0.46	13.43	12.63
MG（N=713）	0.50	0.50	36.21	7.40	0.73	0.45	13.73	13.32
MB（N=477）	0.50	0.50	37.59	8.47	0.64	0.48	12.98	11.53
舟山群岛（N=1150）	0.55	0.50	34.88	8.10	0.64	0.48	16.12	14.55
ZC（N=493）	0.55	0.50	35.07	7.70	0.65	0.48	16.31	15.34
ZB（N=657）	0.56	0.50	34.74	8.39	0.63	0.48	15.98	13.94
三亚及其附近岛屿（N=1901）	0.53	0.50	34.76	8.00	0.75	0.43	15.16	14.09
SC（N=947）	0.58	0.49	34.18	7.86	0.78	0.42	15.62	14.57
SB（N=954）	0.48	0.50	35.33	8.09	0.73	0.44	14.71	13.60
总样本（N=4241）	0.53	0.50	35.35	8.04	0.71	0.46	14.94	13.86

注：a. 性别：男=1，女=0；b. 学历：受过高等教育=1，未受过高等教育=0。

三　样本组间人口社会特征差异

运用 Mann – Whitney U test 和 Kruskal – Wallis test，分别进行两组样

本之间和三组样本之间的人口社会特征差异显著性检验。同一案例地内部两种旅游资源样本组之间，游客受访者的人口社会特征差异较小（因三亚及其附近岛屿珊瑚礁样本组中包含了部分潜水游客，所以海滩和珊瑚礁样本组中受访者的人口社会特征存在差异）；不同案例地两组样本之间或三组样本之间比较，游客受访者的人口社会特征存在较大差异（见表6.3）。

表6.3　　　　　　样本组间人口社会特征差异显著性检验

变量	Mann – Whitney U test			Kruskal – Wallis test	
	MG 和 MB	ZC 和 ZB	SC 和 SB	MG, ZC 和 SC	MB, ZB 和 SB
性别	0.95 (-0.06)	0.63 (0.49)	0.00 (-4.40)	0.01 (10.52)	0.01 (10.25)
年龄	0.01 (2.51)	0.16 (-1.39)	0.00 (3.14)	0.00 (29.21)	0.00 (38.09)
学历	0.00 (-3.04)	0.48 (-0.71)	0.02 (-2.25)	0.00 (27.16)	0.00 (23.03)
收入	0.64 (-0.47)	0.95 (-0.06)	0.01 (-2.61)	0.00 (29.55)	0.00 (29.89)

注：Mann – Whitney U test 括号中为 Z 值；Kruskal – Wallis test 括号中为卡方值。

四　WTP 统计分析

同一案例地内部，相对稀缺型海洋旅游资源与相对充裕型海洋旅游资源的 WTP 比较，相对稀缺型海洋旅游资源 WTP 的低值占比较低、高值占比较高；不同案例地的相对充裕型海洋旅游资源（海滩）之间，舟山群岛海滩、三亚及其附近岛屿海滩与庙岛群岛海滩的 WTP 比较，庙岛群岛海滩 WTP 的低值占比较高、高值占比较低；不同案例地的相对稀缺型海洋旅游资源之间，舟山群岛海洋文化与庙岛群岛海洋地质遗迹或三亚及其附近岛屿珊瑚礁的 WTP 比较，舟山群岛海洋文化 WTP 的低值占比较低、高值占比较高；海洋人文旅游资源与海洋自然旅游资源的 WTP 比较，海洋人文旅游资源 WTP 的低值占比较低、高值占比较高（见表6.4）。

表 6.4　　WTP 分布　　　　　　　　　　　　单位:%

投标值（元）	MG (N=713)	MB (N=477)	ZC (N=493)	ZB (N=657)	SC (N=947)	SB (N=954)
0	1.26	0.84	2.23	2.44	1.48	1.68
1	1.12	1.89	0.81	1.83	1.48	1.26
2	0.28	1.68	0.61	0.30	0.53	0.52
5	3.37	2.94	2.03	2.74	2.43	2.62
10	10.66	16.35	5.88	9.44	9.08	10.27
20	5.19	5.66	5.88	5.48	5.91	7.23
30	1.68	2.94	2.23	1.22	1.69	2.52
50	13.46	15.30	9.33	10.81	14.47	14.15
60	0.84	0.63	0.20	0.61	0.32	0.10
80	0.70	0.84	0.61	0.46	0.11	0.21
100	35.34	30.61	28.60	33.03	30.94	31.55
120	0.00	0.00	0.81	0.15	0.21	0.21
150	0.28	0.42	1.01	1.83	0.84	0.84
200	10.66	7.34	17.44	12.63	14.57	11.11
300	3.09	1.47	5.68	3.65	2.43	2.20
400	0.00	0.42	0.00	0.15	0.11	0.00
500	5.05	5.45	8.11	6.09	5.91	6.71
600	0.98	0.42	1.01	0.91	0.84	0.73
800	0.56	1.47	1.22	0.46	0.63	0.52
1000	4.63	2.73	5.27	3.35	4.33	4.30
1500	0.00	0.63	0.00	0.46	0.11	0.10
2000	0.84	0.00	1.01	1.98	1.58	1.15

五　定序支付意愿变量区间划分

依据 WTP 在 10 元、50 元、100 元和 200 元投标值呈现多峰的特征，并结合划分区间的样本所占比例，将 WTP 划分为≤50、(50, 100]和 >100 三个定序区间（见表 6.5）。

表 6.5　　　　　　　　　WTP_Ordinal 分布

WTP_Ordinal(%)	MG (N=713)	MB (N=477)	ZC (N=493)	ZB (N=657)	SC (N=947)	SB (N=954)
≤50(Level 1)	37.03	47.59	29.01	34.25	37.06	40.25
(50,100](Level 2)	36.89	32.08	29.41	34.09	31.36	31.87
>100(Level 3)	26.09	20.34	41.58	31.66	31.57	27.88

第三节　估值比较Ⅲ WTP 差异性分析

一　定序 logit 模型变量和检验

定序 logit 回归模型的变量定义如表 6.6 所示。

表 6.6　　　　　　　　　变量定义

变量	解释	定义
WTP_Ordinal	定序 WTP 变量	$WTP\_Ordinal=1$，$WTP\leq50$ $WTP\_Ordinal=2$，$50<WTP\leq100$ $WTP\_Ordinal=3$，$WTP>100$
Gender	性别，虚拟变量	男=1，女=0
Age	年龄	2017 减去游客受访者出生年
Education	学历，虚拟变量	受过高等教育=1，未受过高等教育=0
Log of income	家庭年收入对数	家庭年收入取对数
Resource−Scarce	相对稀缺型旅游资源，虚拟变量	模型 1：$Resource-Scarce=MG=1$，$MB=0$ 模型 2：$Resource-Scarce=ZC=1$，$ZB=0$ 模型 3：$Resource-Scarce=SC=1$，$SB=0$
Resource−MG	庙岛群岛海洋地质遗迹，虚拟变量	MG=1，其他=0
Resource−SC	三亚及其附近岛屿珊瑚礁，虚拟变量	SC=1，其他=0
Resource−MB	庙岛群岛海滩，虚拟变量	MB=1，其他=0
Resource−SB	三亚及其附近岛屿海滩，虚拟变量	SB=1，其他=0

模型1至模型3表示三个案例地的同一案例地内部,相对稀缺型旅游资源与相对充裕型旅游资源的 WTP 比较;模型4表示三个案例地之间,相对稀缺型旅游资源的 WTP 比较;模型5表示三个案例地之间,相对充裕型旅游资源的 WTP 比较。运用 Score test 和 Brant test,检验比例比数假设条件是否满足,检验结果如表6.7所示。由表6.7可知,所有模型均满足比例比数假设条件,所以,选择定序 logit 回归模型[①]。

表6.7　　　　　　　　比例比数假设检验

检验		模型1 MG 和 MB	模型2 ZC 和 ZB	模型3 SC 和 SB	模型4 MG, ZC 和 SC	模型5 MB, ZB 和 SB
Score test	χ^2	7.71	5.93	7.06	9.44	7.28
	$Prob > \chi^2$	0.17	0.31	0.22	0.15	0.30
Brant test	χ^2	5.71	6.29	9.04	11.40	6.55
	$Prob > \chi^2$	0.34	0.28	0.11	0.08	0.36

二　定序 logit 模型回归结果

定序 logit 模型回归结果如表6.8所示。在模型1和模型2中,同一案例地内部比较,*Resource - Scarce* 变量与 *WTP - Ordinal* 变量呈正相关,且在1%水平下显著;在模型3中,*Resource - Scarce* 变量的系数是正的。这表明,游客受访者对保护相对稀缺型旅游资源非使用价值的 *WTP* 高于保护相对充裕型旅游资源非使用价值的 *WTP*。也就是,MG 的 *WTP* 比 MB 的 *WTP* 高,ZC 的 *WTP* 比 ZB 的 *WTP* 高,SC 的 *WTP* 比 SB 的 *WTP* 高。从游客受访者的人口社会特征变量来看,收入对 *WTP_Ordinal* 变量有正效应,且在1%水平下显著,即游客受访者收入越高 *WTP* 越高。[②] 三亚及其附近岛屿案例地,学历变量与 *WTP_Ordinal* 变量

---

① J. Scott Long and Jeremy Freese, *Regression Models for Categorical Dependent Variables Using Stata* (3rd ed.), College Station, TX: Stata Press, 2014.

② Emma Risén, et al., "Non - market Values of Algae Beach - cast Management - study Site Trelleborg, Sweden", *Ocean & Coastal Management*, Vol. 140, May 2017; D. Lavee and O. Menachem, "Economic Valuation of the Existence of the Southwestern Basin of the Dead Sea in Israel", *Land Use Policy*, Vol. 71, February 2018; Peter W. Schuhmann, et al., "Visitors' Willingness to Pay Marine Conservation Fees in Barbados", *Tourism Management*, Vol. 71, April 2019.

呈正相关，且在5%水平下显著，庙岛群岛和舟山群岛这一系数为正；这表明受教育程度较高的受访者更能意识到环境退化问题和认识到保护环境的重要性，对保护海洋旅游资源非使用价值的 WTP 较高。①

表6.8　　　　　　　　　　定序 logit 模型回归结果

变量	模型 1 MG 和 MB	模型 2 ZC 和 ZB	模型 3 SC 和 SB	模型 4 MG, ZC 和 SC	模型 5 MB, ZB 和 SB
Gender	0.06 (0.11)	0.19 (0.11)	0.12 (0.09)	0.16* (0.08)	0.08 (0.08)
Age	−0.01 (0.01)	−0.00 (0.01)	−0.01 (0.01)	−0.01 (0.01)	−0.01 (0.01)
Education	0.06 (0.13)	0.08 (0.12)	0.23** (0.11)	0.08 (0.10)	0.17* (0.10)
Log of income	0.77*** (0.10)	1.19*** (0.10)	1.17*** (0.08)	1.07*** (0.07)	1.07*** (0.07)
Resource-Scare	0.37*** (0.11)	0.40*** (0.11)	0.03 (0.09)		
Resource-MG				−0.39*** (0.11)	
Resource-SC				−0.46*** (0.11)	
Resource-MB					−0.36*** (0.12)
Resource-SB					−0.12 (0.10)
τ_1	1.41*** (0.36)	2.34*** (0.34)	2.35*** (0.29)	1.49*** (0.27)	1.96*** (0.27)
τ_2	3.02*** (0.37)	3.86*** (0.35)	3.86*** (0.30)	3.01*** (0.27)	3.51*** (0.27)
Number of observations	1190	1150	1901	2153	2088
Log likelihood	−1234.36	−1169.07	−1921.64	−2213.90	−2121.74

---

① Pankaj Lal, et al., "Valuing Visitor Services and Access to Protected Areas: The Case of Nyungwe National Park in Rwanda", *Tourism Management*, Vol.61, August 2017.

续表

变量	模型 1 MG 和 MB	模型 2 ZC 和 ZB	模型 3 SC 和 SB	模型 4 MG, ZC 和 SC	模型 5 MB, ZB 和 SB
pseudo R^2	0.03	0.07	0.07	0.06	0.07
LR χ^2	87.99	185.26	308.80	299.29	293.62
Prob >χ^2	0.00	0.00	0.00	0.00	0.00

注：a. $*p<0.1$，$**p<0.05$，$***p<0.01$；b. 括号中为标准误。

在模型 4 中，不同案例地之间相对稀缺型海洋旅游资源比较，Resource - MG 变量和 Resource - SC 变量与 WTP_Ordinal 变量均呈负相关，且均在 1% 水平下显著。这表明，游客受访者对保护舟山群岛海洋文化旅游资源非使用价值的 WTP 高于保护庙岛群岛海洋地质遗迹或三亚及其附近岛屿珊瑚礁旅游资源非使用价值的 WTP。在模型 5 中，不同案例地之间相对充裕型海洋旅游资源比较，Resource - MB 变量和 Resource - SB 变量回归系数均为负，且 Resource - MB 变量在 1% 水平下显著。这表明，游客受访者对保护舟山群岛海滩旅游资源非使用价值的 WTP 高于保护庙岛群岛海滩或三亚及其附近岛屿海滩旅游资源的 WTP。从游客受访者的人口社会特征变量来看，模型 4 和模型 5 与模型 1 至模型 3 相似。

三 敏感性分析

将定序 WTP 变量的划分区间界限变换为下一个更高或更低的投标值，重复试验，检验敏感性。提高划分区间界限的定序 WTP 变量：小于等于 60 元、大于 60 元且小于等于 120 元和大于 120 元，分别取值为 1、2 和 3；降低划分区间边界的定序 WTP 变量：小于等于 30 元、大于 30 元且小于等于 80 元和大于 80 元，分别取值为 1、2 和 3。将上述两种情况重复执行定序 logit 模型回归分析，回归结果如表 6.9 和表 6.10 所示。各变量回归系数的正负方向和统计显著性没有显著变化。

表 6.9　提高划分区间边界的定序 logit 模型回归结果

变量	模型 1 MG 和 MB	模型 2 ZC 和 ZB	模型 3 SC 和 SB	模型 4 MG, ZC 和 SC	模型 5 MB, ZB 和 SB
Gender	0.07 (0.11)	0.18 (0.11)	0.11 (0.09)	0.16* (0.08)	0.08 (0.08)

续表

变量	模型1 MG 和 MB	模型2 ZC 和 ZB	模型3 SC 和 SB	模型4 MG, ZC 和 SC	模型5 MB, ZB 和 SB
Age	-0.01 (0.01)	-0.00 (0.01)	-0.01 (0.01)	-0.01 (0.01)	-0.01 (0.01)
$Education$	0.11 (0.13)	0.07 (0.12)	0.24** (0.11)	0.11 (0.10)	0.17* (0.10)
$Log\ of\ income$	0.77*** (0.10)	1.19*** (0.10)	1.16*** (0.08)	1.07*** (0.07)	1.06*** (0.07)
$Resource-Scarce$	0.36*** (0.11)	0.40*** (0.11)	0.03 (0.09)		
$Resource-MG$				-0.39*** (0.11)	
$Resource-SC$				-0.45*** (0.11)	
$Resource-MB$					-0.36*** (0.12)
$Resource-SB$					-0.11 (0.10)
τ_1	1.43*** (0.36)	2.37*** (0.34)	2.37*** (0.29)	1.54*** (0.27)	1.97*** (0.27)
τ_2	3.02*** (0.37)	3.88*** (0.36)	3.88*** (0.30)	3.06*** (0.28)	3.50*** (0.27)
$Number\ of\ observations$	1190	1150	1901	2153	2088
$Log\ likelihood$	-1231.40	-1169.12	-1922.43	-2210.50	-2121.80
$Pseudo\ R^2$	0.04	0.07	0.07	0.06	0.06
$LR\ \chi^2$	90.56	186.19	305.07	304.17	289.05
$Prob>\chi^2$	0.00	0.00	0.00	0.00	0.00

注：a. $*p<0.1$，$**p<0.05$，$***p<0.01$；b. 括号中为标准误。

表 6.10　降低划分区间边界的定序 logit 模型回归结果

变量	Model1 MG 和 MB	Model2 ZC 和 ZB	Model3 SC 和 SB	Model4 MG, ZC 和 SC	Model5 MB, ZB 和 SB
$Gender$	-0.00	0.23*	-0.03	0.07	0.02
	(0.12)	(0.13)	(0.10)	(0.09)	(0.09)
Age	-0.01	-0.00	-0.01	-0.01	-0.01
	(0.01)	(0.01)	(0.01)	(0.01)	(0.01)
$Education$	0.11	0.11	0.32***	0.13	0.26***
	(0.13)	(0.14)	(0.11)	(0.11)	(0.10)
$Log\ of\ income$	0.70***	1.23***	1.28***	1.15***	1.04***
	(0.11)	(0.13)	(0.09)	(0.09)	(0.08)
$Resource-Scarce$	0.41***	0.26**	0.06		
	(0.12)	(0.13)	(0.10)		
$Resource-MG$				-0.17	
				(0.13)	
$Resource-SC$				-0.30**	
				(0.12)	
$Resource-MB$					-0.37***
					(0.12)
$Resource-SB$					-0.14
					(0.11)
τ_1	0.59	1.87***	1.85***	1.12***	1.23***
	(0.37)	(0.39)	(0.31)	(0.30)	(0.28)
τ_2	1.32***	2.50***	2.63***	1.87***	1.94***
	(0.38)	(0.40)	(0.31)	(0.31)	(0.28)
$Number\ of\ observations$	1190	1150	1901	2153	2088
$Log\ likelihood$	-1112.18	-902.01	-1623.46	-1808.07	-1844.59
$Pseudo\ R^2$	0.03	0.07	0.08	0.06	0.06
$LR\ \chi^2$	69.76	138.63	278.73	234.29	236.47
$Prob>\chi^2$	0.00	0.00	0.00	0.00	0.00

注：a. *$p<0.1$，**$p<0.05$，***$p<0.01$；b. 括号中为标准误。

第四节　估值比较Ⅲ WTP 调整

一　WTP 情景

定序 logit 模型回归结果表明，游客受访者对保护不同海洋旅游资源非使用价值的 WTP 存在差异，这种 WTP 的差异由两方面原因引起：一是游客受访者人口社会特征差异引起的 WTP 差异；二是保护不同海洋旅游资源类型引起的 WTP 差异。表 6.3 的 Mann – Whitney U test 和 Kruskal – Wallis test 结果表明，不同样本组之间的游客受访者人口社会特征存在差异。为了研究不同类型海洋旅游资源非使用价值的 WTP 差异，需要剔除不同类型海洋旅游资源样本组之间游客受访者人口社会特征的差异。

参照 Carson 和 Mitchell 及 Borzykowski 等的调整思想[①]，本书研究对游客受访者的 $WTP\_Ordinal$ 取值概率进行预测。首先，对 X 海洋旅游资源子样本进行定序 logit 回归，解释变量为游客受访者的性别、年龄、学历和收入等人口社会特征（变量定义同表 6.6），求得回归系数向量 β_X，即 X 海洋旅游资源非使用价值的 WTP 情景，回归结果如表 6.11 所示；其次，根据式（6–1）至式（6–5），将 Y 海洋旅游资源每个子样本的人口社会特征与 X 海洋旅游资源非使用价值的 WTP 情景结合，得到每个子样本的 $WTP\_Ordinal$ 各个取值的预测概率，将所有子样本的预测概率取均值，即得到 Y 子样本对 X 海洋旅游资源非使用价值 $WTP\_Ordinal$ 取值概率的预测（即 X at Y）。

表 6.11　　　　　　六组子样本定序 logit 模型回归结果

变量	MG	MB	ZC	ZB	SC	SB
Gender	0.02 (0.14)	0.11 (0.17)	0.33* (0.17)	0.08 (0.15)	0.17 (0.13)	0.06 (0.13)

---

① Richard T. Carson and Robert C. Mitchell, "The Issue of Scope in Contingent Valuation Studies", *American Journal of Agricultural Economics*, Vol. 75, No. 5, December 1993; Nicolas Borzykowski, et al., "Scope Effects in Contingent Valuation: Does the Assumed Statistical Distribution of WTP Matter?", *Ecological Economics*, Vol. 144, February 2018.

续表

变量	MG	MB	ZC	ZB	SC	SB
Age	−0.00	−0.01	−0.01	0.00	−0.01	−0.01
	(0.01)	(0.01)	(0.01)	(0.01)	(0.01)	(0.01)
$Education$	0.10	−0.02	0.12	0.04	0.09	0.37**
	(0.17)	(0.19)	(0.18)	(0.17)	(0.16)	(0.15)
$Log\ of\ income$	0.88***	0.58***	0.95***	1.37***	1.27***	1.08***
	(0.13)	(0.16)	(0.15)	(0.14)	(0.11)	(0.11)
τ_1	1.45***	0.75	1.25***	2.86***	2.49***	2.21***
	(0.45)	(0.56)	(0.51)	(0.45)	(0.41)	(0.40)
τ_2	3.14***	2.25***	2.60***	4.52***	3.99***	3.72***
	(0.47)	(0.57)	(0.52)	(0.47)	(0.42)	(0.41)
$Number\ of\ observations$	713	477	493	657	947	954
$Log\ likelihood$	−743.45	−488.62	−507.28	−656.94	−954.62	−965.19
$pseudo\ R^2$	0.04	0.02	0.05	0.09	0.08	0.07
$LR\ \chi^2$	62.15	16.84	54.09	128.85	165.69	143.30
$Prob>\chi^2$	0.00	0.00	0.00	0.00	0.00	0.00

注：a. $*p<0.1$，$**p<0.05$，$***p<0.01$；b. 括号中为标准误。

二　预测概率调整

经调整的预测概率如表 6.12 所示。庙岛群岛海滩旅游资源与海洋地质遗迹旅游资源的 $WTP\_Ordinal$ 预测概率，可从两组数据进行比较：第一组是用庙岛群岛海滩旅游资源子样本的人口社会特征进行调整，即 MB at MB 与 MG at MB 的比较；第二组是用庙岛群岛海洋地质遗迹旅游资源子样本的人口社会特征进行调整，即 MB at MG 与 MG at MG 的比较。如表 6.12 所示，第一组比较中，MG at MB 的 WTP 大于 100 元的概率大于 MB at MB，且 MG at MB 的 WTP 小于等于 50 元的概率小于 MB at MB，这表明通过海滩旅游资源子样本的人口社会特征进行调整，游客受访者对保护海洋地质遗迹旅游资源非使用价值的 WTP 高于保护海滩旅游资源非使用价值的 WTP。同样，在第二组比较中，通过海洋地质遗迹旅游资源子样本的人口社会特征进行调整，相比海滩旅游资源，游客受访者对保护海洋地质遗迹旅游资源非使用价值的 WTP 更高。

在庙岛群岛案例中，剔除人口社会特征差异后，游客受访者对保护相对稀缺型海洋旅游资源非使用价值的 WTP 高于保护相对充裕型旅游资源非使用价值的 WTP，即：MG 的 WTP 高于 MB 的 WTP。与庙岛群岛案例类似，在舟山群岛和三亚及其附近岛屿案例中，游客受访者均是对保护相对稀缺型海洋旅游资源非使用价值的 WTP 高于保护相对充裕型旅游资源非使用价值的 WTP，即：ZC 的 WTP 高于 ZB 的 WTP 和 SC 的 WTP 高于 SB 的 WTP；不同案例地相对稀缺型旅游资源比较，游客受访者对保护舟山群岛海洋文化旅游资源非使用价值的 WTP 最高，三亚及其附近岛屿的珊瑚礁旅游资源与庙岛群岛的海洋地质遗迹旅游资源次之，即：ZC 的 WTP 高于 SC 的 WTP、高于 MG 的 WTP；不同案例地相对充裕型旅游资源比较，游客受访者对保护海滩旅游资源非使用价值的 WTP 排序为：ZB 的 WTP 高于 SB 的 WTP、高于 MB 的 WTP；海洋文化旅游资源与海洋自然旅游资源比较，游客受访者对保护舟山群岛海洋文化旅游资源非使用价值的 WTP 高于保护其他海洋自然旅游资源非使用价值的 WTP，即：ZC 的 WTP 高于 MB 的 WTP、MG 的 WTP、ZB 的 WTP、SB 的 WTP 和 SC 的 WTP。消除各类海洋旅游资源子样本的人口社会特征差异后，不同海洋旅游资源的 WTP 比较结果与原定序 logit 回归结果一致。

表 6.12　　　　　　　　预测概率调整结果

比较研究		$\hat{Pr}$ ($WTP\_Ordinal=1$)	$\hat{Pr}$ ($WTP\_Ordinal=2$)	$\hat{Pr}$ ($WTP\_Ordinal=3$)
MG 和 MB	MG at MG	0.37	0.37	0.26
	MB at MG	0.47	0.32	0.21
MG 和 MB	MG at MB	0.38	0.37	0.25
	MB at MB	0.47	0.32	0.21
ZC 和 ZB	ZC at ZC	0.29	0.29	0.42
	ZB at ZC	0.34	0.34	0.32
ZC 和 ZB	ZC at ZB	0.29	0.29	0.42
	ZB at ZB	0.34	0.34	0.32
SC 和 SB	SC at SC	0.38	0.31	0.31
	SB at SC	0.38	0.32	0.30

续表

比较研究		$\hat{Pr}$ (WTP_Ordinal=1)	$\hat{Pr}$ (WTP_Ordinal=2)	$\hat{Pr}$ (WTP_Ordinal=3)
SC 和 SB	SC at SB	0.40	0.31	0.29
	SB at SB	0.40	0.32	0.28
MG，ZC 和 SC	MG at MG	0.37	0.37	0.26
	ZC at MG	0.32	0.30	0.38
	SC at MG	0.42	0.31	0.27
MG，ZC 和 SC	MG at SC	0.34	0.37	0.29
	ZC at SC	0.29	0.29	0.42
	SC at SC	0.38	0.31	0.31
MG，ZC 和 SC	MG at ZC	0.34	0.37	0.29
	ZC at ZC	0.29	0.29	0.42
	SC at ZC	0.37	0.32	0.32
MB，ZB 和 SB	MB at MB	0.47	0.32	0.21
	ZB at MB	0.39	0.34	0.27
	SB at MB	0.43	0.32	0.25
MB，ZB 和 SB	MB at SB	0.46	0.33	0.22
	ZB at SB	0.38	0.34	0.29
	SB at SB	0.40	0.32	0.28
MB，ZB 和 SB	MB at ZB	0.44	0.33	0.23
	ZB at ZB	0.34	0.34	0.32
	SB at ZB	0.38	0.32	0.30

第五节 估值比较Ⅲ广义定序 logit 模型分析

为了进行稳健性检验，放宽了比例比数模型，采用限制性较小的广义定序 Logit 模型再次回归。运用 Williams（2016）的 Stata 程序 Gologit2 命令，并指定 Autofit 和 Gamma 选项。其中，Autofit 选项设定下，Stata 使用迭代过程确定最适合数据的模型；Gamma 选项设定下，每个解释变量有 1 个 Beta 系数和 M−2 个 Gamma 系数，M 为被解释变量的取值种类，$WTP\_Ordinal$ 是三分类变量，即 M = 3。当某个解释变量满足比例比数假设时，Gamma 系数为 0；当不满足比例比数假设时，Gamma 系数不为 0 并在结果中报告。

广义定序 logit 模型回归结果如表 6.13 所示。从放宽比例比数假设来看，只有模型 1 中的收入变量和模型 4 中的 $Resource-MG$ 变量被放宽，但系数的方向没有改变。因此，从比例比数假设的角度，广义定序 logit 模型回归结果证实了定序 logit 模型回归结果的稳健性。

表 6.13　　　　　　　　广义定序 logit 模型回归结果

	Variables	Model1 MG 和 MB	Model2 ZC 和 ZB	Model3 SC 和 SB	Model4 MG, ZC 和 SC	Model5 MB, ZB 和 SB
Beta	*Gender*	0.06 (0.11)	0.19 (0.11)	0.12 (0.09)	0.15* (0.08)	0.08 (0.08)
	Age	−0.01 (0.01)	−0.00 (0.01)	−0.01 (0.01)	−0.01 (0.01)	−0.01 (0.01)
	Education	0.06 (0.13)	0.08 (0.12)	0.23** (0.11)	0.08 (0.10)	0.17* (0.10)
	Log of income	0.65*** (0.11)	1.19*** (0.10)	1.17*** (0.08)	1.06*** (0.07)	1.07*** (0.07)
	Resource−Scarce	0.36*** (0.11)	0.40*** (0.11)	0.03 (0.09)		
	Resource−MG				−0.25** (0.12)	
	Resource−SC				−0.45*** (0.11)	
	Resource−MB					−0.36*** (0.12)
	Resource−SB					−0.12 (0.10)
Gamma	*Log of income*	0.27** (0.11)				
	Resource−MG				−0.30*** (0.11)	

续表

Variables		Model1 MG 和 MB	Model2 ZC 和 ZB	Model3 SC 和 SB	Model4 MG，ZC 和 SC	Model5 MB，ZB 和 SB
Alpha	Constant1	-1.13***	-2.34***	-2.35***	-1.54***	-1.96***
		(0.37)	(0.34)	(0.29)	(0.27)	(0.27)
	Constant2	-3.39***	-3.86***	-3.86***	-2.97***	-3.51***
		(0.40)	(0.35)	(0.30)	(0.28)	(0.27)
Number of observations		1190	1150	1901	2153	2088
Log likelihood		-1231.69	-1169.07	-1921.64	-2210.12	-2121.74
Pseudo R^2		0.04	0.07	0.07	0.07	0.07
LR χ^2		93.32	185.26	308.80	306.86	293.62
Prob $>\chi^2$		0.00	0.00	0.00	0.00	0.00

注：a. *$p<0.1$，**$p<0.05$，***$p<0.01$；b. 括号中为标准误。

从变量的相关性与显著性来看，两种模型的相关旅游资源虚拟变量回归系数和人口社会特征变量回归系数的方向与显著性一致，这也证实了定序 logit 模型回归结果的稳健性。

第六节　估值比较Ⅲ讨论与结论

一　讨论

（一）WTP 的差异

在海洋旅游资源领域，多数已有的价值评估文献主要集中在特定地理区域的单一旅游资源的使用价值或非市场价值评估上。① 与已有研究不同的是，本书研究从多案例地和多种资源类型视角探索了非使用价值，揭示的结果有益于政策制定。六组子样本估值结果表明，WTP 处于 192.93—373.16 元。结果提供了海洋旅游资源非使用价值在我国存在的证据，进而海洋旅游资源保护或恢复工程的成本—收益分析应包含非使用价值。同一案例地比较，游客对保护相对稀缺型旅游资源的

---

① Edgar Robles‑Zavala and Alejandra Guadalupe Chang Reynoso, "The Recreational Value of Coral Reefs in the Mexican Pacific", *Ocean & Coastal Management*, Vol. 157, May 2018.

WTP 高于保护相对充裕型旅游资源的 WTP。我国大陆和海岛岸线长，多数沿海旅游城市和旅游型海岛有高质量的海滩旅游资源；相对于海滩，海洋地质遗迹、海洋文化和珊瑚礁是相对稀缺型旅游资源，只分布在我国特定区域。此外，公众倾向于对相对独特和稀缺资源支付更多①，与公众偏爱分配保护基金给可爱的和有魅力的物种较为相似②。相对于已有研究多数集中在海滩属性与非市场经济价值尤其是使用价值上③，本书研究集中在海滩旅游资源非使用价值上。结果表明，保护海滩旅游资源非使用价值的 WTP 大小与待估海滩旅游资源的长度一致，即海滩长度越长 WTP 越大；但随着海滩长度增长，WTP 边际递减。前期已有研究发现海洋旅游资源使用价值呈现出边际效应递减。④ 然而，本书研究证实了环境保护非使用价值边际效应递减的已有发现。⑤ 本书研究也揭示了与海洋自然旅游资源相比，游客对海洋文化旅游资源支付更多。海洋文化旅游资源展现出更复杂属性⑥，不仅包含物理属性，还

---

① Allan Provins, et al., "Valuation of the Historic Environment: The Scope for Using Economic Valuation Evidence in the Appraisal of Heritage-related Projects", *Progress in Planning*, Vol. 69, No. 4, May 2008.

② Kristy Wallmo and Daniel K. Lew, "Public Willingness to Pay for Recovering and Downlisting Threatened and Endangered Marine Species", *Conservation Biology*, Vol. 26, No. 5, October 2012.

③ Juliana Castaño-Isaza, et al., "Valuing Beaches to Develop Payment for Ecosystem Services Schemes in Colombia's Seaflower Marine Protected Area", *Ecosystem Services*, Vol. 11, February 2015.

④ Marcus Peng and Kristen L. L. Oleson, "Beach Recreationalists' Willingness to Pay and Economic Implications of Coastal Water Quality Problems in Hawaii", *Ecological Economics*, Vol. 136, June 2017; Peter W. Schuhmann, et al., "Recreational SCUBA Divers' Willingness to Pay for Marine Biodiversity in Barbados", *Journal of Environmental Management*, Vol. 121, May 2013; Michelle Cazabon-Mannette, et al., "Estimates of the Non-market Value of Sea Turtles in Tobago Using Stated Preference Techniques", *Journal of Environmental Management*, Vol. 192, May 2017.

⑤ Vito Frontuto, et al., "Earmarking Conservation: Further Inquiry on Scope Effects in Stated Preference Methods Applied to Nature-based Tourism", *Tourism Management*, Vol. 60, June 2017.

⑥ Sini Miller, et al., "Estimating Indigenous Cultural Values of Freshwater: A Choice Experiment Approach to Māori Values in New Zealand", *Ecological Economics*, Vol. 118, October 2015; E. C. M. Ruijgrok, "The three Economic Values of Cultural Heritage: A Case Study in the Netherlands", *Journal of Cultural Heritage*, Vol. 7, July-September 2006.

包含社会和想象属性①，同时与历史和文化联系紧密②。所以，海洋文化旅游资源具有异质性，更难发现替代品。同时，游客感知文化遗产作为他们自己遗产的一部分③，更加重视文化遗产传承给下一代，确保社会文化的可持续性。④ 而且，更高的文化意识和更高的经济水平，提高了对文化旅游资源的关注⑤。上述结果证实了公众保护不同类型海洋旅游资源非使用价值的差异，与前期已有文献只关注海洋生物一类资源不同⑥，本书研究集中在不同类型海洋旅游资源 WTP 的差异。公众保护海洋旅游资源非使用价值的偏好也影响管理决策：一方面，在资源保护资金有限的情况下，证实的偏好差异为确定优先保护项目和资金再分配提供了理论支持⑦；另一方面，具有更高非使用价值的更具吸引力的海洋旅游资源在保护中扮演着关键角色，这类似于旗舰物种效应。在政策设计中强调更具吸引力的资源，提高公众对保护海洋旅游资源非使用价值的意识和参与度。

（二）CVM 有效性和可靠性检验

范围检验、加总检验等内部一致性检验是 NOAA 和一些重要经济

---

① Erwin Dekker, "Two Approaches to Study the Value of Art and Culture, and the Emergence of a Third", *Journal of Cultural Economics*, Vol. 39, No. 4, November 2014.

② Allan Provins, et al., "Valuation of the Historic Environment: The Scope for Using Economic Valuation Evidence in the Appraisal of Heritage – related Projects", *Progress in Planning*, Vol. 69, No. 4, May 2008.

③ Yaniv Poria, et al., "Heritage Site Perceptions and Motivations to Visit", *Journal of Travel Research*, Vol. 44, February 2006.

④ Kirsten L. L. Oleson, et al., "Cultural Bequest Values for Ecosystem Service Flows among Indigenous Fishers: A Discrete Choice Experiment Validated with Mixed Methods", *Ecological Economics*, Vol. 114, June 2015; E. C. M. Ruijgrok, "The three Economic Values of Cultural Heritage: A Case Study in the Netherlands", *Journal of Cultural Heritage*, Vol. 7, July – September 2006.

⑤ Ana Bedate, et al., "Economic Valuation of the Cultural Heritage: Application to four Case Studies in Spain", *Journal of Cultural Heritage*, Vol. 5, No. 1, January – March 2004.

⑥ Kristy Wallmo and Daniel K. Lew, "Public Willingness to Pay for Recovering and Downlisting Threatened and Endangered Marine Species", *Conservation Biology*, Vol. 26, No. 5, October 2012; Adriana Ressurreição, et al., "Different Cultures, Different Values: The Role of Cultural Variation in Public's WTP for Marine Species Conservation", *Biological Conservation*, Vol. 145, No. 1, January 2012.

⑦ Peter W. Schuhmann, et al., "Visitors' Willingness to Pay Marine Conservation Fees in Barbados", *Tourism Management*, Vol. 71, April 2019.

学家推荐的评估 CVM 研究有效性和可靠性的方法。① Arrow 等提出对范围的充分反应是检验 CVM 研究可靠性的重要标准。在资源与环境经济学领域，范围检验通常集中在检验同一类资源，是否 WTP 随着待估公共物品范围变化而变化。对同一类资源不同范围的 WTP 可能被边际效应递减和饱和程度影响，导致范围检验结果不能用于验证对范围反应的充分性或合理性。② 加总检验通常也集中在同一类资源验证是否总体的 WTP 等于个体增量的 WTP 之和，这不仅受到收入效应的影响③，而且决定是否对范围反应是充分的也有缺陷④。本书研究提供了衡量 CVM 研究有效性和可靠性新视角，即通过探索是否和怎样不同类型海洋旅游资源的 WTP 不同。结果表明，资源虚拟变量对 WTP_Ordinal 变量有显著影响，WTP 随着待估资源类型的变化而调整，这证明了陈述性偏好方法 CVM 在非使用价值估值中是有效的和可靠的。同时，从不同资源类型视角探索 WTP 的差异，可能是评估 CVM 特定研究有效性和可靠性的一种方法，作为范围检验和加总检验的有益补充。这种方法不仅能避免边际效应递减和饱和程度对范围检验的影响，也能避免收入效应对加总检验的影响。

二 结论

（1）公众对保护海洋旅游资源非使用价值具有非常强的支付意愿，六组游客受访者样本的正支付意愿率分别为 99.16%、98.74%、97.56%、97.77%、98.32% 和 98.52%，均高于 95%。这证实了我国

---

① Kenneth Arrow, et al., "Report of the NOAA Panel on Contingent Valuation", *Federal Register*, Vol. 58, No. 10, January 1993; Peter A. Diamond and Jerry A. Hausman, "Contingent Valuation: Is Some Number better than no Number?", *The Journal of Economic Perspectives*, Vol. 8, No. 4, Fall 1994; William Desvousges, et al., "An Adding-up Test on Contingent Valuations of River and Lake Quality", *Land Economics*, Vol. 91, No. 3, August 2015.

② Kenneth Arrow, et al., *Comments on Proposed NOAA Scope Test. Appendix D of Comments on Proposed NOAA/DOI Regulations on Natural Resource Damage Assessment*, U.S.: Environmental Protection Agency, 1994, pp. D1 - D2; William Desvousges, et al., "An Adding-up Test on Contingent Valuations of River and Lake Quality", *Land Economics*, Vol. 91, No. 3, August 2015.

③ Levan Elbakidze and Rodolfo M. Nayga Jr., "The Adding-up Test in an Incentivized Value Elicitation Mechanism: The Role of the Income Effect", *Environmental and Resource Economics*, Vol. 71, No. 3, November 2018.

④ John C. Whitehead, "Plausible Responsiveness to Scope in Contingent Valuation", *Ecological Economics*, Vol. 128, August 2016.

海洋旅游资源非使用价值的存在。

（2）同一个案例地内部之间，游客受访者对保护相对稀缺型旅游资源非使用价值的 WTP 比保护相对充裕型旅游资源的 WTP 高。定序 logit 模型回归结果与调整的预测概率结果显示，庙岛群岛案例地的游客受访者对保护海洋地质遗迹旅游资源非使用价值的 WTP 大于 100 元的概率比保护海滩旅游资源的高，WTP 小于等于 50 元的概率比海滩旅游资源的低；舟山群岛和三亚及其附近岛屿案例地结果与之相似。同时，广义定序 logit 模型回归结果证实了以上结果具有稳健性。

（3）不同案例地之间相对稀缺型旅游资源比较，游客受访者对保护海洋文化旅游资源非使用价值的 WTP 最高，保护珊瑚礁旅游资源非使用价值的 WTP 次之，保护海洋地质遗迹旅游资源非使用价值的 WTP 最低。定序 logit 模型、广义定序 logit 模型的回归结果均证实此结论。

（4）不同案例地之间相对充裕型旅游资源比较，游客受访者对保护海滩旅游资源非使用价值的 WTP 排序为：舟山群岛海滩的 WTP > 三亚及其附近岛屿海滩的 WTP > 庙岛群岛海滩的 WTP。定序 logit 模型、广义定序 logit 模型的回归结果均证实此结论。同时，随着海滩长度的增加呈现边际效应递减。

（5）游客受访者对保护海洋文化旅游资源非使用价值的 WTP 高于保护海洋自然旅游资源非使用价值的 WTP。定序 logit 模型、广义定序 logit 模型回归结果均证实此结论。

第三篇　群岛旅游资源非使用价值评估嵌入效应问题研究

第七章

嵌入效应问题研究总体框架和研究思路

第一节 总体框架

一 嵌入效应研究方案设计

我国群岛旅游资源主要包括海滩、海洋文化、海洋地质遗迹和珊瑚礁。同一群岛的海滩之间和珊瑚礁之间较为相似，具有竞争替代性，将其称为竞争替代型旅游资源；同一群岛的海洋（宗教、沙雕艺术、影视）文化之间和海洋地质（海积地貌、海蚀地貌）遗迹之间存在显著差异，具有合作互补性，将其称为合作互补型旅游资源；同时，将同一群岛拥有海滩与海洋文化两类旅游资源称为复合型旅游资源。本书分别设计竞争替代型海滩旅游资源、竞争替代型珊瑚礁旅游资源、合作互补型海洋文化旅游资源、合作互补型海洋地质遗迹旅游资源和复合型海滩与海洋文化旅游资源的嵌入效应研究方案。每一类旅游资源（或复合型旅游资源）的嵌入效应研究方案拟分别设计3—5个独立子样本，通过独立子样本之间的比较，验证外部范围嵌入效应问题；每个独立子样本内部拟分别设计1—4个旅游资源非使用价值待估对象，通过独立子样本内部的比较，验证内部范围嵌入效应问题。

二 范围检验假设和计量经济模型

以每一类旅游资源（或复合型旅游资源）设计的3—5个独立子样

本和独立子样本内部设计的1—4个旅游资源非使用价值待估对象为基础，每一类旅游资源（或复合型旅游资源）拟分别设计1—3个外部范围检验零假设和2—4个内部范围检验零假设。本书研究CVM支付意愿的引导技术采用支付卡式，外部范围和内部范围假设检验方法采用T检验、Mann–Whitney U检验（两独立样本）、Kruskal–Wallis检验（多独立样本）和单因素方差分析，回归模型拟选取IR模型、Logit模型和OLS模型。

三 不同群岛典型案例研究

综合考虑群岛旅游资源类型和地理位置，选取我国四大海区3个旅游群岛的10个典型旅游岛和2个海湾作为研究案例地，以10个旅游岛和2个海湾的典型旅游资源作为案例研究对象（见表7.1），开展群岛旅游资源非使用价值评估嵌入效应问题的案例研究工作。其中，庙岛群岛的南长山岛、北长山岛和大黑山岛案例地，重点研究海积地貌遗迹和海蚀地貌遗迹（合作互补型）和海滩旅游资源的嵌入效应问题；舟山群岛的普陀山岛、朱家尖岛、桃花岛、岱山岛和泗礁山岛案例地，重点研究海滩（竞争替代型）旅游资源的嵌入效应问题；舟山群岛的普陀山岛、朱家尖岛和桃花岛案例地，重点研究海洋文化（合作互补型）旅游资源的嵌入效应问题和海滩与海洋文化（复合型）旅游资源的嵌入效应问题；三亚及其附近岛屿的西岛、蜈支洲岛、亚龙湾和大东海案例地，重点研究海滩（竞争替代型）旅游资源的嵌入效应问题和珊瑚礁（竞争替代型）旅游资源的嵌入效应问题。

表7.1　　　　研究选取的典型旅游岛、海湾和典型旅游资源

海域	群岛	典型旅游岛、海湾	典型旅游资源
黄渤海区	庙岛群岛	南长山岛	海滩、海积地貌遗迹—海蚀地貌遗迹
		北长山岛	海滩、海积地貌遗迹—海蚀地貌遗迹
		大黑山岛	海积地貌遗迹—海蚀地貌遗迹
东海区	舟山群岛	普陀山岛	海滩、海洋宗教文化
		朱家尖岛	海滩、海洋沙雕艺术文化

续表

海域	群岛	典型旅游岛、海湾	典型旅游资源
东海区	舟山群岛	桃花岛	海滩、海洋影视文化
		岱山岛	海滩
		泗礁山岛	海滩
南海区	三亚及其附近岛屿	西岛	海滩、珊瑚礁
		蜈支洲岛	海滩、珊瑚礁
		亚龙湾	海滩、珊瑚礁
		大东海	海滩、珊瑚礁

四 嵌入效应问题识别

对比研究 3 个群岛竞争替代型旅游资源（海滩、珊瑚礁）、合作互补型旅游资源（海洋文化、海洋地质遗迹）和复合型旅游资源（海滩与海洋文化）的嵌入效应验证结果，本书重点研究识别以下主要因素对 3 类旅游资源嵌入效应问题的影响：替代效应、边际效应递减、收入效应、饱和程度等对竞争替代型旅游资源（海滩、珊瑚礁）嵌入效应问题的影响；收入效应、边际效应递减等对合作互补型旅游资源（海洋文化、海洋地质遗迹）嵌入效应问题的影响；替代效应、边际效应递减和收入效应对复合型旅游资源（海滩与海洋文化）嵌入效应问题的影响。

第二节 研究思路

研究基本思路：嵌入效应研究方案设计、假设和模型、典型案例和嵌入效应问题识别（见图 7.1）。

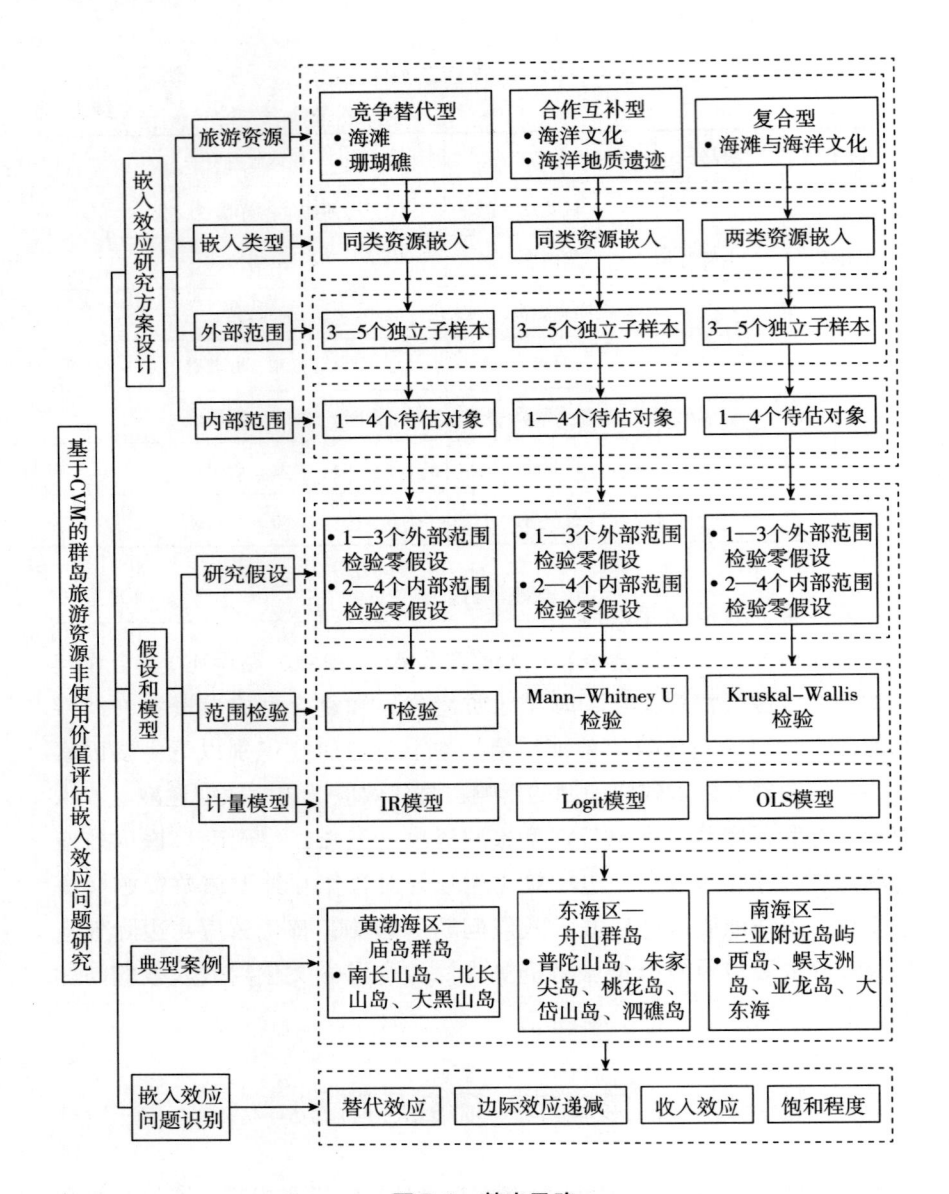

图 7.1 基本思路

第八章

嵌入效应问题研究庙岛群岛案例

第一节 庙岛群岛嵌入效应验证方案设计

参照嵌入物品、序列物品等已有研究成果,本书采用的海滩旅游资源和海洋地质遗迹旅游资源嵌入设计方案①:独立列表(Exclusive List)方法、预先披露(Advanced Disclosure)信息设计和自上而下(Top - down)及自下而上(Bottom - up)相结合的估值问题顺序。本书研究设计5组独立子样本,其中海滩旅游资源设计2组独立子样本,每组独

---

① Ian J. Bateman, et al., *Visible Choice Sets and Scope Sensitivity: An Experimental and Field Test of Study Design Effects upon Nested Contingent Values*, UK: The Centre for Social and Economic Research on the Global Environmental (CSERGE), University of East Anglia, Working Paper EDM, NO. 01 - 01, 2001, pp. 4 - 7; Ian J. Bateman, et al., "On Visible Choice Sets and Scope Sensitivity", *Journal of Environmental Economics and Management*, Vol. 47, No. 1, January 2004; Nick Hanley, et al., "Aggregating the Benefits of Environmental Improvements: Distance - decay Functions for Use and Non - use Values", *Journal of Environmental Management*, Vol. 68, No. 3, July 2003; Richard T. Carson and Robert Cameron Mitchell, "Sequencing and Nesting in Contingent Valuation Surveys", *Journal of Environmental Economics and Management*, Vol. 28, No. 2, March 1995; N. A. Powe and I. J. Bateman, "Ordering Effects in Nested 'Top - down' and 'Bottom - up' Contingent Valuation Designs", *Ecological Economics*, Vol. 45, No. 2, June 2003; Bente Halvorsen, "Ordering Effects in Contingent Valuation Surveys: Willingness to Pay for Reduced Health Damage from Air Pollution", *Environmental and Resource Economics*, Vol. 8, No. 4, December 1996; Timothy L. McDaniels, et al., "Decision Structuring to Alleviate Embedding in Environmental Valuation", *Ecological Economics*, Vol. 46, No. 1, August 2003.

立子样本设计1—2个待估海滩旅游资源非使用价值评估的核心估值问题（见表8.1）；海洋地质遗迹旅游资源设计3组独立子样本，每组独立子样本设计1—3个待估海洋地质遗迹旅游资源非使用价值评估的核心估值问题（见表8.2）。

一　海滩旅游资源嵌入效应验证方案设计

（一）海滩旅游资源设计思路

海滩旅游资源嵌入效应验证方案设计思路如表8.1所示。

表8.1　　海滩旅游资源嵌入效应验证方案设计思路

海滩旅游资源——S-子样本Ⅰ	海滩旅游资源——S-子样本Ⅱ
$MS_{Ⅰ}^{1}$	$MS_{Ⅱ}^{1}$
—	$bs_{Ⅱ}^{2}$

注：下角标"Ⅰ—Ⅱ"表示子样本之间的价值序号；上角标"1—2"表示子样本内部的价值序号；MS表示庙岛群岛待估海滩旅游资源，$MS = bs + ns$；bs和ns分别表示北长山岛和南长山岛待估海滩旅游资源。

（二）海滩旅游资源研究假设

依据表8.1设计思路，提出各待估海滩旅游资源非使用价值评估数量范围嵌入效应验证的外部范围检验零假设和内部范围检验零假设。

海滩旅游资源外部范围检验零假设：

①$ex^s - H_1^0$：$WTP[MS_{Ⅰ}^{1}] = WTP[MS_{Ⅱ}^{1}]$

②$ex^s - H_2^0$：$WTP[bs_{Ⅱ}^{2}] \leq WTP[MS_{Ⅰ}^{1}]$

海滩旅游资源内部范围检验零假设：

$in^s - H_1^0$：$WTP[bs_{Ⅱ}^{2}] \leq WTP[MS_{Ⅱ}^{1}]$

二　海洋地质遗迹旅游资源嵌入效应验证方案设计

（一）海洋地质遗迹旅游资源设计思路

海洋地质遗迹旅游资源嵌入效应验证方案设计思路如表8.2所示。

（二）海洋地质遗迹旅游资源研究假设

依据表8.2设计思路，提出各待估海洋地质遗迹旅游资源非使用价值评估数量范围嵌入效应验证的外部范围检验零假设和内部范围检验零假设。

表 8.2　海洋地质遗迹旅游资源嵌入效应验证方案设计思路

海洋地质遗迹旅游资源 G – 子样本 I	海洋地质遗迹旅游资源 G – 子样本 II	海洋地质遗迹旅游资源 G – 子样本 III
MG_{I}^{1}	MG_{II}^{1}	MG_{III}^{1}
—	bg_{II}^{2}	ng_{III}^{2}
—	—	$(bg+ng)_{\mathrm{III}}^{3}$

注：下角标"I—III"表示子样本之间的价值序号；上角标"1—3"表示子样本内部的价值序号；MG 表示庙岛群岛待估海洋地质遗迹旅游资源，$MG=bg+ng+dg$；bg、ng 和 dg 分别表示北长山岛、南长山岛和大黑山岛待估海洋地质遗迹旅游资源；$(bg+ng)$ 表示北长山岛加南长山岛待估海洋地质遗迹旅游资源。

海洋地质遗迹旅游资源外部范围检验零假设：

①$ex^{g} - H_{1}^{0}$：$WTP[MG_{\mathrm{I}}^{1}] = WTP[MG_{\mathrm{II}}^{1}] = WTP[MG_{\mathrm{III}}^{1}]$

②$ex^{g} - H_{2}^{0}$：$WTP[bg_{\mathrm{II}}^{2}] \leqslant WTP[(bg+ng)_{\mathrm{III}}^{3}] \leqslant WTP[MG_{\mathrm{I}}^{1}]$

③$ex^{g} - H_{3}^{0}$：$WTP[ng_{\mathrm{III}}^{2}] \leqslant WTP[MG_{\mathrm{I}}^{1}]$

海洋地质遗迹旅游资源内部范围检验零假设：

①$in^{g} - H_{1}^{0}$：$WTP[bg_{\mathrm{II}}^{2}] \leqslant WTP[MG_{\mathrm{II}}^{1}]$

②$in^{g} - H_{2}^{0}$：$WTP[ng_{\mathrm{III}}^{2}] \leqslant WTP[(bg+ng)_{\mathrm{III}}^{3}] \leqslant WTP[MG_{\mathrm{III}}^{1}]$

第二节　庙岛群岛嵌入效应验证方案实施

一　核心估值问题

庙岛群岛海滩旅游资源共设计了 2 种独立子样本调查问卷，每种问卷的核心估值问题采用嵌入方式（见表 8.1），以表 8.1 "S – 子样本 II" 为例，MS_{II}^{1} 和 bs_{II}^{2} 核心估值问题分别为："台风等极端天气和旅游等人类活动将对北长山岛月牙湾海滩和南长山岛明珠广场海滩等庙岛群岛主要海岛的海滩旅游资源造成严重影响，为了保护这两个海岛的海滩旅游资源，使其可持续存在、子孙后代使用或自己未来使用，设想成立一个海滩旅游资源保护基金，若该基金正在筹集资金阶段，您是否愿意通过一次性捐款的方式支持这项海滩旅游资源保护活动？"和"……将对北长山岛月牙湾海滩旅游资源……，为了保护北长山岛的海滩旅游资源……"。

庙岛群岛海洋地质遗迹旅游资源共设计了3种独立子样本调查问卷，每种问卷的核心估值问题采用嵌入方式（见表8.2），以表8.2"G-子样本Ⅲ"为例，$MG_{Ⅲ}^1$、$ng_{Ⅲ}^2$和$(bg+ng)_{Ⅲ}^3$核心估值问题分别为："旅游开发等人类活动及海水侵蚀、风化作用等自然活动将对北长山岛九丈崖和月牙湾、南长山岛黄渤海分界线和望夫礁、大黑山岛龙爪山等庙岛群岛主要海岛的海洋地质遗迹旅游资源造成严重影响，为了保护这三个海岛的海洋地质遗迹旅游资源，使其可持续存在、子孙后代使用或自己未来使用，设想成立一个海洋地质遗迹旅游资源保护基金，若该基金正在筹集资金阶段，您是否愿意通过一次性捐款的方式支持这项海洋地质遗迹旅游资源保护活动？"、"……将对南长山岛黄渤海分界线和望夫礁海洋地质遗迹旅游资源……，为了保护南长山岛的海洋地质遗迹旅游资源……"和"……将对北长山岛九丈崖和月牙湾、南长山岛黄渤海分界线和望夫礁等海洋地质遗迹旅游资源……，为了保护北长山岛和南长山岛的海洋地质遗迹旅游资源……"。

海滩和海洋地质遗迹旅游资源支付卡式投标值：1、2、5、10、20、30、50、60、80、100、120、150、200、300、400、500、600、800、1000、1500、2000。

二 样本分布

共获得居民和游客面对面调查问卷1706份，其中，有效问卷1679份，有效率98.42%；其中包含零样本36份，真零样本20份，抗议性零样本16份；进一步分析时剔除了16份抗议性零支付样本，最终分析的样本量为1663份（见表8.3）。

表8.3　　　　　　　　有效样本分布

调查地点	海滩			海洋地质遗迹		
	居民+游客	居民	游客	居民+游客	居民	游客
九丈崖景区	193	1	192	286	1	285
月牙湾景区	193	4	189	284	0	284
望夫礁景区	96	1	95	142	1	141
南长山岛和北长山岛	189	188	1	280	277	3
合计	671	194	477	992	279	713

注：表中有效样本未包含抗议性零样本。

三 描述性统计分析

在 1663 份样本中，18—65 周岁样本占比为 99.58%，17 周岁和 66—69 周岁样本占比为 0.42%。受访者中男性占比为 48%，平均年龄处于 38—39 周岁，平均学历低于大专水平，平均家庭年收入为 12.37 万元；短途游客、中途游客、长途游客和居民样本占比分别为 25.44%、23.27%、22.85% 和 28.44%（见表 8.4）。

表 8.4　　　　　　　　　　样本人口社会特征

旅游资源	样本量	性别	年龄（岁）	学历	家庭年收入（万元）	居民比例（%）	短途游客比例（%）	中途游客比例（%）	长途游客比例（%）
海滩	671	0.47	39	2.60	11.89	28.91	26.83	22.21	22.06
海洋地质遗迹	992	0.48	38	2.80	12.70	28.13	24.50	23.99	23.39
总样本	1663	0.48	38	2.70	12.37	28.44	25.44	23.27	22.85

注：性别：男 =1，女 =0；年龄：2017 - 出生年；学历：1 = 初中及以下，2 = 高中、中专、技校，3 = 大专，4 = 本科，5 = 研究生；短途客源地为山东，中途客源地为北京、天津和河北；长途客源地为大陆其他省（市、区）。

运用两独立样本参数 t – test 和两独立样本非参数 Mann – Whitney U test，进行海滩两组独立子样本人口社会特征差异显著性检验；运用多独立样本参数 one – way ANOVA 和多独立样本非参数 Kruskal – Wallis test，进行海洋地质遗迹三组独立子样本人口社会特征差异显著性检验。海滩旅游资源两组独立子样本之间或海洋地质遗迹旅游资源三组独立子样本之间人口社会特征比较，均通过了参数检验和非参数检验，表明海滩旅游资源样本组之间或海洋地质遗迹旅游资源样本组之间人口社会特征不存在显著差异（见表 8.5）。

表 8.5　　　　样本组之间人口社会特征差异显著性检验

样本组	参数和非参数检验	性别	年龄	学历	家庭年收入
S 子样本 I—II	独立样本 t – test	0.85(-0.19)	0.06(1.86)	0.70(-0.38)	0.14(-1.49)
	Mann – Whitney U test	0.85(-0.19)	0.13(-1.51)	0.76(-0.31)	0.36(-0.91)

续表

样本组	参数和非参数检验	性别	年龄	学历	家庭年收入
G-子样本 I—Ⅲ	one-way ANOVA	0.68(0.39)	0.34(1.07)	0.51(0.68)	0.27(1.31)
	Kruskal-Wallis test	0.68(0.78)	0.28(2.54)	0.51(1.33)	0.31(2.36)

注：括号中数值为 F、Z 或卡方值。

第三节 庙岛群岛结果分析

一 WTP 结果分析

本书研究运用最小二乘（Ordinary Least Square, OLS）回归和区间回归（Interval Regression, IR）①，计算受访者对保护海滩和海洋地质遗迹的 9 种待估海洋旅游资源非使用价值的 WTP（详细计算参见附录1）。9 种待估海洋旅游资源非使用价值 WTP 的原始均值、OLS 均值和 IR 均值如表 8.6 所示。

表 8.6　　　　　　　　　WTP 均值

变量	原始均值（元）	OLS 均值（元）	IR 均值（元）	三种方法均值（元）
$WTP[MS^1_{\mathrm{I}}]$	147.46	170.01(75.10)	163.99(69.37)	160.49
$WTP[MS^1_{\mathrm{II}}]$	148.02	167.54(83.75)	163.74(81.62)	159.77
$WTP[bs^2_{\mathrm{II}}]$	128.82	146.86(84.62)	143.40(78.98)	139.69
$WTP[MG^1_{\mathrm{I}}]$	185.64	215.51(122.94)	206.81(115.08)	202.65
$WTP[MG^1_{\mathrm{II}}]$	191.10	221.46(148.03)	213.03(140.14)	208.53
$WTP[MG^1_{\mathrm{III}}]$	183.41	209.12(120.23)	203.41(115.34)	198.65
$WTP[bg^2_{\mathrm{II}}]$	159.20	184.03(138.90)	177.74(131.18)	173.66
$WTP[ng^2_{\mathrm{III}}]$	155.92	176.99(95.53)	172.37(92.26)	168.43
$WTP[(bg+ng)^3_{\mathrm{III}}]$	178.98	203.62(119.44)	198.23(114.96)	193.61

注：各符号含义同表 8.1 和表 8.2；括号中数值为稳健标准误。

---

① Trudy Ann Cameron and Daniel D. Huppert, "OLS Versus ML Estimation of Non-market Resource Values with Payment Card Interval Data", *Journal of Environmental Economics and Management*, Vol. 17, No. 3, November 1989; Stefania Tonin, "Citizens' Perspectives on Marine Protected Areas as a Governance Strategy to Effectively Preserve Marine Ecosystem Services and Biodiversity", *Ecosystem Services*, Vol. 34, December 2018.

二 范围检验结果分析

内部范围检验两组配对样本比较，采用两配对样本参数 t – test 和两配对样本非参数 Wilcoxon signed – rank test；三组配对样本比较，采用非参数多配对样本 Friedman test。外部范围检验两组独立样本比较，采用两独立样本参数 t – test 和两独立样本非参数 Mann – Whitney U test；三组独立样本比较，采用多独立样本参数 one – way ANOVA 和多独立样本非参数 Kruskal – Wallis test。因可能存在"过度嵌入效应"（Over – embedding）现象，所以，本书研究两者之间比较用的都是双尾（2 – tailed）。

从海滩或海洋地质遗迹旅游资源范围检验结果来看（见表 8.7、表 8.8），各待估海滩旅游资源或海洋地质遗迹旅游资源内部范围检验全部通过；不同独立子样本调查同一待估海滩旅游资源（MS_I^1 和 MS_{II}^1）估值比较，2 组独立子样本最大范围 WTP 估值结果较稳定，通过了外部范围检验；不同独立子样本调查同一待估海洋地质遗迹旅游资源（MG_I^1、MG_{II}^1 和 MG_{III}^1）估值比较，3 组独立子样本最大范围 WTP 估值结果较稳定，通过了外部范围检验；这证明本研究的问卷设计、调查实施和 WTP 估值结果具有可靠性（Reliability）。除了 $ex^g – H_3^0$ 的非参数检验外，其他各待估海滩旅游资源 WTP 估值比较或各待估海洋地质遗迹旅游资源 WTP 估值比较，均未通过外部范围参数检验和非参数检验。从各待估海滩旅游资源 WTP 估值比较或各待估海洋地质遗迹旅游资源 WTP 估值比较来看，受访者能够感知到各待估海滩旅游资源或各待估海洋地质遗迹旅游资源内部数量范围或外部数量范围的变化，并且 WTP 估值大小的变化方向与数量范围大小的变化方向一致（见图 8.1、图 8.3）。

表 8.7　海滩和海洋地质遗迹旅游资源内部范围检验结果

零假设检验		非参数检验		参数检验	
		Z/Chi – Square	Asymp. Sig.	t	Sig.
$in^s – H_1^0$	$WTP[bs_{II}^2] = WTP[MS_{II}^1]$	–4.71	0.00	–3.10	0.00
$in^g – H_1^0$	$WTP[bg_{II}^2] = WTP[MG_{II}^1]$	–6.45	0.00	–4.93	0.00
$in^g – H_2^0$	$WTP[ng_{III}^2] = WTP[(bg+ng)_{III}^3] = WTP[MG_{III}^1]$	110.33	0.00	—	—
	$WTP[(bg+ng)_{III}^3] = WTP[MG_{III}^1]$	–3.93	0.00	–2.36	0.02
	$WTP[ng_{III}^2] = WTP[(bg+ng)_{III}^3]$	–6.08	0.00	–2.44	0.02
	$WTP[ng_{III}^2] = WTP[MG_{III}^1]$	–6.99	0.00	–2.90	0.00

注：各符号含义同表 8.1 和表 8.2。

表 8.8　　海滩和海洋地质遗迹旅游资源外部范围检验结果

零假设检验		非参数检验		参数检验	
		$Z/Chi-Square$	$Asymp.\ Sig.$	t/F	$Sig.$
$ex^s - H_1^0$	$WTP[MS_I^1] = WTP[MS_{II}^1]$	-0.07	0.94	-0.03	0.98
$ex^s - H_2^0$	$WTP[bs_{II}^2] = WTP[MS_I^1]$	-1.33	0.19	0.99	0.32
$ex^g - H_1^0$	$WTP[MG_I^1] = WTP[MG_{II}^1] = WTP[MG_{III}^1]$	0.92	0.63	0.05	0.95
	$WTP[bg_I^2] = WTP[(bg+ng)_{III}^3] = WTP[MG_I^1]$	0.99	0.61	0.67	0.51
$ex^g - H_2^0$	$WTP[(bg+ng)_{III}^3] = WTP[MG_I^1]$	-0.23	0.82	0.27	0.79
	$WTP[bg_{II}^2] = WTP[(bg+ng)_{III}^3]$	-0.75	0.46	-0.85	0.40
	$WTP[bg_{II}^2] = WTP[MG_I^1]$	-0.94	0.35	1.15	0.25
$ex^g - H_3^0$	$WTP[ng_{III}^2] = WTP[MG_{II}^1]$	-2.76	0.01	1.52	0.13

注：各符号含义同表 8.1 和表 8.2。

数量范围检验的首要经济问题是饱和程度，WTP 是否增加取决于受访者关于海滩或海洋地质遗迹旅游资源供给水平的饱和程度。从各待估海滩或海洋地质遗迹旅游资源估值比较来看，内部数量范围变化的边际 WTP 增加值均较低（见图 8.1），外部数量范围变化的边际 WTP 增加值同样均较低（见图 8.3）；同时，各待估海滩或海洋地质遗迹旅游资源非使用价值呈现出边际递减（见图 8.2、图 8.4），并且各条曲线均逐渐趋于平坦，受访者效用趋于饱和。研究表明，饱和程度和边际效应递减是各待估海滩或海洋地质遗迹旅游资源数量范围变化边际 WTP 增加值大小和范围敏感性的主要影响因素。同时，待估海滩或海洋地质遗迹旅游资源内部之间和与外部同类旅游资源之间存在竞争替代性，替代效应也是各待估海滩或海洋地质遗迹旅游资源数量范围变化边际 WTP 增加值大小和范围敏感性的主要影响因素。

$$in^s - H_1^0: WTP[bs_{II}^2] \xrightarrow{20} WTP[MS_{II}^1]$$

$$in^g - H_1^0: WTP[bg_{II}^2] \xrightarrow{35} WTP[MG_{II}^1]$$

$$in^g - H_2^0: WTP[ng_{III}^2] \xrightarrow{26} WTP[(bg+ng)_{III}^3] \xrightarrow{5} WTP[MG_{III}^1]$$

图 8.1　各待估海滩或海洋地质遗迹旅游资源内部
数量范围变化 WTP 估值比较

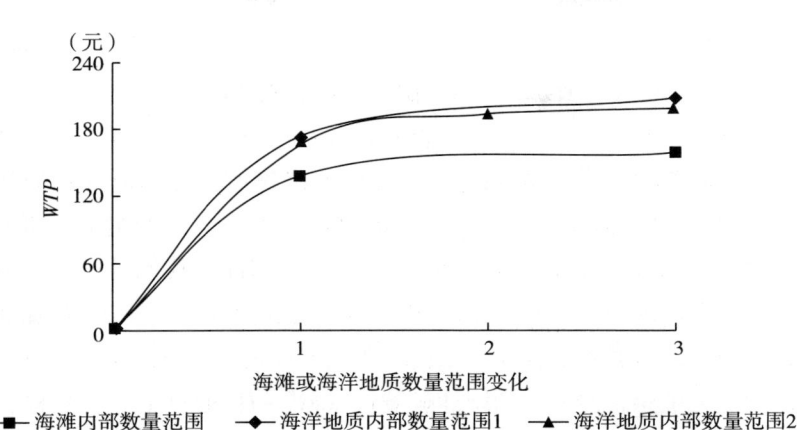

图 8.2　各待估海滩或海洋地质遗迹旅游资源非使用价值
边际递减——内部数量范围

$$ex^s - H_2^0: WTP[bs_{II}^2] \xrightarrow{21} WTP[MS_I^1]$$

$$ex^g - H_2^0: WTP[bg_{II}^2] \xrightarrow{20} WTP[(bg+ng)_{III}^3] \xrightarrow{9} WTP[MG_I^1]$$

$$ex^g - H_3^0: WTP[ng_{III}^2] \xrightarrow{41} WTP[MG_{II}^1]$$

图 8.3　各待估海滩或海洋地质遗迹旅游资源外部数量
范围变化 WTP 估值比较

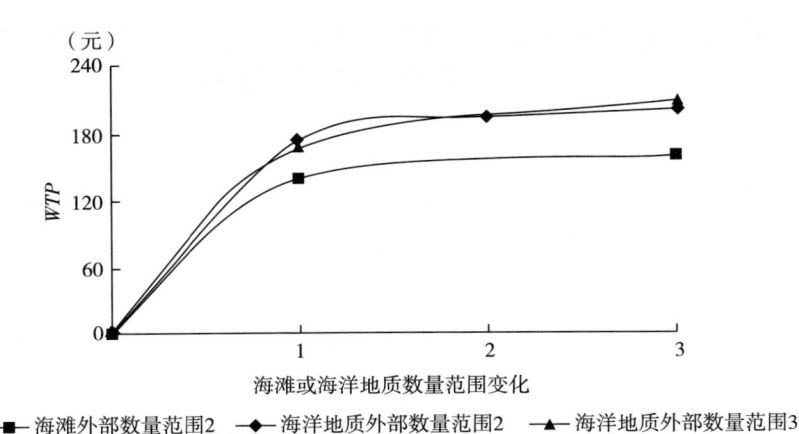

图 8.4　各待估海滩或海洋地质遗迹旅游资源非使用价值
边际递减——外部数量范围

第四节　庙岛群岛结论

（1）不同独立子样本调查同一待估海滩旅游资源或海洋地质遗迹旅游资源 WTP 估值比较，通过了外部数量范围检验，表明本书研究的问卷设计、调查实施和 WTP 估值结果具有可靠性。其他各待估海滩旅游资源或海洋地质遗迹旅游资源外部数量范围估值比较，WTP 存在差异；表明受访者对各待估海滩旅游资源或海洋地质遗迹旅游资源外部数量范围变化敏感，但未达到统计显著性（$ex^g - H_3^0$ 通过了非参数检验）。各待估海洋旅游资源或海洋地质遗迹旅游资源内部范围检验全部通过，表明受访者对各待估海滩旅游资源或海洋地质遗迹旅游资源内部数量范围变化敏感，且达到了统计显著性。

（2）各待估海滩旅游资源或海洋地质遗迹旅游资源数量范围变化，在保护1个海岛的海滩旅游资源或海洋地质遗迹旅游资源后，受访者效用逐渐趋于饱和（曲线较平坦），边际效应迅速递减；同时，海滩旅游资源或海洋地质遗迹旅游资源替代品的存在，加速了边际 WTP 增加值下降的速度。饱和程度、边际效应递减和/或替代效应是边际 WTP 增加值大小变化的主要影响因素，它们为各待估海滩旅游资源或海洋地质遗迹旅游资源的（部分）外部数量范围检验未达到统计显著性提供了依据。所以，范围检验不应作为 CVM 研究有效性的唯一判断标准，检验结果需要通过经济学相关理论更仔细地考虑和解释。

第九章
嵌入效应问题研究舟山群岛案例

第一节 舟山群岛研究框架

舟山群岛案例研究框架包括：旅游型海岛、海洋旅游资源、嵌入效应验证方案设计和嵌入效应验证方案实施四部分（见图9.1）。

第二节 舟山群岛嵌入效应验证方案设计

参照 Bateman 等关于嵌入物品、序列物品的田野实验及实验室实验研究成果[①]，本书研究嵌入公共物品估值问题设计：列表采用独立列表

---

① Ian J. Bateman, et al., *Visible Choice Sets and Scope Sensitivity: An Experimental and Field Test of Study Design Effects upon Nested Contingent Values*, UK: The Centre for Social and Economic Research on the Global Environmental (CSERGE), University of East Anglia, Working Paper EDM, NO. 01 - 01, 2001, pp. 4 - 7; Ian J. Bateman, et al., "On Visible Choice Sets and Scope Sensitivity", *Journal of Environmental Economics and Management*, Vol. 47, No. 1, January 2004; Nick Hanley, et al., "Aggregating the Benefits of Environmental Improvements: Distance - decay Functions for Use and Non - use Values", *Journal of Environmental Management*, Vol. 68, No. 3, July 2003; Richard T. Carson and Robert Cameron Mitchell, "Sequencing and Nesting in Contingent Valuation Surveys", *Journal of Environmental Economics and Management*, Vol. 28, No. 2, March 1995; N. A. Powe and I. J. Bateman, "Ordering Effects in Nested 'Top - down' and 'Bottom - up' Contingent Valuation Designs", *Ecological Economics*, Vol. 45, No. 2, June 2003; Bente Halvorsen, "Ordering Effects in Contingent Valuation Surveys: Willingness to Pay for Reduced Health Damage from Air Pollution", *Environmental and Resource Economics*, Vol. 8, No. 4, December 1996; Timothy L. McDaniels, et al., "Decision Structuring to Alleviate Embedding in Environmental Valuation", *Ecological Economics*, Vol. 46, No. 1, August 2003.

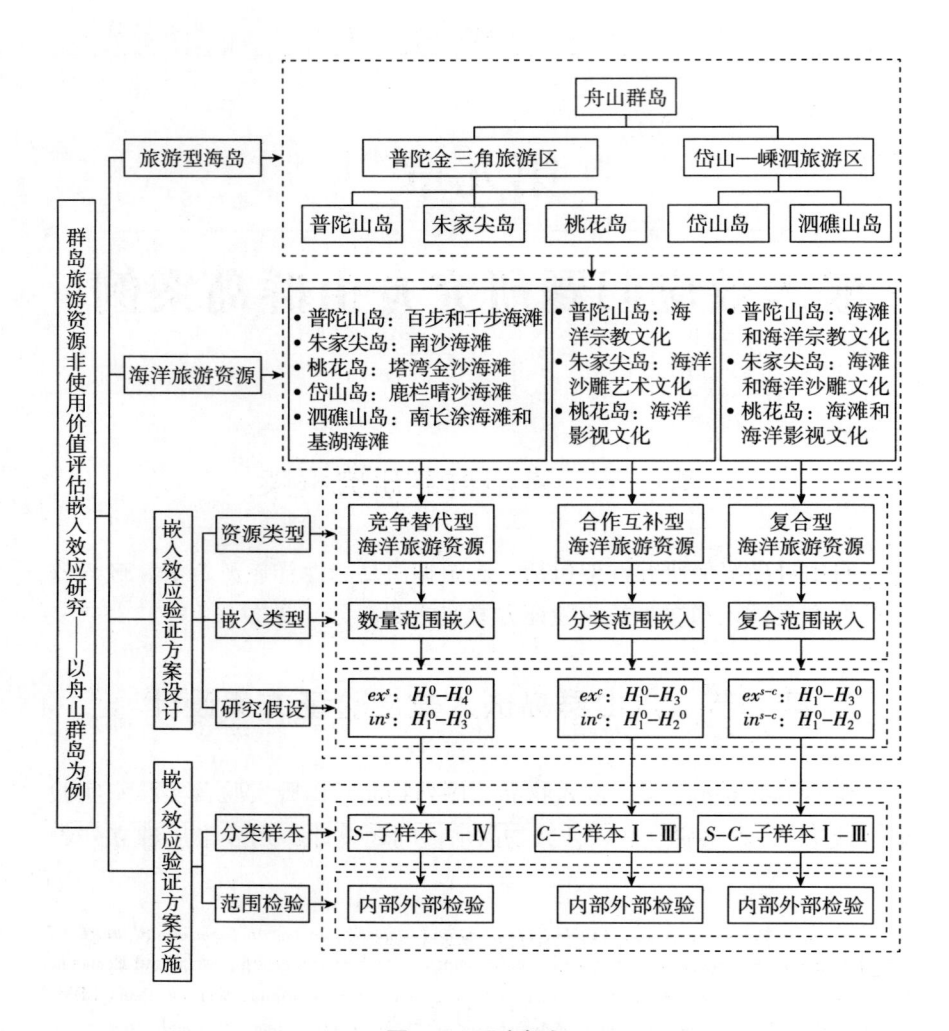

图 9.1 研究框架

（Exclusive List）方法，信息披露采用预先披露（Advanced Disclosure）设计，估值问题顺序采用自上而下（Top-down）和自下而上（Bottom-up）相结合方法。

一　符号含义

嵌入效应验证方案设计与实施中各符号的含义如图 9.2 所示。

群岛	旅游区	旅游岛	海滩、海洋文化旅游资源
A：舟山群岛 AS：舟山群岛主要海滩旅游资源 $AS = BS + CS$ $AS = as + bs + cs + ds + es$	B：普陀金三角 BS：普陀金三角主要海滩旅游资源 $BS = as + bs + cs$	a：普陀山岛 b：朱家尖岛 c：桃花岛	as：百步沙海滩、千步沙海滩 bs：南沙海滩 cs：塔湾金沙海滩
	C：岱山—嵊泗 CS：岱山—嵊泗主要海滩旅游资源 $CS = ds + es$	d：岱山岛 e：泗礁山岛	ds：鹿栏晴沙海滩 es：南长涂海滩、基湖海滩
A：舟山群岛 AC：舟山群岛主要海洋文化旅游资源 $AC = BC$ $AC = ac + bc + cc$	B：普陀金三角 BC：普陀金三角主要海洋文化旅游资源 $BC = ac + bc + cc$	a：普陀山岛 b：朱家尖岛 c：桃花岛	ac：海洋宗教文化 bc：海洋沙雕艺术文化 cc：海洋影视文化
A：舟山群岛 $AS - AC$：舟山群岛主要海滩旅游资源和主要海洋文化旅游资源 $AS - AC = BS - BC + CS$ $AS - AC = as - ac + bs - bc + cs - cc - ds + es$	B：普陀金三角 $BS - BC$：普陀金三角主要海滩旅游资源和主要海洋文化旅游资源 $BS - BC = as - ac + bs - bc + cs - cc$	a：普陀山岛 b：朱家尖岛 c：桃花岛	$as - ac$：百步沙海滩、千步沙海滩和海洋宗教文化 $bs - bc$：南沙海滩和海洋沙雕艺术文化 $cs - cc$：塔湾金沙海滩和海洋影视文化

图9.2 符号含义

二 竞争替代型海滩旅游资源

（一）海滩旅游资源设计思路

海滩属于竞争替代型旅游资源，选取舟山群岛典型的海滩旅游资源（见图9.1至图9.2），从数量范围视角，设计4组海滩旅游资源独立子样本，每组独立子样本设置1—3个海滩旅游资源非使用价值评估的核心估值问题（见表9.1）。

表 9.1　　　　　海滩旅游资源嵌入效应验证方案设计

海滩旅游资源 S-子样本 Ⅰ	海滩旅游资源 S-子样本 Ⅱ	海滩旅游资源 S-子样本 Ⅲ	海滩旅游资源 S-子样本 Ⅳ
$AS_{Ⅰ}^{1}$	$AS_{Ⅱ}^{1}$	$AS_{Ⅲ}^{1}$	$AS_{Ⅳ}^{1}$
—	$bs_{Ⅱ}^{2}$	$es_{Ⅲ}^{2}$	$ds_{Ⅳ}^{2}$
—	—	$(bs+es)_{Ⅲ}^{3}$	$(ds+es)_{Ⅳ}^{3}$

注：下角标"Ⅰ—Ⅳ"表示子样本之间的价值序号；上角标"1—3"表示子样本内部的价值序号；其他各符号的含义参见图 9.2。

(二) 海滩旅游资源研究假设

依据表 9.1 设计思路，提出各待估海滩旅游资源非使用价值评估数量范围嵌入效应验证的外部范围检验零假设和内部范围检验零假设。

海滩旅游资源外部范围检验零假设：

① $ex^s - H_1^0$：$WTP[AS_Ⅰ^1] = WTP[AS_Ⅱ^1] = WTP[AS_Ⅲ^1] = WTP[AS_Ⅳ^1]$

② $ex^s - H_2^0$：$WTP[bs_Ⅱ^2] \leqslant WTP[(bs+es)_Ⅲ^3] \leqslant WTP[AS_Ⅰ^1]$

③ $ex^s - H_3^0$：$WTP[es_Ⅲ^2] \leqslant WTP[(ds+es)_Ⅳ^3] \leqslant WTP[AS_Ⅱ^1]$

④ $ex^s - H_4^0$：$WTP[ds_Ⅳ^2] \leqslant WTP[AS_Ⅲ^1]$

海滩旅游资源内部范围检验零假设：

① $in^s - H_1^0$：$WTP[bs_Ⅱ^2] \leqslant WTP[AS_Ⅱ^1]$

② $in^s - H_2^0$：$WTP[es_Ⅲ^2] \leqslant WTP[(bs+es)_Ⅲ^3] \leqslant WTP[AS_Ⅲ^1]$

③ $in^s - H_3^0$：$WTP[ds_Ⅳ^2] \leqslant WTP[(ds+es)_Ⅳ^3] \leqslant WTP[AS_Ⅳ^1]$

三　合作互补型海洋文化旅游资源

(一) 海洋文化旅游资源设计思路

海洋文化旅游资源属于合作互补型旅游资源，选取舟山群岛典型的海洋文化旅游资源（见图 9.1 至图 9.2），从分类范围视角，设计 3 组海洋文化旅游资源独立子样本，每组独立子样本设置 1—3 个海洋文化旅游资源非使用价值评估的核心估值问题（见表 9.2）。

(二) 海洋文化旅游资源研究假设

依据表 9.2 设计思路，提出各待估海洋文化旅游资源非使用价值评估分类范围嵌入效应验证的外部范围检验零假设和内部范围检验零假设。

表 9.2　　海洋文化旅游资源嵌入效应验证方案设计

海洋文化旅游资源 C - 子样本 I	海洋文化旅游资源 C - 子样本 II	海洋文化旅游资源 C - 子样本 III
BC_{I}^{1}	BC_{II}^{1}	BC_{III}^{1}
—	ac_{II}^{2}	bc_{III}^{2}
—	—	$(ac+bc)_{\mathrm{III}}^{3}$

注：下角标"Ⅰ—Ⅲ"表示子样本之间的价值序号；上角标"1—3"表示子样本内部的价值序号；其他各符号的含义参见图9.2。

海洋文化旅游资源外部范围检验零假设：

①$ex^{c} - H_{1}^{0}$：$WTP[BC_{\mathrm{I}}^{1}] = WTP[BC_{\mathrm{II}}^{1}] = WTP[BC_{\mathrm{III}}^{1}]$

②$ex^{c} - H_{2}^{0}$：$WTP[ac_{\mathrm{II}}^{2}] \leqslant WTP[(ac+bc)_{\mathrm{III}}^{3}] \leqslant WTP[BC_{\mathrm{I}}^{1}]$

③$ex^{c} - H_{3}^{0}$：$WTP[bc_{\mathrm{III}}^{2}] \leqslant WTP[BC_{\mathrm{II}}^{1}]$

海洋文化旅游资源内部范围检验零假设：

①$in^{c} - H_{1}^{0}$：$WTP[ac_{\mathrm{II}}^{2}] \leqslant WTP[BC_{\mathrm{II}}^{1}]$

②$in^{c} - H_{2}^{0}$：$WTP[bc_{\mathrm{III}}^{2}] \leqslant WTP[(ac+bc)_{\mathrm{III}}^{3}] \leqslant WTP[BC_{\mathrm{III}}^{1}]$

四　复合型海滩与海洋文化旅游资源

(一) 海滩与海洋文化旅游资源设计思路

舟山群岛的普陀山岛、朱家尖岛和桃花岛三个海岛，同时包含海滩旅游资源和海洋文化旅游资源（见图9.1至图9.2），从数量范围和分类范围视角，设计3组海滩与海洋文化旅游资源独立子样本，每组独立子样本设置1—3个海滩与海洋文化旅游资源非使用价值评估的核心估值问题（见表9.3）。

表 9.3　　海滩与海洋文化旅游资源嵌入效应验证方案设计

海滩与海洋文化旅游资源 $S-C$ - 子样本 I	海滩与海洋文化旅游资源 $S-C$ - 子样本 II	海滩与海洋文化旅游资源 $S-C$ - 子样本 III
$BS-BC_{\mathrm{I}}^{1}$	$BS-BC_{\mathrm{II}}^{1}$	$BS-BC_{\mathrm{III}}^{1}$
—	ac_{II}^{2*}	as_{III}^{2}
—	—	$as-ac_{\mathrm{III}}^{3}$

注：下角标"Ⅰ—Ⅲ"表示子样本之间的价值序号；上角标"1—3"表示子样本内部的价值序号；其他各符号的含义参见图9.2；"ac_{II}^{2*}"为了与表9.2的"ac_{II}^{2}"区别，加了星号。

（二）海滩与海洋文化旅游资源研究假设

依据表9.3设计思路，提出各待估海滩与海洋文化旅游资源非使用价值评估数量范围与分类范围嵌入效应验证的外部范围检验零假设和内部范围检验零假设。

海滩与海洋文化旅游资源外部范围检验零假设：

①$ex^{s-c} - H_1^0$：$WTP[BS - BC_Ⅰ^1] = WTP[BS - BC_Ⅱ^1] = WTP[BS - BC_Ⅲ^1]$

②$ex^{s-c} - H_2^0$：$WTP[ac_Ⅱ^{2*}] \leq WTP[as - ac_Ⅲ^3] \leq WTP[BS - BC_Ⅰ^1]$

③$ex^{s-c} - H_3^0$：$WTP[as_Ⅲ^2] \leq WTP[BS - BC_Ⅱ^1]$

海滩与海洋文化旅游资源内部范围检验零假设：

①$in^{s-c} - H_1^0$：$WTP[ac_Ⅱ^{2*}] \leq WTP[BS - BC_Ⅱ^1]$

②$in^{s-c} - H_2^0$：$WTP[as_Ⅲ^2] \leq WTP[as - ac_Ⅲ^3] \leq WTP[BS - BC_Ⅲ^1]$

第三节　舟山群岛嵌入效应验证方案实施

一　问卷设计

调查问卷结构包括：待估海滩（或海洋文化、或海滩与海洋文化）旅游资源的研究范围、基本信息（含简图）、受访者人口社会特征（性别、年龄、学历、家庭收入、常住地）、不愿意支付原因选项、核心估值问题等。共设计了10种独立子样本调查问卷，每种问卷的核心估值问题采用嵌入方式（见表9.1至表9.3）：

（1）海滩旅游资源以表9.1的"S–子样本Ⅲ"为例，$AS_Ⅲ^1$、$es_Ⅲ^2$和$(bs+es)_Ⅲ^3$的核心估值问题分别为："台风等极端天气和旅游等人类活动将对普陀山岛百步沙海滩和千步沙海滩、朱家尖岛南沙海滩、桃花岛塔湾金沙海滩、岱山岛鹿栏晴沙海滩、泗礁山岛南长涂海滩和基湖海滩等舟山群岛主要海岛的海滩旅游资源造成严重影响，为了保护这五个海岛的海滩旅游资源，使其可持续存在、子孙后代使用或自己未来使用，设想成立一个海滩旅游资源保护基金，若该基金正在筹集资金阶段，您是否愿意通过一次性捐款的方式支持这项海滩旅游资源保护活动？""……将对泗礁山岛南长涂海滩和基湖海滩旅游资源……，为了保护泗礁山岛的海滩旅游资源……？"和"……将对朱家尖岛南沙海滩、泗礁山岛南长涂海滩和基湖海滩旅游资源……，为了保护朱家尖岛和泗礁山岛的海滩旅游资源……？"。

（2）海洋文化旅游资源以表9.2的"$C-$子样本Ⅲ"为例，BC_{III}^{1}、bc_{III}^{2}和$(ac+bc)_{\mathrm{III}}^{3}$的核心估值问题分别为："台风等极端天气和旅游等人类活动将对普陀山岛寺院建筑、朱家尖岛沙雕艺术主题公园、桃花岛射雕影城等舟山群岛主要海岛的海洋文化旅游资源造成严重影响，为了保护这三个海岛的海洋文化旅游资源，使其可持续存在、子孙后代使用或自己未来使用，设想成立一个海洋文化旅游资源保护基金，若该基金正在筹集资金阶段，您是否愿意通过一次性捐款的方式支持这项海洋文化旅游资源保护活动？""……将对朱家尖岛沙雕艺术主题公园海洋文化旅游资源……，为了保护朱家尖岛的海洋文化旅游资源……？"和"……将对普陀山岛寺院建筑和朱家尖岛沙雕艺术主题公园海洋文化旅游资源……，为了保护普陀山岛和朱家尖岛的海洋文化旅游资源……？"。

（3）海滩与海洋文化旅游资源以表9.3的"$S-C-$子样本Ⅲ"为例，$BS-BC_{\mathrm{III}}^{1}$、as_{III}^{2}和$as-ac_{\mathrm{III}}^{3}$的核心估值问题分别为："台风等极端天气和旅游等人类活动将对普陀山岛百步沙海滩和千步沙海滩、寺院建筑，朱家尖岛南沙海滩、沙雕艺术主题公园，桃花岛塔湾金沙海滩、射雕影城等舟山群岛主要海岛的海滩旅游资源和海洋文化旅游资源造成严重影响，为了保护这三个海岛的海滩旅游资源和海洋文化旅游资源，使其可持续存在、子孙后代使用或自己未来使用，设想成立一个海滩旅游资源和海洋文化旅游资源保护基金，若该基金正在筹集资金阶段，您是否愿意通过一次性捐款的方式支持这项海滩旅游资源和海洋文化旅游资源保护活动？""……将对普陀山岛百步沙海滩和千步沙海滩旅游资源……，为了保护普陀山岛的海滩旅游资源……，……海滩旅游资源保护基金，……海滩旅游资源保护活动？"和"……将对普陀山岛百步沙海滩和千步沙海滩、寺院建筑等海滩旅游资源和海洋文化旅游资源……，为了保护普陀山岛的海滩旅游资源和海洋文化旅游资源……海滩旅游资源和海洋文化旅游资源保护基金，……海滩旅游资源和海洋文化旅游资源保护活动？"。

海滩、海洋文化和海滩与海洋文化旅游资源支付卡式投标值：1、2、5、10、20、30、50、60、80、100、120、150、200、300、400、

500、600、800、1000、1500、2000。

二 样本分布

共获得居民和游客面对面调查问卷 3048 份，其中有效问卷 2929 份，有效率 96.10%。在 2929 份有效样本中，包含了 133 份零支付样本。将对支付意愿或资源保护不感兴趣、排斥捐款或基金形式、因景区管理或旅游物价问题拒绝支付、与自己没关系等不愿意支付的原因确定为抗议性零支付[①]，共计 46 份样本，占有效样本量的 1.57%。本书研究分析中剔除了 46 份抗议性零支付样本，包含了 87 份真零样本[②]，分析样本总计 2883 份。

表 9.4　　　　　　　　　　有效样本分布

调查地点	海滩			海洋文化			海滩与海洋文化		
	居民+游客	居民	游客	居民+游客	居民	游客	居民+游客	居民	游客
普陀山岛	361	90	271	272	59	213	272	55	217
朱家尖岛	176	54	122	130	34	96	131	31	100
桃花岛	154	58	96	107	39	68	96	31	65
岱山岛	137	71	66	99	41	58	85	41	44
泗礁山岛	189	89	100	121	63	58	116	61	55
舟山市区	178	176	2	135	135	0	124	122	2
合计	1195	538	657	864	371	493	824	341	483

注：表中有效样本未包含抗议性零样本。

三 描述性统计分析

（一）受访者人口社会特征

在 2883 份分析总样本中，18—65 周岁的样本占总样本的 99.76%，

[①] Dominika A. Dziegielewska and Robert Mendelsohn, "Does 'No' Mean 'No'? A Protest Methodology", *Environmental and Resource Economics*, Vol. 38, No. 1, September 2007; Alex Y. Lo and C. Y. Jim, "Protest Response and Willingness to Pay for Culturally Significant Urban Trees: Implications for Contingent Valuation Method", *Ecological Economics*, Vol. 114, June 2015.

[②] Adriana Ressurreição, et al., "Economic Valuation of Species Loss in the Open Sea", *Ecological Economics*, Vol. 70, No. 4, February 2011; Robert Cameron Mitchell and Richard T. Carson, *Using Surveys to Value Public Goods: The Contingent Valuation Method*, Washington: Resources for the Future, 1989, pp. 107–126.

16—17周岁和66—68周岁样本占总样本的0.24%。从样本人口社会特征来看（见表9.5），男女比例基本相当，年龄均值处于36—37岁之间，受过高等教育比例不足一半，家庭年收入均值在14万元左右，短途游客、中途游客和长途游客所占比例递减，长三角地区是舟山群岛游客的主要客源市场。

表9.5　　　　　　　　　　样本人口社会特征

待估旅游资源	样本量	性别	年龄（岁）	学历	家庭年收入（万元）	居民比例（%）	短途游客比例（%）	中途游客比例（%）	长途游客比例（%）
海滩资源	1195	0.51	37	0.47	13.79	45.02	21.09	17.91	15.98
海洋文化资源	864	0.50	37	0.47	13.92	42.94	20.72	18.87	17.48
海滩与海洋文化资源	824	0.50	37	0.49	14.29	41.38	22.69	18.57	17.35
总样本	2883	0.51	37	0.48	13.97	43.36	21.44	18.38	16.82

注：性别：男=1，女=0；年龄：2017－出生年；学历：1=接受过高等教育，0=未接受过高等教育；短途客源地为浙江省，中途客源地为江苏省、上海市和安徽省，长途客源地为大陆其他省（市、区）。

（二）样本组间人口社会特征差异

运用Kruskal–Wallis检验，进行海滩4组独立子样本之间、海洋文化3组独立子样本之间、海滩与海洋文化3组独立子样本之间的人口社会特征差异显著性检验；并进行海滩、海洋文化和海滩与海洋文化3组合并样本之间的人口社会特征差异显著性检验。从检验结果来看（见表9.6），在0.05显著性水平下，海滩与海洋文化3组独立子样本的学历和家庭年收入存在显著差异，但这一差异并未引起最大范围WTP之间的显著差异；海滩独立子样本之间、海洋文化独立子样本之间、海滩与海洋文化独立子样本之间的最大范围WTP均不存在显著差异，表明问卷设计和调查过程具有可靠性；海滩合并样本、海洋文化合并样本和海滩与海洋文化合并样本的最大范围WTP存在显著差异，表明受访者能够感知到资源类型的差异。

表 9.6　　　　　　样本组间人口社会特征差异显著性检验

样本组	最大范围 WTP	性别	年龄	学历	家庭年收入
S 子样本 Ⅰ—Ⅳ	0.32 (3.54)	0.70 (1.41)	0.74 (1.27)	0.50 (2.35)	0.06 (7.45)
C 子样本 Ⅰ—Ⅲ	0.87 (0.29)	0.87 (0.29)	0.82 (0.41)	0.93 (0.14)	0.66 (0.84)
$S-C$ 子样本 Ⅰ—Ⅲ	0.29 (2.49)	0.35 (2.11)	0.45 (1.58)	0.02 (8.18)	0.05 (6.02)
S、C 与 $S-C$ 之间	0.00 (19.04)	0.76 (0.54)	0.87 (0.28)	0.86 (0.30)	0.20 (3.20)

注：括号中数值为 Kruskal–Wallis 检验卡方值。

（三）最大范围 WTP 分布特征

从最大范围海滩、海洋文化、海滩与海洋文化及总样本 WTP 累积百分比来看（见图 9.3），各种类型资源的 WTP 主要位于 200 元及以下，500 元及以下的样本占比均超过 90%。将 WTP 分成五个 WTP 区间，从最大范围海滩、海洋文化、海滩与海洋文化及总样本的各 WTP 区间样本量所占比例来看（见图 9.4），随着 WTP 区间增长，样本所占比例下降，这符合经济学的消费理论，即随着价格上升，需求下降。[①]

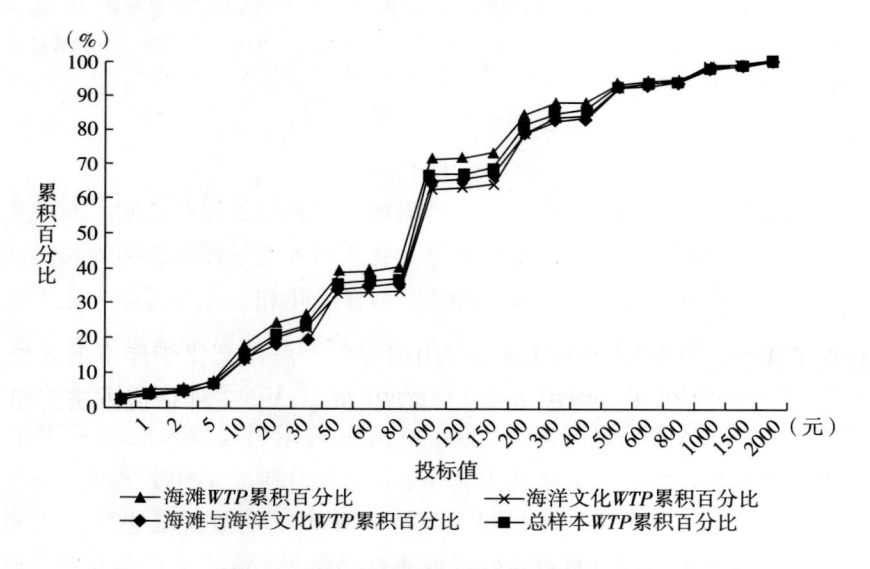

图 9.3　最大范围待估资源 WTP 累积分布

---

① Richard T. Carson, et al., "Contingent Valuation: Controversies and Evidence", *Environmental and Resource Economics*, Vol. 19, No. 2, June 2001.

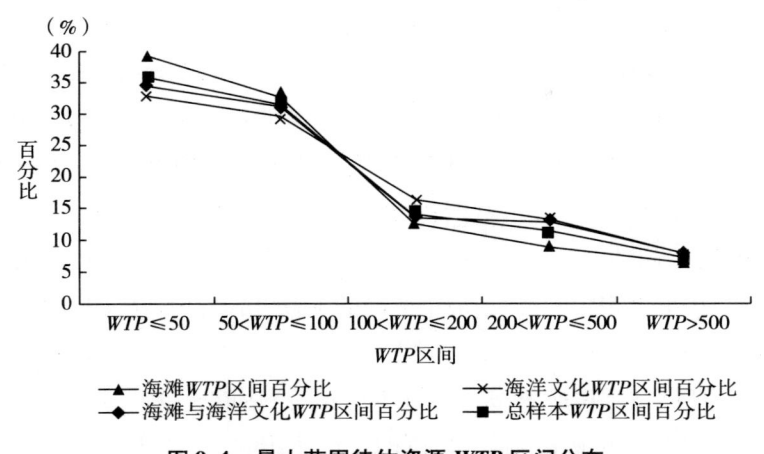

图9.4 最大范围待估资源 WTP 区间分布

第四节 舟山群岛结果分析

一 WTP 结果分析

本书研究运用最小二乘（Ordinary Least Square，OLS）回归和区间回归（Interval Regression，IR）[①]，计算受访者对保护海滩、海洋文化和海滩与海洋文化的21种待估海洋旅游资源非使用价值的 WTP（详细计算参见附录2）。21种待估海洋旅游资源非使用价值 WTP 的原始均值、OLS 均值和 IR 均值如表9.7所示。从原始均值、OLS 均值和 IR 均值结果来看，表现出两个主要特征：①海滩独立子样本最大范围估值（$WTP[AS_\mathrm{I}^1]$、$WTP[AS_\mathrm{II}^1]$、$WTP[AS_\mathrm{III}^1]$、$WTP[AS_\mathrm{IV}^1]$），三种估值方法四组独立子样本之间 WTP 的最大差异均小于3%；海洋文化子样本最大范围估值（$WTP[BC_\mathrm{I}^1]$、$WTP[BC_\mathrm{II}^1]$、$WTP[BC_\mathrm{III}^1]$），三种估值方法三组独立子样本之间 WTP 的最大差异均小于4%；海滩与海洋文化最大范围估值（$WTP[BS-BC_\mathrm{I}^1]$、$WTP[BS-BC_\mathrm{II}^1]$、$WTP[BS-BC_\mathrm{III}^1]$），三种

[①] Trudy Ann Cameron and Daniel D. Huppert, "OLS Versus ML Estimate of Non-Market Resource Values with Payment Card Interval Data", *Journal of Environmental Economics and Management*, Vol. 17, No. 3, November 1989. Stefania Tonin, "Citizens' Perspectives on Marine Protected Areas as a Governance Strategy to Effectively Preserve Marine Ecosystem Services and Biodiversity", *Ecosystem Services*, Vol. 34, December 2018.

估值方法三组独立子样本之间 WTP 的最大差异均小于 3%；普陀山文化两次估值（$WTP[ac_{II}^{2*}]$、$WTP[ac_{II}^{2}]$），三种估值方法两组独立子样本之间 WTP 的最大差异均小于 2%。②海滩的最大范围（$WTP[AS_{I}^{1}]$、$WTP[AS_{II}^{1}]$、$WTP[AS_{III}^{1}]$、$WTP[AS_{IV}^{1}]$）、中间范围（$WTP[(bs+es)_{III}^{3}]$、$WTP[(ds+es)_{IV}^{3}]$）与最小范围（$WTP[bs_{II}^{2}]$、$WTP[es_{III}^{2}]$、$WTP[ds_{IV}^{2}]$）估值比较，海滩三种估值方法均值均表现出，最大范围的 WTP 均值大于中间范围的 WTP 均值大于最小范围的 WTP 均值；海洋文化的最大范围（$WTP[BC_{I}^{1}]$、$WTP[BC_{II}^{1}]$、$WTP[BC_{III}^{1}]$）、中间范围（$WTP[(ac+bc)_{III}^{3}]$）与最小范围（$WTP[ac_{II}^{2}]$、$WTP[bc_{III}^{2}]$）估值比较，海洋文化三种估值方法均值均表现出，最大范围的 WTP 均值大于中间范围的 WTP 均值大于最小范围的 WTP 均值；海滩与海洋文化的最大范围（$WTP[BS-BC_{I}^{1}]$、$WTP[BS-BC_{II}^{1}]$、$WTP[BS-BC_{III}^{1}]$）、中间范围（$WTP[as-ac_{III}^{3}]$）与最小范围（$WTP[ac_{II}^{2*}]$、$WTP[as_{III}^{2}]$）估值比较，海滩与海洋文化三种估值方法均值均表现出，最大范围的 WTP 均值大于中间范围的 WTP 均值大于最小范围的 WTP 均值。

表 9.7　　　　　　　　　　　　WTP 均值

待估变量	原始均值（元）	OLS 均值（元）	IR 均值（元）
$WTP[AS_{I}^{1}]$	185.44	211.65(161.94)	205.11(158.38)
$WTP[AS_{II}^{1}]$	183.72	207.89(163.31)	202.88(158.26)
$WTP[AS_{III}^{1}]$	183.35	209.26(157.83)	203.68(151.12)
$WTP[AS_{IV}^{1}]$	180.39	207.54(142.96)	201.84(137.07)
$WTP[bs_{II}^{2}]$	142.13	160.51(140.61)	157.23(135.42)
$WTP[es_{III}^{2}]$	144.97	165.89(138.23)	161.36(131.36)
$WTP[ds_{IV}^{2}]$	139.37	159.92(103.96)	155.84(100.26)
$WTP[(bs+es)_{III}^{3}]$	159.04	183.76(146.81)	176.88(137.62)
$WTP[(ds+es)_{IV}^{3}]$	155.39	176.84(129.49)	173.61(125.43)
$WTP[BC_{I}^{1}]$	206.93	239.90(111.63)	232.31(106.01)
$WTP[BC_{II}^{1}]$	209.67	240.30(150.52)	233.91(146.00)
$WTP[BC_{III}^{1}]$	201.88	236.85(113.71)	227.42(105.16)
$WTP[ac_{II}^{2}]$	181.13	209.76(129.64)	202.55(121.56)
$WTP[bc_{III}^{2}]$	145.96	169.33(67.83)	163.46(64.01)
$WTP[(ac+bc)_{III}^{3}]$	188.22	221.69(106.65)	212.17(99.46)
$WTP[BS-BC_{I}^{1}]$	214.57	243.92(176.58)	238.32(171.50)

续表

待估变量	原始均值（元）	OLS 均值（元）	IR 均值（元）
$WTP[BS-BC_{II}^1]$	214.70	249.53(163.71)	239.37(156.29)
$WTP[BS-BC_{III}^1]$	212.34	243.46(136.63)	237.20(132.88)
$WTP[ac_{II}^{2*}]$	183.79	213.06(125.04)	204.26(117.76)
$WTP[as_{III}^2]$	154.41	175.80(95.34)	172.30(95.67)
$WTP[as-ac_{III}^3]$	193.15	223.40(133.84)	216.09(128.60)

注：各符号含义如图 9.2 所示；括号中数值为稳健标准误。

二 范围检验结果分析

内部范围检验设计了 2—3 个水平，外部范围检验设计了 2—4 个水平（见表 9.1 至表 9.3）。[1] 两组配对样本比较，同时进行参数检验和非参数检验[2]，采用两配对样本 t – test 和两配对样本 Wilcoxon signed – rank test[3]；三组配对样本比较，采用非参数多配对样本 Friedman test[4]。外部范围检验两组独立样本比较，同时进行参数检验和非参数检验[5]，采用两独立样本 t – test 和两独立样本 Mann – Whitney U test[6]；外部范

---

[1] John C. Whitehead and Todd L. Cherry, "Willingness to Pay for a Green Energy Program: A Comparison of Ex – ante and Ex – post Hypothetical Bias Mitigation Approaches", *Resource and Energy Economics*, Vol. 29, No. 4, November 2007.

[2] R. P. Berrens, et al., "Contingent Values for New Mexico Instream Flows: With Tests of Scope, Group – size Reminder and Temporal Reliability", *Journal of Environmental Management*, Vol. 58, No. 1, January 2000.

[3] Kevin J. Boyle, et al., "An Investigation of Part – whole Biases in Contingent – Valuation Studies", *Journal of Environmental Economics and Management*, Vol. 27, No. 1, July 1994; M. Christie, "A Comparison of Alternative Contingent Valuation Elicitation Treatments for the Evaluation of Complex Environmental Policy", *Journal of Environmental Management*, Vol. 62, No. 3, July 2001; Anna Norinder, et al., "Scope and Scale Insensitivities in a Contingent Valuation Study of Risk Reductions", *Health Policy*, Vol. 57, No. 2, August 2001.

[4] M. Christie, "A Comparison of Alternative Contingent Valuation Elicitation Treatments for the Evaluation of Complex Environmental Policy", *Journal of Environmental Management*, Vol. 62, No. 3, July 2001.

[5] R. P. Berrens, et al., "Contingent Values for New Mexico Instream Flows: With Tests of Scope, Group – size Reminder and Temporal Reliability", *Journal of Environmental Management*, Vol. 58, No. 1, January 2000.

[6] M. Christie, "A Comparison of Alternative Contingent Valuation Elicitation Treatments for the Evaluation of Complex Environmental Policy", *Journal of Environmental Management*, Vol. 62, No. 3, July 2001; Anna Norinder, et al., "Scope and Scale Insensitivities in a Contingent Valuation Study of Risk Reductions", *Health Policy*, Vol. 57, No. 2, August 2001.

围检验三组独立样本和四组独立样本比较,同时进行参数检验和非参数检验①,采用多独立样本 one – way ANOVA 和多独立样本 Kruskal – Wallis test②。因有一些 CVM 案例出现了部分估值大于整体估值的"过度嵌入效应"(Over – embedding)现象③,所以,本书研究两两比较检验用的都是双尾(2 – tailed)。

从范围检验结果来看,内部范围检验全部通过(见表 9.8),外部范围检验结果混合(见表 9.9),CVM 的许多案例都出现了外部范围检验结果混合的现象。④ 从各待估旅游资源 WTP 估值结果来看(见表 9.7),海滩、海洋文化或海滩与海洋文化的受访者能够感知到各待估

---

① R. P. Berrens, et al., "Contingent Values for New Mexico Instream Flows: With Tests of Scope, Group – size Reminder and Temporal Reliability", *Journal of Environmental Management*, Vol. 58, No. 1, January 2000.

② Henrik Svedsäter, "Contingent Valuation of Global Environmental Resources: Test of Perfect and Regular Embedding", *Journal of Economic Psychology*, Vol. 21, No. 6, December 2000; M. Christie, "A Comparison of Alternative Contingent Valuation Elicitation Treatments for the Evaluation of Complex Environmental Policy", *Journal of Environmental Management*, Vol. 62, No. 3, July 2001; Anna Norinder, et al., "Scope and Scale Insensitivities in a Contingent Valuation Study of Risk Reductions", *Health Policy*, Vol. 57, No. 2, August 2001.

③ Thomas A. Heberlein, et al., "Rethinking the Scope Test as a Criterion for Validity in Contingent Valuation", *Journal of Environmental Economics and Management*, Vol. 50, No. 1, July 2005; Neil A. Powe and Ian J. Bateman, "Investigating Insensitivity to Scope: A Split – sample Test of Perceived Scheme Realism", *Land Economics*, Vol. 80, No. 2, May 2004; Vito Frontuto, et al., "Earmarking Conservation: Further Inquiry on Scope Effects in Stated Preference Methods Applied to Nature – based Tourism", *Tourism Management*, Vol. 60, June 2017.

④ Ian J. Bateman, et al., "On Visible Choice Sets and Scope Sensitivity", *Journal of Environmental Economics and Management*, Vol. 47, No. 1, January 2004; William D. Schulze, et al., "Embedding and Calibration in Measuring Non – use Values", *Resource and Energy Economics*, Vol. 20, No. 2, June 1998; John C. Whitehead, et al., "Part – whole Bias in Contingent Valuation: Will Scope Effects be Detected with Inexpensive Survey Methods?", *Southern Economic Journal*, Vol. 65, No. 1, July 1998; John B. Loomis, et al., "Some Empirical Evidence on Embedding Effects in Contingent Valuation of Forest Protection", *Journal of Environmental Economics and Management*, Vol. 25, No. 1, July 1993; Kimberly Rollins and Audrey Lyke, "The Case for Diminishing Marginal Existence Values", *Journal of Environmental Economics and Management*, Vol. 36, No. 3, November 1998; K. L. Giraud, et al., "Internal and External Scope in Willingness – to – pay Estimates for Threatened and Endangered Wildlife", *Journal of Environmental Management*, Vol. 56, No. 3, July 1999; Thomas A. Heberlein, et al., "Rethinking the Scope Test as a Criterion for Validity in Contingent Valuation", *Journal of Environmental Economics and Management*, Vol. 50, No. 1, July 2005; William Desvousges, et al., "Adequate Responsiveness to Scope in Contingent Valuation", *Ecological Economics*, Vol. 84, December 2012.

旅游资源估值范围的差异，并且 WTP 大小的变化方向与各待估旅游资源估值范围大小的变化方向一致；有些待估旅游资源 WTP 估值之间的差异统计不显著，不足以通过所谓的"范围检验"。[①]

表 9.8　　　　　　　　　　内部范围检验结果

零假设检验		非参数检验		参数检验	
		$Z/Chi-Square$	$Asymp. Sig.$	t	$Sig.$
$in^s - H_1^0$	$WTP[bs_{II}^2] = WTP[AS_{II}^1]$	-7.88	0.00	-5.94	0.00
$in^s - H_2^0$	$WTP[es_{III}^2] = WTP[(bs+es)_{III}^3] = WTP[AS_{III}^1]$	86.60	0.00	—	—
	$WTP[(bs+es)_{III}^3] = WTP[AS_{III}^1]$	-5.43	0.00	-3.42	0.00
	$WTP[es_{III}^2] = WTP[(bs+es)_{III}^3]$	-4.62	0.00	-3.77	0.00
	$WTP[es_{III}^2] = WTP[AS_{III}^1]$	-6.59	0.00	-4.61	0.00
$in^s - H_3^0$	$WTP[ds_{IV}^2] = WTP[(ds+es)_{IV}^3] = WTP[AS_{IV}^1]$	98.94	0.00	—	—
	$WTP[(ds+es)_{IV}^3] = WTP[AS_{IV}^1]$	-5.34	0.00	-3.67	0.00
	$WTP[ds_{IV}^2] = WTP[(ds+es)_{IV}^3]$	-4.31	0.00	-2.14	0.03
	$WTP[ds_{IV}^2] = WTP[AS_{IV}^1]$	-6.88	0.00	-4.01	0.00
$in^c - H_1^0$	$WTP[ac_{II}^2] = WTP[BC_{II}^1]$	-3.23	0.00	-2.17	0.03
$in^c - H_2^0$	$WTP[bc_{III}^2] = WTP[(ac+bc)_{III}^3] = WTP[BC_{III}^1]$	113.93	0.00	—	—
	$WTP[(ac+bc)_{III}^3] = WTP[BC_{III}^1]$	-2.65	0.01	-2.04	0.04
	$WTP[bc_{III}^2] = WTP[(ac+bc)_{III}^3]$	-7.05	0.00	-5.95	0.00
	$WTP[bc_{III}^2] = WTP[BC_{III}^1]$	-7.17	0.00	-5.41	0.00
$in^{s-c} - H_1^0$	$WTP[ac_{II}^{2*}] = WTP[BS-BC_{II}^1]$	-3.70	0.00	-2.96	0.00
$in^{s-c} - H_2^0$	$WTP[as_{III}^2] = WTP[as-ac_{III}^3] = WTP[BS-BC_{III}^1]$	124.45	0.00	—	—
	$WTP[as-ac_{III}^3] = WTP[BS-BC_{III}^1]$	-4.23	0.00	-3.41	0.00
	$WTP[as_{III}^2] = WTP[as-ac_{III}^3]$	-6.57	0.00	-3.75	0.00
	$WTP[as_{III}^2] = WTP[BS-BC_{III}^1]$	-7.90	0.00	-5.58	0.00

注：各符号含义如图 9.2 所示。

[①] Roy Brouwer, et al., "Economic Valuation of Groundwater Protection Using a Groundwater Quality Ladder Based on Chemical Threshold Levels", *Ecological Indicators*, Vol. 88, May 2018.

(1) 海滩、海洋文化或海滩与海洋文化旅游资源不同独立子样本的同一待估旅游资源比较，WTP 估值结果非常稳定，均接受了外部范围检验零假设（$ex^s - H_1^0$、$ex^c - H_1^0$、$ex^{s-c} - H_1^0$），这表明本书研究 CVM 的问卷设计、调查实施和 WTP 结果具有可靠性（Reliability）或可信性（Credibility）。[①]

(2) 海滩旅游资源外部范围检验考查的是数量范围嵌入效应。舟山群岛一个海岛的海滩旅游资源（$bs_{II}^2/es_{III}^2/ds_{IV}^2$）与两个海岛的海滩旅游资源 $[(bs+es)_{III}^3/(ds+es)_{IV}^3]$，或两个海岛的海滩旅游资源与五个海岛的海滩旅游资源（$AS_I^1/AS_{II}^1/AS_{III}^1/AS_{IV}^1$）比较，WTP 估值存在差异（见图9.5），这表明受访者对数量范围敏感，但差异未达到统计显著性（见表9.9）。舟山群岛一个海岛的海滩旅游资源与两个海岛的海滩旅游资源比较，边际 WTP 增加值为 20 元或 12 元（各待估旅游资源的 WTP 取原始、OLS 和 IR 三种方法计算结果的平均值，以下相同）；两个海岛的海滩旅游资源与五个海岛的海滩旅游资源比较，边际 WTP 增加值为 28 元或 29 元；一个海岛的海滩旅游资源与五个海岛的海滩旅游资源比较，边际 WTP 增加值为 47 元（见图9.5）。各边际 WTP 增加值均较低，且呈现出海滩旅游资源非使用价值边际递减的趋势（见图9.6）。

$$ex^s - H_2^0: WTP[bs_{II}^2] \xrightarrow{20} WTP[(bs+es)_{III}^3] \xrightarrow{28} WTP[AS_I^1]$$

$$ex^s - H_3^0: WTP[es_{III}^2] \xrightarrow{12} WTP[(ds+es)_{IV}^3] \xrightarrow{29} WTP[AS_{II}^1]$$

$$ex^s - H_4^0: WTP[ds_{IV}^2] \xrightarrow{47} WTP[AS_{III}^1]$$

图 9.5　海滩旅游资源 WTP 比较——外部范围

[①] Richard T. Carson, et al., "Contingent Valuation: Controversies and Evidence", *Environmental and Resource Economics*, Vol. 19, No. 2, June 2001; M. Christie, "A Comparison of Alternative Contingent Valuation Elicitation Treatments for the Evaluation of Complex Environmental Policy", *Journal of Environmental Management*, Vol. 62, No. 3, July 2001; Mary Jo Kealy, et al., "Reliability and Predictive Validity of Contingent Values: Does the Nature of the Good Matter?", *Journal of Environmental Economics and Management*, Vol. 19, No. 3, November 1990.

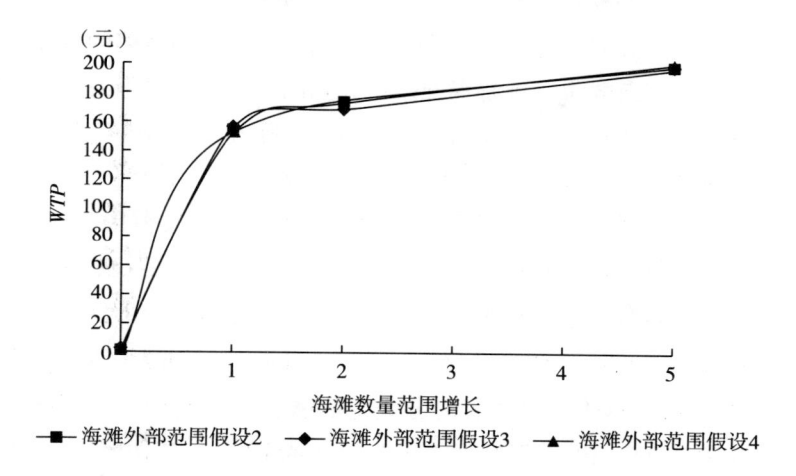

```
 (元)
 200
 180
 160
 140
W 120
T 100
P  80
    60
    40
    20
     0
        1      2      3      4      5
              海滩数量范围增长
   ─■─ 海滩外部范围假设2  ─◆─ 海滩外部范围假设3  ─▲─ 海滩外部范围假设4
```

图9.6　海滩旅游资源非使用价值边际递减

数量范围检验的首要经济问题是饱和程度[①], WTP是否增加取决于受访者关于公共物品供给水平的饱和程度[②]。Rollins和Lyke（1998）研究十个荒野公园案例得出, 受访者接近饱和时边际 WTP 非常低。海滩是沿海地区比较常见的旅游资源, 舟山群岛外部和内部的海滩旅游资源均存在竞争替代性；海滩旅游资源替代品的存在改变了其稀缺条件, 进而对各待估海滩旅游资源 WTP 的估值产生影响[③]；舟山群岛五个海岛

---

① Ian J. Bateman, et al., *Visible Choice Sets and Scope Sensitivity: An Experimental and Field Test of Study Design Effects upon Nested Contingent Values*, UK: The Centre for Social and Economic Research on the Global Environmental (CSERGE), University of East Anglia, Working Paper EDM, NO. 01-01, 2001, pp. 4-7; Ian J. Bateman, et al., "On Visible Choice Sets and Scope Sensitivity", *Journal of Environmental Economics and Management*, Vol. 47, No. 1, January 2004; Kimberly Rollins and Audrey Lyke, "The Case for Diminishing Marginal Existence Values", *Journal of Environmental Economics and Management*, Vol. 36, No. 3, November 1998.

② S. M. Chilton and W. G. Hutchinson, "A Note on the Warm Glow of Giving and Scope Sensitivity in Contingent Valuation Studies", *Journal of Economic Psychology*, Vol. 21, No. 4, August 2000.

③ Jeremy De Valck and John Rolfe, "Spatial Heterogeneity in Stated Preference Valuation: Status, Challenges and Road Ahead", *International Review of Environmental and Resource Economics*, Vol. 11, No. 4, August 2018; Alan Randall and John P. Hoehn, "Embedding in Market Demand Systems", *Journal of Environmental Economics and Management*, Vol. 30, No. 3, May 1996; Richard T. Carson, et al., "Sequencing and Valuing Public Goods", *Journal of Environmental Economics and Management*, Vol. 36, No. 3, November 1998.

中每一个海岛的海滩旅游资源，均为华东地区较大的和著名的海滩旅游资源，由一个海岛的海滩旅游资源，扩大到两个海岛、五个海岛的海滩旅游资源，从图9.6三条曲线的趋势可知，边际效应递减和饱和程度对各待估海滩旅游资源 WTP 的估值产生了重要影响。①

（3）海洋文化旅游资源外部范围检验考查的是分类范围嵌入效应。普陀山海洋宗教文化旅游资源（ac_{II}^2）、普陀山海洋宗教文化旅游资源和朱家尖海洋沙雕艺术文化旅游资源 [$(ac+bc)_{III}^3$] 与舟山群岛（普陀金三角）海洋文化旅游资源（BC_I^1）三者之间比较，WTP 估值存在差异（见图9.7），这表明受访者对分类范围敏感，但差异未达到统计显著性（见表9.9）；边际 WTP 增加值为9元或19元，各边际 WTP 增加值均较低（见图9.7）。朱家尖海洋沙雕艺术文化旅游资源（bc_{III}^2）与舟山群岛（普陀金三角）海洋文化旅游资源（BC_{II}^1）比较，WTP 估值存在显著差异，边际 WTP 增加值为68元（见图9.7），通过了外部范围检验（见表9.9）。

$$ex^c - H_2^0: WTP[\,ac_{II}^2\,] \xrightarrow{9} WTP[\,(ac+bc)_{III}^3\,] \xrightarrow{19} WTP[\,BC_I^1\,]$$

$$ex^c - H_3^0: WTP[\,bc_{III}^2\,] \xrightarrow{68} WTP[\,BC_{II}^1\,]$$

图9.7 海洋文化旅游资源 WTP 比较——外部范围

---

① Kevin J. Boyle, et al., "An Investigation of Part – whole Biases in Contingent – valuation Studies", *Journal of Environmental Economics and Management*, Vol. 27, No. 1, July 1994; Jeremy De Valck and John Rolfe, "Spatial Heterogeneity in Stated Preference Valuation: Status, Challenges and Road Ahead", *International Review of Environmental and Resource Economics*, Vol. 11, No. 4, August 2018; Kimberly Rollins and Audrey Lyke, "The Case for Diminishing Marginal Existence Values", *Journal of Environmental Economics and Management*, Vol. 36, No. 3, November 1998; Alan Randall and John P. Hoehn, "Embedding in Market Demand Systems", *Journal of Environmental Economics and Management*, Vol. 30, No. 3, May 1996; Neil A. Powe and Ian J. Bateman, "Investigating Insensitivity to Scope: A Split – sample Test of Perceived Scheme Realism", *Land Economics*, Vol. 80, No. 2, May 2004; Richard T. Carson, et al., "Sequencing and Valuing Public Goods", *Journal of Environmental Economics and Management*, Vol. 36, No. 3, November 1998.

第九章 | 嵌入效应问题研究舟山群岛案例

分类范围检验的首要经济问题是替代与补偿关系。① 舟山群岛海洋文化旅游资源（普陀山海洋宗教文化、朱家尖海洋沙雕艺术文化和桃花岛海洋影视文化）具有独特性，很少有替代品，普陀山海洋宗教文化旅游资源是其最核心资源；三类海洋文化旅游资源之间不存在竞争替代性，是一种合作互补关系。受访者对保护舟山群岛海洋文化最核心旅游资源（ac_{II}^2）的 WTP 较高（198 元），受访者对保护包含最核心旅游资源的更大范围的海洋文化旅游资源［$(ac+bc)_{III}^3/BC_I^1$］的 WTP 更高（207 元或 226 元），但 WTP 之间差异不显著；而未包含最核心旅游资源的朱家尖沙雕艺术文化旅游资源（bc_{III}^2）与包含最核心旅游资源的舟山群岛（普陀金三角）海洋文化旅游资源（BC_I^1）比较，WTP 之间存在显著差异。本书研究待估旅游资源中是否包含"最核心旅游资源"对 WTP 估值影响较大，这里的"最核心旅游资源"效应类似于 Kontoleon 和 Swanson、Molina 等、White 等物种保护经济价值评估中的"旗舰物种"效应。② 本书研究参照旗舰物种效应，将最核心旅游资源效应称为旗舰资源（Flagship Resource）效应。同时，虽然 WTP 相对于家庭收入占比较低，但多数家庭的收入已被提前预算，真正可支配收入较少。③ 旗舰资源效应引起 WTP 估值均较高，虽然文化旅游资源之间存在互补关系，但因受预

---

① Richard T. Carson, et al., "Sequencing and Valuing Public Goods", *Journal of Environmental Economics and Management*, Vol. 36, No. 3, November 1998; Ian J. Bateman, et al., *Visible Choice Sets and Scope Sensitivity: An Experimental and Field Test of Study Design Effects upon Nested Contingent Values*, UK: The Centre for Social and Economic Research on the Global Environmental (CSERGE), University of East Anglia, Working Paper EDM, NO. 01-01, 2001, pp. 4-7; Ian J. Bateman, et al., "On Visible Choice Sets and Scope Sensitivity", *Journal of Environmental Economics and Management*, Vol. 47, No. 1, January 2004.

② Andreas Kontoleon and Timothy Swanson, "The Willingness to Pay for Property Rights for the Giant Panda: Can a Charismatic Species be an Instrument for Nature Conservation?", *Land Economics*, Vol. 79, No. 4, November 2003; J. R. Molina, et al., "The Role of Flagship Species in the Economic Valuation of Wildfire Impacts: An Application to two Mediterranean Protected Areas", *Science of the Total Environment*, Vol. 675, July 2019; Piran C. L. White, et al., "Economic Values of Threatened Mammals in Britain: A Case Study of the Otter Lutra Lutra and the Water Vole Arvicola Terrestris", *Biological Conservation*, Vol. 82, No. 3, December 1997.

③ Richard T. Carson, et al., "Contingent Valuation: Controversies and Evidence", *Environmental and Resource Economics*, Vol. 19, No. 2, June 2001.

算限制①，边际 WTP 增加值仍然较低。这表明，预算限制对各待估海洋文化旅游资源 WTP 的估值也产生了重要影响。②

（4）海滩与海洋文化旅游资源外部范围检验考查的是数量范围与分类范围复合嵌入效应。普陀山海洋文化旅游资源（ac_{II}^{2*}）、普陀山海滩与海洋文化旅游资源（$as-ac_{III}^{3}$）和舟山群岛（普陀金三角）海滩与海洋文化旅游资源（$BS-BC_{I}^{1}$）三者之间比较，WTP 估值存在差异（见图9.8），这表明受访者对复合范围敏感，但差异未达到统计显著性（见表9.9）；边际 WTP 增加值为11元或21元，各边际 WTP 增加值均较低（见图9.8）。普陀山海滩旅游资源（as_{III}^{2}）与舟山群岛（普陀金三角）海滩与海洋文化旅游资源（$BS-BC_{II}^{1}$）比较，WTP 估值存在显著差异（见图9.8），边际 WTP 增加值为67元，通过了外部范围检验（见表9.9）。与海洋文化旅游资源同样道理，ac_{II}^{2*}、$as-ac_{III}^{3}$ 和 $BS-BC_{I}^{1}$ 均包含旗舰资源，受旗舰资源效应的影响，WTP 估值均较高；同时，虽然它们之间存在互补关系，但因受预算限制③及海滩旅游资源替代品存在④的影响，边际 WTP 增加值仍然较低。

$$ex^{s-c}-H_2^0: WTP[ac_{II}^{2*}]\xrightarrow{11}WTP[as-ac_{III}^{3}]\xrightarrow{21}WTP[BS-BC_{I}^{1}]$$

$$ex^{s-c}-H_3^0: WTP[as_{III}^{2}]\xrightarrow{67}WTP[BS-BC_{II}^{1}]$$

图9.8 海滩与海洋文化旅游资源 WTP 比较——外部范围

---

① Alan Randall and John P. Hoehn, "Embedding in Market Demand Systems", *Journal of Environmental Economics and Management*, Vol. 30, No. 3, May 1996; Kunt Veisten, et al., "Scope Insensitivity in Contingent Valuation of Complex Environmental Amenities", *Journal of Environmental Management*, Vol. 73, No. 4, December 2004.

② Richard T. Carson, et al., "Contingent Valuation: Controversies and Evidence", *Environmental and Resource Economics*, Vol. 19, No. 2, June 2001.

③ Alan Randall and John P. Hoehn, "Embedding in Market Demand Systems", *Journal of Environmental Economics and Management*, Vol. 30, No. 3, May 1996; Kunt Veisten, et al., "Scope Insensitivity in Contingent Valuation of Complex Environmental Amenities", *Journal of Environmental Management*, Vol. 73, No. 4, December 2004.

④ Alan Randall and John P. Hoehn, "Embedding in Market Demand Systems", *Journal of Environmental Economics and Management*, Vol. 30, No. 3, May 1996; Richard T. Carson, et al., "Sequencing and Valuing Public Goods", *Journal of Environmental Economics and Management*, Vol. 36, No. 3, November 1998; Jeremy De Valck and John Rolfe, "Spatial Heterogeneity in Stated Preference Valuation: Status, Challenges and Road Ahead", *International Review of Environmental and Resource Economics*, Vol. 11, No. 4, August 2018.

(5) 海滩、海洋文化和海滩与海洋文化旅游资源样本组之间,受访者的人口社会特征不存在显著差异(见表9.6);所以,可以对同一资源或存在嵌入关系的资源进行跨样本组比较。结果表明,普陀山海洋宗教文化同一旅游资源(ac_{II}^{2}、ac_{II}^{2*})WTP估值基本一致(见图9.9),接受了外部范围检验零假设(见表9.9),这再次验证了本书研究CVM的问卷设计、调查实施和WTP结果具有可靠性[①];同时,外部范围检验"$WTP[ac_{II}^{2}]=WTP[ac_{II}^{2*}]$"接受零假设,进一步验证了Bateman et al.(2001,2004)田野实验及实验室实验的结果:采用独立列表和预先披露方式,自上而下和自下而上估值顺序均能得到可靠的结果。[②] 朱家尖海滩旅游资源(bs_{II}^{2})、海洋沙雕艺术文化旅游资源(bc_{II}^{2})分别与舟山群岛(普陀金三角)海滩与海洋文化旅游资源($BS-BC_{I}^{1}$)比较,WTP估值存在显著差异(见图9.9),均通过了外部范围检验(见表9.9)。与海洋文化旅游资源和海滩与海洋文化旅游资源同样道理,普陀山海洋宗教—朱家尖海洋沙雕艺术文化旅游资源$[(ac+bc)_{III}^{3}]$、舟山群岛(普陀金三角)海洋文化旅游资源(BC_{I}^{1})和舟山群岛(普陀金三角)海滩与海洋文化旅游资源($BS-BC_{I}^{1}$)均包含旗舰资源,因受旗舰资源效应及预算限制的影响,三者之间比较,边际WTP增加值较低(见图9.9),均未通过外部范围检验(见表9.9);与海滩旅游资源同样道理,普陀山海滩旅游资源(as_{III}^{2})与舟山群岛五个海岛海滩旅游资源(AS_{I}^{1})的WTP估值比较,因受边际效应递减、饱和程度及替代效应等因素影响,边际WTP增加值较低(见图9.9),未通过外部范围检验(见表9.9)。跨样本组外部范围检验结果,进一步强化了海

[①] Mary Jo Kealy, et al., "Reliability and Predictive Validity of Contingent Values: Does the Nature of the Good Matter?", *Journal of Environmental Economics and Management*, Vol. 19, No. 3, November 1990; Richard T. Carson, et al., "Contingent Valuation: Controversies and Evidence", *Environmental and Resource Economics*, Vol. 19, No. 2, June 2001; M. Christie, "A Comparison of Alternative Contingent Valuation Elicitation Treatments for the Evaluation of Complex Environmental Policy", *Journal of Environmental Management*, Vol. 62, No. 3, July 2001.

[②] Ian J. Bateman, et al., *Visible Choice Sets and Scope Sensitivity: An Experimental and Field Test of Study Design Effects upon Nested Contingent Values*, UK: The Centre for Social and Economic Research on the Global Environmental (CSERGE), University of East Anglia, Working Paper EDM, NO. 01-01, 2001, pp. 4-7; Ian J. Bateman, et al., "On Visible Choice Sets and Scope Sensitivity", *Journal of Environmental Economics and Management*, Vol. 47, No. 1, January 2004.

滩旅游资源、海洋文化旅游资源或海滩与海洋文化旅游资源各组独立子样本之间的外部范围检验结果。

跨样本组外部范围：$WTP[ac_{II}^{2*}] \xrightarrow{2} WTP[ac_{II}^{2*}]$

跨样本组外部范围：$WTP[bs_{II}^{2}] \xrightarrow{79} WTP[BS-BC_{I}^{1}]$

跨样本组外部范围：$WTP[bc_{II}^{2}] \xrightarrow{72} WTP[BS-BC_{I}^{1}]$

跨样本组外部范围：$WTP[(ac+bc)_{III}^{3}] \xrightarrow{25} WTP[BS-BC_{I}^{1}]$

跨样本组外部范围：$WTP[BC_{I}^{1}] \xrightarrow{6} WTP[BS-BC_{I}^{1}]$

跨样本组外部范围：$WTP[as_{II}^{2}] \xrightarrow{33} WTP[AS_{I}^{1}]$

图 9.9 待估旅游资源 WTP 比较——跨样本组

表 9.9 外部范围检验结果

零假设检验		非参数检验		参数检验	
		Z/Chi-Square	Asymp. Sig.	t/F	Sig.
$ex^s - H_1^0$	$WTP[AS_I^1] = WTP[AS_{II}^1] =$ $WTP[AS_{III}^1] = WTP[AS_{IV}^1]$	3.54	0.32	0.01	1.00
$ex^s - H_2^0$	$WTP[bs_{II}^2] = WTP[(bs+es)_{III}^3] =$ $WTP[AS_I^1]$	1.95	0.38	1.58	0.21
	$WTP[(bs+es)_{III}^3] = WTP[AS_I^1]$	-0.06	0.95	1.05	0.29
	$WTP[bs_{II}^2] = WTP[(bs+es)_{III}^3]$	-1.30	0.20	0.75	0.45
	$WTP[bs_{II}^2] = WTP[AS_I^1]$	-1.12	0.26	1.68	0.10
$ex^s - H_3^0$	$WTP[es_{III}^2] = WTP[(ds+es)_{IV}^3] =$ $WTP[AS_{II}^1]$	4.47	0.11	1.46	0.23
	$WTP[(ds+es)_{IV}^3] = WTP[AS_{II}^1]$	-1.50	0.13	1.13	0.26
	$WTP[es_{III}^2] = WTP[(ds+es)_{IV}^3]$	-0.51	0.61	0.49	0.62
	$WTP[es_{III}^2] = WTP[AS_{II}^1]$	-2.06	0.04	1.60	0.11
$ex^s - H_4^0$	$WTP[ds_{IV}^2] = WTP[AS_{III}^1]$	-2.67	0.01	1.96	0.05
$ex^c - H_1^0$	$WTP[BC_I^1] = WTP[BC_{II}^1] =$ $WTP[BC_{III}^1]$	0.29	0.87	0.05	0.95

续表

零假设检验		非参数检验		参数检验	
		Z/Chi−Square	Asymp. Sig.	t/F	Sig.
$ex^c-H_2^0$	$WTP[ac_{II}^2]=WTP[(ac+bc)_{III}^3]=WTP[BC_I^1]$	3.92	0.14	0.69	0.50
	$WTP[(ac+bc)_{III}^3]=WTP[BC_I^1]$	−0.06	0.95	0.82	0.41
	$WTP[ac_{II}^2]=WTP[(ac+bc)_{III}^3]$	−1.75	0.08	0.33	0.74
	$WTP[ac_{II}^2]=WTP[BC_I^1]$	−1.67	0.10	1.08	0.28
$ex^c-H_3^0$	$WTP[bc_{III}^3]=WTP[BC_I^1]$	−3.23	0.00	2.91	0.00
$ex^{s-c}-H_1^0$	$WTP[BS-BC_I^1]=WTP[BS-BC_{II}^1]=WTP[BS-BC_{III}^1]$	2.49	0.29	0.00	1.00
$ex^{s-c}-H_2^0$	$WTP[ac_{II}^{2*}]=WTP[as-ac_{III}^3]=WTP[BS-BC_I^1]$	2.80	0.25	0.73	0.48
	$WTP[as-ac_{III}^3]=WTP[BS-BC_I^1]$	−0.38	0.71	0.78	0.44
	$WTP[ac_{II}^{2*}]=WTP[as-ac_{III}^3]$	−1.58	0.11	0.40	0.69
	$WTP[ac_{II}^{2*}]=WTP[BS-BC_I^1]$	−1.26	0.21	1.13	0.26
$ex^{s-c}-H_3^0$	$WTP[as_{III}^2]=WTP[BS-BC_I^1]$	−2.53	0.01	2.50	0.01
跨样本组检验	$WTP[ac_{II}^2]=WTP[ac_{II}^{2*}]$	−0.19	0.85	−0.12	0.91
	$WTP[bs_{II}^2]=WTP[BS-BC_I^1]$	−3.46	0.00	−2.67	0.01
	$WTP[bc_{III}^2]=WTP[BS-BC_I^1]$	−2.24	0.03	−2.79	0.01
	$WTP[(ac+bc)_{III}^3]=WTP[BS-BC_I^1]$	−0.76	0.45	−1.02	0.31
	$WTP[BC_I^1]=WTP[BS-BC_I^1]$	−0.69	0.49	−0.28	0.78
	$WTP[as_{III}^2]=WTP[AS_I^1]$	−0.10	0.92	−1.24	0.22

注：各符号含义如图 9.2 所示。

第五节 舟山群岛结论

（1）海滩、海洋文化和海滩与海洋文化旅游资源的 10 组独立子样本，共设计了 7 个内部范围检验、10 个同样本组外部范围检验和 6 个跨样本组外部范围检验。范围检验结果表明：内部范围检验全部通过，同样本组外部范围检验 5 个通过、5 个未通过，跨样本组外部范围检验 3 个通过、3 个未通过。同一待估旅游资源不同调查形成的 3 个同样本组外部范围检验和 1 个跨样本组外部范围检验全部通过，这验证了本书研究 CVM 的问卷设计、调查实施和 WTP 结果具有可靠性。

（2）舟山群岛不同数量范围海滩旅游资源之间比较，WTP 估值大小的变化方向与数量范围大小的变化方向保持一致，这表明受访者能够感知到数量范围的变化，对不同数量范围海滩旅游资源的 WTP 不同；但各边际 WTP 增加值均较低，且呈现出海滩旅游资源非使用价值边际递减的趋势；同时，舟山群岛五个海岛的海滩均较大，且各海岛海滩旅游资源之间和与舟山群岛外部海滩旅游资源之间均存在竞争替代性。边际效应递减、饱和程度及替代效应等因素存在，导致舟山群岛特定海滩旅游资源与更具包容性海滩旅游资源比较，WTP 估值差异统计不显著，海滩数量范围嵌入效应的外部范围检验未通过。

（3）舟山群岛不同分类范围海洋文化旅游资源之间比较或不同复合范围海滩与海洋文化旅游资源之间比较，WTP 估值存在差异，且估值大小的变化方向与分类范围或复合范围大小的变化方向一致，这表明受访者对分类范围或复合范围敏感。其中，未包含旗舰资源的分类范围或复合范围待估旅游资源与包含旗舰资源的分类范围或复合范围待估旅游资源的 WTP 估值比较，边际 WTP 增加值均较高，同样本组的 2 个外部范围检验和跨样本组的 2 个外部范围检验均通过；而对于都包含旗舰资源的不同分类范围或不同复合范围待估旅游资源的 WTP 估值比较，边际 WTP 增加值均较低，未通过外部范围检验。舟山群岛海洋文化旅游资源之间是一种互补关系，具有独特性，很少有替代品；同时，舟山群岛海滩旅游资源与海洋文化旅游资源也存在互补关系。包含旗舰资源的不同分类范围或不同复合范围旅游资源的 WTP 估值均较高，因受旗舰资源效应及预算限制的影响，即使存在互补关系，也未能通过分类范围或复合范围嵌入效应的外部范围检验。

（4）边际效应递减、饱和程度、替代效应、旗舰资源效应、预算限制等因素存在，可能会导致部分独立估值加总高估整体估值，所以，在成本—收益分析中，对舟山群岛（或一个区域）的海滩旅游资源、或海洋文化旅游资源、或海滩与海洋文化旅游资源，进行整体估值更为可靠；这一点同样适用于复杂公共物品估值。

（5）范围检验结果需要更仔细地考量，范围检验结果失败可以用适合的经济理论来解释，不应该将范围检验作为 CVM 研究有效性的唯一判断标准；同时，在 CVM 环境资源和文化资源非使用价值评估中，弱比例标准更为适用。

第十章

嵌入效应问题研究三亚及其附近岛屿案例

第一节 三亚及其附近岛屿嵌入效应验证方案设计

参照嵌入物品、序列物品等已有研究成果,本研究采用的海滩旅游资源和珊瑚礁旅游资源嵌入设计方案[①]:独立列表(Exclusive List)方法、预先披露(Advanced Disclosure)信息设计和自上而下(Top - down)及自下而上(Bottom - up)相结合的估值问题顺序。本书研究

---

① Ian J. Bateman, et al., *Visible Choice Sets and Scope Sensitivity: An Experimental and Field Test of Study Design Effects upon Nested Contingent Values*, UK: The Centre for Social and Economic Research on the Global Environmental (CSERGE), University of East Anglia, Working Paper EDM, NO. 01 - 01, 2001, pp. 4 - 7; Ian J. Bateman, et al., "On Visible Choice Sets and Scope Sensitivity", *Journal of Environmental Economics and Management*, Vol. 47, No. 1, January 2004; Nick Hanley, et al., "Aggregating the Benefits of Environmental Improvements: Distance - decay Functions for Use and Non - use Values", *Journal of Environmental Management*, Vol. 68, No. 3, July 2003; Richard T. Carson and Robert Cameron Mitchell, "Sequencing and Nesting in Contingent Valuation Surveys", *Journal of Environmental Economics and Management*, Vol. 28, No. 2, March 1995; N. A. Powe and I. J. Bateman, "Ordering Effects in Nested 'Top - down' and 'Bottom - up' Contingent Valuation Designs", *Ecological Economics*, Vol. 45, No. 2, June 2003; Bente Halvorsen, "Ordering Effects in Contingent Valuation Surveys: Willingness to Pay for Reduced Health Damage from Air Pollution", *Environmental and Resource Economics*, Vol. 8, No. 4, December 1996; Timothy L. McDaniels, et al., "Decision Structuring to Alleviate Embedding in Environmental Valuation", *Ecological Economics*, Vol. 46, No. 1, August 2003.

从数量范围嵌入效应视角，设计 10 组独立子样本，其中海滩旅游资源和珊瑚礁旅游资源各 5 组独立子样本；每组独立子样本设计 1—3 个待估海滩旅游资源或待估珊瑚礁旅游资源保护非使用价值评估的核心估值问题（见表 10.1、表 10.2）。

一 海滩旅游资源嵌入效应验证方案设计

（一）海滩旅游资源设计思路

海滩旅游资源嵌入效应验证方案设计思路如表 10.1 所示。

表 10.1　　海滩旅游资源嵌入效应验证方案设计思路

海滩旅游资源 S-子样本 I	海滩旅游资源 S-子样本 II	海滩旅游资源 S-子样本 III	海滩旅游资源 S-子样本 IV	海滩旅游资源 S-子样本 V
SS_{I}^1	SS_{II}^1	SS_{III}^1	SS_{IV}^1	SS_{V}^1
—	xs_{II}^2	ws_{III}^2	ys_{IV}^2	ds_{V}^2
—	—	$(xs+ws)_{\text{III}}^3$	$(xs+ys)_{\text{IV}}^3$	$(xs+ds)_{\text{V}}^3$

注：下角标"I—V"表示子样本之间的价值序号；上角标"1—3"表示子样本内部的价值序号；SS 表示三亚及其附近岛屿待估海滩旅游资源，$SS = xs + ws + ys + ds$；xs、ws、ys 和 ds 分别表示西岛、蜈支洲岛、亚龙湾和大东海待估海滩旅游资源；$(xs+ws)$、$(xs+ys)$ 和 $(xs+ds)$ 分别表示西岛加蜈支洲岛、西岛加亚龙湾和西岛加大东海待估海滩旅游资源。

（二）海滩旅游资源研究假设

依据表 10.1 设计思路，提出各待估海滩旅游资源非使用价值评估数量范围嵌入效应验证的外部范围检验零假设和内部范围检验零假设。

海滩旅游资源外部范围检验零假设：

①$ex^s - H_1^0$：$WTP[SS_{\text{I}}^1] = WTP[SS_{\text{II}}^1] = WTP[SS_{\text{III}}^1] = WTP[SS_{\text{IV}}^1] = WTP[SS_{\text{V}}^1]$

②$ex^s - H_2^0$：$WTP[xs_{\text{II}}^2]$，$WTP[(xs+ws)_{\text{III}}^3] \leqslant WTP[SS_{\text{I}}^1]$

③$ex^s - H_3^0$：$WTP[ws_{\text{III}}^2]$，$WTP[(xs+ys)_{\text{IV}}^3] \leqslant WTP[SS_{\text{II}}^1]$

④$ex^s - H_4^0$：$WTP[ys_{\text{IV}}^2]$，$WTP[(xs+ds)_{\text{V}}^3] \leqslant WTP[SS_{\text{III}}^1]$

⑤$ex^s - H_5^0$：$WTP[ds_{\text{V}}^2] \leqslant WTP[SS_{\text{IV}}^1]$

⑥$ex^s - H_6^0$：$WTP[xs_{\text{II}}^2] \leqslant WTP[(xs+ws)_{\text{III}}^3]$，$WTP[(xs+ys)_{\text{IV}}^3]$，$WTP[(xs+ds)_{\text{V}}^3]$

海滩旅游资源内部范围检验零假设：

①$in^s - H_1^0$：$WTP[xs_{\mathrm{II}}^2] \leqslant WTP[SS_{\mathrm{II}}^1]$

②$in^s - H_2^0$：$WTP[ws_{\mathrm{III}}^2] \leqslant WTP[(xs+ws)_{\mathrm{III}}^3] \leqslant WTP[SS_{\mathrm{III}}^1]$

③$in^s - H_3^0$：$WTP[ys_{\mathrm{IV}}^2] \leqslant WTP[(xs+ys)_{\mathrm{IV}}^3] \leqslant WTP[SS_{\mathrm{IV}}^1]$

④$in^s - H_4^0$：$WTP[ds_{\mathrm{V}}^2] \leqslant WTP[(xs+ds)_{\mathrm{V}}^3] \leqslant WTP[SS_{\mathrm{V}}^1]$

二 珊瑚礁旅游资源嵌入效应验证方案设计

（一）珊瑚礁旅游资源设计思路

珊瑚礁旅游资源嵌入效应验证方案设计思路如表10.2所示。

表10.2　珊瑚礁旅游资源嵌入效应验证方案设计思路

珊瑚礁旅游资源 R - 子样本Ⅰ	珊瑚礁旅游资源 R - 子样本Ⅱ	珊瑚礁旅游资源 R - 子样本Ⅲ	珊瑚礁旅游资源 R - 子样本Ⅳ	珊瑚礁旅游资源 R - 子样本Ⅴ
SR_{I}^1	SR_{II}^1	SR_{III}^1	SR_{IV}^1	SR_{V}^1
—	xr_{II}^2	wr_{III}^2	yr_{IV}^2	dr_{V}^2
—	—	$(xr+wr)_{\mathrm{III}}^3$	$(xr+yr)_{\mathrm{IV}}^3$	$(xr+dr)_{\mathrm{V}}^3$

注：下角标"Ⅰ—Ⅴ"表示子样本之间的价值序号；上角标"1—3"表示子样本内部的价值序号；SR表示三亚及其附近岛屿待估珊瑚礁旅游资源，$SR = xr + wr + yr + dr$；xr、wr、yr和dr分别表示西岛、蜈支洲岛、亚龙湾和大东海待估珊瑚礁旅游资源；$(xr+wr)$、$(xr+yr)$和$(xr+dr)$分别表示西岛加蜈支洲岛、西岛加亚龙湾和西岛加大东海待估珊瑚礁旅游资源。

（二）珊瑚礁旅游资源研究假设

依据表10.2设计思路，提出各待估珊瑚礁旅游资源非使用价值评估数量范围嵌入效应验证的外部范围检验零假设和内部范围检验零假设。

珊瑚礁旅游资源外部范围检验零假设：

①$ex^r - H_1^0$：$WTP[SR_{\mathrm{I}}^1] = WTP[SR_{\mathrm{II}}^1] = WTP[SR_{\mathrm{III}}^1] = WTP[SR_{\mathrm{IV}}^1] = WTP[SR_{\mathrm{V}}^1]$

②$ex^r - H_2^0$：$WTP[xr_{\mathrm{II}}^2]$，$WTP[(xr+wr)_{\mathrm{III}}^3] \leqslant WTP[SR_{\mathrm{I}}^1]$

③$ex^r - H_3^0$：$WTP[wr_{\mathrm{III}}^2]$，$WTP[(xr+yr)_{\mathrm{IV}}^3] \leqslant WTP[SR_{\mathrm{II}}^1]$

④$ex^r - H_4^0$：$WTP[yr_{\mathrm{IV}}^2]$，$WTP[(xr+dr)_{\mathrm{V}}^3] \leqslant WTP[SR_{\mathrm{III}}^1]$

⑤ $ex^r - H_5^0$：$WTP[\,dr_V^2\,] \leq WTP[\,SR_{IV}^1\,]$

⑥ $ex^r - H_6^0$：$WTP[\,xr_{II}^2\,] \leq WTP[\,(xr+wr)_{III}^3\,]$，$WTP[\,(xr+yr)_{IV}^3\,]$，$WTP[\,(xr+dr)_V^3\,]$

珊瑚礁旅游资源内部范围检验零假设：

① $in^r - H_1^0$：$WTP[\,xr_{II}^2\,] \leq WTP[\,SR_{II}^1\,]$

② $in^r - H_2^0$：$WTP[\,wr_{III}^2\,] \leq WTP[\,(xr+wr)_{III}^3\,] \leq WTP[\,SR_{III}^1\,]$

③ $in^r - H_3^0$：$WTP[\,yr_{IV}^2\,] \leq WTP[\,(xr+yr)_{IV}^3\,] \leq WTP[\,SR_{IV}^1\,]$

④ $in^r - H_4^0$：$WTP[\,dr_V^2\,] \leq WTP[\,(xr+dr)_V^3\,] \leq WTP[\,SR_V^1\,]$

第二节　三亚及其附近岛屿嵌入效应验证方案实施

一　核心估值问题

三亚及其附近岛屿海滩旅游资源共设计了5种独立子样本调查问卷，每种问卷的核心估值问题采用嵌入方式（见表10.1），以表10.1 "S-子样本Ⅲ" 为例，SS_{III}^1、ws_{III}^2 和 $(xs+ws)_{III}^3$ 核心估值问题分别为："台风等极端天气和旅游等人类活动将对西岛海滩、蜈支洲岛海滩、亚龙湾海滩、大东海海滩等三亚主要海岛和海湾的海滩旅游资源造成严重影响，为了保护这两个海岛和两个海湾的海滩旅游资源，使其可持续存在、子孙后代使用或自己未来使用，设想成立一个海滩旅游资源保护基金，若该基金正在筹集资金阶段，您是否愿意通过一次性捐款的方式支持这项海滩旅游资源保护活动？"、"……将对蜈支洲岛海滩……，为了保护蜈支洲岛……" 和 "……将对西岛海滩和蜈支洲岛海滩……，为了保护西岛和蜈支洲岛……"。

三亚及其附近岛屿珊瑚礁旅游资源共设计了5种独立子样本调查问卷，每种问卷的核心估值问题采用嵌入方式（见表10.2），以表10.2 "R-子样本Ⅲ" 为例，SR_{III}^1、wr_{III}^2 和 $(xr+wr)_{III}^3$ 核心估值问题分别为："污水、泥沙、潜水旅游等人类活动将对西岛附近海域、蜈支洲岛附近海域、亚龙湾附近海域、大东海附近海域等三亚主要海岛和海湾附近海域的珊瑚礁旅游资源造成严重影响，为了保护这两个海岛和两个海湾附近海域的珊瑚礁旅游资源，使其可持续存在、子孙后代使用或自己未来使用，设想成立一个珊瑚礁旅游资源保护基金，若该基金正在筹集资金阶段，您是否愿意通过一次性捐款的方式支持这项珊瑚礁旅游资源保护活动？""……将对蜈支洲岛附近海域……，为了保护蜈支洲岛……"和"……将对西岛附近海域和蜈支洲岛附近海域……，为了保护西岛和蜈支洲岛……"。

海滩和珊瑚礁旅游资源支付卡式投标值：1、2、5、10、20、30、50、60、80、100、120、150、200、300、400、500、600、800、1000、1500、2000。

二 样本分布

共获得居民和游客面对面调查问卷2793份，其中有效问卷2724份，有效率为97.53%；其中包含零样本59份，真零样本39份，抗议性零样本20份；剔除20份抗议性零支付，最终分析问卷2704份（见表10.3）。

表10.3　　　　　　　　有效样本分布

调查地点	海滩			珊瑚礁		
	居民+游客	居民	游客	居民+游客	居民	游客
亚龙湾景区	368	17	351	347	21	326
大东海景区	196	15	181	192	13	179
蜈支洲岛景区	241	21	220	246	10	236
西岛景区	219	18	201	218	13	205
三亚市区	340	339	1	337	336	1
合计	1364	410	954	1340	393	947

注：三亚市区调查范围包括新风街、金鸡岭街、吉祥街、凤凰路、榆亚路、河东路、解放路、迎宾路等市区内的主要街区。

三 描述性统计分析

在2704份样本中，18—65周岁样本占比为99.85%，17周岁和66—69周岁样本占比为0.15%。受访者中男性占比为53%，平均年龄处于33—34周岁，平均学历接近大专水平，平均家庭年收入处于13.50万元左右；短途游客、中途游客、长途游客和居民样本占比分别为

25.04%、20.53%、24.74%和29.70%（见表10.4）。运用多独立样本参数 one-way ANOVA 和多独立样本非参数 Kruskal-Wallis test，进行5组海滩旅游资源独立子样本之间和5组珊瑚礁旅游资源独立子样本之间的人口社会特征差异显著性检验，结果表明：独立子样本之间的人口社会特征不存在显著差异（见表10.5）。

表 10.4　样本人口社会特征

旅游资源	样本量	性别	年龄（岁）	学历	家庭年收入（万元）	居民比例（%）	短途游客比例（%）	中途游客比例（%）	长途游客比例（%）
海滩	1364	0.49	34.10	2.84	13.15	30.06	26.17	18.62	25.15
珊瑚礁	1340	0.57	33.41	3.01	13.86	29.33	23.88	22.46	24.33
总样本	2704	0.53	33.76	2.93	13.50	29.70	25.04	20.53	24.74

注：性别：男=1，女=0；年龄：2017－出生年；学历：1=初中及以下，2=高中、中专、技校，3=大专，4=本科，5=研究生；短途客源地为海南、广东、广西、湖南、贵州、云南、福建和江西，中途客源地为四川、重庆、湖北、安徽、浙江、上海和江苏；长途客源地为大陆其他省（市、区）。

表 10.5　样本组间人口社会特征差异显著性检验

样本组	参数和非参数检验	性别	年龄	学历	家庭年收入
S 子样本 I—V	one-way ANOVA	0.45 (0.93)	0.63 (0.64)	0.07 (2.15)	0.11 (1.89)
	Kruskal-Wallis test	0.44 (3.73)	0.53 (3.20)	0.06 (8.90)	0.56 (3.00)
R 子样本 I—V	one-way ANOVA	0.16 (1.64)	0.52 (0.81)	0.70 (0.55)	0.59 (0.70)
	Kruskal-Wallis test	0.16 (6.55)	0.78 (1.76)	0.67 (2.37)	0.76 (1.86)

注：括号中数值为 one-way ANOVA F 值或 Kruskal-Wallis test 卡方值。

第三节　三亚及其附近岛屿结果分析

一　WTP 结果分析

本书研究运用最小二乘（Ordinary Least Square，OLS）回归和区间回归（Interval Regression，IR）[①]，计算受访者对保护海滩和珊瑚礁的24种待估海洋旅游资源非使用价值的 WTP（详细计算参见附录3）。24种待估海洋旅游资源非使用价值 WTP 的原始均值、OLS 均值和 IR 均值如表10.6 所示。

表10.6　　　　　　　　　　WTP 均值

变量	原始均值（元）	OLS 均值（元）	IR 均值（元）	三种方法均值（元）
$WTP[SS_I^1]$	174.01	200.25(156.35)	193.92(146.46)	189.39
$WTP[SS_{II}^1]$	172.74	199.89(117.61)	192.35(110.19)	188.33
$WTP[SS_{III}^1]$	172.19	198.51(163.89)	190.80(155.25)	187.17
$WTP[SS_{IV}^1]$	175.77	198.69(96.00)	194.62(92.60)	189.69
$WTP[SS_V^1]$	175.20	201.51(123.73)	195.19(118.59)	190.63
$WTP[xs_{II}^2]$	134.63	154.50(100.02)	148.84(92.20)	145.99
$WTP[ws_{III}^2]$	134.22	154.37(141.89)	148.51(134.06)	145.70
$WTP[ys_{IV}^2]$	142.66	162.96(91.86)	158.01(88.61)	154.54
$WTP[ds_V^2]$	135.99	158.23(108.53)	152.40(100.00)	148.87
$WTP[(xs+ws)_{III}^3]$	150.26	173.34(145.39)	166.52(136.41)	163.37
$WTP[(xs+ys)_{IV}^3]$	159.89	181.02(100.64)	177.01(97.18)	172.64
$WTP[(xs+ds)_V^3]$	153.81	180.09(116.42)	171.54(105.83)	168.48
$WTP[SR_I^1]$	187.16	215.23(176.42)	209.38(167.94)	203.92
$WTP[SR_{II}^1]$	187.86	217.42(172.13)	209.67(162.56)	204.98
$WTP[SR_{III}^1]$	180.29	209.30(116.38)	200.86(111.85)	196.82
$WTP[SR_{IV}^1]$	189.35	217.79(147.28)	210.70(142.15)	205.95
$WTP[SR_V^1]$	180.68	205.31(156.66)	200.97(151.83)	195.65
$WTP[xr_{II}^2]$	159.48	181.59(146.02)	176.74(141.46)	172.60
$WTP[wr_{III}^2]$	152.62	177.05(110.58)	169.88(106.74)	166.52

[①] Trudy Ann Cameron and Daniel D. Huppert, "OLS Versus ML Estimation of Non‑market Resource Values with Payment Card Interval Data", *Journal of Environmental Economics and Management*, Vol. 17, No. 3, November 1989; Stefania Tonin, "Citizens' Perspectives on Marine Protected Areas as a Governance Strategy to Effectively Preserve Marine Ecosystem Services and Biodiversity", *Ecosystem Services*, Vol. 34, December 2018.

续表

变量	原始均值（元）	OLS 均值（元）	IR 均值（元）	三种方法均值（元）
$WTP[yr_{IV}^2]$	167.93	193.70(145.53)	187.32(138.81)	182.98
$WTP[dr_V^2]$	148.68	171.18(126.35)	165.91(117.30)	161.92
$WTP[(xr+wr)_{III}^3]$	159.05	183.00(110.24)	176.02(106.61)	172.69
$WTP[(xr+yr)_{IV}^3]$	177.62	205.04(145.35)	198.19(139.54)	193.62
$WTP[(xr+dr)_V^3]$	161.23	184.53(144.74)	178.92(138.27)	174.89

注：各符号含义同表10.1和表10.2；括号中数值为稳健标准误。

二 范围检验结果分析

内部范围检验两组配对样本比较，采用两配对样本参数 t–test 和两配对样本非参数 Wilcoxon signed–rank test；三组配对样本比较，采用非参数多配对样本 Friedman test。外部范围检验两组独立样本比较，采用两独立样本参数 t–test 和两独立样本非参数 Mann–Whitney U test；三组独立样本和四组独立样本比较，采用多独立样本参数 one–way ANOVA 和多独立样本非参数 Kruskal–Wallis test。因可能存在"过度嵌入效应"（Over–embedding）现象，所以，本书研究两者之间比较用的都是双尾（2–tailed）。

（一）海滩旅游资源范围检验结果分析

从海滩旅游资源范围检验结果来看（见表10.7和表10.8），各待估海滩旅游资源内部范围检验全部通过；不同独立子样本调查同一待估海滩旅游资源（SS_I^1、SS_{II}^1、SS_{III}^1、SS_{IV}^1、SS_V^1）估值比较，5组独立子样本最大范围 WTP 估值结果较稳定，通过了外部范围检验；这证明本书研究的问卷设计、调查实施和 WTP 估值结果具有可靠性（Reliability）；蜈支洲岛待估海滩旅游资源（ws_{III}^2）与三亚（四地）待估海滩旅游资源（SS_{II}^1）估值比较，通过了外部范围非参数检验；其他各待估海滩旅游资源估值比较，均未通过外部范围参数和非参数检验。从各待估海滩旅游资源 WTP 估值比较来看，受访者能够感知到待估海滩旅游资源内部数量范围或外部数量范围的变化，并且 WTP 估值大小的变化方向与数量范围大小的变化方向一致（见图10.1、图10.3、图10.5、图10.7）。

表 10.7　　　　　　　海滩旅游资源内部范围检验结果

零假设检验		非参数检验		参数检验	
		$Z/Chi-Square$	$Asymp.\ Sig.$	t	$Sig.$
$in^s-H_1^0$	$WTP[xs_{II}^2]=WTP[SS_{II}^1]$	-6.83	0.00	-4.18	0.00
$in^s-H_2^0$	$WTP[ws_{III}^2]=WTP[(xs+ws)_{III}^3]=WTP[SS_{III}^1]$	106.57	0.00	—	—
	$WTP[(xs+ws)_{III}^3]=WTP[SS_{III}^1]$	-5.15	0.00	-3.43	0.00
	$WTP[ws_{III}^2]=WTP[(xs+ws)_{III}^3]$	-5.95	0.00	-4.46	0.00
	$WTP[ws_{III}^2]=WTP[SS_{III}^1]$	-7.67	0.00	-4.62	0.00
$in^s-H_3^0$	$WTP[ys_{IV}^2]=WTP[(xs+ys)_{IV}^3]=WTP[SS_{IV}^1]$	79.91	0.00	—	—
	$WTP[(xs+ys)_{IV}^3]=WTP[SS_{IV}^1]$	-5.23	0.00	-3.05	0.00
	$WTP[ys_{IV}^2]=WTP[(xs+ys)_{IV}^3]$	-4.64	0.00	-2.73	0.01
	$WTP[ys_{IV}^2]=WTP[SS_{IV}^1]$	-6.48	0.00	-4.23	0.00
$in^s-H_4^0$	$WTP[ds_V^2]=WTP[(xs+ds)_V^3]=WTP[SS_V^1]$	99.13	0.00	—	—
	$WTP[(xs+ds)_V^3]=WTP[SS_V^1]$	-4.92	0.00	-2.64	0.01
	$WTP[ds_V^2]=WTP[(xs+ds)_V^3]$	-5.28	0.00	-2.77	0.01
	$WTP[ds_V^2]=WTP[SS_V^1]$	-7.09	0.00	-3.20	0.00

注：各符号含义同表 10.1。

表 10.8　　　　　　　海滩旅游资源外部范围检验结果

零假设检验		非参数检验		参数检验	
		$Z/Chi-Square$	$Asymp.\ Sig.$	t/F	$Sig.$
$ex^s-H_1^0$	$WTP[SS_I^1]=WTP[SS_{II}^1]=WTP[SS_{III}^1]=WTP[SS_{IV}^1]=WTP[SS_V^1]$	1.61	0.81	0.01	1.00
$ex^s-H_2^0$	$WTP[(xs+ws)_{III}^3]=WTP[SS_I^1]$	-1.30	0.19	0.97	0.33
	$WTP[xs_{II}^2]=WTP[SS_I^1]$	-1.75	0.08	1.64	0.10
$ex^s-H_3^0$	$WTP[(xs+ys)_{IV}^3]=WTP[SS_{II}^1]$	-1.75	0.08	0.50	0.62
	$WTP[ws_{III}^2]=WTP[SS_{II}^1]$	-3.85	0.00	1.61	0.11

续表

零假设检验		非参数检验		参数检验	
		$Z/Chi-Square$	$Asymp.\ Sig.$	t/F	$Sig.$
$ex^s-H_4^0$	$WTP[(xs+ds)_V^3]=WTP[SS_{III}^1]$	-0.17	0.87	0.80	0.42
	$WTP[ys_{IV}^2]=WTP[SS_{III}^1]$	-1.94	0.05	1.18	0.24
$ex^s-H_5^0$	$WTP[ds_V^2]=WTP[SS_{IV}^1]$	-1.50	0.13	1.67	0.10
$ex^s-H_6^0$	$WTP[xs_{II}^2]=WTP[(xs+ws)_{III}^3]$	-0.36	0.72	-0.69	0.49
	$WTP[xs_{II}^2]=WTP[(xs+ys)_{IV}^3]$	-0.82	0.41	-1.06	0.29
	$WTP[xs_{II}^2]=WTP[(xs+ds)_V^3]$	-1.47	0.14	-0.93	0.35

注：各符号含义同表 10.1。

从各待估海滩旅游资源估值比较来看，内部数量范围变化的边际 WTP 增加值均较低（见图 10.1），外部数量范围变化的边际 WTP 增加值同样均较低（见图 10.3、图 10.5、图 10.7）；同时，各待估海滩旅游资源保护的非使用价值呈现出边际递减（见图 10.2、图 10.4、图 10.6、图 10.8），并且各条曲线均逐渐趋于平坦，受访者效用趋于饱和。研究表明，饱和程度和边际效应递减是各待估海滩旅游资源数量范围变化边际 WTP 增加值大小和范围敏感性的主要影响因素。西岛、蜈支洲岛、亚龙湾和大东海四个片区的海滩旅游资源内部之间和与外部海滩旅游资源之间存在竞争替代性，替代效应也是各待估海滩旅游资源数量范围变化边际 WTP 增加值大小和范围敏感性的主要影响因素。

$in^s-H_1^0: WTP[xs_{II}^2] \xrightarrow{42} WTP[SS_{II}^1]$

$in^s-H_2^0: WTP[ws_{III}^2] \xrightarrow{17} WTP[(xs+ws)_{III}^3] \xrightarrow{24} WTP[SS_{III}^1]$

$in^s-H_3^0: WTP[ys_{IV}^2] \xrightarrow{18} WTP[(xs+ys)_{IV}^3] \xrightarrow{17} WTP[SS_{IV}^1]$

$in^s-H_4^0: WTP[ds_V^2] \xrightarrow{19} WTP[(xs+ds)_V^3] \xrightarrow{23} WTP[SS_V^1]$

图 10.1　各待估海滩旅游资源内部数量范围变化 WTP 估值比较

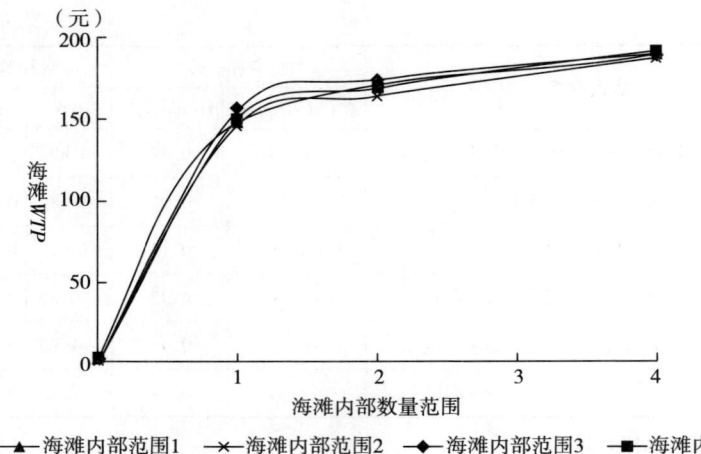

图 10.2　各待估海滩旅游资源非使用价值边际递减——内部数量范围

$$ex^s - H_2^0: WTP[\,xs_{\mathrm{II}}^2\,] \xrightarrow{43} WTP[\,SS_{\mathrm{I}}^1\,]$$

$$ex^s - H_3^0: WTP[\,ws_{\mathrm{III}}^2\,] \xrightarrow{42} WTP[\,SS_{\mathrm{II}}^1\,]$$

$$ex^s - H_4^0: WTP[\,ys_{\mathrm{IV}}^2\,] \xrightarrow{32} WTP[\,SS_{\mathrm{III}}^1\,]$$

$$ex^s - H_5^0: WTP[\,ds_{\mathrm{V}}^2\,] \xrightarrow{41} WTP[\,SS_{\mathrm{IV}}^1\,]$$

图 10.3　各待估海滩旅游资源外部数量范围变化（0 – 1 – 4）WTP 估值比较

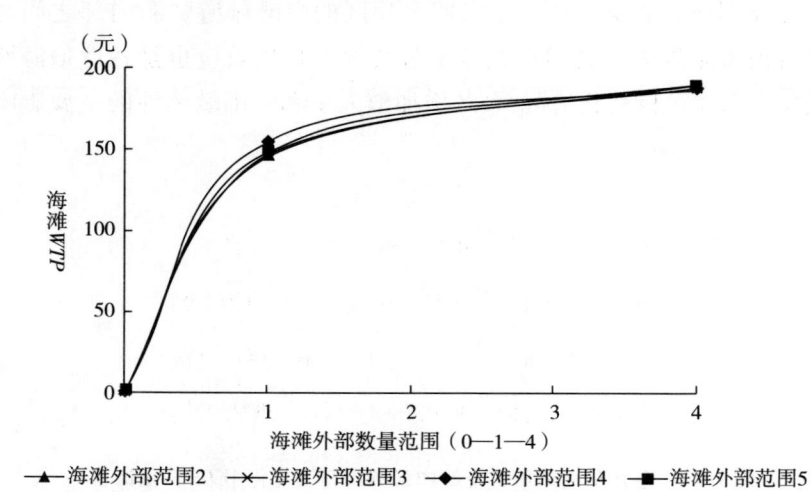

图 10.4　各待估海滩旅游资源非使用价值边际递减——外部数量范围（0 – 1 – 4）

$$ex^s - H_2^0: WTP[\,(xs+ws)_{\text{III}}^3\,] \xrightarrow{26} WTP[\,SS_{\text{I}}^1\,]$$

$$ex^s - H_3^0: WTP[\,(xs+ys)_{\text{IV}}^3\,] \xrightarrow{15} WTP[\,SS_{\text{II}}^1\,]$$

$$ex^s - H_4^0: WTP[\,(xs+ds)_{\text{V}}^3\,] \xrightarrow{19} WTP[\,SS_{\text{III}}^1\,]$$

图 10.5　各待估海滩旅游资源外部数量范围变化（0－2－4）WTP 估值比较

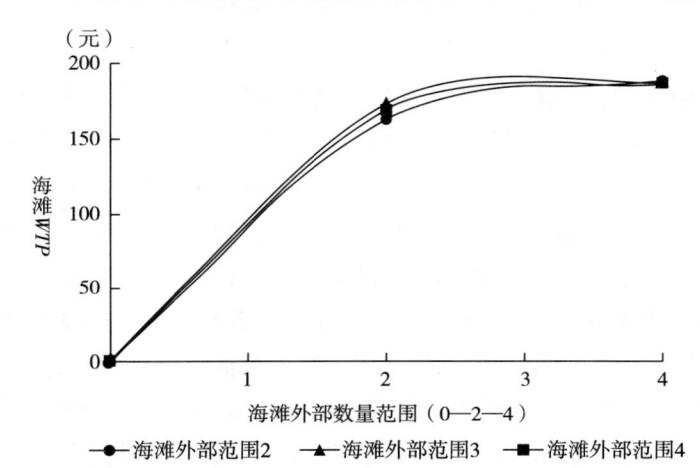

图 10.6　各待估海滩旅游资源非使用价值边际递减——外部数量范围（0－2－4）

$$ex^s - H_6^0: WTP[\,xs_{\text{II}}^2\,] \xrightarrow{17} WTP[\,(xs+ws)_{\text{III}}^3\,]$$

$$ex^s - H_6^0: WTP[\,xs_{\text{II}}^2\,] \xrightarrow{27} WTP[\,(xs+ys)_{\text{IV}}^3\,]$$

$$ex^s - H_6^0: WTP[\,xs_{\text{II}}^2\,] \xrightarrow{22} WTP[\,(xs+ds)_{\text{V}}^3\,]$$

图 10.7　各待估海滩旅游资源外部数量范围变化（0－1－2）WTP 估值比较

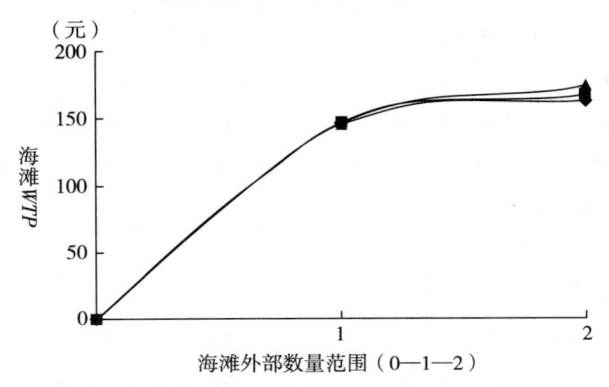

图 10.8　各待估海滩旅游资源非使用价值边际递减——外部数量范围（0－1－2）

(二) 珊瑚礁旅游资源范围检验结果分析

从珊瑚礁旅游资源范围检验结果来看，蜈支洲岛待估珊瑚礁旅游资源（$wr_{Ⅲ}^2$）与西岛加蜈支洲岛待估珊瑚礁旅游资源 $[(xr+wr)_{Ⅲ}^3]$ 估值比较，未通过两配对样本内部范围参数检验；其他各待估珊瑚礁旅游资源估值比较，均通过了内部范围参数和非参数检验（见表10.9）。不同独立子样本调查同一待估珊瑚礁旅游资源（$SR_{Ⅰ}^1$、$SR_{Ⅱ}^1$、$SR_{Ⅲ}^1$、$SR_{Ⅳ}^1$、$SR_{Ⅴ}^1$）估值比较，5组独立子样本最大范围WTP估值结果较稳定，通过了外部范围检验；这证明本书研究的问卷设计、调查实施和WTP估值结果具有可靠性（Reliability）。西岛待估珊瑚礁旅游资源（$xr_{Ⅱ}^2$）与三亚（四地）待估珊瑚礁旅游资源（$SR_{Ⅰ}^1$）估值比较，通过了外部范围非参数检验；其他各待估珊瑚礁旅游资源估值比较，均未通过外部范围参数和非参数检验（见表10.10）。从各待估珊瑚礁旅游资源WTP估值比较来看，受访者能够感知到待估珊瑚礁旅游资源内部数量范围或外部数量范围的变化，并且WTP估值大小的变化方向与数量范围大小的变化方向一致（见图10.9、图10.11、图10.13、图10.15）。

表10.9　　　　　　　珊瑚海旅游资源内部范围检验结果

零假设检验		非参数检验		参数检验	
		Z/Chi–Square	Asymp. Sig.	t	Sig.
$in^r - H_1^0$	$WTP[xr_{Ⅱ}^2] = WTP[SR_{Ⅱ}^1]$	-5.96	0.00	-3.35	0.00
$in^r - H_2^0$	$WTP[wr_{Ⅲ}^2] = WTP[(xr+wr)_{Ⅲ}^3] = WTP[SR_{Ⅲ}^1]$	52.63	0.00	—	—
	$WTP[(xr+wr)_{Ⅲ}^3] = WTP[SR_{Ⅲ}^1]$	-4.81	0.00	-2.93	0.00
	$WTP[wr_{Ⅲ}^2] = WTP[(xr+wr)_{Ⅲ}^3]$	-2.19	0.03	-1.93	0.06
	$WTP[wr_{Ⅲ}^2] = WTP[SR_{Ⅲ}^1]$	-4.98	0.00	-3.65	0.00
$in^r - H_3^0$	$WTP[yr_{Ⅳ}^2] = WTP[(xr+yr)_{Ⅳ}^3] = WTP[SR_{Ⅳ}^1]$	29.79	0.00	—	—
	$WTP[(xr+yr)_{Ⅳ}^3] = WTP[SR_{Ⅳ}^1]$	-3.01	0.00	-1.97	0.05
	$WTP[yr_{Ⅳ}^2] = WTP[(xr+yr)_{Ⅳ}^3]$	-2.14	0.03	-2.05	0.04
	$WTP[yr_{Ⅳ}^2] = WTP[SR_{Ⅳ}^1]$	-3.52	0.00	-2.85	0.01

续表

零假设检验		非参数检验		参数检验	
		$Z/Chi-Square$	Asymp. Sig.	t	Sig.
$in^r - H_4^0$	$WTP[dr_V^2] = WTP[(xr+dr)_V^3] = WTP[SR_V^1]$	85.83	0.00	—	—
	$WTP[(xr+dr)_V^3] = WTP[SR_V^1]$	-6.16	0.00	-3.69	0.00
	$WTP[dr_V^2] = WTP[(xr+dr)_V^3]$	-2.64	0.01	-1.99	0.05
	$WTP[dr_V^2] = WTP[SR_V^1]$	-6.31	0.00	-3.92	0.00

注：各符号含义同表 10.2。

表 10.10　珊瑚礁旅游资源外部范围检验结果

零假设检验		非参数检验		参数检验	
		$Z/Chi-Square$	Asymp. Sig.	t/F	Sig.
$ex^r - H_1^0$	$WTP[SR_I^1] = WTP[SR_{II}^1] = WTP[SR_{III}^1] = WTP[SR_{IV}^1] = WTP[SR_V^1]$	2.92	0.57	0.05	1.00
$ex^r - H_2^0$	$WTP[(xr+wr)_{III}^3] = WTP[SR_I^1]$	-1.38	0.17	1.13	0.26
	$WTP[xr_{II}^2] = WTP[SR_I^1]$	-2.35	0.02	1.05	0.30
$ex^r - H_3^0$	$WTP[(xr+yr)_{IV}^3] = WTP[SR_{II}^1]$	-0.76	0.45	0.38	0.70
	$WTP[wr_{III}^2] = WTP[SR_{II}^1]$	-1.76	0.08	1.46	0.14
$ex^r - H_4^0$	$WTP[(xr+dr)_V^3] = WTP[SR_{III}^1]$	-0.96	0.34	0.78	0.43
	$WTP[yr_{IV}^2] = WTP[SR_{III}^1]$	-1.79	0.07	0.49	0.63
$ex^r - H_5^0$	$WTP[dr_V^2] = WTP[SR_{IV}^1]$	-0.81	0.42	1.54	0.12
$ex^r - H_6^0$	$WTP[xr_{II}^2] = WTP[(xr+wr)_{III}^3]$	-1.05	0.30	0.02	0.99
	$WTP[xr_{II}^2] = WTP[(xr+yr)_{IV}^3]$	-1.24	0.21	-0.68	0.50
	$WTP[xr_{II}^2] = WTP[(xr+dr)_V^3]$	-1.74	0.08	-0.07	0.95

注：各符号含义同表 10.2。

数量范围检验的首要经济问题是饱和程度，WTP 是否增加取决于受访者关于珊瑚礁旅游资源供给水平的饱和程度。从各待估珊瑚礁旅游资源估值比较来看，内部数量范围变化的边际 WTP 增加值均较低（见图 10.9），外部数量范围变化的边际 WTP 增加值同样均较低（见图 10.11、图 10.13、图 10.15）。同时，各待估珊瑚礁旅游资源保护的非使用价值呈现出边际递减（见图 10.10、图 10.12、图 10.14、图 10.16），并且保护 1 个片区的珊瑚礁旅游资源后，各条曲线均趋于平坦（见图 10.10、图 10.12、图 10.16），受访者效用趋于饱和。研究表明，饱和程度和边际效应递减是各待估珊瑚礁旅游资源数量范围变化边际 WTP 增加值大小和范围敏感性的主要影响因素。

$$in^r - H_1^0: WTP[xr_{II}^2] \xrightarrow{32} WTP[SR_{II}^1]$$

$$in^r - H_2^0: WTP[wr_{III}^2] \xrightarrow{6} WTP[(xr+wr)_{III}^3] \xrightarrow{24} WTP[SR_{III}^1]$$

$$in^r - H_3^0: WTP[yr_{IV}^2] \xrightarrow{11} WTP[(xr+yr)_{IV}^3] \xrightarrow{12} WTP[SR_{IV}^1]$$

$$in^r - H_4^0: WTP[dr_V^2] \xrightarrow{13} WTP[(xr+dr)_V^3] \xrightarrow{21} WTP[SR_V^1]$$

图 10.9　各待估珊瑚礁旅游资源内部数量范围变化 *WTP* 估值比较

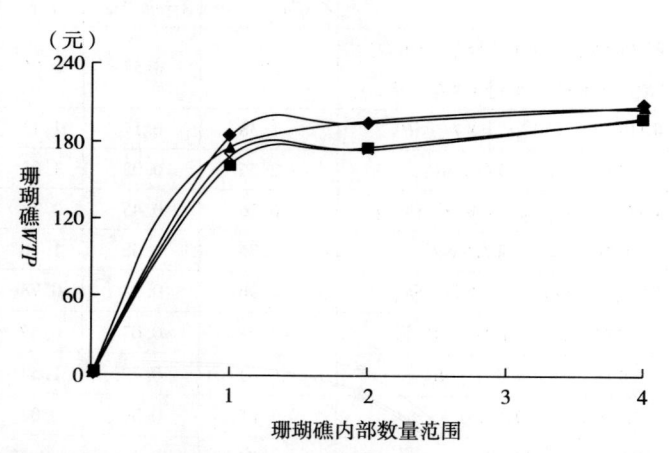

图 10.10　各待估珊瑚礁旅游资源非使用价值边际递减——内部数量范围

$$ex^r - H_2^0: WTP[xr_{II}^2] \xrightarrow{31} WTP[SR_I^1]$$

$$ex^r - H_3^0: WTP[wr_{III}^2] \xrightarrow{38} WTP[SR_{II}^1]$$

$$ex^r - H_4^0: WTP[yr_{IV}^2] \xrightarrow{14} WTP[SR_{III}^1]$$

$$ex^r - H_5^0: WTP[dr_V^2] \xrightarrow{44} WTP[SR_{IV}^1]$$

图 10.11　各待估珊瑚礁旅游资源外部数量范围变化（0 – 1 – 4）*WTP* 估值比较

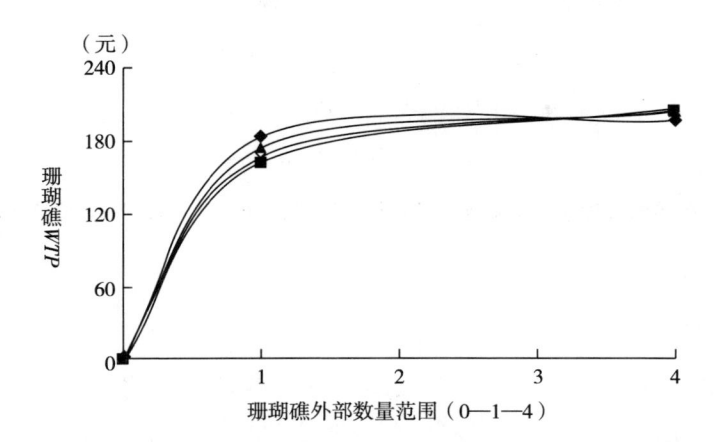

第十章 | 嵌入效应问题研究三亚及其附近岛屿案例

(元)

珊瑚礁 WTP

珊瑚礁外部数量范围（0—1—4）

──▲── 珊瑚礁外部范围2　──×── 珊瑚礁外部范围3　──◆── 珊瑚礁外部范围4　──■── 珊瑚礁外部范围5

图 10.12　各待估珊瑚礁旅游资源非使用价值边际递减——外部数量范围（0－1－4）

$$ex^r - H_2^0: WTP[(xr+wr)_{\mathrm{III}}^3] \xrightarrow{31} WTP[SR_{\mathrm{I}}^1]$$

$$ex^r - H_3^0: WTP[(xr+yr)_{\mathrm{IV}}^3] \xrightarrow{11} WTP[SR_{\mathrm{II}}^1]$$

$$ex^r - H_4^0: WTP[(xr+dr)_{\mathrm{V}}^3] \xrightarrow{22} WTP[SR_{\mathrm{III}}^1]$$

图 10.13　各待估珊瑚礁旅游资源外部数量范围变化（0－2－4）WTP 估值比较

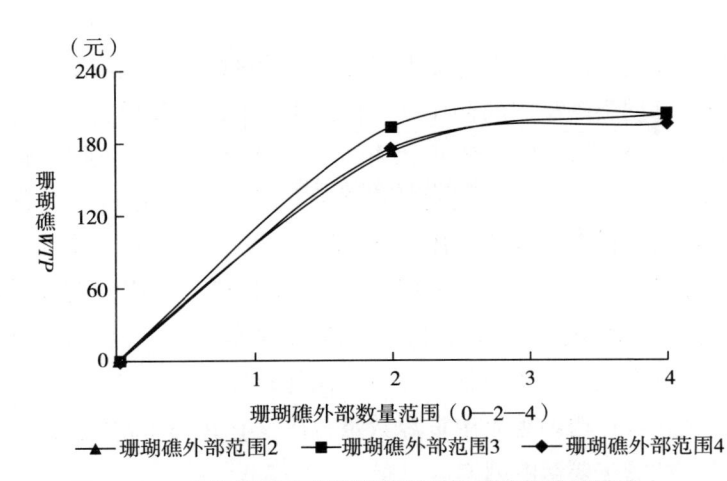

(元)

珊瑚礁 WTP

珊瑚礁外部数量范围（0—2—4）

──▲── 珊瑚礁外部范围2　──■── 珊瑚礁外部范围3　──◆── 珊瑚礁外部范围4

图 10.14　各待估珊瑚礁旅游资源非使用价值边际递减——外部数量范围（0－2－4）

$$ex^r - H_6^0 : WTP[xr_{\mathrm{II}}^2] \xrightarrow{0} WTP[(xr+wr)_{\mathrm{III}}^3]$$

$$ex^r - H_6^0 : WTP[xr_{\mathrm{II}}^2] \xrightarrow{21} WTP[(xr+yr)_{\mathrm{IV}}^3]$$

$$ex^r - H_6^0 : WTP[xr_{\mathrm{II}}^2] \xrightarrow{2} WTP[(xr+dr)_{\mathrm{V}}^3]$$

图 10.15　各待估珊瑚礁旅游资源外部数量范围变化（0 – 1 – 2）WTP 估值比较

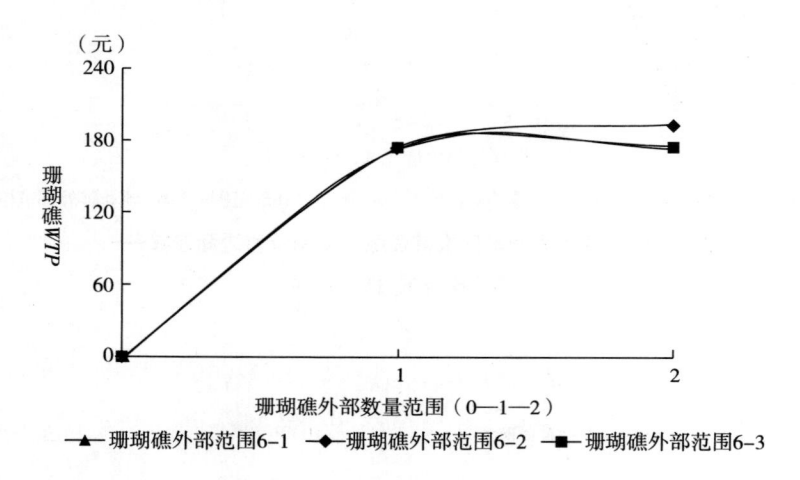

图 10.16　各待估珊瑚礁旅游资源非使用价值边际递减——
外部数量范围（0 – 1 – 2）

西岛、蜈支洲岛、亚龙湾和大东海四个片区的珊瑚礁旅游资源内部之间和与外部同类资源之间存在竞争替代性。如西岛和蜈支洲岛均为离岸小岛屿，珊瑚礁旅游资源极为相似；西岛待估珊瑚礁旅游资源（xr_{II}^2）与西岛加蜈支洲岛待估珊瑚礁旅游资源 [$(xr+wr)_{\mathrm{III}}^3$] 外部数量范围估值比较，边际 WTP 增加值为 0 元（见图 10.15）；蜈支洲岛待估珊瑚礁旅游资源（wr_{III}^2）与西岛加蜈支洲岛待估珊瑚礁旅游资源 [$(xr+wr)_{\mathrm{III}}^3$] 内部数量范围估值比较，边际 WTP 增加值为 6 元（见图 10.9）；其他各待估珊瑚礁旅游资源估值比较，同样存在替代效应。研究表明，替代效应是各待估珊瑚礁旅游资源数量范围变化边际 WTP 增加值大小和范围敏感性的主要影响因素。

第四节　三亚及其附近岛屿结论

（1）不同独立子样本调查同一待估海滩旅游资源或珊瑚礁旅游资源 *WTP* 估值比较，通过了外部数量范围检验，表明本书研究的问卷设计、调查实施和 *WTP* 估值结果具有可靠性。其他各待估海滩旅游资源或珊瑚礁旅游资源外部数量范围估值比较，*WTP* 存在差异；表明受访者对各待估海滩旅游资源或珊瑚礁旅游资源外部数量范围变化敏感，但未达到统计显著性（$ex^s - H_3^0$ 的一部分非参数检验通过）。内部范围检验除 $in^r - H_2^0$ 的一部分参数检验未通过外，其他检验全部通过；表明受访者对各待估海滩旅游资源或珊瑚礁旅游资源内部数量范围变化敏感，且达到了统计显著性。

（2）各待估海滩旅游资源或珊瑚礁旅游资源数量范围变化，受访者在保护 1 个片区的海滩旅游资源或珊瑚礁旅游资源后，受访者效用逐渐趋于饱和（曲线较平坦），边际效应迅速递减；同时，海滩旅游资源或珊瑚礁旅游资源替代品的存在，加速了边际 *WTP* 增加值下降的速度。饱和程度、边际效应递减和/或替代效应是边际 *WTP* 增加值大小变化的主要影响因素，它们为各待估海滩旅游资源或珊瑚礁旅游资源外部数量范围检验和内部数量范围检验未达到统计显著性提供了依据。所以，范围检验不应作为 CVM 研究有效性的唯一判断标准，检验结果需要通过经济学相关理论更仔细的考虑和解释。

（3）四个片区的海滩旅游资源（xs_{II}^2、ws_{III}^2、ys_{IV}^2、ds_V^2）分别估值，*WTP* 之和为 595 元；四个片区的海滩旅游资源整体（SS_I^1、SS_{II}^1、SS_{III}^1、SS_{IV}^1、SS_V^1）估值，五组独立子样本 *WTP* 均值为 189 元；珊瑚礁旅游资源（xr_{II}^2、wr_{III}^2、yr_{IV}^2、dr_V^2）分别估值，*WTP* 之和为 684 元；四个片区的珊瑚礁旅游资源整体（SR_I^1、SR_{II}^1、SR_{III}^1、SR_{IV}^1、SR_V^1）估值，五组独立子样本 *WTP* 均值为 201 元。四个片区待估海滩旅游资源独立估值加总之和是其整体估值的 3.10 倍，四个片区待估珊瑚礁旅游资源独立估值加总之和是其整体估值的 3.40 倍。因受饱和程度、边际效应递减、替代效应等因素影响，在成本—收益分析中，利用各待估海滩旅游资源或珊瑚礁旅游资源的整体估值结果更为科学；这一结论同样适用于存在包含关系的复杂公共物品非使用价值估值。

第四篇 研究结论

第十一章

群岛旅游资源非使用价值估值比较

　　本书研究运用条件价值评估法（CVM），基于黄渤海区—山东庙岛群岛、东海区—浙江舟山群岛和南海区—海南三亚及其附近岛屿的居民和游客问卷调查数据，比较研究公众对保护海滩、海洋地质遗迹、海洋文化和珊瑚礁等典型海洋旅游资源非使用价值支付意愿的偏好。结果表明：①公众对保护四种典型海洋旅游资源非使用价值的支付意愿具有显著差异性，即不同资源类型非使用价值的支付意愿不同；②公众不但能够感知到海洋旅游资源非使用价值的存在，还能够识别出不同类型海洋旅游资源差异化的非使用价值；③公众保护海洋相对稀缺型旅游资源（海洋地质遗迹、海洋文化、珊瑚礁）非使用价值比保护海洋相对充裕型旅游资源（海滩）非使用价值的平均支付意愿高；④公众保护海洋人文旅游资源（海洋文化）非使用价值比保护海洋自然旅游资源（海滩、海洋地质遗迹、珊瑚礁）非使用价值的平均支付意愿高。

　　以居民和游客合并数据为例：①公众保护庙岛群岛海洋地质遗迹、舟山群岛海洋文化、三亚及其附近岛屿珊瑚礁旅游资源非使用价值的平均支付意愿分别为 251 元/人、359 元/人、266 元/人，消除样本组之间受访者人口社会特征差异，调整后的两个平均支付意愿分别为 245 元/人和 271 元/人、360 元/人和 353 元/人、258 元/人和 257 元/人；②公众保护庙岛群岛海滩、舟山群岛海滩、三亚及其附近岛屿海滩旅游资源非使用价值的平均支付意愿分别为 201 元/人、298 元/人、250 元/人，调整后的两个平均支付意愿分别为 205 元/人和 219 元/人、299 元/人和 279 元/人、257 元/人和 241 元/人。

依据分位数回归结果，庙岛群岛海滩和海洋地质遗迹、舟山群岛海滩和海洋文化、三亚及其附近岛屿海滩和珊瑚礁等各案例地各类资源，从总体来看：收入变量的回归系数在多个分位数回归模型中都呈现出统计显著性，收入变量回归系数为正值，这表明受访者的支付意愿与收入成正比，收入越高的受访者支付意愿越高；并且，收入变量的回归系数随着分位点的增加呈现递增趋势，这表明收入变化对支付意愿较高的受访者影响更大。

本书研究揭示了我国公众保护海洋旅游资源非使用价值的偏好，为海洋旅游资源非使用价值的存在性提供了实验证据，也为将非使用价值纳入到中国海洋旅游资源保护或恢复工程成本—收益分析中的必要性提供了理论支撑；研究成果同时为海洋旅游资源保护政策制定和 CVM 有效性、可靠性检验提供了新思路。分位数回归研究结果为预测随着公众生活水平的提高，支付意愿的变化趋势提供了参考。

第十二章

群岛旅游资源非使用价值评估嵌入效应问题

本书研究基于庙岛群岛海滩和海洋地质遗迹，舟山群岛海滩、海洋文化和海滩与海洋文化，三亚及其附近岛屿海滩和珊瑚礁的居民和游客问卷调查数据，在"群岛旅游资源非使用价值估值比较"研究的基础上，对基于 CVM 的群岛旅游资源非使用价值评估嵌入效应问题进行了研究。庙岛群岛案例结果表明：①不同独立子样本调查同一待估海滩旅游资源或海洋地质遗迹旅游资源支付意愿估值比较，通过了外部数量范围检验，表明本书研究的问卷设计、调查实施和支付意愿估值结果具有可靠性。其他各待估海滩旅游资源或海洋地质遗迹旅游资源外部数量范围估值比较，支付意愿存在差异；表明受访者对各待估海滩旅游资源或海洋地质遗迹旅游资源外部数量范围变化敏感，但未达到统计显著性。各待估海洋旅游资源或海洋地质遗迹旅游资源内部范围检验全部通过；表明受访者对各待估海滩旅游资源或海洋地质遗迹旅游资源内部数量范围变化敏感，且达到了统计显著性。②各待估海滩旅游资源或海洋地质遗迹旅游资源数量范围变化，在保护 1 个海岛的海滩旅游资源或海洋地质遗迹旅游资源后，受访者效用逐渐趋于饱和（曲线较平坦），边际效应迅速递减；同时，海滩旅游资源或海洋地质遗迹旅游资源替代品的存在，加速了边际支付意愿增加值下降的速度。饱和程度、边际效应递减和/或替代效应是边际支付意愿增加值大小变化的主要影响因素，它们为各待估海滩旅游资源或海洋地质遗迹旅游资源的（部分）外部数量范围检验未达到统计显著性提供了依据。

舟山群岛案例结果表明：①内部范围检验全部通过，外部范围检验结果混合；同一待估旅游资源不同调查的外部范围检验全部通过，这验证了本书研究 CVM 的问卷设计、调查实施和支付意愿结果具有可靠性。②受访者能够感知到海滩旅游资源数量范围或海洋文化旅游资源分类范围或海滩与海洋文化旅游资源复合范围的变化，并且支付意愿估值的变化方向与数量范围或分类范围或复合范围的变化方向一致。③边际效应递减、饱和程度及替代效应是海滩旅游资源数量范围嵌入效应外部范围检验不敏感的主要影响因素；旗舰资源效应及预算限制是海洋文化旅游资源分类范围或海滩与海洋文化旅游资源复合范围嵌入效应外部范围检验不敏感的主要影响因素。

三亚及其附近岛屿案例结果表明：①不同独立子样本调查的同一待估海滩旅游资源或珊瑚礁旅游资源支付意愿估值比较，通过了外部数量范围检验，表明本书研究的问卷设计、调查实施和支付意愿估值结果具有可靠性；②受访者能够感知到各待估海滩旅游资源或珊瑚礁旅游资源外部数量范围和内部数量范围的变化，且边际支付意愿增加值大小的变化方向与数量范围大小的变化方向一致；③饱和程度、边际效应递减和替代效应是边际支付意愿增加值较低和嵌入效应的主要影响因素；保护超过 1 个片区的海滩旅游资源或珊瑚礁旅游资源，受访者效用趋于饱和（曲线较平坦），边际支付意愿非常低；④因受上述各因素影响，四个片区海滩旅游资源或珊瑚礁旅游资源独立估值的支付意愿之和是四个片区海滩旅游资源或珊瑚礁旅游资源整体估值支付意愿的 3.10 倍或 3.40 倍。

本书研究建议：①范围检验结果需要更仔细的考量，一些范围检验结果失败可以用适合的经济理论来解释，不应该将范围检验作为 CVM 研究有效性的唯一判断标准；②在成本—收益分析中，对复杂公共物品（如群岛海滩或海洋文化或海滩与海洋文化旅游资源）进行整体估值是一种更为可靠的方法。

附　录

附录 1　庙岛群岛 OLS 和 IR 详细计算结果

庙岛群岛各待估海滩旅游资源和各待估海洋地质遗迹旅游资源 OLS 和 IR 详细计算结果如附表 1.1 至附表 1.9 所示，各符号含义同正文表 8.1 和表 8.2。

附表 1.1　　　庙岛群岛海滩 WTP [MS_1^1]

变量	OLS	IR
Sex	14.64 (30.05)	14.79 (27.60)
Age	-21.00* (11.13)	-19.53* (10.32)
Ages	28.34* (14.42)	26.29** (13.31)
Edu	-4.10 (39.87)	-1.77 (35.83)
Lninc	119.96*** (30.23)	110.57*** (27.86)
Resp	-10.98 (38.68)	-13.82 (34.99)
Constant	-842.47** (336.33)	-764.14** (309.16)
Lnsigma	—	5.55*** (0.12)
Sigma	278.36	256.57 (30.91)
N	337	337
R^2	0.07	—
F	3.08	—
Prob > F	0.01	—

续表

变量	OLS	IR
Log pseudolikelihood	—	-1356.18
Wald χ^2	—	18.47
Prob > χ^2	—	0.01
Median	159.81	155.82
Mean	170.01（75.10）	163.99（69.37）

注：括号中数值为稳健标准误；$*p<0.1$，$**p<0.05$，$***p<0.01$。

附表1.2　　庙岛群岛海滩 WTP [MS_{II}^1]

变量	OLS	IR
Sex	6.14（33.16）	6.19（31.71）
Age	-20.23*（11.90）	-18.93*（11.23）
Ages	23.16（15.30）	21.88（14.63）
Edu	-3.05（33.79）	-4.05（31.77）
Lninc	135.12***（45.33）	132.91***（44.39）
Resp	-35.12（40.78）	-35.87（39.38）
Constant	-948.08**（436.01）	-955.60**（422.67）
Lnsigma	—	5.62***（0.13）
Sigma	290.70	276.53（34.93）
N	334	334
R^2	0.08	—
F	3.08	—
Prob > F	0.01	—
Log pseudolikelihood	—	-1400.69
Wald χ^2	—	18.11
Prob > χ^2	—	0.01
Median	153.96	151.24
Mean	167.54（83.75）	163.74（81.62）

注：括号中数值为稳健标准误；$*p<0.1$，$**p<0.05$，$***p<0.01$。

附表1.3　庙岛群岛海滩 WTP $[bs_{II}^2]$

变量	OLS	IR
Sex	-13.96（28.16）	-11.20（26.63）
Age	-27.26**（11.07）	-25.01**（10.21）
$Ages$	32.00**（14.06）	29.32**（13.00）
Edu	-6.93（27.85）	-6.36（26.75）
$Lninc$	134.56***（39.12）	125.87***（36.06）
$Resp$	-23.00（31.77）	-20.22（30.07）
$Constant$	-827.67**（359.38）	-779.23**（336.26）
$Lnsigma$	—	5.46***（0.14）
$Sigma$	248.84	235.02（32.91）
N	334	334
R^2	0.11	—
F	3.13	—
$Prob>F$	0.01	—
$Log\ pseudolikelihood$	—	-1367.55
$Wald\ \chi^2$	—	19.24
$Prob>\chi^2$	—	0.00
$Median$	135.22	133.54
$Mean$	146.86（84.62）	143.40（78.98）

注：括号中数值为稳健标准误；* $p<0.1$，** $p<0.05$，*** $p<0.01$。

附表1.4　庙岛群岛海洋地质遗迹 WTP $[MG_I^1]$

变量	OLS	IR
Sex	42.49（37.77）	41.60（35.51）
Age	6.34（13.92）	6.36（12.80）
$Ages$	-10.81（17.02）	-10.83（15.52）
Edu	53.31（54.61）	51.03（52.34）
$Lninc$	163.77***（37.79）	152.29***（35.75）
$Resp$	-179.22***（61.14）	-166.63***（58.82）
$Constant$	-1669.90***（467.52）	-1553.61***（439.75）
$Lnsigma$	—	5.76***（0.10）
$Sigma$	341.07	316.38（32.13）

续表

变量	OLS	IR
N	337	337
R^2	0.12	—
F	5.11	—
$Prob > F$	0.00	—
$Log\ pseudolikelihood$	—	-1389.41
$Wald\ \chi^2$	—	28.96
$Prob > \chi^2$	—	0.00
$Median$	201.05	193.78
$Mean$	215.51（122.94）	206.81（115.08）

注：括号中数值为稳健标准误；$*p<0.1$，$**p<0.05$，$***p<0.01$。

附表1.5　庙岛群岛海洋地质遗迹 $WTP\ [MG_{II}^{1}]$

变量	OLS	IR
Sex	101.35***（33.62）	96.60***（31.06）
Age	-6.88（9.70）	-7.15（8.83）
$Ages$	8.50（11.03）	8.90（10.16）
Edu	-35.03（45.84）	-33.70（43.28）
$Lninc$	212.69***（43.00）	201.12***（42.14）
$Resp$	-40.13（39.39）	-42.36（37.48）
$Constant$	-2101.00***（457.11）	-1968.35***（438.60）
$Lnsigma$	—	5.65***（0.09）
$Sigma$	308.62	283.57（26.33）
N	322	322
R^2	0.19	—
F	5.75	—
$Prob > F$	0.00	—
$Log\ pseudolikelihood$	—	-1255.77
$Wald\ \chi^2$	—	33.69
$Prob > \chi^2$	—	0.00
$Median$	211.13	202.41
$Mean$	221.46（148.03）	213.03（140.14）

注：括号中数值为稳健标准误；$*p<0.1$，$**p<0.05$，$***p<0.01$。

附表1.6　　　庙岛群岛海洋地质遗迹 WTP [bg_{II}^2]

变量	OLS	IR
Sex	92.91*** (29.15)	86.48*** (27.21)
Age	-6.70 (9.14)	-6.49 (8.16)
Ages	7.17 (10.15)	6.89 (9.14)
Edu	-12.64 (38.85)	-13.59 (37.35)
Lninc	195.78*** (41.39)	185.12*** (40.41)
Resp	-71.34** (35.15)	-71.64** (34.21)
Constant	-1917.32*** (433.33)	-1800.42*** (413.94)
Lnsigma	—	5.54*** (0.11)
Sigma	274.74	253.86 (28.34)
N	322	322
R^2	0.21	—
F	6.65	—
Prob > F	0.00	—
Log pseudolikelihood	—	-1275.50
Wald χ^2	—	39.58
Prob > χ^2	—	0.00
Median	171.74	167.24
Mean	184.03 (138.90)	177.74 (131.18)

注：括号中数值为稳健标准误；*$p<0.1$，**$p<0.05$，***$p<0.01$。

附表1.7　　　庙岛群岛海洋地质遗迹 WTP [MG_{III}^1]

变量	OLS	IR
Sex	-11.26 (37.91)	-10.44 (36.20)
Age	5.29 (8.13)	5.92 (7.48)
Ages	-7.68 (10.21)	-8.49 (9.38)
Edu	-19.84 (42.48)	-18.84 (40.76)
Lninc	205.18*** (48.14)	196.12*** (47.19)
Resp	-81.34 (50.18)	-79.68 (48.80)
Constant	-2152.25*** (526.51)	-2067.92*** (519.47)
Lnsigma	—	5.76*** (0.11)
Sigma	333.65	316.04 (33.98)

续表

变量	OLS	IR
N	333	333
R^2	0.12	—
F	3.50	—
$Prob > F$	0.00	—
$Log\ pseudolikelihood$	—	−1359.16
$Wald\ \chi^2$	—	19.90
$Prob > \chi^2$	—	0.00
$Median$	196.94	191.00
$Mean$	209.12（120.23）	203.41（115.34）

注：括号中数值为稳健标准误；$*p<0.1$，$**p<0.05$，$***p<0.01$。

附表1.8　庙岛群岛海洋地质遗迹 $WTP\ [ng_{\text{Ⅲ}}^2]$

变量	OLS	IR
Sex	−22.94（34.43）	−25.70（32.76）
Age	−3.16（8.64）	−2.64（8.12）
$Ages$	2.31（10.26）	1.50（9.44）
Edu	−25.16（40.09）	−26.89（38.84）
$Lninc$	167.20***（44.69）	160.95***（43.53）
$Resp$	−36.93（37.66）	−34.86（36.03）
$Constant$	−1603.77***（446.36）	−1543.06***（435.77）
$Lnsigma$	—	5.68***（0.12）
$Sigma$	309.36	293.04（35.64）
N	333	333
R^2	0.09	—
F	3.01	—
$Prob > F$	0.01	—
$Log\ pseudolikelihood$	—	−1393.04
$Wald\ \chi^2$	—	17.46
$Prob > \chi^2$	—	0.01
$Median$	166.81	163.71
$Mean$	176.99（95.53）	172.37（92.26）

注：括号中数值为稳健标准误；$*p<0.1$，$**p<0.05$，$***p<0.01$。

附表 1.9　庙岛群岛海洋地质遗迹 $WTP\ [\ (bg+ng)_{III}^{3}\ ]$

变量	OLS	IR
Sex	-8.01（37.68）	-7.95（36.05）
Age	6.54（7.99）	7.24（7.34）
$Ages$	-9.58（10.10）	-10.47（9.25）
Edu	-20.76（42.59）	-19.51（40.88）
$Lninc$	202.30***（48.04）	193.87***（47.05）
$Resp$	-85.48*（50.10）	-83.71*（48.70）
$Constant$	-2141.25***（520.37）	-2065.35***（513.58）
$Lnsigma$	—	5.75***（0.11）
$Sigma$	332.38	315.49（34.09）
N	333	333
R^2	0.12	—
F	3.58	—
$Prob>F$	0.00	—
$Log\ pseudolikelihood$	—	-1374.40
$Wald\ \chi^2$	—	20.60
$Prob>\chi^2$	—	0.00
$Median$	189.55	184.76
$Mean$	203.62（119.44）	198.23（114.96）

注：括号中数值为稳健标准误；*$p<0.1$，**$p<0.05$，***$p<0.01$。

附录2　舟山群岛 OLS 和 IR 详细计算结果

舟山群岛各待估海滩旅游资源和各待估海洋文化旅游资源 OLS 和 IR 详细计算结果如附表 2.1 至附表 2.21 所示，各符号含义同正文图 9.2。

附表2.1　　　舟山群岛海滩 $WTP\ [AS^1_I]$

变量	OLS	IR
Sex	66.95*（39.28）	64.45*（37.01）
Age	-0.87（9.59）	-1.95（9.05）
$Ages$	-1.64（11.88）	-0.42（11.18）
Edu	-90.13*（46.73）	-86.00*（44.23）
$Lninc$	274.51***（61.38）	268.90***（61.29）
$Resp$	-11.08（41.45）	-13.43（39.13）
$Constant$	-2894.71***（660.52）	-2813.65***（660.78）
$Lnsigma$	—	5.78***（0.09）
$Sigma$	345.53	324.58（29.26）
N	303	303
R^2	0.18	—
F	3.77	—
$Prob > F$	0.00	—
$Log\ pseudolikelihood$	—	-1309.74
$Wald\ \chi^2$	—	21.26
$Prob > \chi^2$	—	0.00
$Median$	203.18	197.89
$Mean$	211.65（161.94）	205.11（158.38）

注：括号中数值为稳健标准误；*$p<0.1$，**$p<0.05$，***$p<0.01$。

附表2.2　　　舟山群岛海滩 $WTP\ [AS^1_{II}]$

变量	OLS	IR
Sex	16.76（40.40）	11.54（38.70）
Age	-14.22（12.25）	-12.77（11.79）
$Ages$	19.60（15.66）	18.02（15.21）
Edu	2.95（45.74）	5.59（44.00）
$Lninc$	244.76***（52.04）	236.68***（51.46）
$Resp$	-12.30（40.46）	-8.52（37.69）
$Constant$	-2412.61***（546.38）	-2354.44***（538.34）
$Lnsigma$	—	5.74***（0.11）
$Sigma$	326.78	310.52（32.65）

续表

变量	OLS	IR
N	296	296
R^2	0.20	—
F	4.58	—
$Prob > F$	0.00	—
$Log\ pseudolikelihood$	—	-1228.24
$Wald\ \chi^2$	—	26.87
$Prob > \chi^2$	—	0.00
$Median$	190.43	182.89
$Mean$	207.89（163.31）	202.88（158.26）

注：括号中数值为稳健标准误；$*p<0.1$，$**p<0.05$，$***p<0.01$。

附表2.3　　　　舟山群岛海滩 $WTP\ [bs_{II}^2]$

变量	OLS	IR
Sex	-17.21（35.75）	-22.11（34.36）
Age	-16.20（11.32）	-15.26（10.96）
$Ages$	23.09（14.87）	21.92（14.50）
Edu	7.45（39.90）	7.16（38.92）
$Lninc$	210.80***（50.31）	202.43***（48.83）
$Resp$	0.45（31.41）	5.81（28.97）
$Constant$	-2034.89***（500.64）	-1958.41***（487.69）
$Lnsigma$	—	5.56***（0.13）
$Sigma$	274.00	259.84（33.35）
N	296	296
R^2	0.21	—
F	3.55	—
$Prob > F$	0.00	—
$Log\ pseudolikelihood$	—	-1236.65
$Wald\ \chi^2$	—	21.49
$Prob > \chi^2$	—	0.00
$Median$	149.05	146.68
$Mean$	160.51（140.61）	157.23（135.42）

注：括号中数值为稳健标准误；$*p<0.1$，$**p<0.05$，$***p<0.01$。

附表 2.4　　　　舟山群岛海滩 WTP $[AS_{\text{III}}^1]$

变量	OLS	IR
Sex	-59.32（38.68）	-54.12（36.72）
Age	-16.88（16.57）	-16.14（16.28）
Ages	25.91（22.32）	24.74（21.89）
Edu	-11.26（43.93）	-6.51（40.50）
Lninc	271.86***（50.29）	258.91***（50.03）
Resp	15.18（40.39）	15.23（38.21）
Constant	-2652.31***（440.76）	-2524.03***（427.36）
Lnsigma	—	5.65***（0.11）
Sigma	302.12	284.43（30.28）
N	302	302
R^2	0.22	—
F	7.03	—
Prob > F	0.00	—
Log pseudolikelihood	—	-1212.17
Wald χ^2	—	41.22
Prob > χ^2	—	0.00
Median	194.82	188.87
Mean	209.26（157.83）	203.68（151.12）

注：括号中数值为稳健标准误；*$p<0.1$，**$p<0.05$，***$p<0.01$。

附表 2.5　　　　舟山群岛海滩 WTP $[es_{\text{III}}^2]$

变量	OLS	IR
Sex	-74.36**（31.63）	-68.54**（29.18）
Age	-21.92（15.91）	-21.35（15.71）
Ages	31.97（21.69）	30.99（21.43）
Edu	-13.84（40.42）	-10.78（36.83）
Lninc	223.42***（47.91）	211.64***（47.20）
Resp	70.72**（30.47）	67.18**（28.18）
Constant	-2059.48***（394.39）	-1937.65***（370.91）
Lnsigma	—	5.42***（0.12）
Sigma	243.33	226.09（26.20）

续表

变量	OLS	IR
N	302	302
R^2	0.25	—
F	5.97	—
$Prob > F$	0.00	—
$Log\ pseudolikelihood$	—	-1213.49
$Wald\ \chi^2$	—	36.70
$Prob > \chi^2$	—	0.00
$Median$	154.66	149.07
$Mean$	165.89（138.23）	161.36（131.36）

注：括号中数值为稳健标准误；$*p<0.1$，$**p<0.05$，$***p<0.01$。

附表2.6　舟山群岛海滩 $WTP\ [\ (bs+es)_{\mathrm{III}}^{3}\ ]$

变量	OLS	IR
Sex	-64.32*（33.57）	-61.05**（30.57）
Age	-21.94（16.03）	-20.65（15.72）
$Ages$	31.82（21.85）	29.86（21.43）
Edu	-21.40（41.64）	-17.71（38.01）
$Lninc$	241.37***（48.93）	224.85***（48.14）
$Resp$	71.59**（33.65）	68.92**（30.67）
$Constant$	-2248.36***（416.21）	-2085.93***（389.96）
$Lnsigma$	—	5.50***（0.10）
$Sigma$	268.59	244.68（25.33）
N	302	302
R^2	0.23	—
F	6.05	—
$Prob > F$	0.00	—
$Log\ pseudolikelihood$	—	-1209.57
$Wald\ \chi^2$	—	36.68
$Prob > \chi^2$	—	0.00
$Median$	170.06	164.17
$Mean$	183.76（146.81）	176.88（137.62）

注：括号中数值为稳健标准误；$*p<0.1$，$**p<0.05$，$***p<0.01$。

附表2.7　　　　舟山群岛海滩 WTP $[AS_{IV}^1]$

变量	OLS	IR
Sex	26.86（32.17）	24.68（30.15）
Age	-45.80***（16.88）	-43.43***（16.11）
Ages	61.77***（22.48）	58.57***（21.61）
Edu	97.44**（46.58）	93.75**（44.06）
Lninc	196.15***（36.48）	188.73***（34.64）
Resp	-73.88*（38.71）	-71.37*（37.05）
Constant	-1307.42***（433.95）	-1266.03***（402.89）
Lnsigma	—	5.60***（0.11）
Sigma	288.87	269.46（30.60）
N	294	294
R^2	0.20	—
F	6.25	—
Prob > F	0.00	—
Log pseudolikelihood	—	-1134.37
Wald χ^2	—	37.51
Prob > χ^2	—	0.00
Median	194.62	188.48
Mean	207.54（142.96）	201.84（137.07）

注：括号中数值为稳健标准误 * $p<0.1$，** $p<0.05$，*** $p<0.01$。

附表2.8　　　　舟山群岛海滩 WTP $[ds_{IV}^2]$

变量	OLS	IR
Sex	2.52（27.01）	1.13（25.29）
Age	-28.44**（13.34）	-25.75**（12.31）
Ages	36.10**（16.57）	32.71**（15.26）
Edu	56.35*（32.29）	52.78*（30.38）
Lninc	155.92***（30.54）	152.37***（29.96）
Resp	-31.62（33.26）	-30.03（32.05）
Constant	-1145.30***（340.78）	-1156.43***（314.43）
Lnsigma	—	5.44***（0.15）
Sigma	245.64	229.62（33.46）

续表

变量	OLS	IR
N	294	294
R^2	0.16	—
F	5.89	—
$Prob > F$	0.00	—
$Log\ pseudolikelihood$	—	-1181.49
$Wald\ \chi^2$	—	35.42
$Prob > \chi^2$	—	0.00
$Median$	149.00	146.42
$Mean$	159.92 (103.96)	155.84 (100.26)

注:括号中数值为稳健标准误;$*p<0.1$,$**p<0.05$,$***p<0.01$。

附表2.9 舟山群岛海滩 $WTP\ [(ds+es)^3_{IV}]$

变量	OLS	IR
Sex	25.85 (28.80)	23.25 (27.59)
Age	-42.92*** (16.52)	-40.46** (15.83)
$Ages$	57.68** (22.28)	54.49** (21.46)
Edu	106.99** (41.84)	101.60** (40.73)
$Lninc$	165.94*** (30.69)	163.58*** (30.07)
$Resp$	-52.26 (36.15)	-51.88 (35.12)
$Constant$	-1048.49*** (380.71)	-1064.56*** (359.74)
$Lnsigma$	—	5.52*** (0.13)
$Sigma$	261.99	249.35 (32.77)
N	294	294
R^2	0.20	—
F	6.65	—
$Prob > F$	0.00	—
$Log\ pseudolikelihood$	—	-1180.69
$Wald\ \chi^2$	—	40.08
$Prob > \chi^2$	—	0.00
$Median$	172.80	169.64
$Mean$	176.84 (129.49)	173.61 (125.43)

注:括号中数值为稳健标准误;$*p<0.1$,$**p<0.05$,$***p<0.01$。

附表 2.10　舟山群岛海洋文化 WTP $[BC_I^1]$

变量	OLS	IR
Sex	43.89 (35.80)	37.94 (33.70)
Age	-0.01 (12.02)	-0.18 (11.28)
Ages	-1.14 (15.57)	-0.79 (14.68)
Edu	39.66 (45.88)	36.71 (42.30)
Lninc	170.03*** (43.38)	163.45*** (40.62)
Resp	-8.90 (45.09)	-9.58 (42.53)
Constant	-1752.76*** (481.58)	-1677.93*** (457.46)
Lnsigma	—	5.71*** (0.10)
Sigma	325.69	302.92 (31.64)
N	290	290
R^2	0.11	—
F	3.80	—
Prob > F	0.00	—
Log pseudolikelihood	—	-1124.95
Wald χ^2	—	22.02
Prob > χ^2	—	0.00
Median	231.02	224.99
Mean	239.90 (111.63)	232.31 (106.01)

注：括号中数值为稳健标准误；$*p<0.1$，$**p<0.05$，$***p<0.01$。

附表 2.11　舟山群岛海洋文化 WTP $[BC_{II}^1]$

变量	OLS	IR
Sex	24.22 (37.45)	22.46 (35.29)
Age	2.44 (10.48)	1.58 (10.11)
Ages	-1.62 (14.01)	-0.48 (13.56)
Edu	-21.91 (45.25)	-20.71 (43.30)
Lninc	230.37*** (45.72)	223.36*** (45.69)
Resp	-28.50 (39.16)	-25.34 (36.71)
Constant	-2492.86*** (547.69)	-2404.04*** (545.72)
Lnsigma	—	5.69*** (0.10)
Sigma	315.33	295.73 (30.25)

续表

变量	OLS	IR
N	293	293
R^2	0.19	—
F	4.96	—
$Prob > F$	0.00	—
$Log\ pseudolikelihood$	—	-1136.60
$Wald\ \chi^2$	—	28.78
$Prob > \chi^2$	—	0.00
$Median$	226.22	219.73
$Mean$	240.30（150.52）	233.91（146.00）

注：括号中数值为稳健标准误；$*p<0.1$，$**p<0.05$，$***p<0.01$。

附表 2.12　舟山群岛海洋文化 WTP [ac_{II}^2]

变量	OLS	IR
Sex	11.38（32.87）	6.79（30.17）
Age	-1.35（13.33）	-0.95（12.22）
$Ages$	4.24（18.35）	3.63（16.94）
Edu	-8.99（41.77）	-6.32（38.43）
$Lninc$	191.18***（45.66）	180.01***（44.74）
$Resp$	12.80（39.10）	8.85（36.24）
$Constant$	-2034.92***（511.77）	-1914.93***（496.57）
$Lnsigma$	—	5.58***（0.10）
$Sigma$	287.96	265.00（27.10）
N	293	293
R^2	0.17	—
F	4.02	—
$Prob > F$	0.00	—
$Log\ pseudolikelihood$	—	-1168.32
$Wald\ \chi^2$	—	23.33
$Prob > \chi^2$	—	0.00
$Median$	194.91	188.30
$Mean$	209.76（129.64）	202.55（121.56）

注：括号中数值为稳健标准误；$*p<0.1$，$**p<0.05$，$***p<0.01$。

附表 2.13　舟山群岛海洋文化 WTP $[BC_{\mathrm{III}}^{1}]$

变量	OLS	IR
Sex	-1.11（34.77）	-0.27（31.72）
Age	-11.60（10.83）	-12.92（10.20）
Ages	14.85（13.43）	15.93（12.57）
Edu	73.16（47.39）	67.56（43.89）
Lninc	164.67***（33.97）	151.74***（30.79）
Resp	-90.61**（45.84）	-83.42**（42.48）
Constant	-1438.09***（434.18）	-1266.91***（392.87）
Lnsigma	—	5.61***（0.10）
Sigma	301.07	272.02（27.26）
N	281	281
R^2	0.13	—
F	5.51	—
Prob > F	0.00	—
Log pseudolikelihood	—	-1034.33
Wald χ^2	—	34.12
Prob > χ^2	—	0.00
Median	229.08	223.42
Mean	236.85（113.71）	227.42（105.16）

注：括号中数值为稳健标准误；*$p<0.1$，**$p<0.05$，***$p<0.01$。

附表 2.14　舟山群岛海洋文化 WTP $[bc_{\mathrm{III}}^{2}]$

变量	OLS	IR
Sex	-13.97（27.07）	-13.21（24.43）
Age	-6.21（7.30）	-6.49（6.82）
Ages	7.20（9.21）	7.27（8.54）
Edu	31.22（37.06）	26.87（32.72）
Lninc	102.07***（24.21）	96.68***（22.33）
Resp	-41.57（33.67）	-37.24（29.95）
Constant	-871.47***（310.89）	-806.71***（284.61）
Lnsigma	—	5.33***（0.09）
Sigma	231.08	206.98（18.12）

续表

变量	OLS	IR
N	281	281
R^2	0.08	—
F	4.36	—
$Prob > F$	0.00	—
$Log\ pseudolikelihood$	—	-1075.99
$Wald\ \chi^2$	—	27.32
$Prob > \chi^2$	—	0.00
$Median$	165.04	158.92
$Mean$	169.33（67.83）	163.46（64.01）

注：括号中数值为稳健标准误；*$p<0.1$，**$p<0.05$，***$p<0.01$。

附表 2.15　舟山群岛海洋文化 $WTP\ [(ac+bc)_{\mathrm{III}}^{3}]$

变量	OLS	IR
Sex	0.13（31.40）	-1.31（28.06）
Age	-13.44（9.47）	-13.89（8.80）
$Ages$	17.46（11.96）	17.56（11.07）
Edu	53.53（43.98）	47.08（38.47）
$Lninc$	159.24***（30.40）	149.21***（27.86）
$Resp$	-39.99（39.71）	-36.27（34.65）
$Constant$	-1381.19***（388.01）	-1258.02***（348.96）
$Lnsigma$	—	5.49***（0.08）
$Sigma$	274.07	241.48（19.08）
N	281	281
R^2	0.13	—
F	6.68	—
$Prob > F$	0.00	—
$Log\ pseudolikelihood$	—	-1012.05
$Wald\ \chi^2$	—	41.09
$Prob > \chi^2$	—	0.00
$Median$	218.52	208.96
$Mean$	221.69（106.65）	212.17（99.46）

注：括号中数值为稳健标准误；*$p<0.1$，**$p<0.05$，***$p<0.01$。

附表2.16　舟山群岛海滩与海洋文化 WTP $[BS-BC_I^1]$

变量	OLS	IR
Sex	63.64（40.54）	61.23（39.24）
Age	-13.78（14.28）	-12.81（13.63）
$Ages$	19.20（18.15）	18.03（17.42）
Edu	-77.11（58.07）	-70.22（56.60）
$Lninc$	297.49*** （54.64）	288.89*** （54.47）
$Resp$	-33.61（48.04）	-35.76（46.29）
$Constant$	-2952.78*** （607.06）	-2878.06*** （605.01）
$Lnsigma$	—	5.83*** （0.10）
$Sigma$	354.99	339.20（33.83）
N	286	286
R^2	0.20	—
F	5.17	—
$Prob > F$	0.00	—
$Log\ pseudolikelihood$	—	-1189.82
$Wald\ \chi^2$	—	29.87
$Prob > \chi^2$	—	0.00
$Median$	225.61	221.42
$Mean$	243.92（176.58）	238.32（171.50）

注：括号中数值为稳健标准误；$*p<0.1$，$**p<0.05$，$***p<0.01$。

附表2.17　舟山群岛海滩与海洋文化 WTP $[BS-BC_{II}^1]$

变量	OLS	IR
Sex	28.16（39.44）	26.85（35.76）
Age	-0.78（10.59）	-0.89（9.63）
$Ages$	-2.11（13.28）	-1.81（12.10）
Edu	-36.97（36.90）	-32.21（33.52）
$Lninc$	272.55*** （46.43）	259.73*** （45.08）
$Resp$	-27.53（36.76）	-26.74（33.22）
$Constant$	-2853.39*** （544.14）	-2716.11*** （532.76）
$Lnsigma$	—	5.68*** （0.09）
$Sigma$	322.18	292.86（25.85）

续表

变量	OLS	IR
N	270	270
R^2	0.21	—
F	7.01	—
$Prob > F$	0.00	—
$Log\ pseudolikelihood$	—	-1050.09
$Wald\ \chi^2$	—	39.68
$Prob > \chi^2$	—	0.00
$Median$	233.67	224.14
$Mean$	249.53（163.71）	239.37（156.29）

注：括号中数值为稳健标准误；$*p<0.1$，$**p<0.05$，$***p<0.01$。

附表 2.18　舟山群岛海滩与海洋文化 WTP $[ac_{II}^{2*}]$

变量	OLS	IR
Sex	14.76（34.61）	11.56（31.32）
Age	-1.68（10.62）	-1.51（9.59）
$Ages$	1.31（13.00）	0.98（11.77）
Edu	-40.80（35.55）	-37.79（32.22）
$Lninc$	208.65***（42.58）	196.55***（40.37）
$Resp$	1.93（34.67）	1.76（31.20）
$Constant$	-2167.32***（491.99）	-2036.27***（469.92）
$Lnsigma$	—	5.58***（0.09）
$Sigma$	292.81	264.04（24.54）
N	270	270
R^2	0.16	—
F	4.55	—
$Prob > F$	0.00	—
$Log\ pseudolikelihood$	—	-1093.58
$Wald\ \chi^2$	—	26.79
$Prob > \chi^2$	—	0.00
$Median$	203.49	194.83
$Mean$	213.06（125.04）	204.26（117.76）

注：括号中数值为稳健标准误；$*p<0.1$，$**p<0.05$，$***p<0.01$。

附表 2.19　舟山群岛海滩与海洋文化 $WTP\ [BS-BC_{\text{III}}^1]$

变量	OLS	IR
Sex	43.48（34.06）	41.71（31.86）
Age	−14.65（13.43）	−13.85（12.24）
$Ages$	21.53（18.30）	20.06（16.62）
Edu	−44.69（45.76）	−41.11（42.06）
$Lninc$	209.86***（45.58）	204.77***（44.08）
$Resp$	23.21（41.80）	19.75（39.01）
$Constant$	−1993.83***（508.02）	−1947.74***（487.88）
$Lnsigma$	—	5.67***（0.11）
$Sigma$	311.10	289.86（31.85）
N	268	268
R^2	0.17	—
F	4.03	—
$Prob>F$	0.00	—
$Log\ pseudolikelihood$	—	−1012.87
$Wald\ \chi^2$	—	24.35
$Prob>\chi^2$	—	0.00
$Median$	229.62	221.55
$Mean$	243.46（136.63）	237.20（132.88）

注：括号中数值为稳健标准误；*$p<0.1$，**$p<0.05$，***$p<0.01$。

附表 2.20　舟山群岛海滩与海洋文化 $WTP\ [as_{\text{III}}^2]$

变量	OLS	IR
Sex	5.29（29.52）	5.70（27.50）
Age	−12.24（10.45）	−12.54（9.94）
$Ages$	14.11（13.51）	14.60（12.83）
Edu	−29.48（35.46）	−30.67（33.04）
$Lninc$	155.26***（40.10）	155.77***（39.14）
$Resp$	−1.82（30.37）	0.31（27.75）
$Constant$	−1380.58***（450.51）	−1386.78***（435.30）
$Lnsigma$	—	5.50***（0.14）
$Sigma$	258.26	243.90（33.06）

续表

变量	OLS	IR
N	268	268
R^2	0.12	—
F	2.95	—
$Prob > F$	0.01	—
$Log\ pseudolikelihood$	—	-1066.67
$Wald\ \chi^2$	—	17.94
$Prob > \chi^2$	—	0.01
$Median$	163.87	159.55
$Mean$	175.80（95.34）	172.30（95.67）

注：括号中数值为稳健标准误；$*p<0.1$，$**p<0.05$，$***p<0.01$。

附表 2.21　舟山群岛海滩与海洋文化 $WTP\ [as-ac_{\text{III}}^3]$

变量	OLS	IR
Sex	38.96（32.73）	36.09（30.21）
Age	-13.98（13.66）	-12.80（12.27）
$Ages$	20.72（18.63）	18.78（16.68）
Edu	-44.72（44.31）	-40.65（40.14）
$Lninc$	208.25***（44.20）	200.94***（42.44）
$Resp$	15.72（40.80）	12.06（37.71）
$Constant$	-2000.99***（493.97）	-1937.08***（472.79）
$Lnsigma$	—	5.59***（0.11）
$Sigma$	290.69	266.33（29.57）
N	268	268
R^2	0.18	—
F	4.36	—
$Prob > F$	0.00	—
$Log\ pseudolikelihood$	—	-1015.62
$Wald\ \chi^2$	—	26.04
$Prob > \chi^2$	—	0.00
$Median$	209.96	203.90
$Mean$	223.40（133.84）	216.09（128.60）

注：括号中数值为稳健标准误；$*p<0.1$，$**p<0.05$，$***p<0.01$。

附录3 三亚及其附近岛屿 OLS 和 IR 详细计算结果

三亚及其附近岛屿各待估海滩旅游资源和各待估珊瑚礁旅游资源 OLS 和 IR 详细计算结果如附表 3.1 至附表 3.24 所示，各符号含义同正文表 10.1 和表 10.2。

附表 3.1　　三亚及其附近岛屿海滩 WTP $[SS_1^1]$

变量	OLS	IR
Sex	25.20（36.67）	23.41（34.64）
Age	-7.54（11.39）	-6.92（10.82）
Ages	6.65（13.36）	6.04（12.71）
Edu	-99.00**（40.68）	-89.96**（37.56）
Lninc	249.93***（41.46）	234.17***（39.67）
Resp	11.64（48.67）	11.43（45.56）
Constant	-2472.84***（416.34）	-2314.73***（401.97）
Lnsigma	—	5.66***（0.13）
Sigma	305.04	285.81（36.64）
N	275	275
R^2	0.21	—
F	7.45	—
Prob > F	0.00	—
Log pseudolikelihood	—	-1120.46
Wald χ^2	—	43.10
Prob > χ^2	—	0.00
Median	170.59	167.54
Mean	200.25（156.35）	193.92（146.46）

注：括号中数值为稳健标准误；*$p<0.1$，**$p<0.05$，***$p<0.01$。

附表 3.2　　三亚及其附近岛屿海滩 $WTP\left[xs_{II}^{2}\right]$

变量	OLS	IR
Sex	13.76（35.76）	18.19（32.75）
Age	-16.56（12.40）	-15.95（11.63）
$Ages$	25.96（18.29）	24.56（17.20）
Edu	4.46（37.02）	5.64（34.79）
$Lninc$	173.95*** （41.54）	159.68*** （37.98）
$Resp$	-51.42（37.07）	-44.10（33.64）
$Constant$	-1568.86*** （468.81）	-1422.24*** （428.68）
$Lnsigma$	—	5.53*** （0.15）
$Sigma$	275.35	253.09（37.15）
N	276	276
R^2	0.12	—
F	3.44	—
$Prob > F$	0.00	—
$Log\ pseudolikelihood$	—	-1152.62
$Wald\ \chi^2$	—	20.58
$Prob > \chi^2$	—	0.00
$Median$	140.06	136.11
$Mean$	154.50（100.02）	148.84（92.20）

注：括号中数值为稳健标准误；$*p<0.1,**p<0.05,***p<0.01$。

附表 3.3　　三亚及其附近岛屿海滩 $WTP\left[SS_{II}^{1}\right]$

变量	OLS	IR
Sex	46.89（40.30）	49.23（37.36）
Age	-16.27（15.15）	-15.32（13.89）
$Ages$	24.50（20.94）	22.97（19.41）
Edu	6.88（45.32）	11.73（41.24）
$Lninc$	200.62*** （44.46）	185.56*** （41.92）
$Resp$	-47.24（44.61）	-41.63（39.85）
$Constant$	-1840.37*** （504.85）	-1696.50*** （473.17）
$Lnsigma$	—	5.68*** （0.12）
$Sigma$	318.10	294.13（34.80）

续表

变量	OLS	IR
N	276	276
R^2	0.12	—
F	3.72	—
$Prob > F$	0.00	—
$Log\ pseudolikelihood$	—	-1122.78
$Wald\ \chi^2$	—	21.20
$Prob > \chi^2$	—	0.00
$Median$	182.17	178.11
$Mean$	199.89（117.61）	192.35（110.19）

注：括号中数值为稳健标准误；$*p<0.1$，$**p<0.05$，$***p<0.01$。

附表3.4　三亚及其附近岛屿海滩 $WTP\ [ws^2_{\text{III}}]$

变量	OLS	IR
Sex	14.53（28.79）	12.67（25.74）
Age	-6.47（8.78）	-6.92（8.45）
$Ages$	5.89（11.40）	6.66（10.82）
Edu	-60.68（49.90）	-53.53（46.50）
$Lninc$	211.92***（47.32）	200.95***（46.97）
$Resp$	10.30（51.98）	2.43（50.06）
$Constant$	-2118.73***（467.56）	-1990.21***（458.42）
$Lnsigma$	—	5.46***（0.12）
$Sigma$	256.81	235.35（29.17）
N	266	266
R^2	0.24	—
F	5.58	—
$Prob > F$	0.00	—
$Log\ pseudolikelihood$	—	-1108.59
$Wald\ \chi^2$	—	33.48
$Prob > \chi^2$	—	0.00
$Median$	128.35	124.73
$Mean$	154.37（141.89）	148.51（134.06）

注：括号中数值为稳健标准误；$*p<0.1$，$**p<0.05$，$***p<0.01$。

附表3.5　三亚及其附近岛屿海滩 WTP $[(xs+ws)_{\mathrm{III}}^{3}]$

变量	OLS	IR
Sex	4.56（31.59）	4.23（28.01）
Age	-3.05（9.04）	-3.87（8.63）
Ages	2.46（11.61）	3.48（10.96）
Edu	-41.83（51.66）	-38.22（47.89）
Lninc	217.88***（48.03）	204.93***（47.58）
Resp	-9.09（56.70）	-12.10（53.52）
Constant	-2235.05***（480.98）	-2077.30***（469.20）
Lnsigma	—	5.50***（0.11）
Sigma	268.36	244.81（27.82）
N	266	266
R^2	0.23	—
F	5.66	—
Prob > F	0.00	—
Log pseudolikelihood	—	-1074.22
Wald χ^2	—	33.86
Prob > χ^2	—	0.00
Median	145.56	139.23
Mean	173.34（145.39）	166.52（136.41）

注：括号中数值为稳健标准误；$*p<0.1$，$**p<0.05$，$***p<0.01$。

附表3.6　三亚及其附近岛屿海滩 WTP $[SS_{\mathrm{III}}^{1}]$

变量	OLS	IR
Sex	-15.85（38.84）	-16.42（36.01）
Age	-3.41（9.90）	-3.69（9.50）
Ages	4.31（12.59）	4.77（11.94）
Edu	-9.20（55.51）	-7.09（52.80）
Lninc	246.79***（49.00）	233.97***（48.87）
Resp	-57.19（66.86）	-62.10（65.15）
Constant	-2529.83***（501.20）	-2383.46***（497.29）
Lnsigma	—	5.63***（0.11）
Sigma	302.28	278.48（29.38）

续表

变量	OLS	IR
N	266	266
R^2	0.23	—
F	5.96	—
$Prob > F$	0.00	—
$Log\ pseudolikelihood$	—	-1084.06
$Wald\ \chi^2$	—	33.87
$Prob > \chi^2$	—	0.00
$Median$	165.15	157.95
$Mean$	198.51 (163.89)	190.80 (155.25)

注：括号中数值为稳健标准误；$*p<0.1$，$**p<0.05$，$***p<0.01$。

附表3.7　三亚及其附近岛屿海滩 $WTP\ [ys^2_{\mathrm{IV}}]$

变量	OLS	IR
Sex	30.63 (37.00)	30.77 (34.92)
Age	-1.94 (12.37)	-0.71 (11.29)
$Ages$	0.92 (17.50)	-0.84 (15.90)
Edu	20.19 (36.56)	21.22 (33.56)
$Lninc$	125.14*** (29.13)	119.69*** (26.96)
$Resp$	-1.71 (38.14)	-2.36 (34.51)
$Constant$	-1255.48*** (349.25)	-1217.67*** (323.46)
$Lnsigma$	—	5.62*** (0.15)
$Sigma$	295.28	276.52 (42.49)
N	271	271
R^2	0.09	—
F	4.60	—
$Prob > F$	0.00	—
$Log\ pseudolikelihood$	—	-1158.60
$Wald\ \chi^2$	—	28.70
$Prob > \chi^2$	—	0.00
$Median$	150.36	146.53
$Mean$	162.96 (91.86)	158.01 (88.61)

注：括号中数值为稳健标准误；$*p<0.1$，$**p<0.05$，$***p<0.01$。

附表3.8　　三亚及其附近岛屿海滩 $WTP\ [(xs+ys)_{IV}^{3}]$

变量	OLS	IR
Sex	7.60 (39.91)	8.39 (38.18)
Age	-4.72 (14.13)	-4.33 (13.39)
Ages	5.81 (20.67)	5.33 (19.67)
Edu	1.96 (40.19)	2.19 (38.53)
Lninc	143.22*** (30.92)	138.34*** (29.34)
Resp	13.37 (36.63)	11.30 (35.29)
Constant	-1399.41*** (375.98)	-1353.61*** (355.49)
Lnsigma	—	5.70*** (0.15)
Sigma	312.50	297.90 (44.06)
N	271	271
R^2	0.10	—
F	5.26	—
Prob > F	0.00	—
Log pseudolikelihood	—	-1153.58
Wald χ^2	—	32.33
Prob > χ^2	—	0.00
Median	169.06	166.11
Mean	181.02 (100.64)	177.01 (97.18)

注：括号中数值为稳健标准误；$*p<0.1$，$**p<0.05$，$***p<0.01$。

附表3.9　　三亚及其附近岛屿海滩 $WTP\ [SS_{IV}^{1}]$

变量	OLS	IR
Sex	18.63 (42.20)	19.24 (40.60)
Age	-6.26 (16.00)	-6.91 (15.30)
Ages	7.45 (23.42)	8.51 (22.58)
Edu	4.09 (43.55)	7.88 (41.56)
Lninc	133.44*** (30.49)	127.67*** (28.42)
Resp	20.77 (38.64)	20.33 (36.32)
Constant	-1248.59*** (403.75)	-1179.21*** (380.78)
Lnsigma	—	5.77*** (0.14)
Sigma	335.56	321.20 (44.30)

续表

变量	OLS	IR
N	271	271
R^2	0.08	—
F	4.36	—
$Prob > F$	0.00	—
$Log\ pseudolikelihood$	—	-1149.89
$Wald\ \chi^2$	—	27.75
$Prob > \chi^2$	—	0.00
$Median$	188.73	185.08
$Mean$	198.69（96.00）	194.62（92.60）

注：括号中数值为稳健标准误；*$p<0.1$，**$p<0.05$，***$p<0.01$。

附表3.10　三亚及其附近岛屿海滩 $WTP\ [ds_V^2]$

变量	OLS	IR
Sex	46.55（28.88）	45.24*（26.14）
Age	-11.42（14.51）	-11.62（14.11）
$Ages$	17.41（21.55）	17.38（21.03）
Edu	-21.99（43.26）	-19.90（39.43）
$Lninc$	155.38***（34.43）	142.59***（31.86）
$Resp$	-29.71（39.80）	-26.94（36.10）
$Constant$	-1448.39***（360.48）	-1301.83***（320.30）
$Lnsigma$	—	5.39***（0.13）
$Sigma$	241.96	220.17（28.13）
N	276	276
R^2	0.17	—
F	4.12	—
$Prob > F$	0.00	—
$Log\ pseudolikelihood$	—	-1076.20
$Wald\ \chi^2$	—	25.42
$Prob > \chi^2$	—	0.00
$Median$	140.65	136.65
$Mean$	158.23（108.53）	152.40（100.00）

注：括号中数值为稳健标准误；*$p<0.1$，**$p<0.05$，***$p<0.01$。

附表 3.11　三亚及其附近岛屿海滩 $WTP\left[(xs+ds)_V^3\right]$

变量	OLS	IR
Sex	60.57*（31.64）	54.66**（27.89）
Age	-4.66（11.35）	-3.45（10.06）
Ages	6.47（15.91）	4.48（13.91）
Edu	-0.40（42.08）	3.69（36.87）
Lninc	163.85***（33.83）	148.41***（29.85）
Resp	-55.28（41.56）	-53.24（36.83）
Constant	-1622.54***（373.77）	-1470.81***（326.11）
Lnsigma	—	5.39***（0.08）
Sigma	251.10	220.02（18.50）
N	276	276
R^2	0.18	—
F	5.34	—
Prob > F	0.00	—
Log pseudolikelihood	—	-1045.04
Wald χ^2	—	33.93
Prob > χ^2	—	0.00
Median	154.86	149.72
Mean	180.09（116.42）	171.54（105.83）

注：括号中数值为稳健标准误；*$p<0.1$，**$p<0.05$，***$p<0.01$。

附表 3.12　三亚及其附近岛屿海滩 $WTP\left[SS_V^1\right]$

变量	OLS	IR
Sex	38.08（33.55）	39.50（30.89）
Age	10.13（10.24）	9.33（9.68）
Ages	-15.42（13.08）	-14.71（12.29）
Edu	-20.85（51.81）	-23.38（49.54）
Lninc	175.70***（42.88）	167.83***（42.05）
Resp	-49.31（45.78）	-47.92（43.20）
Constant	-1952.54***（454.61）	-1849.51***（442.01）
Lnsigma	—	5.57***（0.11）
Sigma	283.64	262.06（27.82）

续表

变量	OLS	IR
N	276	276
R^2	0.16	—
F	5.02	—
$Prob > F$	0.00	—
$Log\ pseudolikelihood$	—	−1073.16
$Wald\ \chi^2$	—	30.75
$Prob > \chi^2$	—	0.00
$Median$	180.15	171.25
$Mean$	201.51（123.73）	195.19（118.59）

注：括号中数值为稳健标准误；$*p<0.1$，$**p<0.05$，$***p<0.01$。

附表3.13　三亚及其附近岛屿珊瑚礁 $WTP\ [SR_1^1]$

变量	OLS	IR
Sex	−15.72（34.20）	−14.58（32.18）
Age	−19.76（19.65）	−19.62（19.38）
$Ages$	30.59（29.01）	30.48（28.74）
Edu	−7.93（44.55）	−8.61（42.65）
$Lninc$	264.03***（50.04）	251.16***（50.12）
$Resp$	−25.15（36.37）	−25.71（35.38）
$Constant$	−2518.29***（573.98）	−2378.06***（564.31）
$Lnsigma$	—	5.66***（0.12）
$Sigma$	303.69	287.11（33.39）
N	267	267
R^2	0.26	—
F	6.11	—
$Prob > F$	0.00	—
$Log\ pseudolikelihood$	—	−1064.49
$Wald\ \chi^2$	—	33.60
$Prob > \chi^2$	—	0.00
$Median$	190.82	184.39
$Mean$	215.23（176.42）	209.38（167.94）

注：括号中数值为稳健标准误；$*p<0.1$，$**p<0.05$，$***p<0.01$。

附表 3.14　三亚及其附近岛屿珊瑚礁 WTP $[xr_{II}^2]$

变量	OLS	IR
Sex	49.88（31.43）	50.36*（28.86）
Age	-6.34（12.44）	-6.12（11.36）
Ages	6.54（16.22）	6.40（14.93）
Edu	-55.73（54.79）	-53.51（52.85）
Lninc	223.37***（51.44）	215.83***（50.93）
Resp	-18.96（52.29）	-17.22（50.12）
Constant	-2245.88***（620.05）	-2172.31***（599.48）
Lnsigma	—	5.63***（0.13）
Sigma	296.69	279.77（35.18）
N	276	276
R^2	0.20	—
F	3.87	—
Prob > F	0.00	—
Log pseudolikelihood	—	-1157.54
Wald χ^2	—	22.90
Prob > χ^2	—	0.00
Median	163.89	158.56
Mean	181.59（146.02）	176.74（141.46）

注：括号中数值为稳健标准误；*p<0.1，**p<0.05，***p<0.01。

附表 3.15　三亚及其附近岛屿珊瑚礁 WTP $[SR_{II}^1]$

变量	OLS	IR
Sex	92.76***（32.51）	89.46***（29.99）
Age	0.47（12.23）	0.47（11.08）
Ages	-3.14（15.45）	-3.07（14.06）
Edu	-59.46（52.74）	-61.52（50.70）
Lninc	254.29***（48.60）	239.16***（47.84）
Resp	-37.39（48.04）	-29.14（43.73）
Constant	-2690.71***（592.17）	-2527.15***（573.11）
Lnsigma	—	5.64***（0.11）
Sigma	303.92	281.75（30.24）

续表

变量	OLS	IR
N	276	276
R^2	0.25	—
F	6.11	—
$Prob > F$	0.00	—
$Log\ pseudolikelihood$	—	−1098.25
$Wald\ \chi^2$	—	33.92
$Prob > \chi^2$	—	0.00
$Median$	190.17	186.38
$Mean$	217.42 (172.13)	209.67 (162.56)

注：括号中数值为稳健标准误；$*p<0.1$，$**p<0.05$，$***p<0.01$。

附表 3.16　三亚及其附近岛屿珊瑚礁 $WTP\ [wr_{\mathrm{III}}^2]$

变量	OLS	IR
Sex	−6.74 (34.23)	−3.16 (30.43)
Age	6.02 (12.21)	3.04 (11.40)
$Ages$	−12.22 (17.08)	−7.62 (15.92)
Edu	−64.80 (47.28)	−64.49 (44.57)
$Lninc$	180.75*** (45.33)	175.37*** (43.99)
$Resp$	−20.47 (37.81)	−22.88 (34.09)
$Constant$	−1913.65*** (526.75)	−1813.47*** (511.16)
$Lnsigma$	—	5.51*** (0.11)
$Sigma$	274.10	245.83 (27.00)
N	268	268
R^2	0.14	—
F	3.36	—
$Prob > F$	0.00	—
$Log\ pseudolikelihood$	—	−1080.79
$Wald\ \chi^2$	—	20.36
$Prob > \chi^2$	—	0.00
$Median$	162.23	154.18
$Mean$	177.05 (110.58)	169.88 (106.74)

注：括号中数值为稳健标准误；$*p<0.1$，$**p<0.05$，$***p<0.01$。

附表3.17　三亚及其附近岛屿珊瑚礁 WTP $[(xr+wr)_{III}^{3}]$

变量	OLS	IR
Sex	-19.07（35.33）	-15.15（31.53）
Age	3.10（12.57）	0.17（11.70）
Ages	-7.46（17.69）	-2.96（16.47）
Edu	-51.32（47.75）	-51.44（44.88）
Lninc	181.88***（45.19）	176.85***（43.78）
Resp	-27.44（43.21）	-29.66（38.92）
Constant	-1876.33***（533.42）	-1780.71***（515.97）
Lnsigma	—	5.53***（0.11）
Sigma	281.08	252.37（28.80）
N	268	268
R^2	0.14	—
F	3.41	—
Prob > F	0.00	—
Log pseudolikelihood	—	-1072.11
Wald χ^2	—	21.14
Prob > χ^2	—	0.00
Median	166.36	159.86
Mean	183.00（110.24）	176.02（106.61）

注：括号中数值为稳健标准误；*p<0.1，**p<0.05，***p<0.01。

附表3.18　三亚及其附近岛屿珊瑚礁 WTP $[SR_{III}^{1}]$

变量	OLS	IR
Sex	-45.23（37.68）	-39.49（33.70）
Age	-0.81（17.27）	-2.62（15.50）
Ages	-1.80（23.80）	1.33（21.39）
Edu	-58.60（50.30）	-54.91（46.98）
Lninc	192.05***（46.04）	185.45***（44.63）
Resp	-28.57（43.82）	-31.97（39.44）
Constant	-1883.42***（562.28）	-1794.97***（540.95）
Lnsigma	—	5.59***（0.10）
Sigma	299.67	268.41（27.49）

续表

变量	OLS	IR
N	268	268
R^2	0.13	—
F	3.43	—
$Prob > F$	0.00	—
Log pseudolikelihood	—	−1040.10
Wald χ^2	—	21.25
$Prob > \chi^2$	—	0.00
Median	195.36	186.10
Mean	209.30 (116.38)	200.86 (111.85)

注：括号中数值为稳健标准误；$*p<0.1$，$**p<0.05$，$***p<0.01$。

附表3.19　三亚及其附近岛屿珊瑚礁 $WTP\ [yr_{\text{IV}}^2]$

变量	OLS	IR
Sex	16.17 (34.70)	19.75 (31.63)
Age	−13.55 (15.48)	−12.47 (14.17)
Ages	21.75 (23.61)	19.47 (21.43)
Edu	36.40 (42.11)	28.71 (39.86)
Lninc	222.84*** (53.93)	213.39*** (53.16)
Resp	−76.58 (50.00)	−70.04 (46.68)
Constant	−2173.65*** (637.58)	−2081.47*** (626.64)
Lnsigma	—	5.70*** (0.12)
Sigma	317.77	297.40 (35.02)
N	267	267
R^2	0.18	—
F	3.91	—
$Prob > F$	0.00	—
Log pseudolikelihood	—	−1102.92
Wald χ^2	—	22.06
$Prob > \chi^2$	—	0.00
Median	173.53	164.20
Mean	193.70 (145.53)	187.32 (138.81)

注：括号中数值为稳健标准误；$*p<0.1$，$**p<0.05$，$***p<0.01$。

附表 3.20　　三亚及其附近岛屿珊瑚礁 $WTP\ [\ (xr+yr)_{\mathrm{IV}}^{3}\ ]$

变量	OLS	IR
Sex	24.56（36.41）	26.51（33.22）
Age	-8.96（14.42）	-8.05（13.17）
Ages	14.30（22.37）	12.41（20.26）
Edu	17.18（44.25）	11.55（41.76）
Lninc	225.48***（53.74）	216.85***（52.93）
Resp	-83.21（51.23）	-75.72（47.86）
Constant	-2246.25***（618.78）	-2163.72***（608.00）
Lnsigma	—	5.72***（0.11）
Sigma	326.59	305.05（34.08）
N	267	267
R^2	0.17	—
F	3.51	—
Prob > F	0.00	—
Log pseudolikelihood	—	-1096.08
Wald χ^2	—	20.29
Prob > χ^2	—	0.00
Median	179.08	177.38
Mean	205.04（145.35）	198.19（139.54）

注：括号中数值为稳健标准误；$*p<0.1$，$**p<0.05$，$***p<0.01$。

附表 3.21　　三亚及其附近岛屿珊瑚礁 $WTP\ [\ SR_{\mathrm{IV}}^{1}\ ]$

变量	OLS	IR
Sex	13.32（41.58）	15.11（38.67）
Age	0.79（14.42）	1.07（13.23）
Ages	-0.31（22.25）	-1.26（20.26）
Edu	13.19（45.79）	7.33（43.44）
Lninc	228.13***（54.79）	220.80***（54.02）
Resp	-76.78（52.08）	-70.72（48.90）
Constant	-2414.22***（627.75）	-2336.15***（618.99）
Lnsigma	—	5.80***（0.11）
Sigma	351.77	330.31（35.63）

续表

变量	OLS	IR
N	267	267
R^2	0.15	—
F	3.51	—
$Prob > F$	0.00	—
$Log\ pseudolikelihood$	—	-1115.75
$Wald\ \chi^2$	—	20.16
$Prob > \chi^2$	—	0.00
$Median$	194.81	190.24
$Mean$	217.79（147.28）	210.70（142.15）

注：括号中数值为稳健标准误；$*p<0.1$，$**p<0.05$，$***p<0.01$。

附表3.22　　三亚及其附近岛屿珊瑚礁WTP $[dr_V^2]$

变量	OLS	IR
Sex	26.44（32.40）	24.78（30.06）
Age	-31.36**（14.81）	-29.13**（13.50）
$Ages$	41.20**（20.92）	37.98**（18.97）
Edu	-22.41（48.33）	-23.80（45.82）
$Lninc$	207.81***（41.60）	192.81***（38.93）
$Resp$	-72.03（51.69）	-58.46（46.53）
$Constant$	-1624.63***（461.36）	-1500.24***（426.94）
$Lnsigma$	—	5.51***（0.15）
$Sigma$	266.16	246.79（37.29）
N	262	262
R^2	0.19	—
F	4.57	—
$Prob > F$	0.00	—
$Log\ pseudolikelihood$	—	-1031.76
$Wald\ \chi^2$	—	27.00
$Prob > \chi^2$	—	0.00
$Median$	150.66	146.31
$Mean$	171.18（126.35）	165.91（117.30）

注：括号中数值为稳健标准误；$*p<0.1$，$**p<0.05$，$***p<0.01$。

附表 3.23　三亚及其附近岛屿珊瑚礁 $WTP\ [(xr+dr)_V^3]$

变量	OLS	IR
Sex	38.99（35.14）	38.17（32.62）
Age	-54.03**（21.66）	-54.00**（21.41）
$Ages$	75.66**（31.73）	75.59**（31.40）
Edu	-25.05（52.46）	-21.31（50.16）
$Lninc$	208.37***（44.73）	194.39***（41.84）
$Resp$	-51.87（54.87）	-38.26（49.32）
$Constant$	-1292.13**（508.28）	-1147.75**（474.06）
$Lnsigma$	—	5.58***（0.14）
$Sigma$	285.33	264.87（35.78）
N	262	262
R^2	0.21	—
F	4.20	—
$Prob>F$	0.00	—
$Log\ pseudolikelihood$	—	-1039.33
$Wald\ \chi^2$	—	24.52
$Prob>\chi^2$	—	0.00
$Median$	164.92	159.36
$Mean$	184.53（144.74）	178.92（138.27）

注：括号中数值为稳健标准误；$*p<0.1$，$**p<0.05$，$***p<0.01$。

附表 3.24　三亚及其附近岛屿珊瑚礁 $WTP\ [SR_V^1]$

变量	OLS	IR
Sex	46.70（36.74）	47.68（34.85）
Age	-58.45***（21.52）	-58.93***（21.01）
$Ages$	82.73***（31.70）	83.62***（31.01）
Edu	-25.49（54.49）	-19.85（53.14）
$Lninc$	221.78***（46.27）	209.58***（44.45）
$Resp$	-70.74（60.16）	-59.58（58.09）
$Constant$	-1353.59***（519.49）	-1223.49**（496.18）
$Lnsigma$	—	5.66***（0.13）
$Sigma$	302.40	288.00（37.13）

续表

变量	OLS	IR
N	262	262
R^2	0.22	—
F	4.58	—
$Prob > F$	0.00	—
$Log\ pseudolikelihood$	—	−1031.53
$Wald\ \chi^2$	—	26.91
$Prob > \chi^2$	—	0.00
Median	183.20	178.29
Mean	205.31 (156.66)	200.97 (151.83)

注：括号中数值为稳健标准误；$*p<0.1$，$**p<0.05$，$***p<0.01$。

参考文献

敖长林等：《空间尺度下公众对环境保护的支付意愿度量方法及实证研究》，《资源科学》2015年第11期。

蔡志坚等：《条件价值评估的有效性与可靠性改善——理论、方法与应用》，《生态学报》2011年第10期。

董雪旺等：《条件价值法中的偏差分析及信度和效度检验——以九寨沟游憩价值评估为例》，《地理学报》2011年第2期。

金建君等：《条件价值法在澳门固体废弃物管理经济价值评估中的比较研究》，《地球科学进展》2006年第6期。

李作志等：《滨海旅游活动的经济价值评价——以大连为例》，《中国人口·资源与环境》2010年第10期。

刘佳等：《浒苔绿潮影响下滨海旅游环境价值损失及影响因素——以青岛市海水浴场为例》，《资源科学》2018年第2期。

刘亚萍等：《环境价值评估中的WTP值和WTA值测算与非对称性——以广西北部湾经济区滨海生态环境保护为例》，《生态学报》2015年第9期。

阮氏春香等：《条件价值评估法在森林生态旅游非使用价值评估中范围效应的研究》，《南京林业大学学报》（自然科学版）2013年第1期。

肖建红等：《基于CVM的旅游相关资源价值评估总体范围扩展方法研究》，《自然资源学报》2013年第9期。

肖建红等：《条件价值评估法自愿支付工具与强制支付工具比较研

究——以沂蒙湖国家水利风景区游憩价值评估为例》,《中国人口·资源与环境》2018年第3期。

肖建红等:《不同资源类型不同非使用价值——四种典型海洋旅游资源非使用价值支付意愿研究》,《旅游科学》2019年第4期。

肖建红等:《群岛旅游地海洋旅游资源非使用价值支付意愿偏好研究——以山东庙岛群岛、浙江舟山群岛和海南三亚及其岛屿为例》,《中国人口·资源与环境》2019年第8期。

徐大伟等:《流域生态补偿意愿的WTP与WTA差异性研究:基于辽河中游地区居民的CVM调查》,《自然资源学报》2013年第3期。

徐中民等:《额济纳旗生态系统服务恢复价值评估方法的比较与应用》,《生态学报》2003年第9期。

许丽忠等:《条件价值法评估旅游资源非使用价值的可靠性检验》,《生态学报》2007年第10期。

赵军等:《环境与生态系统服务价值的WTA/WTP不对称》,《环境科学学报》2007年第5期。

曾贤刚等:《基于CVM的城市大气细颗粒物健康风险的经济评估——以北京市为例》,《中国环境科学》2015年第7期。

张明军等:《不确定性影响下的平均支付意愿参数估计》,《生态学报》2007年第9期。

张翼飞:《CVM研究中支付意愿问卷"内容依赖性"的实证研究——以上海城市内河生态恢复CVM评估为例》,《中国人口·资源与环境》2012年第6期。

张翼飞等:《大城市非本地户籍人口对城市河流治理支付意愿的特征研究——基于上海和南京样本的CVM调查》,《复旦学报》(自然科学版)2014年第1期。

张茵等:《用条件估值法评估九寨沟的游憩价值——CVM方法的校正与比较》,《经济地理》2010年第7期。

张志强等:《黑河流域张掖市生态系统服务恢复价值评估研究——连续型和离散型条件价值评估方法的比较应用》,《自然资源学报》2004年第2期。

A. Kontogianni, et al., "Service Providing Units, Existence Values and the Valuation of Endangered Species: A Methodological Test", *Ecological Economics*, Vol. 79, July 2012.

A. Kontogianni, et al., "Eliciting Beach Users' Willingness to Pay for Protecting European Beaches from Beachrock Processes", *Ocean & Coastal Management*, Vol. 98, September 2014.

Abderraouf Dribek and Louinord Voltaire. "Contingent Valuation Analysis of Willingness to Pay for Beach Erosion Control through the Stabiplage Technique: A Study in Djerba (Tunisia)", *Marine Policy*, Vol. 86, December 2017.

Adriana Ressurreição, et al., "Economic Valuation of Species Loss in the Open Sea", *Ecological Economics*, Vol. 70, No. 4, February 2011.

Adriana Ressurreição, et al., "Different Cultures, Different Values: The Role of Cultural Variation in Public's WTP for Marine Species Conservation", *Biological Conservation*, Vol. 145, No. 1, January 2012.

Alan Randall and John P. Hoehn, "Embedding in Market Demand Systems", *Journal of Environmental Economics and Management*, Vol. 30, No. 3, May 1996.

Alan Shiell and Lisa Gold, "Contingent Valuation in Health Care and the Persistence of Embedding Effects without the Warm Glow", *Journal of Economic Psychology*, Vol. 23, No. 2, April 2002.

Alex Y. Lo and C. Y. Jim, "Protest Response and Willingness to Pay for Culturally Significant Urban Trees: Implications for Contingent Valuation Method", *Ecological Economics*, Vol. 114, June 2015.

Allan Provins, et al., "Valuation of the Historic Environment: The Scope for Using Economic Valuation Evidence in the Appraisal of Heritage-related Projects", *Progress in Planning*, Vol. 69, No. 4, May 2008.

A. Myrick Freeman III, et al., *The Measurement of Environmental and Resource Values: Theory and Measure* (2nd ed.), Washington D C: Resource for the Future Press, 2003.

Ana Bedate, et al., "Economic Valuation of the Cultural Heritage: Application to four Case Studies in Spain", *Journal of Cultural Heritage*,

Vol. 5, No. 1, January – March 2004.

Anatoli Togridou, et al. , "Determinants of Visitors' Willingness to Pay for the National Marine Park of Zakynthos, Greece", *Ecological Economics*, Vol. 60, No. 1, November 2006.

Andrea M. Leiter and Gerald J. Pruckner, "Proportionality of Willingness to Pay Small Changes in Risk: The Impact of Attitudinal Factors in Scope Tests", *Environmental and Resource Economics*, Vol. 42, No. 2, February 2009.

Andreas Kontoleon and Timothy Swanson, "The Willingness to Pay for Property Rights for the Giant Panda: Can a Charismatic Species be an Instrument for Nature Conservation?", *Land Economics*, Vol. 79, No. 4, November 2003.

Annabelle Cruz – Trinidad, et al. , "How Much are the Bolinao – Anda Coral Reefs Worth?", *Ocean & Coastal Management*, Vol. 54, No. 9, September 2011.

Anna Norinder, et al. , "Scope and Scale Insensitivities in a Contingent Valuation Study of Risk Reductions", *Health Policy*, Vol. 57, No. 2, August 2001.

Annika Batel, et al. , "Valuing Visitor Willingness to Pay for Marine Conservation: The Case of the Proposed Cres – Lošinj Marine Protected Area, Croatia", *Ocean & Coastal Management*, Vol. 95, July 2014.

Bente Halvorsen, "Ordering Effects in Contingent Valuation Surveys: Willingness to Pay for Reduced Health Damage from Air Pollution", *Environmental and Resource Economics*, Vol. 8, No. 4, December 1996.

Berta Martín – López, et al. , "The Non – economic Motives behind the Willingness to Pay for Biodiversity Conservation", *Biological Conservation*, Vol. 139, No. 1 – 2, September 2007.

Brian R. Binger, et al. , "Contingent Valuation Methodology in the Natural Resource Damage Regulatory Process: Choice Theory and the Embedding Phenomenon", *Natural Resources Journal*, Vol. 35, No. 3, July 1995.

Bruna Alves, et al. , "Coastal Erosion Perception and Willingness to

Pay for Beach Management (Cadiz, Spain)", *Journal of Coastal Conservation*, Vol. 19, No. 3, June 2015.

Carlisle A. Pemberton, et al., "Cultural Bias in Contingent Valuation of Copper Mining in the Commonwealth of Dominica", *Ecological Economics*, Vol. 70, No. 1, November 2010.

Chiradip Chatterjee, et al., "Willingness to Pay for Safe Drinking Water: A Contingent Valuation Study in Jacksonville, FL", *Journal of Environmental Management*, Vol. 203, December 2017.

Choong - Ki Lee and James W. Mjelde, "Valuation of Ecotourism Resources Using a Contingent Valuation Method: The Case of the Korean DMZ", *Ecological Economics*, Vol. 63, No. 2-3, August 2007.

Choong - Ki Lee and Sang - Yoel Han, "Estimating the Use and Preservation Values of National Parks' Tourism Resources Using a Contingent Valuation Method", *Tourism Management*, Vol. 23, No. 5, October 2002.

Christian A. Vossler and Sharon B. Watson, "Understanding the Consequences of Consequentiality: Testing the Validity of Stated Preferences in the Field", *Journal of Economic Behavior & Organization*, Vol. 86, February 2013.

Christopher Giguere, et al., "Valuing Hemlock Woolly Adelgid Control in Public Forests: Scope Effects with Attribute Nonattendance", *Land Economics*, Vol. 96, No. 1, February 2020.

Dambala Gelo and Steven F. Koch, "Contingent Valuation of Community Forestry Programs in Ethiopia: Controlling for Preference Anomalies in Double - bounded CVM", *Ecological Economics*, Vol. 114, June 2015.

Daniel Kahneman, *Comments. In Brookshire D, Cummings R G, Schulze W D. (Eds.). Valuing Environmental Goods: An Assessment of the Contingent Valuation Method*, Totowa, New Jersey: Rowman & Littlefield, 1986, pp. 61 - 62.

Daniel Kahneman and Ilana Ritov, "Determinants of Stated Willingness to Pay for Public Goods: A Study in the Headline Method", *Journal of Risk and Uncertainty*, Vol. 9, No. 1, July 1994.

Daniel Kahneman and Jack L. Knetsch, "Valuing Public Goods: The

Purchase of Moral Satisfaction", *Journal of Environmental Economics and Management*, Vol. 22, No. 1, January 1992.

Daniel Kahneman, et al., "Stated Willingness to Pay for Public Goods: A Psychological Perspective", *Psychological Science*, Vol. 4, No. 5, September 1993.

Daniel R. Petrolia and Tae – Goun Kim, "Preventing Land Loss in Coastal Louisiana: Estimates of WTP and WTA", *Journal of Environmental Management*, Vol. 92, No. 3, March 2011.

Daniel R. Petrolia, et al., "America's Wetland? A National Survey of Willingness to Pay for Restoration of Louisiana's Coastal Wetlands", *Marine Resources Economics*, Vol. 29, No. 1, January 2014.

David J. Chapman, et al., "On the Adequacy of Scope Test Results: Comments on Desvousges, Mathews, and Train", *Ecological Economics*, Vol. 130, October 2016.

Diane P. Dupont, "CVM Embedding Effects When There are Active, Potentially Active and Passive Users of Environmental Goods", *Environmental and Resource Economics*, Vol. 25, No. 3, July 2003.

D. Gyrd – Hansen, et al., "Scope Insensitivity in Contingent Valuation Studies of Health Care Services: Should We Ask Twice?", *Health Economics*, Vol. 21, No. 2, February 2012.

D. Lavee and O. Menachem, "Economic Valuation of the Existence of the Southwestern Basin of the Dead Sea in Israel", *Land Use Policy*, Vol. 71, February 2018.

Dominika A. Dziegielewska and Robert Mendelsohn, "Does 'No' Mean 'No'? A Protest Methodology", *Environmental and Resource Economics*, Vol. 38, No. 1, September 2007.

Donald Philip Green, et al., "How the Scope and Method of Public Funding Affect Willingness to Pay for Public Goods", *The Public Opinion Quarterly*, Vol. 58, No. 1, January 1994.

E. C. M. Ruijgrok, "The three Economic Values of Cultural Heritage: A Case Study in the Netherlands", *Journal of Cultural Heritage*, Vol. 7,

July – September 2006.

Edgar Robles – Zavala and Alejandra Guadalupe Chang Reynoso, "The Recreational Value of Coral Reefs in the Mexican Pacific", *Ocean & Coastal Management*, Vol. 157, May 2018.

Edoh Y. Amiran and Daniel A. Hagen, "The Scope Trials: Variation in Sensitivity to Scope and WTP with Directionally Bounded Utility Functions", *Journal of Environmental Economics and Management*, Vol. 59, No. 3, May 2010.

E. Koutrakis, et al., "ICZM and Coastal Defence Perception by Beach Users: Lessons from the Mediterranean Coastal Area", *Ocean & Coastal Management*, Vol. 54, No. 11, November 2011.

Elcin Akcura, "Mandatory Versus Voluntary Payment for Green Electricity", *Ecological Economics*, Vol. 116, August 2015.

Elena Ojea and Maria L. Loureiro, "Valuing the Recovery of Overexploited Fish Stocks in the Context of Existence and Option Values", *Marine Policy*, Vol. 34, No. 3, May 2010.

Elena Ojea and Maria L. Loureiro, "Identifying the Scope Effect on a Meta – analysis of Biodiversity Valuation Studies", *Resource and Energy Economics*, Vol. 33, No. 3, September 2011.

Emma Risén, et al., "Non – market Values of Algae Beach – cast Management – study Site Trelleborg, Sweden", *Ocean & Coastal Management*, Vol. 140, May 2017.

Erwin Dekker, "Two Approaches to Study the Value of Art and Culture, and the Emergence of a Third", *Journal of Cultural Economics*, Vol. 39, No. 4, November 2014.

Glenn W. Harrison, "Valuing Public Goods with the Contingent Valuation Method: A Critique of Kahneman and Knetsch", *Journal of Environmental Economics and Management*, Vol. 23, No. 3, November 1992.

Heidi Crumpler and Philip J. Grossman, "An Experimental Test of Warm Glow Giving", *Journal of Public Economics*, Vol. 92, No. 5 – 6, June 2008.

Henrik Andersson and Mikael Svensson, "Cognitive Ability and Scale Bias in the Contingent Valuation Method: An Analysis of Willingness to Pay to Reduce Mortality Risk", *Environmental and Resource Economics*, Vol. 39, No. 4, April 2008.

Henrik Svedsäter, "Contingent Valuation of Global Environmental Resources: Test of Perfect and Regular Embedding", *Journal of Economic Psychology*, Vol. 21, No. 6, December 2000.

Hilary Ndambiri, et al., "Scope Effects of Respondent Uncertainty in Contingent Valuation: Evidence from Motorized Emission Reductions in the City of Nairobi, Kenya", *Journal of Environmental Planning and Management*, Vol. 60, No. 1, January 2017.

Hilary Nixon and Jean-Daniel Saphores, "Financing Electronic Waste Recycling Californian Households' Willingness to Pay Advanced Recycling Fees", *Journal of Environmental Management*, Vol. 84, No. 4, September 2007.

Ian J. Bateman, et al., "Does Part-whole Bias Exist? An Experimental Investigation", *The Economic Journal*, Vol. 107, March 1997.

Ian J. Bateman, et al., "Estimating four Hicksian Welfare Measures for a Public Good: A Contingent Valuation Investigation", *Land Economics*, Vol. 76, No. 3, August 2000.

Ian J. Bateman, et al., *Visible Choice Sets and Scope Sensitivity: An Experimental and Field Test of Study Design Effects upon Nested Contingent Values*, UK: The Centre for Social and Economic Research on the Global Environmental (CSERGE), University of East Anglia, Working Paper EDM, NO. 01-01, 2001, pp. 4-7.

Ian J. Bateman, et al., "On Visible Choice Sets and Scope Sensitivity", *Journal of Environmental Economics and Management*, Vol. 47, No. 1, January 2004.

Ian J. Bateman, et al., "Economic Valuation of Policies for Managing Acidity in Remote Mountain Lakes: Examining Validity through Scope Sensitivity Testing", *Aquatic Sciences*, Vol. 67, No. 3, September 2005.

Ian J. Bateman and Roy Brouwer, "Consistency and Construction in

Stated WTP for Health Risk Reductions: A Novel Scope – sensitivity Test", *Resource and Energy Economics*, Vol. 28, No. 3, August 2006.

Ian J. Bateman, et al., "The Aggregation of Environmental Benefit Values: Welfare Measures, Distance Decay and Total WTP", *Ecological Economics*, Vol. 60, No. 2, December 2006.

Ian J. Bateman, *Valid Value Estimates and Value Estimate Validation: Better Methods and Better Testing for Stated Preference Research*, Cheltenham UK: Edward Elgar Publishing, 2011, pp. 322 – 352.

Icek Ajzen, et al., "Information Bias in Contingent Valuation: Effects of Personal Relevance, Quality of Information, and Motivational Orientation", *Journal of Environmental Economics and Management*, Vol. 30, No. 1, January 1996.

Ioanna Grammatikopoulou and Søren Bøye Olsen, "Accounting Protesting and Warm Glow Bidding in Contingent Valuation Surveys Considering the Management of Environmental Goods: An Empirical Case Study Assessing the Value of Protecting a Natura 2000 Wetland Area in Greece", *Journal of Environmental Management*, Vol. 130, November 2013.

Ivana Logar and Jeroen C. J. M. van den Bergh, "Respondent Uncertainty in Contingent Valuation of Preventing Beach Erosion: An Analysis with a Polychotomous Choice Question", *Journal of Environmental Management*, Vol. 113, December 2012.

James Francis Casey, et al., "Are Tourists Willing to Pay Additional Fees to Protect Corals in Mexico?", *Journal of Sustainable Tourism*, Vol. 18, No. 4, May 2010.

James J. Murphy, et al., "A Meta – analysis of Hypothetical Bias in Stated Preference Valuation", *Environmental and Resource Economics*, Vol. 30, No. 3, March 2005.

James K. Hammitt, "Evaluating Contingent Valuation of Environmental Health Risks: The Proportionality Test", *Association of Environmental and Resource Economists Newsletter*, Vol. 20, No. 1, January 2000.

James R. Meldrum, "Comparing Different Attitude Statements in Latent

Class Models of Stated Preferences for Managing an Invasive Forest Pathogen", *Ecological Economics*, Vol. 120, December 2015.

Jennifer Pate and John B. Loomis, "The Effect of Distance on Willingness to Pay Values: A Case Study of Wetlands and Salmon in California", *Ecological Economics*, Vol. 20, No. 3, March 1997.

Jeremy De Valck and John Rolfe, "Spatial Heterogeneity in Stated Preference Valuation: Status, Challenges and Road Ahead", *International Review of Environmental and Resource Economics*, Vol. 11, No. 4, August 2018.

Jerry Hausman, "Contingent Valuation: From Dubious to Hopeless", *The Journal of Economic Perspective*, Vol. 26, No. 4, Fall 2012.

John A. List, "Do Explicit Warnings Eliminate the Hypothetical Bias in Elicitation Procedures? Evidence from Field Auctions for Sportscards", *The American Economics Review*, Vol. 91, No. 5, December 2001.

John Armbrecht, "Use Value of Cultural Experiences: A Comparison of Contingent Valuation and Travel Cost", *Tourism Management*, Vol. 42, June 2014.

John Asafu – Adjaye and Sorada Tapsuwan, "A Contingent Valuation Study of Scuba Diving Benefits: Case Study in Mu Ko Similan Marine National Park, Thailand", *Tourism Management*, Vol. 29, No. 6, December 2008.

John B. Loomis, et al., "Some Empirical Evidence on Embedding Effects in Contingent Valuation of Forest Protection", *Journal of Environmental Economics and Management*, Vol. 25, No. 1, July 1993.

John B. Loomis, "How Large is the Extent of the Market for Public Goods: Evidence from a Nationwide Contingent Valuation Survey", *Applied Economics*, Vol. 28, No. 7, February 1996.

John B. Loomis and Armando González – Cabán, "The Importance of the Market Area Determination for Estimating Aggregate Benefits of Public Goods: Testing Differences in Resident and Nonresident Willingness to Pay", *Agricultural and Resource Economics Review*, Vol. 25, No. 2, October 1996.

John B. Loomis and Armando González – Cabán, "A Willingness – to – pay Function for Protecting Acres of Spotted Owl Habitat from Fire", *Ecological Economics, Vol. 25, No. 3, June 1998.

John C. Bergstrom, et al., "The Impact of Information on Environmental Commodity Valuation Decisions", American Journal of Agricultural Economics, Vol. 72, No. 3, August 1990.

John C. Whitehead, "Differentiating Use and Non-use Values with the Properties of the Variation Function", Applied Economics Letters, Vol. 2, No. 10, February 1995.

John C. Whitehead, et al., "Assessing the Validity and Reliability of Contingent Values: A Comparison of On-site Users, Off-site Users, and Non-users", Journal of Environmental Economics and Management, Vol. 29, No. 2, September 1995.

John C. Whitehead, et al., "Part-whole Bias in Contingent Valuation: Will Scope Effects be Detected with Inexpensive Survey Methods?", Southern Economic Journal, Vol. 65, No. 1, July 1998.

John C. Whitehead and Suzanne S. Finney, "Willingness to Pay for Submerged Maritime Cultural Resources", Journal of Cultural Economics, Vol. 27, No. 3-4, November 2003.

John C. Whitehead and Todd L. Cherry, "Willingness to Pay for a Green Energy Program: A Comparison of Ex-ante and Ex-post Hypothetical Bias Mitigation Approaches", Resource and Energy Economics, Vol. 29, No. 4, November 2007.

John C. Whitehead, "Albemarle-Pamlico Sounds Revealed and Stated Preference Data", Data in Brief, Vol. 3, June 2015.

John C. Whitehead, "Plausible Responsiveness to Scope in Contingent Valuation", Ecological Economics, Vol. 128, August 2016.

John B. Loomis, et al., "Improving Validity Experiments of Contingent Valuation Methods: Results of Efforts to Reduce the Disparity of Hypothetical and Actual Willingness to Pay", Land Economics, Vol. 72, No. 4, November 1996.

John B. Loomis, and Luis E. Santiago, "Testing Differences in Estimation of River Recreation Benefits for International and Domestic Tourists as a

Function of Single – versus Multiple – destination Day Trips", *Journal of Hospitality Marketing & Management*, Vol. 20, No. 2, 2011.

John P. Hoehn and Alan Randall, "Too Many Proposals Pass the Benefit Cost Test", *The American Economic Review*, Vol. 79, No. 3, June 1989.

John V. Krutilla, "Conservation Reconsidered", *The American Economic Review*, Vol. 57, No. 4, September 1967.

Jonathan Baron, "Contingent Valuation: Flawed Logic?", *Science*, Vol. 357, No. 6349, July 2017.

J. R. Molina, et al., "The Role of Flagship Species in the Economic Valuation of Wildfire Impacts: An Application to two Mediterranean Protected Areas", *Science of the Total Environment*, Vol. 675, July 2019.

J. Scott Long and Jeremy Freese, *Regression Models for Categorical Dependent Variables Using Stata (3rd ed.)*, College Station, TX: Stata Press, 2014.

Juan C. Trujillo, et al., "Coral Reefs Under Threat in a Caribbean Marine Protected Area: Assessing Divers' Willingness to Pay Toward Conservation", *Marine Policy*, Vol. 68, June 2016.

Juliana Castaño – Isaza, et al., "Valuing Beaches to Develop Payment for Ecosystem Services Schemes in Colombia's Seaflower Marine Protected Area", *Ecosystem Services*, Vol. 11, February 2015.

Jürgen Meyerhoff and Ulf Liebe, "Protest Beliefs in Contingent Valuation: Explaining Their Motivation", *Ecological Economics*, Vol. 57, No. 4, June 2006.

Jürgen Meyerhoff, et al., "A Meta – study Investigating the Sources of Protest Behaviour in Stated Preference Surveys", *Environmental and Resource Economics*, Vol. 58, No. 1, May 2014.

Ju – Yeon Kim, et al., "Comparing Willingness – to – pay between Residents and Non – residents when Correcting Hypothetical Bias: Case of Endangered Spotted Seal in South Korea", *Ecological Economics*, Vol. 78, June 2012.

Kenneth Arrow, et al., "Report of the NOAA Panel on Contingent Valuation", *Federal Register*, Vol. 58, No. 10, January 1993.

Kenneth Arrow, et al., *Comments on Proposed NOAA Scope Test. Appendix D of Comments on Proposed NOAA/DOI Regulations on Natural Resource Damage Assessment*, U. S.: Environmental Protection Agency, 1994, pp. D1 – D2.

Kevin J. Boyle, et al., "An Investigation of Part – whole Biases in Contingent – valuation Studies", *Journal of Environmental Economics and Management*, Vol. 27, No. 1, July 1994.

Kevin P. Ransom and Stephen C. Mangi, "Valuing Recreational Benefits of Coral Reefs: The Case of Mombasa Marine National Park and Reserve, Kenya", *Environmental Management*, Vol. 45, No. 1, January 2010.

Kimberly Rollins and Audrey Lyke, "The Case for Diminishing Marginal Existence Values", *Journal of Environmental Economics and Management*, Vol. 36, No. 3, November 1998.

Kirsten L. L. Oleson, et al., "Cultural Bequest Values for Ecosystem Service Flows among Indigenous Fishers: A Discrete Choice Experiment Validated with Mixed Methods", *Ecological Economics*, Vol. 114, June 2015.

Kristy Wallmo and Daniel K. Lew, "Public Willingness to Pay for Recovering and Downlisting Threatened and Endangered Marine Species", *Conservation Biology*, Vol. 26, No. 5, October 2012.

K. L. Giraud, et al., "Internal and External Scope in Willingness – to – pay Estimates for Threatened and Endangered Wildlife", *Journal of Environmental Management*, Vol. 56, No. 3, July 1999.

Kunt Veisten, et al., "Scope Insensitivity in Contingent Valuation of Complex Environmental Amenities", *Journal of Environmental Management*, Vol. 73, No. 4, December 2004.

Levan Elbakidze and Rodolfo M. Nayga Jr., "The Adding – up Test in an Incentivized Value Elicitation Mechanism: The Role of the Income Effect", *Environmental and Resource Economics*, Vol. 71, No. 3, November 2018.

Louinord Voltaire, et al., "Dealing with Preference Uncertainty in

Contingent Willingness to Pay for a Nature Protection Program: A New Approach", *Ecological Economics*, Vol. 88, April 2013.

Luke Fitzpatrick, et al., "Threshold Effects in Meta – analyses with Application to Benefit Transfer for Coral Reef Valuation", *Ecological Economics*, Vol. 133, March 2017.

L. Venkatachalam, "The Contingent Valuation Method: A Review", *Environmental Impact Assessment Review*, Vol. 24, No. 1, January 2004.

Magnus Aa. Skeie, et al., "Smartphone and Tablet Effects in Contingent Valuation Web Surveys – No Reason to Worry?", *Ecological Economics*, Vol. 165, November 2019.

Magnus Johannesson, et al., "An Experimental Comparison of Dichotomous Choice Contingent Valuation Questions and Real Purchase Decisions", *Applied Economics*, Vol. 30, No. 5, February 1998.

Mahfuzuddin Ahmed, et al., "Valuing Recreational and Conservation Benefits of Coral Reefs: The Case of Bolinao, Philippines", *Ocean & Coastal Management*, Vol. 50, No. 1 – 2, January 2007.

Mani Nepal, et al., "Assessing Perceived Consequentiality: Evidence from a Contingent Valuation Survey on Global Climate Change", *International Journal of Ecological Economics and Statistics*, Vol. 14, No. P09, June 2009.

Marcus Peng and Kristen L. L. Oleson, "Beach Recreationalists' Willingness to Pay and Economic Implications of Coastal Water Quality Problems in Hawaii", *Ecological Economics*, Vol. 136, June 2017.

Maria L. Loureiro, et al., "Do Experimental Auction Estimates Pass the Scope Test?", *Journal of Economic Psychology*, Vol. 37, No. 4, August 2013.

Marina Farr, et al., "The Non – consumptive (tourism) 'Value' of Marine Species in the Northern Section of the Great Barrier Reef", *Marine Policy*, Vol. 43, January 2014.

Mary Jo Kealy, et al., "Reliability and Predictive Validity of Contingent Values: Does the Nature of the Good Matter?", *Journal of Environmen-*

tal Economics and Management, Vol. 19, No. 3, November 1990.

Massimo Paradiso and Antoenlla Trisorio, "The Effect of Knowledge on the Disparity Between Hypothetical and Real Willingness to Pay", *Applied Economics*, Vol. 33, No. 11, September 2001.

Matleena Kniivilä, "Users and Non – users of Conservation Areas: Are there Differences in WTP, Motives and the Validity of Responses in CVM Surveys?", *Ecological Economics*, Vol. 59, No. 4, October 2006.

Matthew J. Kotchen and Stephen D. Reiling, "Environmental Attitudes, Motivations, and Contingent Valuation of Nonuse Values: A Case Study Involving Endangered Species", *Ecological Economics*, Vol. 32, No. 1, January 2000.

Mavra Stithou and Riccardo Scarpa, "Collective Versus Voluntary Payment in Contingent Valuation for the Conservation of Marine Biodiversity: An Exploratory Study from Zakynthos, Greece", *Ocean & Coastal Management*, Vol. 56, February 2012.

M. Christie, "A Comparison of Alternative Contingent Valuation Elicitation Treatments for the Evaluation of Complex Environmental Policy", *Journal of Environmental Management*, Vol. 62, No. 3, July 2001.

Melville Saayman, et al., "Willingness to Pay: Who are the Cheap Talkers?", *Annals of Tourism Research*, Vol. 56, January 2016.

Michelle Cazabon – Mannette, et al., "Estimates of the Non – market Value of Sea Turtles in Tobago Using Stated Preference Techniques", *Journal of Environmental Management*, Vol. 192, May 2017.

Mikołaj Czajkowski and Nick Hanley, "Using Labels to Investigate Scope Effects in Stated Preference Methods", *Environmental and Resource Economics*, Vol. 44, No. 4, December 2009.

Min Gong and Jonathan Baron, "The Generality of the Emotion Effect on Magnitude Sensitivity", *Journal of Economic Psychology*, Vol. 32, No. 1, February 2011.

Mohammed Hussen Alemu, et al., "Attending to the Reasons for Attribute Non – attendance in Choice Experiments", *Environmental and Resource Economics, Vol. 54, No. 3, March 2013.

Murugadas Ramdas and Badaruddin Mohamed, "Impacts of Tourism on Environmental Attributes, Environmental Literacy and Willingness to Pay: A Conceptual and Theoretical Review", *Procedia - Social and Behavioral Sciences*, Vol. 144, August 2014.

Mushtaq Ahmed Memon and Shunji Matsuoka, "Validity of Contingent Valuation Estimates from Developing Countries: Scope Sensitivity Analysis", *Environmental Economics and Policy Studies*, Vol. 5, No. 1, September 2002.

N. A. Powe and I. J. Bateman, "Ordering Effects in Nested 'Top - down' and 'Bottom - up' Contingent Valuation Designs", *Ecological Economics*, Vol. 45, No. 2, June 2003.

Natasha Charmaine A. Tamayo, et al. , "National Estimates of Values of Philippine Reefs' Ecosystem Services", *Ecological Economics*, Vol. 146, April 2018.

Neil A. Powe and Ian J. Bateman, "Investigating Insensitivity to Scope: A Split - sample Test of Perceived Scheme Realism", *Land Economics*, Vol. 80, No. 2, May 2004.

Nick Hanley, et al. , "Aggregating the Benefits of Environmental Improvements: Distance - decay Functions for Use and Non - use Values", *Journal of Environmental Management*, Vol. 68, No. 3, July 2003.

Nicolas Borzykowski, et al. , "Scope Effects in Contingent Valuation: Does the Assumed Statistical Distribution of WTP Matter?", *Ecological Economics*, Vol. 144, February 2018.

Niels Jobstvogt, et al. , "Looking Below the Surface: The Cultural Ecosystem Service Values of UK Marine Protected Areas (MPAs)", *Ecosystem Services*, Vol. 10, December 2014.

Nikoleta Jones, "Visitors' Perceptions on the Management of an Important Nesting Site for Loggerhead Sea Turtle (Caretta Caretta L.): The Case of Rethymno Coastal Area in Greece", *Ocean & Coastal Management*, Vol. 54, No. 8, August 2011.

N. J. Beaumont, et al. , "Identification, Definition and Quantification of Goods and Services Provided by Marine Biodiversity: Implications for the Ecosystem Approach", *Marine Pollution Bulletin*, Vol. 54, No. 3, March 2007.

Pallab Mozumder, et al., "Consumers' Preference for Renewable Energy in the Southwest USA", *Energy Economics*, Vol. 33, No. 6, November 2011.

Pankaj Lal, et al., "Valuing Visitor Services and Access to Protected Areas: The Case of Nyungwe National Park in Rwanda", *Tourism Management*, Vol. 61, August 2017.

Patricia A. Champ, et al., "Using Donation Mechanisms to Value Nonuse Benefits from Public Goods", *Journal of Environmental Economics and Management*, Vol. 33, No. 2, June 1997.

Patrick Lloyd-Smith, et al., "Moving Beyond the Contingent Valuation Versus Choice Experiment Debate: Presentation Effects in Stated Preference", *Land Economics*, Vol. 96, No. 1, February 2020.

Paulo A. L. D. Nunes and Erik Schokkaert, "Identifying the Warm Glow Effect in Contingent Valuation", *Journal of Environmental Economics and Management*, Vol. 45, No. 2, March 2003.

Paulo A. L. D. Nunes and Jeroen C. J. M. van den Bergh, "Can People Value Protection Against Invasive Marine Species? Evidence from a Joint TC-CV Survey in the Netherlands", *Environmental and Resource Economics*, Vol. 28, No. 4, August 2004.

Paulo Torres, et al., "Dead or Alive: The Growing Importance of Shark Diving in the Mid-Atlantic Region", *Journal of Nature Conservation*, Vol. 36, April 2017.

P. C. Boxall, et al., "Analysis of the Economic Benefits Associated with the Recovery of Threatened Marine Mammal Species in the Canadian St. Lawrence Estuary", *Marine Policy*, Vol. 36, No. 1, January 2012.

Peter A. Diamond and Jerry A. Hausman, *On Contingent Valuation Measurement of Nonuse Values. In Hausman J. A. (Ed.). Contingent Valuation: A Critical Assessment*, UK: Bingley: Emerald Group Publishing Limited, 1993, pp. 3 - 38.

Peter A. Diamond, et al., *Does Contingent Valuation Measure Preferences? Experimental Evidence*. In Hausman J A (Ed.). *Contingent Valuation: A Critical Assessment*, UK: Bingley: Emerald Group Publishing Limited, 1993, pp. 41 - 89.

Peter A. Diamond and Jerry A. Hausman, "Contingent Valuation: Is Some Number Better than no Number?", *The Journal of Economic Perspectives*, Vol. 8, No. 4, Fall 1994.

Peter A. Diamond, "Testing the Internal Consistency of Contingent Valuation Surveys", *Journal of Environmental Economics and Management*, Vol. 30, No. 3, May 1996.

Peter W. Schuhmann, et al., "Recreational SCUBA Divers' Willingness to Pay for Marine Biodiversity in Barbados", *Journal of Environmental Management*, Vol. 121, May 2013.

Peter W. Schuhmann, et al., "Visitors' Willingness to Pay Marine Conservation Fees in Barbados", *Tourism Management*, Vol. 71, April 2019.

Pierre - Alexandre Mahieu, et al., "Stated Preferences: A Unique Database Composed of 1657 Recent Published Articles in Journals Related to Agriculture, Environment, or Health", *Review of Agricultural, Food and Environmental Studies*, Vol. 98, No. 3, November 2017.

Piran C. L. White, et al., "Economic Values of Threatened Mammals in Britain: A Case Study of the Otter Lutra Lutra and the Water Vole Arvicola Terrestris", *Biological Conservation*, Vol. 82, No. 3, December 1997.

P. Mwebaze, et al., "Economic Valuation of the Influence of Invasive Alien Species on the Economy of the Seychelles Islands", *Ecological Economics*, Vol. 69, No. 12, October 2010.

Alan Randall, et al., *The Structure of Contingent Markets: Some Results of a Recent Experiment*. Presented to the annual meeting of the American Economic Association, Washington D. C., 1981.

Rathnayake Mudiyanselage Wasantha Rathnayake, "'Turtle Watching': A Strategy for Endangered Marine Turtle Conservation through Community Participation in Sri Lanka", *Ocean & Coastal Management*, Vol. 119, January 2016.

Raymond J. Kopp, "Why Existence Value Should be Included in Cost-benefit Analysis", *Journal of Policy Analysis and Management*, Vol. 11, No. 1, December 1992.

R. Brouwer, et al., "Public Willingness to Pay for Alternative Management Regimes of Remote Marine Protected Areas in the North Sea", *Marine Policy*, Vol. 68, June 2016.

Richard C. Bishop and Michael P. Welsh, "Existence Values in Benefit-cost Analysis and Damage Assessment", *Land Economics*, Vol. 68, No. 4, November 1992.

Richard C. Bishop, et al., "Putting a Value on Injuries to Natural Assets: The BP Oil Spill", *Science*, Vol. 356, No. 6335, April 2017.

Richard C. Bishop, et al., "Contingent Valuation: Flawed Logic? — Response", *Science*, Vol. 357, No. 6349, July 2017.

Richard C. Bishop, "Warm Glow, Good Feelings, and Contingent Valuation", *Journal of Agricultural and Resource Economics*, Vol. 43, No. 3, September 2018.

Richard T. Carson, et al., *A Contingent Valuation Study of Lost Passive Use Values Resulting from the Exxon Valdez Oil Spill*, Germany: University Library of Munich, 1992, pp. 80 – 125.

Richard T. Carson and Robert Cameron Mitchell, "Sequencing and Nesting in Contingent Valuation Surveys", *Journal of Environmental Economics and Management*, Vol. 28, No. 2, March 1995.

Richard T. Carson and Robert C. Mitchell, "The Issue of Scope in Contingent Valuation Studies", *American Journal of Agricultural Economics*, Vol. 75, No. 5, December 1993.

Richard T. Carson, et al., "Contingent Valuation and Revealed Preference Methodologies: Comparing the Estimates for Quasi-public Goods", *Land Economics*, Vol. 72, No. 1, February 1996.

Richard T. Carson, et al., "Sequencing and Valuing Public Goods",

Journal of Environmental Economics and Management, Vol. 36, No. 3, November 1998.

Richard T. Carson, et al., "Contingent Valuation: Controversies and Evidence", *Environmental and Resource Economics*, Vol. 19, No. 2, June 2001.

I. Ritov and D. Kahneman, "How People Value the Environment: Attitudes Versus Economic Values", In: Bazerman M. H., Messick D. M., Tenbrunzel A. E., et al. (Eds.), *Environment, Ethics and Behaviour: The Psychology of Environmental Valuation and Degradation*, San Francisco, CA: The New Lexington Press, 1997.

R. Kerry Turner, et al., "Valuing Nature: Lessons Learned and Future Research Directions", *Ecological Economics*, Vol. 46, No. 3, October 2003.

Robert Cameron Mitchell and Richard T. Carson, *Using Surveys to Value Public Goods: The Contingent Valuation Method*, Washington: Resources for the Future, 1989, pp. 107–126.

Robert J. Johnston, "Is Hypothetical Bias Universal? Validating Contingent Responses Using a Binding Public Referendum", *Journal of Environmental Economics and Management*, Vol. 52, No. 1, July 2006.

Robert Kenneth Davis, *The Value of Outdoor Recreation: An Economic Study of the Maine Woods*, Cambridge, England: Harvard University, 1963.

Rodelio F. Subade, "Mechanisms to Capture Economic Values of Marine Biodiversity: The Case of Tubbataha Reefs UNESCO World Heritage Site, Philippines", *Marine Policy*, Vol. 31, No. 2, March 2007.

Rodelio F. Subade and Herminia A. Francisco, "Do Non-users Value Coral Reefs? Economic Valuation of Conserving Tubbataha Reefs, Philippines", *Ecological Economics*, Vol. 102, June 2014.

Roger Koenker and Gilbert Bassett, "Regression Quantiles", *Econometrica*, Vol. 46, January 1978.

Ronald G. Cummings and Glenn W. Harrison, "Was the Ohio Court Well Informed in its Assessment of the Accuracy of the Contingent Valuation Method?", *Natural Resources Journal*, Vol. 34, No. 1, Winter 1994.

Ronald G. Cummings and Glenn W. Harrison, "The Measurement and

Decomposition of Nonuse Values: A Critical Review", *Environmental and Resource Economics*, Vol. 5, No. 3, April 1995.

Ronald Sutherland and Richard G. Walsh, "Effect of Distance on the Preservation Value of Water Quality", *Land Economics*, Vol. 61, No. 3, August 1985.

Roy Brouwer and Julia Martín – Ortega, "Modeling Self – censoring of Polluter Pays Protest Votes in Stated Preference Research to Support Resource Damage Estimations in Environmental Liability", *Resource and Energy Economics*, Vol. 34, No. 1, January 2012.

Roy Brouwer, et al., "Economic Valuation of Groundwater Protection Using a Groundwater Quality Ladder Based on Chemical Threshold Levels", *Ecological Indicators*, Vol. 88, May 2018.

R. P. Berrens, et al., "Contingent Values for New Mexico Instream Flows: With Tests of Scope, Group – size Reminder and Temporal Reliability", *Journal of Environmental Management*, Vol. 58, No. 1, January 2000.

R. Pinto, et al., "Valuing the Non – market Benefits of Estuarine Ecosystem Services in a River Basin Context: Testing Sensitivity to Scope and Scale", *Estuarine, Coastal and Shelf Science*, Vol. 169, February 2016.

Seul – Ye Lim, et al., "Public Willingness to Pay for Transforming Jogyesa Buddhist Temple in Seoul, Korea into a Cultural Tourism Resource", *Sustainability*, Vol. 8, No. 9, September 2016.

Sevda Birdir, et al., "Willingness to Pay as an Economic Instrument for Coastal Tourism Management: Cases from Mersin, Turkey", *Tourism Management*, Vol. 36, No. 3, June 2013.

Sini Miller, et al., "Estimating Indigenous Cultural Values of Freshwater: A Choice Experiment Approach to Māori Values in New Zealand", *Ecological Economics*, Vol. 118, October 2015.

Sisse Liv Jørgensen, et al., "Spatially Induced Disparities in Users' and Non – users' WTP for Water Quality Improvements: Testing the Effect of Multiple Substitutes and Distance Decay", *Ecological Economics*, Vol. 92, August 2013.

Siti Aznor Ahmad and Nick Hanley, "Willingness to Pay for Reducing Crowding Effect Damages in Marine Parks in Malaysia", *The Singapore Economic Review*, Vol. 54, No. 1, April 2009.

S. Marzetti, et al., "Visitors' Awareness of ICZM and WTP for Beach Preservation in four European Mediterranean Regions", *Marine Policy*, Vol. 63, January 2016.

S. M. Chilton and W. G. Hutchinson, "A Note on the Warm Glow of Giving and Scope Sensitivity in Contingent Valuation Studies", *Journal of Economic Psychology*, Vol. 21, No. 4, August 2000.

S. M. Chilton and W. G. Hutchinson, "A Qualitative Examination of How Respondents in a Contingent Valuation Study Rationalise their WTP Responses to an Increase in the Quantity of the Environmental Good", *Journal of Economic Psychology*, Vol. 24, No. 1, February 2003.

Stefania Tonin, "Economic Value of Marine Biodiversity Improvement in Coralligenous Habitats", *Ecological Indicators*, Vol. 85, February 2018.

Stefania Tonin, "Citizens' Perspectives on Marine Protected Areas as a Governance Strategy to Effectively Preserve Marine Ecosystem Services and Biodiversity", *Ecosystem Services*, Vol. 34, December 2018.

Steven M. Thur, "User Fees as Sustainable Financing Mechanisms for Marine Protected Areas: An Application to the Bonaire National Marine Park", *Marine Policy*, Vol. 34, No. 1, January 2010.

Susan M. Chilton and W. George Hutchinson, "Some Further Implications of Incorporating the Warm Glow of Giving into Welfare Measures: A Comment on the Use of Donation Mechanisms by Champ et al.", *Journal of Environmental Economics and Management*, Vol. 37, No. 2, March 1999.

S. V. Ciriacy-Wantrup, "Capital Returns from Soil-Conservation Practices", *Journal of Farm Economics*, Vol. 29, No. 4, November 1947.

Tanya O'Garra, "Bequest Values for Marine Resources: How Important for Indigenous Communities in Less-developed Economies?", *Environmental and Resource Economics*, Vol. 44, No. 2, October 2009.

T. Enriquez-Acevedo, et al., "Willingness to Pay for Beach Ecosystem Services: The Case Study of three Colombian Beaches", *Ocean & Coastal Management*, Vol. 161, July 2018.

Thomas A. Heberlein, et al., "Rethinking the Scope Test as a Criterion for Validity in Contingent Valuation", *Journal of Environmental Economics and Management*, Vol. 50, No. 1, July 2005.

Thomas C Brown and John W. Duffield, "Testing Part – whole Valuation Effects in Contingent Valuation of Instream Flow Protection", *Water Resources Research*, Vol. 31, No. 9, September 1995.

Thomas C. Brown, et al., "Does Better Information about the Good Avoid the Embedding Effect?", *Journal of Environmental Management*, Vol. 44, No. 1, May 1995.

Tijen Arin and Randall A. Kramer, "Divers' Willingness to Pay to Visit Marine Sanctuaries: An Exploratory Study", *Ocean & Coastal Management*, Vol. 45, No. 2 – 3, February 2002.

Timothy L. McDaniels, et al., "Decision Structuring to Alleviate Embedding in Environmental Valuation", *Ecological Economics*, Vol. 46, No. 1, August 2003.

Trudy Ann Cameron and Daniel D. Huppert, "OLS Versus ML Estimation of Non – market Resource Values with Payment Card Interval Data", *Journal of Environmental Economics and Management*, Vol. 17, No. 3, November 1989.

Tuba Tunçel and James K. Hammitt, "A New Meta – analysis on the WTP/WTA Disparity", *Journal of Environmental Economics and Management*, Vol. 68, No. 1, July 2014.

Vito Frontuto, et al., "Earmarking Conservation: Further Inquiry on Scope Effects in Stated Preference Methods Applied to Nature – based Tourism", *Tourism Management*, Vol. 60, June 2017.

V. Kerry Smith, "Arbitrary Values, Good Causes, and Premature Verdicts", *Journal of Environmental Economics and Management*, Vol. 22, No. 1, January 1992.

V. Kerry Smith, "Nonmarket Valuation of Environmental Resources: An

Interpretative Appraisal", *Land Economics*, Vol. 69, No. 1, February 1993.

V. Kerry Smith and Laura L. Osborne, "Do Contingent Valuation Estimates Pass a 'Scope' Test? A Meta-analysis", *Journal of Environmental Economics and Management*, Vol. 31, No. 3, November 1996.

W. George Hutchinson, et al., "Measuring Non-use Value of Environmental Goods Using the Contingent Valuation Method: Problems of Information and Cognition and the Application of Cognitive Questionnaire Design Methods", *Journal of Agricultural Economics*, Vol. 46, No. 1, January 1995.

William Desvousges, et al., *Measuring Natural Resource Damages with Contingent Valuation: Tests of Validity and Reliability*, UK: Bingley: Emerald Group Publishing Limited, 1993, pp. 91–164.

William Desvousges, et al., "Adequate Responsiveness to Scope in Contingent Valuation", *Ecological Economics*, Vol. 84, December 2012.

William Desvousges, et al., "An Adding-up Test on Contingent Valuations of River and Lake Quality", *Land Economics*, Vol. 91, No. 3, August 2015.

William Desvousges, et al., "From Curious to Pragmatically Curious: Comment on 'from Hopeless to Curious? Thoughts on Hausman's 'Dubious to Hopeless' Critique of Contingent Valuation'", *Applied Economic Perspectives and Policy*, Vol. 38, No. 1, March 2016.

William Desvousges, et al., "Reply to on the Adequacy of Scope Test Results: Comments on Desvousges, Mathews, and Train", *Ecological Economics*, Vol. 130, October 2016.

William D. Schulze, et al., "Embedding and Calibration in Measuring Non-use Values", *Resource and Energy Economics*, Vol. 20, No. 2, June 1998.

William Wei-Chun Tseng, et al., "Estimating the Willingness to Pay to Protect Coral Reefs from Potential Damage Caused by Climate Change: The Evidence from Taiwan", *Marine Pollution Bulletin*, Vol. 101, No. 2, December 2015.

W. Michael Hanemann, "Valuing the Environment through Contingent

Valuation", *The Journal of Economic Perspectives*, Vol. 8, No. 4, February 1994.

Yaniv Poria, et al., "Heritage Site Perceptions and Motivations to Visit", *Journal of Travel Research*, Vol. 44, February 2006.